DENIAL
HISTORY BETRAYED

DENIAL
HISTORY BETRAYED

TONY TAYLOR

MELBOURNE UNIVERSITY PRESS
An imprint of Melbourne University Publishing Limited
187 Grattan Street, Carlton, Victoria 3053, Australia
mup-info@unimelb.edu.au
www.mup.com.au

First published 2008
Text © Tony Taylor, 2008
Design and typography © Melbourne University Publishing Limited, 2008

This book is copyright. Apart from any use permitted under the *Copyright Act 1968* and subsequent amendments, no part may be reproduced, stored in a retrieval system or transmitted by any means or process whatsoever without the prior written permission of the publisher.

Every attempt has been made to locate the copyright holders for material quoted in this book. Any person or organisation that may have been overlooked or misattributed may contact the publisher.

Designed by Peter Long and Megan Ellis
Typeset by TypeSkill
Printed in Australia by Griffin Press

National Library of Australia Cataloguing-in-Publication entry:

Taylor, Tony.
   Denial: history betrayed / Tony Taylor.
   9780522854824 (pbk.)
   Includes index.
   Bibliography.

   Denial (Psychology). History, Modern—20th century. History, Modern—21st century. Mass media and history.

909.82

This project has been assisted by the Australian Government through the Australia Council, its principal arts funding and advisory body.

CONTENTS

Acknowledgements — VI
Introduction: The Pathology of Historical Denial — VII

1. Under Western Eyes: Armenian Massacres and Turkish Denial — 1
2. Frauds and Fanatics: The Pathology of Western Holocaust Denial — 38
3. A Culture of Denial: Explaining the Politics of Remembrance in Modern Japan — 71
4. British Communism and Two Decades of Denial: From Moscow 1936 to Budapest 1956 — 102
5. Tales of Heartless Denial from the Balkans: Serbian Victimhood and Marxist Conspiracy Theories — 136
6. Failing the Scholarly Test: Australian Denial and the Art of Pseudohistory — 174

Coda — 210
Appendix — 216
Notes — 226
Bibliography — 289
Index — 313

ACKNOWLEDGEMENTS

It is important to recognise, with gratitude, the colleagues, friends and relations who have all played a part in the writing of this book. Starting with Melbourne University Publishing, I should like to thank Louise Adler, who generously gave the project initial support; Foong Ling Kong, whose encouragement throughout was invaluable; and Cinzia Cavallaro, who gave crucial support at the final hurdle. That leaves Penny Mansley, whose meticulous, astute and forbearing copy-editing was both a boon and a blessing.

The support of Monash University colleagues during two periods of research leave in 2007 should also be acknowledged.

I also owe a debt of thanks to Stuart Macintyre, who suggested that I write this book and who gave generous advice on several drafts, and to Anna Clark, Peter Cochrane and Corinne Manning who were also kind enough to review drafts and provide eminently sensible advice.

Finally, closer to home, I owe a debt of thanks to Dan Taylor for advice on politics, Sam Taylor for advice on philosophy and Scilla Taylor for advice on psychology, and for her patience.

INTRODUCTION
The Pathology of Historical Denial

As a defence mechanism, denial is perfectly normal; we use it every day. We may deny to ourselves, perhaps, that we are drinking too much wine in the evening. We may deny that we are neglecting our paid work by taking unauthorised time off to do some shopping. We may also deny that our favourite sports team is tragically incompetent, externalising its run of losses as sheer bad luck. And we see denial all around us. We know senior managers of large organisations who deny that there is a staff morale problem, even though absenteeism rates are high, in-house bickering is endemic and efficiency is low. It is this kind of denial, as a defence mechanism, that helps us and our senior managers to deal with circumstances in life that make us feel uncomfortable or anxious. We tell ourselves and others that things are fine when they aren't, and it is these self-deceptive white lies of denial that keep us going. Denial is a day-to-day transactional business. It's just routine.

Denial becomes troublesome when the game is stepped up a notch or two, when the defence mechanism turns into a self-deceptive refusal to accept significant, life-affecting realities that are obvious to the world at large. When Thabo Mbeki and the South African government asserted (until 2006 at least) that HIV-AIDS was not a serious issue in their country, with the health minister explaining that AIDS was actually an illness that could be cured by garlic, beetroot and lemons, that was denial. When President George W Bush, against growing evidence to the contrary, rejected the criticism that his administration's intelligence failures had led to a faulty strategy in the war against Iraq, that was denial. And when Chinese leader Deng Xiao-Ping denied the scale and character of the massacre at Tiananmen Square, that was denial (along with contempt for human rights and for foreign meddling). These were not white lies told to smooth away anxiety; they were significant misrepresentations, distortions and falsehoods constructed to meet internalised psychological and external political needs. Not only are these self-deceiving deniers stubbornly resistant to external reality; they also occupy positions of authority, meaning that their denial is a powerful political tool. When it comes to denying for personal gratification and for political gain, the deniers hold all the cards, for the time being at least.

With his political denial, Mbeki was probably torn between thinking that he was right but sensing that he was wrong. Bush, in the circumstances, couldn't afford to tell himself that he was wrong. Deng deceived himself by following the expedient party line in refusing to accept a widely held belief (outside China) that the students of Tiananmen were peaceful, pro-democracy demonstrators. Observers and commentators may be angry about these types of contemporary political denials, but with much of the evidence still to be released concerning motivation, occurrence and causation, all they can do is conjecture, search for more clues and grumble about *a half-known and half-explored present.*

In contrast to political denial, with historical denial, it is a self-deceiving fantasy about *a more fully known and explored past* that makes observers angry, bearing in mind that interpretations of the past change, just as times change. Historical denialist fictions may make perfect, delusory sense to deniers, whose motivation to deny, as we shall see, is a self-protective irrationality; but denial provokes astonishment from bemused and exasperated onlookers, who may well think that denialist distortion of key facets of past events is just a spiteful version of flat earthism. More specifically, informed observers, such as working historians, tend to be dismissive of historical denialism, writing off both individual and organisational deniers as cranks motivated by personal or ideological agendas. Indeed, much professional historical commentary takes the phenomenon of denial at face value, treating it as an inexplicable, marginal activity peopled by stubborn fantasists.

Even when historical denial is taken seriously, individual historians have tended to confine themselves to examining it on a topic-by-topic basis. There are books about Holocaust denial, communist denial and Turkish denial, for example, but there is little written on denial as a historical genre in its own right. Even within these specialist historical topics, there is a tendency for historians to become distracted by testing out the content or substance of the denial rather than trying to establish its pathology—what it is that makes these deniers tick. Diverted by denouncing and proving the deniers to be impostors, the opponents of denialism have, in many instances, passed up the chance either to explain why deniers do what they do or to seek any deeper, functional basis for this strange and enduring phenomenon.

The key to historical denial lies in its self-deception transformed into an attempted deception of others, and this process tends to follow certain behavioural patterns. This book will deal with historical denial as an activity that has its own underlying structure based on several observable psychological characteristics. The argument here is that deniers share certain traits that may be categorised in psychological terms, although there are variations in their emphasis and applicability. Historical denial is viewed as about more than a capricious desire to block and shock, more than a personal or political desire to oppose. Once an individual or group wishes to convince others of their self-deceiving distortion of historical reality, the utterances of that individual or group will tend to follow the same processes employed by an individual using psychological denial. For example, to convince oneself that an unpleasant truth of one's own life is not so—no, I do not drink too much wine in the evening—one may repress knowledge of how many bottles of wine one buys, claim to be just a social drinker, point to others who drink much more (whether they do or not), and dismiss, ignore or hide the empty bottles. Similarly, a political leader or a writer who wishes to deny interpretations of past events may repress uncomfortable feelings or thoughts, claim to be an objective observer, discuss others' alleged misdeeds and dismiss, ignore or suppress any contradictory evidence.

Having established this proposition, that historical denial has a psychological dimension, the application of denialism's common characteristics will be considered in detail in this book, through an examination of six illustrative case studies taken from modern history. The case studies chosen are, in chronological order: Turkish denial of genocidal behaviour towards Armenians; Holocaust denial; Japanese denial of wartime atrocities; British communist denial of Stalinist crimes against humanity; Serbian and Marxist denial of genocide in Bosnia; and Australian denial of the maltreatment of Indigenous Australians.

The choice of these particular twentieth-century topics was based on several factors: It is only in the twentieth century that we have seen the promulgation of a series of constraining international conventions and declarations that have attempted to limit, through international condemnation and sanctions, the excesses of brutal regimes and organisations. From 1899 onwards, following the adoption of the first Hague convention, originally framed to govern conduct in war, a growing international awareness of the continuing conflict between human rights on the one hand and ruthless political, religious or economic ambition on the other produced a parallel growth in denialism. Perpetrators and their supporters, trying to stay within the bounds of what has become increasingly accepted as lawful behaviour regarding human rights, rationalise away their excesses through practices of denial, which may vary in character but remain consistent in form and function.

The first of these consistencies in denialist form is hostility by the majority of deniers towards a particular 'other' or group of 'others'. That is to say, they are, as individuals and as groups, bigoted; indeed, in some cases, they are deeply prejudiced to the point of showing intense hatred. For example, Turkish bias against Armenians is still alive and well among some Islamic extremist sections of the Turkish community; neo-Nazis enthusiastically maintain their anti-Semitism; Japanese ultra-nationalists continue to be racially contemptuous of their Chinese and Korean neighbours; Serbian ultra-nationalists loathe their Muslim neighbours to the west and to the south; and some Australians who support the denialist position seem to have an obsession more with the condition of Indigenous history than with the condition of Indigenous Australians. There are exceptions; for example, in their pro-Stalinist condition of denial, British Marxists did not consciously display racist or ethnic intolerance, unlike their hero.

INTRODUCTION

When they do exist, these different prejudicial perspectives occur on a denialist continuum that ranges from those at the extreme end who might sponsor assassinations, bombings and other forms of violence to the relatively restrained deniers whose activities lie mainly in publishing and public speaking, and also generally within the criminal law. This denialist continuum remains a measure of prejudice from the fanatical end of the scale to the merely abhorrent.

To place this kind of prejudice in context and to see how it relates to the functioning of denial, the work of US social psychologist Gordon Allport is particularly valuable. Allport, a pioneer in the field of prejudice whose 1954 classic *The Nature of Prejudice* had a huge impact in the 1960s and thereafter, gave prejudice some theoretical and practical context by moving beyond a merely psychodynamic definition. He described the prejudiced individual as a person who holds a hatred based upon a 'faulty and inflexible generalization'. This was an of-its-time definition that did not, for example, include gender issues, and some of Allport's pre-feminist thinking has since been challenged as the basis of subsequent research. However, the characteristics of prejudiced individuals or groups identified by Allport, and by his successors, include some recognisable traits that hold today among deniers: acquiescence to authority and leaders; emotional inhibition; belief in order and discipline; hostility towards an easy target; distrust of others who are different; simplistic analysis of complex circumstances; antagonism to ideas beyond their frame of reference; belief in the purity of self and in the evil of a different other; and belief that their own group is superior to other groups. As we shall see, these traits manifest themselves repeatedly among individual deniers and, to some extent, form a behavioural basis for institutional denial.

The second consistency in denialist form is the attachment of deniers to outrageous beliefs, an attachment that appears to defy logic and seems only to increase in intensity as yet more evidence comes to light that contradicts the denialist position. Again, in line with the facile view that deniers are misguided idiots, critics of denialism see this simply as an extreme form of obstinacy: the tendency of a denier, drowning in a sea of refutation, to clutch at straws. However, there is more to this stubbornness than meets the eye, and to explain exactly what is going on, the work of Leon Festinger, yet another pioneering US psychologist, who developed the concept of cognitive dissonance, is both apposite and helpful. In his book *A Theory of Cognitive Dissonance* (1957), Festinger argued that the self seeks internal consistency of beliefs, but, if faced with two competing belief systems, resolution of this uncomfortable state of mind may be sought by rejecting one system and by increasing adherence to the remaining system. For example, if a group has an unfolding organisational memory (or history) that imagines Stalin to be especially good, but this organisational memory is increasingly confronted by evidence that unambiguously shows that Stalin was especially bad, the result will be an uncomfortable cognitive dissonance within the group. Festinger's approach, although qualified and modified by later research, thus helps to explain why, when the evidence for one set of denied events becomes increasingly incontrovertible, the deniers simply cling to their original position, tightening their grip and rationalising away any new findings that contradict their beliefs. Festinger also pointed out that when cognitive dissonance reaches breaking point, an individual will either strongly reinforce already held views or reject them. This finding is borne out, for example, when we consider those British Marxists who, after enduring decades of increasing cognitive dissonance, finally broke with communism over the Soviet suppression of the Hungarian uprising in 1956, and at the others, who remained within the Communist Party of Great Britain, notwithstanding the clearly appalling behaviour of Soviet authorities.

The third consistency in denialism is found in the way in which almost all of its attributes can be grouped within the overarching concepts of repression and projection, two key defence mechanisms that were first outlined by Sigmund Freud in a psychoanalytic context and later refined by his daughter Anna.

Repression is a method used by the self (in this case, the denier) to deal with an anxiety-producing condition (in this case, knowledge of a discomfiting past), by blotting out the unsavoury details, contradicting any commentary that may include anxiety-producing symptoms

INTRODUCTION

and fabricating a reassuring, if deluded, worldview. Such is the case, for example, with Marxist denial of Serb atrocities in Bosnia.

To bolster their defences against unwelcome intrusions from more realistically grounded others, deniers may also employ projection as a defence mechanism. This is the attributing of one's own feelings or motivations to others. For example, deniers will commonly accuse their opponents of a conspiracy against the denialist position when, as it happens, the deniers themselves are engaged in a conspiracy or cover-up of their own. Or, if the denialist case is concerned with rejecting accusations of mass murder, the projectionist position will argue that the victims of the mass murder committed murder on the same or similar scale or were so provocative that they brought the punitive killings upon themselves, an argument that contemporary Turkish nationalists have made against their Armenian accusers about the massacres of 1915. This form of projection, which includes the view that the deniers' opponents are out to get them and repression of the idea that it is they, in the first place, who are out to get their opponents, produces in the deniers a feeling of increased self-confirmation and solidarity, which allows them to continue to cope with their fearful version of reality.

Moving beyond her father's basic analysis of repression and projection, Anna Freud extended the ideas by categorising denial, again within a psychoanalytic context, into four major forms, which provide a useful set of behavioural categories.

The first category of denial is simple denial, or a blocking of reality, despite overwhelmingly contrary evidence that is generally regarded as unassailable. In modern Japan, for example, nationalists refuse to believe that imperial Japanese troops carried out countless barbaric atrocities, preferring instead to think that accusations of appalling military behaviour during World War II are part of a foreign conspiracy against the honour of Japan.

The second category lies in deeds, or taking action, to support denial. For example, in Turkey, as we shall see, under Article 301 of the criminal code, it is illegal to defame Turkishness by commenting on the 1915 Armenian massacres in a way that suggests Turkish involvement was a genocidal act.

The third category of denial is fantasy, in other words maintaining a belief in unsound ideas by creating fantasies around the object of the denial. Holocaust deniers provide the most florid examples of fantasy with their view, for example, that Adolf Hitler was a much-maligned leader. And, the deniers may continue, even if it is the case that large numbers of Jews were killed, the Führer was, in reality, both the unwitting chief of organisations staffed by over-zealous underlings and the victim of post-war Jewish conspiracies and lies.

The fourth category is the use of carefully chosen words to perpetuate the mistaken belief. The single most significant word in current denialist vocabulary is 'revisionism', generally the rewriting of history either using new evidence or re-interpreting existing evidence. In making the assertion that they are 'revisionists', the deniers hope to place themselves on a scale of legitimate historical inquiry that ranges from orthodoxy to heterodoxy, with themselves situated at the (respectably) heterodox end.

There are other, less common forms of denial that are clearly manifested in the behaviour of some individual deniers. In Freudian terms, the more specific neuroses of grandiosity and narcissism are often associated with the overarching neuroses of repression and projection. Grandiosity is a boastful and pretentious tendency to regard the self as a mover and shaker when others do not share this view. To deal with possible external rejection, grandiose personalities demand recognition for fantasised achievements and tell lies to gain credibility. There are several deniers discussed in the following chapters who exhibit grandiose behaviour. Narcissists display symptoms similar to grandiosity; indeed, the two are commonly linked. Narcissists inhabit a self-absorbed and conniving world and have a tendency to use and abuse others to gain attention that will prop up their self-regarding fantasies. They become enraged when obstructed or when their defences are broken through and they are revealed for what they are. While conventional narcissists may behave in a callously seductive fashion to achieve their goals, in an inverted form of the neurosis, the more that denialist narcissists behave in an outrageous and manipulative fashion, the more reinforcement they feel they are obtaining for their view of self as the centre of attention. As with grandiosity, this form of narcissism is exhibited in the most extravagant fashion by several of the individual deniers discussed in this book.

A composite picture now begins to emerge of deniers as individuals or groups who, in making false claims, frequently display behaviour and opinions consistent with deep-seated prejudice, including: belief in the wickedness of others, the infallibility of the self and the supremacy of right-minded authority; vindictive attacks on supporters of opposing points of view; obsessive fear, to the point of neuroticism, of attack, while attacking others; stubborn refusal to believe widely accepted rational explanations for past events; defence of their position through actions that, at worst, may include violence, and, at least, may include a vexatious form of litigation; re-emphasis on the strength of their beliefs while rationalising away rebuttals in order to cope with contradictions in their own convictions; and overweening egotism combined with an inability to see themselves as others see them.

When it comes to ego, there is an interesting common feature in the case studies that follow. Without wanting to linger for too long in Freudian constructions, each set of deniers discussed has an ego ideal, an iconic *pater familias*, so to speak. Among Turkish deniers, it is Kemal Ataturk; among Holocaust deniers, Hitler; among Japanese deniers, the emperor; among Marxist deniers, Stalin; among Serb deniers, Milosevic; and among Australian deniers, long-serving prime minister John Howard, a fatherly hero in the battle against progressivist thinking. Not all of these father figures have much in common; their inclusion in the pantheon of denial has more to do with the way in which denialism operates (uncritical respect for a superior authority) than it has to do with universality of behaviour.

Deniers not only appear to have a pathology, or a symptomatic commonality of motivation and process, but also adopt a common set of techniques, including falsely claiming scholarly or technical expertise;

using straw-man reasoning (the attributing of false assertions to others to distract argument); focusing on relatively insignificant and apparently inconsistent events that bolster their argument; forcing the counter-denier into arguing about an event of minor significance in a manner that steers the debate well away from the larger mass of corroborated evidence; attacking minor inconsistencies in the arguments of others while ignoring or denying major flaws in their own position; contradicting widely accepted evidence or deriding it as a product of a conspiracy, thus placing opponents in the position of proving a negative; accepting evidence as proven or corroborated even when there is neither valid proof nor corroboration; misrepresenting the views of opponents; making outrageous statements in public to attract media attention and notoriety; choosing to defy authorities or the law to gain publicity and martyrdom; picking public appearances carefully to take advantage of media ignorance; and telling lies. It is through these techniques that the denialist betrayal of history takes place.

In the first instance, denialism betrays history by attempting to distort our understandings of the actual past, or history, as it was lived. It does this by wilfully bending the evidence to suit the unyielding and self-interested purpose of the deniers. The second betrayal lies in denialism's scorn for the primary principles of historical investigation, which include following the evidence, balancing the arguments and providing a coherent and justified explanation. The third betrayal is found in misrepresentation: not only the deniers' misrepresentation of opponents' arguments, a common enough tactic, but also the false claims of historical authenticity made by the deniers themselves.

Another common feature of historical denial that seems to be almost axiomatic is that the more traumatic the event, the more strenuous the denial. The most strenuous forms of denial surround the issue of genocide and its definition. It is important, therefore, to clarify the exact meaning of the word 'genocide'. It was created by US Justice Department lawyer Raphael Lemkin in his 1944 report 'Axis Rule in Occupied Europe: Laws of Occupation, Analysis of Government, Proposals for Redress', as a context-specific reference to the Holocaust. Lemkin's

INTRODUCTION

term was adopted internationally as one of several 'crimes against humanity' as defined in the Nuremberg Charter (or the Charter of the International Military Tribunal), and later by the United Nations (UN), under Resolution 96-1 of December 1946 and Resolution 260-111 of December 1948. The fact that the term was created at a certain time does not mean, as some deniers assert, that it may not be applied retrospectively to events that preceded its adoption. Indeed, the worst consequences of the Holocaust itself preceded the creation of Lemkin's neologism, which had a precise but generally applicable etymology, from the Greek *genos*, meaning 'people' and the Latin *caedo*, meaning 'I murder', the latter commonly used prior to 1944 in the words patricide and matricide.

During the negotiations that preceded the UN resolutions, however, the Soviet Union, having just done its pre-war best to annihilate the 'counter-revolutionary' Ukrainians and still busily incarcerating and killing its people in the Gulags, was keen to avoid including political crimes within the term 'genocide'. That is why the final UN definition focused on 'intent to destroy, *in whole or in part* [emphasis added], a national, ethnical, racial or religious group', but not a political group. According to the definition, destruction of members of such groups may be through outright killing; causing serious bodily or mental harm; deliberately inflicting conditions of life calculated to bring about a group's physical destruction in whole or in part; imposing measures intended to prevent births within a group; and forcibly transferring children of the group to another group. The important point here is that because the term genocide is so closely associated with such a dreadful event as the Holocaust, delinquent nations, groups and individuals will do all they can to avoid categorisation as genocidal any violent activities for which they may have been responsible.

As tight a definition as it may seem, the UN version of genocide still exhibits some serious semantic flaws, as genocide scholar Eric Weitz has pointed out. For example, the Indonesian campaign against its Chinese minority in the 1960s, which resulted in the deaths of approximately half a million civilians, may be construed by its defenders as a political (hence non-genocidal) campaign, a classic piece of denialist casuistry. On that basis, the Khmer Rouge may technically be accused of genocide only against their minority populations, because their murderous 1970s campaign against their own people was, it may be argued, politically motivated.

Deniers also use the numbers argument to defend their position, adopting a piece of logic chopping known as 'denying the antecedent'. This is how the argument goes: Anything of the nature and numbers of the Holocaust is genocide; if any event does not have the nature and numbers of the Holocaust, it is not genocide. To put it another way, the Holocaust equals genocide; therefore, genocide must equal the Holocaust. The first problem here is that, when it comes to the nature of the event, the Holocaust was a specific historical occurrence that had certain attributes, including intent and a comprehensive, industrially run extermination campaign. If other mass murders do not have these precise attributes, this does not automatically disqualify them from being considered genocidal. The second problem, the numbers debate, is a red herring, since the key phrase in the UN definition is 'with intent to destroy, in whole or in part': under Lemkin's rules, it allows that an intentional plan to harm, for example, part of a small clan, a tribe or an ethnic community of several hundred can be genocidal. Proportion is one thing; numbers are another—it is the proportion that counts. For example, the international legal definition of mass murder has come to include the 1990s euphemism 'ethnic cleansing', but only in certain circumstances is this considered genocidal, as in the case of Bosnia between 1992 and 1995. The Serbian plan to create a Muslim-free zone in the Upper Drina Valley by means of murder, rape and destruction of property was confirmed as genocide by the International Criminal Tribunal for the Former Yugoslavia and by the International Court of Justice in 2007, but solely in the case of the massacre at Srebrenica. In this, the ICTY and ICJ's judgment was not in accord with a broader version of genocide as 'intent to destroy', a formulation agreed upon by a non-binding UN General Assembly resolution in 1993. The 1948 and 2007 definitions currently hold sway in international law.

INTRODUCTION

The UN definition of genocide, while including highly localised atrocities such as Srebrenica, excludes, on the above grounds, such violent incidents as the terror attack on civilians in Guernica in 1937; the indiscriminate bombings of Rotterdam and Coventry, and the London Blitz, in 1940; the fire-bombings of Hamburg in 1943, and of Dresden and Tokyo in 1945; the nuclear attacks on Hiroshima and Nagasaki in 1945; the Red Army violence against German civilians in Berlin in April 1945; the Soviet expulsion of Germans from East Prussia in 1945; and the post-war Czech expulsion of Sudeten Germans from the Czech borderlands, also in 1945. Although all were morally questionable assaults that led to dreadful civilian casualties, their exclusion is based on the view that the Germans and the Allies (in these cases) had no intention of destroying the people of Spain, the Netherlands, England, Japan and Germany 'in whole, or in part'.

Genocide, therefore, is about intent; it is about proportion but not necessarily numbers; it is retrospectively applicable. This definition separates genocide from such terms as massacre (general slaughter), mass murder (killing of many individuals), ethnic cleansing (forced expulsion, usually involving brutality and murder) and Holocaust (a specific historical event, despite attempts to gain ownership of the proper noun by non-Jewish survivor groups).

Finally, a note about *Denial*. This book is intended for the general reader. In presenting its findings as a series of introductory essays, it is based on scholarly and other sources that are, in many cases, relatively inaccessible or highly specialised. The essays themselves cover six discrete areas of modern history, and the structure of each chapter is shaped by its own story. For example, four of the less familiar narratives are given detailed backgrounds (Turkey, Japan, Bosnia and Stalinism), while the Holocaust and Australian chapters focus more on denial and on the arguments about denial than they do on the well-known narrative of the Final Solution and the less well known but fairly easily summarised narrative of the dispossession and deaths of Indigenous Australians.

1

UNDER WESTERN EYES

Armenian Massacres and Turkish Denial

It was Friday 19 January 2007, at about two in the afternoon. Campaigning journalist Hrant Dink was leaving the Istanbul office of his Armenian community newspaper *Agos*. Without warning, gunshots rang out and the Armenian writer fell to the ground. Security cameras recorded images of a young man running away, hastily tucking a pistol into his belt. An eyewitness later told reporters that the fugitive had yelled, 'I killed the infidel'. Dink had been shot twice in the back of the head, and four shell cases were found at the scene, evidence of a nervously effective amateur assassin. Television news footage later showed Dink's body lying prone on the footpath, covered with a white sheet.

On hearing of the murder, Turkish prime minister Recep Tayyip Erdogan [pronounced Erdo-wan] announced that 'dark hands' were behind the assassination, remarking that 'a bullet was fired at freedom of thought and democratic life'. Almost immediately, the conspiracy theory mills began to grind out their fantasies: Dink had been killed by foreign intelligence agencies wanting to block Turkey's entry into the European Union; Armenian *agents provocateurs* were trying to blacken Turkey's name, according to Turkish ultra-nationalists; it was an inter-Armenian squabble and Dink had been caught in the crossfire. Rumours circulated

Istanbul that Nobel Prize–winning novelist Orhan Pamuk, who had previously crossed swords both with the authorities and with ultra-nationalists over Turkey's Armenian question, had quietly and quickly left the country on hearing of Dink's assassination.

If Pamuk had indeed left Turkey in fear of his life, there was good reason. Following a tip-off, police arrested the assassin, Ogun Samast, a solitary teenage dropout from Trabzon, the Black Sea harbour city in north-eastern Anatolia, heartland of provincial conservative Islam. Samast immediately and unrepentantly confessed, telling police that he did it because he had seen on a CNN website that Dink remarked, 'I am from Turkey but Turkish blood is dirty'. The lone gunman's confession then unravelled when it turned out that he was a member of an ultra-nationalist youth group. Further unravelling occurred when it was discovered that Yasin Hayal, a friend of Samast, was a known Islamic extremist. Indeed, back in 2004, Hayal had served eleven months in jail for bombing a McDonald's restaurant in Trabzon. And it had been in Trabzon, in the spring of 2006, that a fundamentalist youth, apparently incensed over the worldwide Mohammed cartoon crisis that had begun in Denmark, had shot an Italian priest in the back of the head.

Hayal was arrested, together with five other fundamentalist suspects. He confessed to supplying Samast with a pistol and some money. By this time, the story of a lone, misguided gunman at work had begun to look shaky. It appeared that Hrant Dink, an opponent of extremism, had been killed by a gang of religious fanatics angered by the journalist's attempts to reconcile Turkish society to the full scale of the Armenian massacres of 1915, which were viewed as genocide by many, but as exaggerated misadventures or even lies by others, particularly those fierce and often violent fundamentalist Turks represented by Hayal.

Notwithstanding the intimidatory act by these extremists, and possibly even because of the assassination, many Istanbul-based Turks protested against the murder by attending Dink's funeral. An estimated 100 000 Turks, Turkish Armenians and expatriate Armenians either marched to the funeral together or stood in tribute on the footpaths. Dink's widow, Rakel, speaking before the cortege moved off, said,

'We are saying goodbye to our brother with a silent walk, without slogans and without asking how a baby became a murderer'. She and Dink's two adult daughters, Beda and Sera, then released doves as a symbol of peace and as a sign of hope for change.

But some things do not change. As the self-confessed ringleader Hayal was being led into an Istanbul court on the day after the funeral, he shouted a defiant warning towards a cluster of journalists. 'Orhan Pamuk, be smart, be smart!' he called out, cautioning the famous author, and everyone else, to stay quiet on the genocide question—or else.

The motivation for killing the journalist was simple enough. Hrant Dink had been attempting to find common ground, but consensual moderates like Dink are even more harmful to an extremist ideology than are opposition activists. So, in some Islamic extremist eyes, he had to be killed. However, the unintended consequence of the murder was a show of harmony, in Istanbul at least. Although the funeral march was meant to be silent, many mourners shouted out slogans, and thousands carried black-and-white placards that read 'We are all Hrant Dink' and 'We are all Armenians'. In this rare and astonishing moment of inter-ethnic solidarity, Prime Minister Erdogan, with one cautious eye on his Islamic-oriented Justice and Development Party (better known as the AKP), sent out a message that his schedule was too busy for him to attend. His deputy went instead.

The Armenian Massacres

Dink's murder was shocking but not unexpected. It was yet another incident in a long and violent conflict over the question of Turkish persecution of its Armenian minority, a campaign of Armenian retribution and intimidation as well as Turkish nationalist retaliation that began when World War I ended and continues to this day.

The conflict is based on the bare fact that, at the beginning of 1915, the Turkish Armenian population numbered an estimated 1.75 million and yet, three years later, only 1.1 million Turkish Armenians were still alive. This meant that, during those three years, more than one in three Turkish Armenians were either killed outright or died as a direct result of forced expulsion at the hands of Turkish authorities. As a consequence, during the post-massacre period, the majority of the remaining Turkish Armenian community scattered to the four winds in a global diaspora. Today, the Armenian population of Turkey is calculated at a mere 80 000. In contrast, the Armenian-descended population of France, one of several major destinations for the Armenian diaspora, is estimated at 750 000. These French descendants of the survivors of the massacres represent an influential anti-Turkish minority within the French republic and it is this kind of globalised minority that contributes to an Armenian campaign to remember the obliteration of the Turkish Armenians, to allege a Turkish cover-up and to seek reparation.

The pro-Armenian allegation, in an almost century-long war of words, bullets and bombs, is that, in 1915, the Turkish government instigated a campaign of expulsions that was directly responsible for murdering somewhere between 500 000 and two million Armenians (the figures vary), in a deliberate and pre-meditated campaign of genocide.

There are two counter-claims, and, oddly, they form the basis of one of the few causes that unites Islamic and secular Turkey. First, Islamic Turkish denial is straightforward enough: the Armenians were, and are, liars. What they claim to have happened is a slur on Islamic Turkish honour. In any case, the infidel Armenians massacred Islamic Turks in eastern Anatolia in 1915, so they probably got what they deserved. In this context, the phrase 'Armenian Massacres' refers to the killing of Islamic Turks by Armenians, not the other way around. Anyone who espouses the Armenian cause is an enemy of Turkish Islam. Second, secular Turkish denialists argue, in a more nuanced fashion, that perhaps hundreds of thousands of Armenians unfortunately perished during a state-auspiced, wartime deportation of a potentially disloyal population. Armenian fatalities, exaggerated by Christian propagandists (Armenian and others), occurred as a consequence of poor planning, bad weather, lack of food and water, and attacks by Kurds and Circassian bandits, but certainly not because of any systematic government plan. In any case, treacherous Armenians had already massacred Turks in eastern Anatolia, so they probably brought it on themselves. Anyone who espouses the Armenian cause is an enemy of the sanctity of the modern Turkish constitution and the revered memory of Kemal Ataturk.

Armenians in Turkey—and an Enormous Crime

> The propaganda work necessary to justify an enormous crime was fully prepared: The Armenians had united with the enemy, revolution was about to break out in Istanbul, they [the Armenians] were going to kill Unionist [government party] leaders, they were going to force open the straits.
>
> Ahmet Refik, Turkish army officer and historian, 1919

In attempting to untangle the thorny problem of what precisely happened to the Turkish Armenians and why so many Turks are in denial, the best place to start is probably with three questions: Who were these Armenians? What were they doing in Turkey? Why did the Turkish government want them expelled?

Turkish Armenians, mainly concentrated in north-eastern Anatolia, formed a substantial Christian minority population within the predominantly Islamic Ottoman, or Turkish, Empire. The Armenians numbered an estimated 1.1 million at the turn of the twentieth century, in a total Anatolian population of just over thirteen million, and their numbers rose to approximately 1.7 million by 1915. As an ethnic group, they were linked with Russian-based Armenians to the north. They were Indo-European in origin, had an ancient culture and a distinct language and were an established Anatolian people, absorbed by the expanding Ottoman Empire and made subject to Islamic rule. Until the mid-1800s, the conditions under which they existed had been more or less oppressive, as were the conditions for all non-Islamic minorities. However, the Ottoman capacity for continuing subjugation of its minorities changed in the nineteenth century, partly as a result of foreign interventions of various kinds and partly because of successful Christian rebellions against Turkish rule.

These foreign interventions, in the form of Capitulations (forced agreements), had begun in a small way in the 1600s, but by the end of the nineteenth century, the once proud Ottoman Empire, humiliatingly labelled the 'sick man of Europe', had been all but booted out of its European possessions and was compelled to accept increased interference in its affairs by Britain, France and Russia, chiefly regarding the protection of its Christian minorities: the Greeks, the Serbs and the Armenians.

These European intrusions did not help the Armenian cause at all. A predominantly rural and provincial group with many prosperous merchants in the various regional towns, Armenians were generally resented by Islamic Turks as an exploitative provincial minority with high-profile intellectual and mercantile communities in the national capital of Istanbul (formerly Constantinople). Attempts to protect the Armenians by European outsiders simply increased this resentment. And there was a widespread view that Armenian loyalties turned more towards Christian Russia, and hence against Islamic Turkey, at a time, in 1915, when Turkey and Russia were at war. This hostile opinion was strengthened by the activities of a small number of recklessly violent Armenian separatists, the Hnchak.

This long-standing prejudicial view of the Armenians as a vexatious, separatist ethnic minority, second-class subjects of Turkey but allegedly too smart and too rich for their own good, had been made even more severe by the slow decline in status of the Turkish Empire, which had led to the growth of post-imperial and irreducible (Anatolian) Turkish nationalism. The consequence was that when World War I broke out, in August 1914, the Turkish government (often referred to as the Porte) sided with the Central Powers of Germany, Austria-Hungary and Italy, against the already loathed Triple Entente powers of Britain, France and Russia. With a fiercely chauvinistic Ittihadist (*Ittihad ve Terakki*, or Young Turks) government in charge, led by the Triumvirate of Enver Pasha, Talat Pasha and Djemal Pasha, Turkish policy was driven by an official strain of Turkish nationalism that saw the war as an opportunity to settle old scores with both internal and external enemies. Moreover, any form of separatism or partition of the residual Anatolian homeland was anathema to the Young Turks.

Accordingly, the disposition of the reforming Turkish Porte was to regard the Armenians as a growing and intractable problem, a problem that was made all the more severe by both the closeness of the Anatolian Armenians to the heartland of the modern, diminished Turkish Empire and their simultaneous closeness to the Russian front. Indeed, Tsarist Armenian officers, acting as recruiters, soon began to cross the border into Turkey to set up insurgent gangs. For the Porte, the provocation was unambiguous and a decisive response was required.

In examining the claims and counter claims surrounding the Armenian question, three aspects of the events of 1915 and 1916 need closer examination. First, there is the question of government intent. That many Armenians died is beyond question, but did they die as part of an intended and comprehensive government-inspired campaign of genocide? Second, if there was intent, was there a state mechanism available to carry out the purpose? Third, allowing for a discussion of intent and state mechanism, can the Armenian massacres be considered as a Holocaust-style atrocity, indeed, the first Holocaust of the twentieth century, a considerable and pointed claim frequently made by supporters of the Armenian position? To deal with these questions, we will examine two features of the Armenian question: first, the role of the government in establishing the deportations and colluding in the massacres, and the nature of the massacres and second, whether or not what happened in Turkey was the first Holocaust of the twentieth century.

Intent to Kill: Countdown to Genocide

> Talat said that they had discussed the matter very thoroughly and arrived at a decision to which they would adhere. When I said they would be condemned by the world, he said they would know how to defend themselves; in other words, he does not give a damn.
>
> Henry Morgenthau, US Ambassador, 1915

The main players in the development of the policy of deportation were closely associated with the Committee for Union and Progress (CUP), a fiercely nationalist Islamic faction in the Young Turk movement, which operated as a government within a government, as did the Communist Party in Soviet Russia. Three senior CUP members in particular, known later as the Triumvirate, stand accused by the Armenians of being directly involved. They are Enver Pasha, Minister of War; Talat Pasha, Minister of the Interior; and Djemal Pasha, Viceroy of Syria, Lebanon and Palestine (although more recent research shows that Djemal may not have been quite so much the villain). The process by which the CUP, as the party of government, and the Triumvirate, as CUP leaders, developed their policy is a complex narrative probably best explained as a series of key events, with a special emphasis on the crucial period of March to May 1915 (bearing in mind that the Turkish cabinet was generally presented with Triumvirate *faits accomplis* and that the parliament was out of session during these months).

To begin with, during the first winter of World War I (1914–15), it was reported by various observers in Istanbul that anti-Armenian sentiment was so powerful in government circles that massacres were imminent and inevitable. This kind of reprisal against minorities was not unusual in the Turkish Empire, where it was standard practice to carry out the occasional large-scale massacre to subdue dissenters, but there appeared to be something new about government attitudes in 1914, due perhaps to the impact of the war. Turkish sociologist-historian Taner Akcam, admittedly using mainly hearsay or journalistic evidence, describes the change at that stage as atmospheric rather than tangible but suggests that the anti-Armenian feeling was almost palpable, and growing in intensity. Official, as well as popular, attitudes appeared to be moving away from sporadic acts of suppression towards something more systematic. To inflame the situation further, small-scale but brutal Armenian nationalist activity was reported in eastern Anatolia, where it was met by equally cruel government-initiated reprisals against Armenian villagers. This tit-for-tat conflict aggravated already strained relations between Turkish and Armenian communities in the east and gave a perfect pretext for governmental repression of Armenians.

At the same time, the Turkish government, bolstered by its participation in the Central Powers alliance, was pressing on with a grandiose plan for a pan–Turkic Islamic empire that would stretch from the Caucasus to North Africa. This ambition came to a sudden and disastrous halt in early January 1915. The previous month, the Turkish Third Army, led by Triumvirate member Enver Pasha, having adopted an over-optimistic strategy of encirclement, had crossed into Russian territory. The Turks could not have begun a military operation in the Transcaucasus at a worse time, and the poorly equipped Third Army floundered in the snow and ice of the mountainous borderlands. The Turkish troops eventually crossed into Russian Armenia, but it was all to no avail. In January 1915, during and following the battle of Sarikamish, the Turks were all but annihilated by the Russians, who had substantial Armenian help. Some 25 000 Turkish soldiers were lost in the week-long struggle, and an estimated 50 000 to 60 000 fatalities occurred during the Third Army's retreat across the mountains to Anatolia. This humiliating defeat immediately brought into play CUP-inspired stab-in-the-back accusations against the Armenians, who, it was alleged, were engaged in a murderous conspiracy to subvert Turkish war aims. One of the main proponents of the backstabbing theory was Enver Pasha, whose ambitious and ill-organised campaign had led to the defeat at Sarikamish. Enver, a man unaccustomed to humiliation, returned to Istanbul and began to use the army's propaganda machinery to attack the Armenians and to deflect attention away from his own shortcomings.

Allowing for the gradual evolution of wartime anti-Armenian policy in Turkey, the defeat at Sarikamish constituted one of the first major turning points in the obliteration of the Turkish Armenians. The defeat and its consequences produced in the CUP leadership a growing belief that the Armenian minority within Turkey's boundaries formed a strong obstacle to any nationalist and pan-Islamic ambitions for a new, homogeneous Turkish empire. After the battle, the official Turkish attitude to its Armenian population quickly changed from one of harsh oppression to one of deportation, and then to one of annihilation. The CUP Central Committee knew that the Armenians were not just going to fade away; on the contrary, in January 1915, with the war going so badly for Turkey, there was every chance that the Armenians and their Russian co-religionists could soon force a dreaded partition arrangement on the Porte.

The Turkish government moved from mere anti-Armenian propaganda to physical action in February 1915 when, in response to supposed Armenian treachery at Sarikamish, Armenian troops serving in the Turkish army were disarmed and recruited into labour or transport units. In these battalions they later proved to be vulnerable to murderous attacks by fully armed Turkish colleagues.

On 19 February, the war stakes were raised when French and British forces began a shelling campaign to demolish the Turkish forts that overlooked the Dardanelles. The threat of imminent attack from the west was now a reality, and the view from Istanbul was that Turkey was facing a fight on four fronts: France and Britain to the west, Russia to the east, British Mesopotamia to the south—and the Armenians within.

In March, the Entente shelling campaign continued, and the CUP Central Committee decided that drastic measures needed to be taken, firstly to deal with the internal enemy. It was at about that time that Enver Pasha reportedly suggested that the solution to the Armenian question was to remove the Armenians from eastern Anatolia and send them elsewhere.

To manage the eastern problem, Sakir Bey of the shadowy Special Organisation, a man aggressively hostile to Armenians, travelled to Istanbul from the eastern regional fortress city of Erzurum and requested that he be relieved of his duties as agitator in foreign parts and put in charge of dealing with domestic enemies, 'the Armenians inside'. He was sent back on the difficult 1200-kilometre journey to the east, this time with new orders and a bag of cash to pay for services about to be rendered. This meant that by the end of March 1915, the stage was set. The CUP Central Committee, the Turkish government in all but name, had decided to commence deportations from the more troublesome areas. How that was to be arranged and with what consequence was not yet clear: the plan was still only a suggestion and a draft government policy. Enver's approach was yet to manifest itself as mass murder.

Sakir Bey, with his new orders and his stash of money, arrived back in the eastern garrison town of Erzurum at the beginning of April. Simultaneously, the introduction of a deportation law aimed at the Armenians was agreed at CUP headquarters in Istanbul.

Events then took a sharp turn in mid-April when Armenians in the eastern regional centre of Van rose up against the Turks, the revolt apparently caused by fear of impending Turkish massacres. The inhabitants of Van held out for a month, further confirming Turkish apprehensions and infuriating the Istanbul authorities. Importantly, however, while the CUP's targeted deportation decision had already been made in March, the events at Van provided the perfect excuse for a series of arrests of Istanbul Armenians (and other local undesirables) on 24 April, followed by mass deportations throughout Anatolia, the next stage in anti-Armenian operations. New Entente activities, including the Gallipoli landings in the west and Russian advances in the east, only added to the urgency of the anti-Armenian measures. Accordingly, early in May, Enver Pasha, as minister of war, ordered the removal of the troublesome Armenians of Van, but, by that time, there was a growing unanimity among CUP leaders that a more radical solution than mere localised deportations had to be brought into play.

There is evidence that local and national CUP leaders were privy to the new direction; for example, at the beginning of April, Ekran Bey, adjutant to Major Lange, a German officer attached to the Turkish army, reportedly said that Turks would exterminate the whole race, a not uncommon remark at that time. Furthermore, Mehmet Vehip, Commander of the Third Army, alleged after the war that the Central Committee of the CUP had sent out deportation orders to provinces by special courier, implying urgency and secrecy.

The plot thickened. Erzincanh Sabit, Governor of Harput (in the Van region) was reported as saying that the Armenians in Turkey were going to be killed, and Ihsan Bey, Head of the Special Bureau of the Interior

Ministry, stated after war that when he was prefect of Kilis (a town in southern Turkey, near the Syrian border), Abdul'ahad Nuri Bey, Deputy Director of the Office for Resettlement of Tribes and Refugees, told him that Talat Pasha's intention behind deportation was extermination.

On 15 May the cabinet rubber-stamped the expulsion process by approving fifteen regulations for the implementation of deportation law and resettlement. Inter-community tensions, already high, were ratcheted up a further notch on 18 May when Russian troops arrived in Van to relieve besieged Armenian inhabitants, bringing with them Armenian volunteers. During and after the fighting, Islamic prisoners and villagers were massacred, possibly in their thousands, in an orgy of revenge killing, which was then followed by counter-atrocities when Ottoman forces briefly re-took the town two months later.

Meanwhile, and crucially, on 24 May the Russians asked the other Entente powers to issue a declaration holding Turks to account for massacres of Christians. British historian Donald Bloxham regards this foreign ultimatum as a major incitement to the already furious Turks. The CUP became agitated at the implied threat, and Bloxham makes a valid suggestion that, as a consequence of the Entente declaration, the CUP had nothing left to lose after yet another example of Franco-British meddling. As far as the Triumvirate was concerned, the CUP might as well be hanged for sheep as for lambs.

Events began to gather speed. On 26 May, in the midst of the Van uprising and two days after the Entente's threat, in a move seen as highly significant by author Taner Akcam, a statement was sent to the grand vizier (the prime minister, but in effect the cabinet secretary) by Talat's ministry of interior which stated that the Armenian question must 'be brought to an end in a comprehensive and absolute way … preparations and presentations have been proposed and considered for a final end in a comprehensive and absolute way, to this issue, which constitutes an important matter among the vital issues for the state'. On the same day, following a pattern established in previous ethnic relocations, the Turkish High Command ordered that there should be a resettlement pattern to avoid concentrations of Armenians—they should not form more than 10 per cent of any local Islamic population. Finally, on 27 May, the cabinet adopted the 'Provisional Law Concerning the Measures to Be Taken by the Military Authorities against Those Who Oppose the Operations of the Government', the implication being that all Armenians opposed the operations of the government. While decisions about the deportation process were being made in Istanbul, the stakes were raised further in late May when a Turkish army, under Generals Cevdet and Halil, took on the invading Russians near Bitlis, a key strategic town close to the Van region, massacring Armenians as they went.

On 14 June, yet another crucial genocidal milestone was reached when Talat Pasha sent an instruction to Erzurum authorising the killing of 'resisters and escapees'—on the face of it, simply a harsh act in a tough wartime environment, but Bloxham reads more significance into Talat's command: as far as he is concerned it is an indirect direction for mass killing, along the lines of 'killed while attempting to escape'.

Finally, on 9 July, Talat Pasha apparently told US ambassador Henry Morgenthau that he did not give a damn. The die had already been cast. By that time, tens of thousands of Armenians were already dead and hundreds of thousands more were destined either for immediate death at the hands of local Turks or for death during journeys to holding camps and in the holding camps themselves.

In conclusion, the argument here is that the Turkish government, in effect the Central Committee of the CUP, originally intended a policy of forced removal in Armenian hot spots as a consequence of external and internal factors. Because of exigent circumstances, in April and May 1915 this position quickly changed into a policy of mass deportation, with the expected destruction, through murder and attrition, of the Armenian population. The deportation policy was accompanied by explicit condemnations of this supposedly tumultuous minority, together with an implicit declaration of open season on any Armenians.

The pronouncement had a powerful impact, first on local CUP officials, who, sometimes with the help of the Special Organisation, willingly helped organise killing sprees; second on established Islamic Turkish villagers who coveted Armenian land, stock and possessions; and third on newly arrived refugee Turks looking for the spoils of deportation. Kurdish tribesmen wanted a piece of the action too. They were traditional enemies of the Armenians and were slowly moving from a nomadic transhumance economy to a settled agricultural economy and, as with many Turkish villagers, they coveted Armenian land.

The general position of the army was to keep its distance unless ordered into action. Local administrators either actively or tacitly supported the deportations and massacres, with just a small minority, punished by execution or removal from office, resisting the inhumane aspects of the CUP's policy.

From Incitement to Genocide

> The authorities talk of an accidental meeting with hostile Kurds, which is the official euphemism for massacre. There have been frequent cases of torture as well ... At Harput our Consul lately saw the deported during the halt there, and related that nothing could equal their misery ... The murder of Armenians has become a sport.
>
> Lewis Einstein, US consular official, 1915

The Turkish government policy of national incitement against the Armenians operated on five levels. First, in the upper echelons of government, the political regime and the army issued national regulations to give the appearance of orderly deportations. Second, at the regional level, provincial CUP authorities, under orders, made plans to deal with 'their' Armenians, either by setting up massacres or by following central directives for deportation, or both. Third, local CUP agents auspiced district-level anti-Armenian activities of an increasingly violent nature in towns and villages, using Special Organisation squads or specially released convicts to do the dirty work or directly encouraging the local residents to take part in round-ups, killings and dispossessions. Fourth, at the local, individual level, Islamic Turks together with Kurdish and Circassian bandits, having understood that their activities would go unpunished, murdered whomever they could find and took whatever they could carry. Fifth, those Armenians who survived both the horrors of the Anatolian massacres and the forced marches over inhospitable territory, mainly women and young children, were eventually corralled in improvised and inadequate camps in Syria and northern Iraq (then Mesopotamia), there to suffer and, all too often, to die.

What happened, therefore, in 1915 and 1916 was not so much a nationally coordinated campaign of extermination as an Istanbul-supported operation that produced myriad events at a local level, in which individuals and groups were murdered or maltreated and deported and there was a deliberately mismanaged policy of expulsion and incarceration of vulnerable survivors. The question is, did all of this amount to a massive act of genocide, for it is the genocidal nature of the tragedy, as well as the intent of the Porte, that is responsible for the creation of the subsequent controversy.

As for the numbers, it is impossible to determine exactly how many Armenian men, women and children died in 1915 and 1916 (and later, since the conflict continued until 1923) while supposedly in the care of the Turkish authorities. Principally, this is because absolutely precise totals for pre- and post-deportation periods are still unavailable, leaving the topic open to distortion by propagandists from either side. There are other complicating factors, however. Because of inefficient and fragmented record-keeping and since many violent incidents took place in isolated areas, often going unrecorded, there is no way of tracking accurate casualty numbers. Furthermore, many Armenian children were abducted or sold, and some adult Armenian survivors were forced to convert to Islam, so these do not appear as Armenian Christians in the relevant post-1916 official figures.

Despite these problems, Guenter Lewy, the US political scientist, in a careful and cautious analysis, has come up with a figure of about 642 000 deaths, which amounts to about 37 per cent of the estimated pre-war Turkish Armenian population. To place the figures in a proper context, Armenians were not the only people to suffer in that period: the Turks too bore military and civilian casualties during the war and in the two years following the war when Turkey was ravaged by invasion and occupation, accompanied, yet again, by the customary massacres. Moreover, during the Turkish War of Independence (1920–23) there were further Turkish casualties. But the Armenians suffered the most: 'Due to famine, epidemics, and warfare, the people of Turkey, both Muslims and Christians, experienced a mortality rate far worse than that of any country during the First World War; but the sad fate of the Armenians will always stand out as a special tragedy'. However, as Lewy points out, the Armenian community of what was then Constantinople, as well as the Armenians of Smyrna and Aleppo, were left largely untouched by the anti-Armenian campaign of 1915 and 1916, suggesting again that what took place was on a large scale but was not a consistent and coherent policy of complete extermination.

While what happened to the Armenians may not therefore have been the result of an *ab initio* governmentally designed genocidal strategy, by targeting Armenians in an undifferentiated fashion, by letting loose the worst elements of a hotly incited society on all Armenians, men, women and children, and by failing in its duty to protect the deportees, the effect was the same: mass murder of genocidal proportions and character.

Allowing that what occurred in Anatolia was genocidal, there is a final issue that needs closer examination: some of the pro-Armenian discourse about the genocide tends to construct these horrific events as a forgotten Holocaust. In other words, Turkish genocidal activity in the war years was a precursor to the Nazis' *Endlösung*, the Final Solution.

The Special Organisation

> Until the main court martial ... of 1919, nobody had linked the SO to the Armenian deportations. The reports and writings of foreign consular officials, missionaries and German officers who served in Turkey are a rich source of information about the deportations and massacres, but the SO is never mentioned.
>
> Guenter Lewy, 2005

The Armenians argue that the Special Organisation (SO) was instrumental in fuelling the already established hatreds that led to Nazi-style massacres of so many Armenians in 1915. The activities of members of the SO squads, so the Armenian story goes, demonstrated complete government complicity in the genocide; but there are, as might be expected, fierce debates about that.

The word 'special' has a particularly sinister connotation in twentieth-century history. As an adjective, it can be a vague indication of some precise but illicit activity that needs to be concealed. For example, when the Romanov royal family was murdered in Ekaterinburg (Sverdlovsk) in 1918, the deed took place in a 'house for a special purpose'. Just over a decade later, the Nazis used the term 'special unit' (Sonderkommando) to describe the squads that were part of the Einsatzgruppen (Operations Group) killing machine that worked with the armed forces and police battalions in the east to eliminate Jews, commissars and other 'enemies of the Reich'. During the Final Solution, the process by which Jews were eliminated was described as Sonderbehandlung, or 'special treatment'. So it is disconcerting to discover that, just before World War I began, the Turkish government set up a unit called the Special Organisation (Teskilati Mahsusa). The precise date of the establishment of the SO is unclear, but the best estimates give its creation as an informal and unnamed outfit at around 1913. It was formally constituted under its official title in July 1914, by which time it was under the control of Enver Pasha and the army.

Originally, the SO's role was to intimidate ethnic enemies of the pan-Turkic movement through externally fomented terror and the repression of insurgents. Led by selected regular army officers and numbering, at the peak of its operations, between 30 000 and 40 000 men, the SO consisted of soldiers from the regular army, members of the gendarmerie, Kurdish tribesmen and resentful Islamic Turkish refugees from newly independent Christian provinces (known as *mujahirs*).

The appearance of the SO in the narrative of Turkish–Armenian relations seems ominous, especially in the context of Balkan and Anatolian history, in which inter-ethnic and inter-religious conflict was commonly conducted through pillage, rape and massacre and in which the Ottoman Empire had, in the past, employed ill-disciplined irregulars to do its dirty work. This had certainly been the case with the Bashi Bazouks (literally 'damaged heads' but more accurately 'leaderless'), who crushed the Bulgarian uprising in 1876 with such ferocity that the Turks later stopped using them. The SO, however, was neither a reincarnation of the Bashi Bazouks, nor a precursor of Heinrich Himmler's *Schutzstaffeln* (SS), as has been claimed: it was a much less enraged group than the Bashi Bazouks, and a much less ideologically coherent group than the SS.

There are two divergent points of view about the role of the SO in the Armenian massacres. The first, put forward forcefully by US Armenian scholar Vahakn Dadrian and supported by several other writers, suggests that the SO was the principal organiser of the genocide. And indeed, it is undeniable that some of its leaders were zealous anti-Armenian members of the CUP and that the SO was implicated in the recruiting of released convicts to carry out particularly brutal operations against the Armenians. However, while Taner Akcam, the otherwise methodical Turkish sociologist-historian, agrees with Dadrian, suggesting that the SO was given the task of directly organising the Armenian 'genocide'. In making his case, he points primarily to the SO's track record in agitational operations in Russia and Iran, and its redirection to eastern Anatolia in 1914 and 1915, during which time the CUP's local agents seem to have been making most of the running when it came to organising the massacres. The contrary view, expressed cogently by Guenter Lewy and followed more or less by Donald Bloxham, is that the SO operated as a paramilitary group that was nationalistic in intent and behaviour, conducting small-scale, and very vicious, guerilla operations in Russia and acting as an intelligence agency, but with much closer ties to the army than with the CUP. Lewy goes further, alleging that Dadrian has ignored evidence that contradicts the thesis that the SO was the principal agent of the genocide.

Although the SO was heavily involved in what are now called black operations, these activities were carried out mainly beyond Turkey's borders. But it is possible, and even likely, that the gangs of cut-throats established by the SO to perform their terroristic work in the Caucasus were then recruited by the CUP into local operations in eastern Anatolia. Because SO documents were largely destroyed after the war, however, there is little evidence of direct and considered SO involvement in a policy of genocidal massacres.

A Case Study: Incident at Kemakh Gorge

> The first convoy set off on June 7th. Rich people hired carts. (Again, one is amazed by their simple trust in Turkish words.) They were to go in the first place, to Kharput, taking the lengthy, semi-circular route via the Kemakh gorge, a rough road full of twists and turns.
>
> Christopher Walker, 1990

The details of how the massacres were carried out varied from locality to locality. For example, those Armenians who travelled to northern Syria arrived relatively unmolested, only to find themselves camped in a lethally hostile desert. In eastern, inland Anatolia, the process began with the disarming of Armenian villagers, whose hunting rifles, shotguns and other weapons were seized and sometimes displayed for official photographs as evidence of their insurgent intentions. The next stage was a pronouncement that the villagers or townspeople were to be resettled, away from the front, for their own protection. When the deportation assembly began, local men and youths were culled, usually murdered out of sight (or even in plain sight) by gendarmes (armed Turkish police under military command), irregulars or Turkish villagers, or by all three. The remaining, terrified refugees, predominantly women, girls and children, and the older men, may have been told that they could take their possessions to make the resettlement easier. Caravans were then formed and the refugees set off, normally guarded by a few gendarmes. Before long, the caravans were attacked, either by Turkish villagers or by Kurdish bandits. The gendarmes sometimes advised the refugees to leave their possessions to appease the bandits, but it was all to no avail. In general, the gendarmes took no action, watched or even colluded as the Armenian men who had survived the pre-caravan round-up were murdered, the women raped and killed, the children abducted. Infants were murdered or abandoned to die, and the rest of the children were left to manage for themselves. These officially sanctioned attacks, which went largely unpunished, occurred time and time again, all over eastern Turkey, as the caravans wended their way over difficult mountain tracks and across the valleys of the unforgiving Anatolian ranges. Hundreds of thousands of Armenians were hacked to death, shot one by one or in groups, or murdered in mass killings carried out mainly in remote areas.

There were variations. Some gendarmes tried to protect their caravans but were often outnumbered. Some local officials protested but were removed from office or even executed. Some Islamic villagers sheltered refugees, normally for a fee, while others adopted children as potential converts; still others took girls or young women into their harems. Infants, extra mouths to feed for 'rescuers', seem generally to have been left to die.

The general pattern therefore was for the eastern Armenians to be massacred in their own towns and villages or in nearby locations. One such isolated location was Kemakh gorge. This beautiful, rugged, ravine, which acts as a notched pass through the high peaks of the Munzur Ranges, lies 15 kilometres to the south and west of the town of Erzincan. The mountains separate the Erzincan plateau from the Christian centre of Harput, in southern Turkey, the purported destination of the Erzincan refugees. The gorge itself is a steep and rocky chasm through which flows the upper part of the western Euphrates, at that time known as the Kara Su (black water) or Frat Su (as in the Armenian Ephrat). The narrow track that ran alongside the gorge was once part of a major camel route from Persia to the west. Further south along the track are steep canyons, one of which, at downstream Avshin, is 300 metres high on each side.

According to the pattern described above, the Armenians who lived in Erzincan were gathered together in early June 1915 for deportation.

At that time, the garrison town was a regional centre situated in a relatively fertile and well-watered plain and surrounded by small villages, with a population of around 15 000. It was a relatively prosperous provincial town, with a half-Armenian and half–Islamic Turkish population. It had old and new barracks buildings, a textile factory, a boot factory and a tannery. The Armenians played an active, if subservient, part in the economic life of the region. Identifying and gathering those for deportation was simple enough because some villages (small hamlets, in truth) were Armenian and others were Turkish, while town-dwelling Armenians were quartered in their own section.

As they were rounded up from their fields and homes, the Erzincan Armenians could probably see the smoke rising above the surrounding mountains, a sign of the campfires of nomadic Kurds. And wandering unseen along the mountain tracks were mounted Kurdish and Circassian vagabonds. Both were bandit groups with an appetite for easy pickings. On the pretext that they were protecting the Armenians from these predatory Kurds and Circassians, gendarmes accompanied the caravan that had taken four days to assemble. The refugees were marched along the flatlands towards the Kemakh pass. After 15 kilometres, the caravan reached the gorge, where the hapless refugees were hemmed in on the right by the steep slope and on the left by the Euphrates. It was the perfect site for a killing ground.

As the gendarmes abandoned their caravan and moved up the sides of the ravine, with the help of Kurdish tribesmen and *chetes* (Turkish irregulars, mainly Kurdish), they began a fusillade, shooting onto the refugees, who turned back in panic, only to encounter their former neighbours, the Islamic Turks of the Erzincan plateau, armed with guns and sabres. At that point, many Armenian women, fearing the worst, began to jump into the Euphrates.

> The whole surface of the river was covered with them ... The Turks were slaughtering in great numbers, but the Armenians were many, and by rushing upon them they managed to break through the line of Turks and reach the plain ... a few days later there was

a mopping-up operation since many little children were still alive and wandering about beside their dead parents, the *chetes* were sent to round them up and kill them. They collected thousands of children and brought them to the banks of the Euphrates, where seizing them by the feet, they dashed their heads against the rocks. And while a child was still in its death throes they would throw it into the river.

The terrible events at Kemakh were repeated as refugees from further afield were forced south through the gorge, resulting, over time, in the deaths of an unknown number of Armenians. But while this one incident at Kemakh tells us something about both the operational method and the motivation of the murderers, it also tells us something about the mythology of the Armenian massacres.

In a small provincial centre such as Erzincan, it is not inconceivable that the killers had surreptitiously planned the whole event in the days before the assembly took place, for it is quite clear from this eyewitness account and from other evidence that the attack was both premeditated and coordinated. The act of carnage at Kemakh gorge forms a useful case study in the attempted annihilation of a local ethnic minority, involving, as it did, CUP officials and local government authorities who instigated the deportation and supervised subsequent auctions of Armenian property, the gendarmes who shepherded the Armenians to their fate, the irregulars who were already in position, ready for pillage and murder, the Kurds who may have had an interest in some of the farming properties once held by the Armenians and, finally, the Islamic Turks who, having determined that half of the area's assets would adventitiously come their way, were not going to hand anything back. In this one appalling incident we find official sanction for and complicity in dispossession, robbery, looting and mass murder, along with authorised banditry and a homicidally rapacious peasantry.

The incident at Kemakh represents, in microcosm, a policy of mass murder, but it is not part of an Istanbul-based and tightly controlled campaign of genocide; on the contrary, Kemakh was a locally conducted and frenzied genocidal act carried out in a centrally fomented climate of resentment, fear and greed. At the same time, there is no point in attempting to minimise the suffering by saying that, as one of thousands of such localised acts, Kemakh was any less awful than a similar incident in any Istanbul-instigated policy of deliberate, total extermination. Locally organised or centrally directed, the Armenian victims were still very much dead.

However, some problems remain with Kemakh gorge's place in the mythology of the Armenian massacres. To begin with, an inspection of the site raises doubts over the alleged scale of the murder. Casualties from Erzincan totalled 20 000 killed, according to Christopher Walker (who uses as a source Johannes Lepsius's *Der Todesgang des Armenischen Volkes*, published in Potsdam in 1919), but this figure is highly improbable. To begin with, the camel track would at the time have been about 3 metres wide, which would have allowed caravans to pass by each other. Fitting 20 000 refugees along the track, even over several days, and then murdering them with rifle fire from the hills, is an unlikely occurrence for several reasons. First, the ambushers would have been using single-shot hunting rifles or, at best, five-shot Mausers, which would severely limit their killing power. Second, the refugees, in a column of several thousands, would have stretched back almost to the town of Erzincan itself. Third, there seems to be no eyewitness account of what actually happened at Kemakh gorge, only hearsay evidence by a Greek town dweller and the testimony of two Danish Red Cross nurses who were passing through on their way to Sivas and who subsequently reported what they saw (but not the massacre itself) to Lepsius, a German missionary. Fourth, the total population of Erzincan at that time was an estimated 5000 fewer than the 20 000 fatal casualties suggested by Lepsius.

What probably occurred, therefore, is this: in Erzincan, the local authorities rounded up as many Armenians as they could find, but some Armenians, realising what was about to happen, may have already slipped away into the hills, to an uncertain fate. The remaining able-bodied males were taken away and murdered, probably in their several hundreds; some of the women were taken by local Turks as concubines or domestic servants; children of working age were adopted for conversion; others, generally the old and the very young, were formed into caravans and sent on their way to be ambushed and eliminated at Kemakh, with the help of bandits who were almost certainly after women and booty. Neighbouring Turks, keen to make sure that there would be no survivors to reclaim any newly acquired assets, acted as back-up to the ambushes, which probably killed about 2000 refugees over several days. The survivors of the ambushes, arguably in their hundreds at most, were then hunted down and shot, stabbed or thrown into the river. Together, these events formed the end of the Armenian presence in Erzincan.

Ironically, there was a terrible aftermath to the extermination of the Armenian population of Erzincan: shortly afterwards, Russian and Armenian forces took the town and massacred its Islamic inhabitants, whose bodies, eyewitnesses said, were piled high in the streets.

Blaming the Victim—and Turkish Denial

> Since both the Turkish government and the nation were forced to take punitive measures and to respond fully, but always and without exception only after their patience was exhausted, the responsibility for the disasters that befell the Armenian community within the Turkish Empire belongs entirely to the Armenian community.
>
> Ismet Inonu, Turkish negotiator, 1923

The continuing phenomenon of Turkish denial of the Armenian genocide may be put down, at a fairly superficial level, to a national character of stubbornness. After all, the Turks obstinately and skilfully held out against combined British and French imperial forces at Gallipoli, inflicting on the western powers their only major naval and land defeat of World War I. This kind of defiance is characteristic: Turkey is a nation proud of its Ottoman history, including the legacy that saw dominion over the Mediterranean and south-eastern European regions from the conquest of Constantinople in 1453 until the late nineteenth century, and a nation certain of its racial and cultural superiority over the Arabs and Iranians to the south, the Russians, Armenians and Caucasians to the north and the Greeks and Balkan Slavs to the west. Into this mix we can throw the traditionalist Islamist view that coloured Turkish–Armenian relations for centuries: infidels are an inferior and subversive form of humanity, which means that they may legitimately be subjected to unlimited oppressive or aggressive measures. Probably most important of all, there is the more recent secularist Turkish position on the re-creation of itself as a modern republic, which includes the inviolability of the Young Turk movement to criticism and the sanctity of the reputation of Kemal Ataturk.

These factors have produced a particular psychological construct of Turkish national infallibility combined with the sanctity of the reputation of the Turkish republic, leading to the 2005 promulgation of the notorious Article 301, which forbids the 'denigration' of Turkishness, of the Turkish government and of its origins. Tellingly, any Turkish citizen who breaches this law overseas may be given an additional one-third penalty on the standard sentence options of six months to two years for the particularly treacherous act of washing dirty linen in front of foreigners. External image has been important to modern Turkish governments who are only too aware that they are constantly under the gaze of sceptical, even hostile, western eyes, a scrutiny seen by some as the same kind of meddling dynamic that once produced the hated Capitulations. One factor that has raised levels of hostility towards external scrutiny is Turkey's proposed and troubled admission to full membership of the European Union, a process that has intensified nationalist and isolationist elements in the Turkish game of denial.

At the same time, in the records of post-war courts martial held by the Turkish authorities lies evidence of official connivance in genocide, although it was not called that at the time. The irony here is that while the Kemalist government itself documented the Armenian massacres, modern Turkish governments have refused to accept the published evidence and have unsurprisingly limited access to these archives to 'reliable' scholars.

In the face of overwhelming evidence to the contrary, the official Turkish position was, and remains, that what happened from 1915 onwards was not a genocidal act. Indeed, the Armenian genocide, according to majority opinion in Turkey, is based on a fabrication brought about at best by a deluded and misguided ethnic minority and at worst by Turk-haters who openly and erroneously draw comparisons between the events of 1915 and the Holocaust.

> All we can rely on are cold, hard FACTS. Certainly Armenians were killed as a result of massacres ... often by their Muslim neighbours, in reprisal for murderous acts committed by the Armenians ... but anybody who calls acts of massacres 'genocide' doesn't even know the meaning of the word ... (At least the way most of us perceive the meaning, as with what Hitler did to the Jews; the legal definition of genocide is essentially meaningless, and can be applied to almost any conflict.)
>
> Tall Armenian Tale website

Anyone who is familiar with the shrill and unrelenting propaganda war between Turkish supporters and Armenian accusers will know that it is a bitter struggle. The Turkish denial defence is built on three main theses.

The first of these arguments is the 'hard-denial' view that there was no intention to conduct a systematic policy of Holocaust-style genocide against a helpless minority. How can we tell that this was the case? First, because there is no direct evidence of an Istanbul-based order to exterminate the Armenians—not on paper, at any rate. Second, Armenians were not a helpless minority, because they participated in treacherous acts themselves, thus provoking the massacres because of their support for the Russian enemy. Third, the 'genocide' was really a necessary wartime deportation policy that was handled badly, so Armenian deaths were partly a series of terrible misadventures caused by human error. Fourth, it all occurred long ago, and modern Turkish governments have no retrospective responsibility for matters in which they were not involved: what happened in 1915 was then, and this is now. Time to move on.

The second group, of 'soft denial' arguments, is about both numbers and morality. In the first instance, the number of Armenians killed is greatly exaggerated by the genocide camp (implying that Armenians are liars). Second, Armenians participated in massacres of Turks prior to, during and after World War I (implying that if the Armenian claims are even half true, they are morally responsible for their own fate). Third, more Turks were killed between 1914 and 1918 than Armenians (implying that it wasn't just Armenians who suffered). Fourth, modern Armenian terrorists have been involved in anti-Turkish campaigns of bombing and assassinations (implying that with friends like these, the Armenians are morally bankrupt).

The third argument is that what happened in 1915 and 1916 occurred under a misguided and paranoid Ottoman regime and not during the Ittihadist government of the benign and revered Kemal Ataturk. This would be a reasonably accurate representation of events if we forgot altogether that the Ittihadists were in *de facto* charge before World War I and if we ignored the active role of the Ittihadist Armenian-haters Enver Pasha, Talat Pasha and their accomplices. Admittedly, their work preceded Kemal Ataturk's regime, and the founder of modern Turkey did not display the same murderous intentions as his colleagues, but in 1915 Turkey was already formally under the control of an Ittihadist regime and had been since the 1913 assumption of power by the Triumvirate. So the suggested purity of Ittihadism was firmly compromised within two years of the Young Turks taking control of their new nation.

The principal agents and advocates of the comprehensive campaign of denial range from senior members of the Ankara-based government to individual bloggers. Nationalist parliamentarians such as Cemil Cicek consistently denounce the treacherous mentality of Turks who support the intentional genocide thesis. Ankara supports lobbyists in Washington, and the Turkish Ministry of Culture and Tourism supports a website that consistently and persistently responds to old and new accusations of intentional genocide. Within the parliamentary system, nationalist members frequently vent their spleen, and Article 301 was introduced and passed in order to replace the less draconian Article 159.

Next comes the judicial system, in which activists and writers who 'denigrate Turkishness' by supporting the idea of genocide are prosecuted. Within the legal system itself, there is a nationalist group of lawyers, called Unity of Jurists, which instigates legal actions against its ideological opponents.

Alongside the judicial system we have the media. Most Turkish mass media is hostile to Armenian claims, with the exception of the English-language *Turkish Daily News*. To complement official online Turkish denial, any internet-based counter-accusations have been interdicted by Turkish authorities. For example, on 6 March 2007, as part of the nationalist campaign against 'insulting' the memory of Ataturk online, Turk Telecom was ordered by an Istanbul court to close access to YouTube because of anti-Ataturk content, a ban that was lifted two days later when the allegedly offensive material was removed. On 4 May 2007, a Bill was passed in the Turkish parliament (ratified as Law 5651 on 22 May) that allowed the government to block websites that 'insulted' Kemal Ataturk's memory—code for, among other things, mentioning the Armenian genocide in terms considered unfavourable to Turkish memory. As well as punishing 'crimes against Ataturk', Law 5651 outlaws using the internet for inciting suicide, the sexual abuse of children, prostitution and drug use.

Next in the list of agencies of denial comes the higher education system, in which selected Turkish scholars are supported by government grants and given privileged access to state archives. The Ministry of Culture and Tourism selectively supports research centres and republishes scholarly articles and monographs that are favourable to the official position. Overseas universities are given Turkish government endowments to set up centres for Turkish studies. At the school level, history textbooks used to omit any mention of the Armenian genocide. Even as late as 2006, schools catering to the small Armenian population were not allowed to teach strategic subjects such as history.

Finally, angered by what they see as Armenian domination of the international debate, Turkish groups such as the Assembly of Turkish American Associations have been formed in several western countries to act as expatriate propagandists for the official Turkish view; in a case in 2005, one such group took Massachusetts education officials to court over the genocide issue.

The Armenian Point of View

> The Armenian Genocide, perpetrated by the Ottoman Empire, cost the lives of about 1.5 million Armenians in the midst of the WWI chaos. The Turkish government has adamantly denied the occurrence of the Armenian Genocide and insists that such a mass murder never took place.
>
> Armenian Genocide Information & Recognition website

The Armenian position is not helped by the strident exaggerations of its adherents. Much of the Armenian propaganda that promotes the genocide point of view is exaggerated, wildly tendentious, relies on suspect, even forged, evidence and is unremittingly anti-Turkish. Indeed, the tone of some of the writings in favour of the Armenian case is hysterical.

The Armenian case seems obsessed with payback. Supported from a distance by the Ministry of Foreign Affairs of the former soviet republic of Armenia, anti-Turkish websites and online articles and blogs pour out rants of the most abusive kind. Even otherwise respectable pro-Armenian scholars are selective in the evidence that they cite and have a tendency to string together atrocity stories in the hope, presumably, that the overwhelming barbarity described in these anecdotes will result in universal condemnation of the Turks, sometimes gilding the lily by attributing eyewitness accounts to observers who were not there.

To illustrate more completely the partisan nature of the Armenian controversy, in a 2007 *London Review of Books* article, 'The Mass Murder They Still Deny', Michael Oren, a respected American-Israeli scholar in the field, wrote: 'Lewis Einstein, yet another American Jewish diplomat assigned to the Istanbul embassy, tells of watching as an elderly Turkish woman borrowed an officer's pistol and shot a passing Armenian refugee in the head'. (Morgenthau was the other American Jewish diplomat that Oren had in mind.) This, however, is what Einstein, safely in Istanbul and relying on the eyewitness accounts of others, actually wrote: 'The murder of Armenians has become almost a sport, and one Turkish lady passing one of these caravans [in eastern Turkey], and thinking she too would relish killing an Armenian, on the guards' invitation took out a revolver and shot the first wretch she saw', which is not exactly the first-hand account suggested by Oren.

The Politics of the Holocaust Distraction

> This year, Congress established April 15 as Holocaust Memorial Day, commemorating the Nazi genocide of European Jewry. Just nine days later, on April 24, Armenians throughout the world observed the commemoration of *their* great tragedy: the massacre of as many as 1.5 million Armenians at the hands of the Turks that began in 1915.
>
> In many ways, it was the 20th century's first genocide that helped set the stage for its largest, including Rwanda and now Darfur. Adolf Hitler reportedly said, on the eve of his invasion of Poland in 1939, 'Who, after all, speaks today of the annihilation of the Armenians?'
>
> *Los Angeles Times*, 11 June 2007

The Holocaust comparison remains a powerful element in Armenian rhetoric, based on the view that the Turkish Armenians, like the Jews, constituted a minority envied for its commercial and cultural success, hated for its religious difference and despised for its racial or ethnic origins. Moreover, runs the argument, the Turkish state apparatus created its own, less structured version of the SS using the local CUP secretaries and the SO squads, with the eliminationist Talat Pasha as Heinrich Himmler's Turkish equivalent. This larger Holocaust comparison is a huge distraction from the reality of the Armenian genocide, serving neither side well. Indeed, the diversionary argument is characteristic of the whole furious debate. As far as the official Turkish position is concerned, the 'Armenian Holocaust' creates a convenient straw-man argument, since comparisons between the Turks in 1915 and 1916 and the Nazis between 1942 and 1945 are highly, and conveniently, questionable.

But some in the pro-Armenian camp remain undeterred in setting up yet another emotive but inaccurate front in the war against the deniers. In this context, nothing characterises the contentiousness of the Final Solution comparison as clearly as the much used, and much abused, Hitler quote that even the best known commentators can occasionally get wrong, as did the usually knowledgeable (if tendentious) Robert Fisk in a January 2000 article, 'Remember the First Holocaust'. Here is how Fisk, *The Independent*'s senior Middle East correspondent, began his piece on the 1915 attempt by the Turkish government to purge their Armenian people: '"Who now remembers the Armenians?" Hitler asked, just before he embarked on the destruction of European Jewry. Precious few, it seems'. The article then goes on to assert that the Armenian massacres were the first and forgotten Holocaust.

The problem is that Hitler's rhetorical question, supposedly asked in August 1939, may never have been uttered. But that small detail does not stop the pro-Armenian side from emulating Fisk and quoting Hitler time and again, often in fuzzily inaccurate versions. The link being made here is that the Nazi leader, remembering apparent European insensibility to the plight of the Armenians in 1915, was inspired to begin his campaign of European and Russian genocide. The consequent assertion is that Hitler's intentional genocide against the Jews was based on a successful campaign of genocide against the Armenians by the

Turks, in the so-called 'First Holocaust'. But the record of what Hitler actually said in the summer of 1939 is imprecise and is still of disputed provenance.

What happened is this: In August 1939, Hitler assembled his general staff at noon in his Bavarian retreat, the Berghof. As he leaned against a piano, Hitler spoke about the Polish crisis, extemporising from a brief set of notes and carefully outlining an imminent war of total brutality, conquest and elimination. No official record of what he said was taken, but three participants, Admiral Canaris, General Böhm and General Halder, made informal notes (which were leaked to a US journalist in 1942). In one of these sets of notes (thought to be Canaris's), Hitler is recorded as ending his speech with the controversial sentence 'Who, after all, speaks today of the annihilation of the Armenians?'

Was Hitler telling his High Command that he felt encouraged to follow a Turkish precedent because the Turks had effectively got away with genocide twenty years previously? Turkish nationalists and deniers don't think so. Their position is that both the origins and the integrity of the quote are suspect. They say that the quote appears in only one of the three sets of surviving notes, and, although the 'Canaris' notes were offered in evidence at the Nuremberg War Crimes Tribunal, they were not used, thus casting doubts on their reliability. Moreover, even if Hitler did make that remark, it pre-dated, by more than two years, any decision that the Nazi government made about a genocidal campaign against the Jews: the genocide intent became serious only at the notorious Wannsee Conference of 20 January 1942 when Heydrich, ostensibly at Goering's command, outlined the Nazi plans for implementation of the Final Solution. Hitler's remark, Turkish nationalists continue, authentic or not, refers to Poles, not Jews, and to Lebensraum, not genocide. Finally, the pro-Turkish argument suggests that Hitler's reference to brutality was a take-no-prisoners allusion to dealing with supposedly subhuman Slavic opposition and resistance. The implication is that he was referring to a commonplace kind of battlefield cruelty that was functional rather than ideological and that Hitler's supposed threat of severe measures was completely in line with the German military's long track record of punitive sanctions and mass reprisals against civilians.

The Armenian response to this is that while the Nazi campaign of genocide actually started in Poland, the Nazis stepped up the tempo in late 1941 during their war of extermination in Soviet Russia, which was just as brutal as Hitler had originally suggested in 1939. And, the Armenians claim, the fact that the Canaris notes were not used at Nuremberg was more to do with there being quite enough evidence available at the time, and nothing to do with unreliability.

The point here is that even a few words in a speech by Hitler, who was accustomed to improvising and rambling at length in this kind of forum, have been seized on by both sides of the argument as a monumentalised point of contention embedded in a web of propaganda, leaving the outside observer as mystified as ever. Moreover, if anything, the Hitler quote was a reference to the proposed subjugation, removal and extermination of the Slavic peoples west of the Urals, a plan much more in line with the Turkish aims for eastern Anatolia.

In summary, the reference in Hitler's speech may have some significance. Or it may not. If it happened at all. Which it may not have done.

Moving away from this Hitler distraction to a more realistic appraisal of the Holocaust connection, US scholar Robert Melson has argued, quite convincingly, that, from a comparative view, the Armenian massacres may have more to do with events in Africa and Asia (he later included the Balkans) than they do with the Holocaust. In Nigeria, for example, more than a million Biafrans died as a consequence of the post-colonial Nigerian federal military government's blocking of supplies to its minority population. As for events in the Balkans in the early 1990s, the post-colonial Serbian government invented the phrase 'ethnic cleansing' in an attempt to cosmeticise their murderous activities in Croatia and Bosnia. Melson's point is that, in these scenarios, as in Turkey, the dominant ethnic group in a pluralistic society tries to institute a power monopoly and in doing so is resisted by minority groups attempting to establish greater independence, a classification that clearly did not apply to Hitler's Reich. Melson does discuss significant differences between the Armenian massacres and the Nigerian and Balkan atrocities, but his substantive point is that the Armenian genocide is actually a precursor more of post-1945 genocides (including, by extrapolation, the Rwandan genocide) than of the Holocaust, which, he argues (less convincingly), is more a forerunner of what happened under Pol Pot in Cambodia.

Some Progress

In recent years, there have been small signs of a shift in opinion among some sections of the Turkish population. For example, in 1998, Armenian-American academic Ronald Suny was asked to lecture in Turkey, where, as he puts it, he was met with curiosity rather than hostility. In the same year, at the University of Michigan, Suny hosted a workshop on genocide attended by Turkish scholars. A few years on and there was even more progress, of sorts. By 2005, the Armenian question, previously examined from only a partisan Turkish viewpoint, had reached such a state of national importance in Turkish schools that the minister of education announced that both sides of the question could now be presented in history textbooks. And in 2007, notwithstanding frozen Armenian–Turkish diplomatic relations and the virulent Armenian foreign affairs ministry's anti-Turkish propaganda, the Armenian republic's deputy foreign minister Arman Kirakossian attended Hrant Dink's funeral, sitting behind the Turkish officials. Finally, Recep Tayyip Erdogan, the prime minister, who had himself been jailed in 1998 for publicly reading a pro-Islamic poem, showed some willingness, following Dink's assassination, to review Article 301.

But prejudices die hard. In May 2005 a conference on the topic of the Armenian genocide was scheduled to take place at Istanbul's Bogazici University. The conference was to be attended by Turkish scholars who had rejected the official line. Interior Minister Cicek immediately denounced the academics as traitors and the governor of Istanbul summoned the rector of Bogazici University, commanding her to cancel the conference. She refused. At the same time, the Turkish chief public prosecutor demanded of her an advance sighting of the papers. She refused again, but the conference was proscribed and official intimidation won the day. Later in the year, Bogazici University tried again, only to have the conference shut down by a court order instigated by nationalist lawyers. The court's hostile decision was criticised by Prime Minister Erdogan himself. The organisers then cleverly circumvented the ban by moving their forum to Istanbul's Bilgi University, a private college over which the authorities had no jurisdiction. Modifying the government's position, foreign minister Abdullah Gul sent what might be regarded as an even-handedly conciliatory message to the conference, and a participant, Professor Baskin Oran of Ankara University, commented on the significance of the occasion: 'This conference proves that the Armenian question is no longer a taboo subject in Turkey. Armenia should give up the demand of territory, compensation and the recognition of genocide'. The pointed reference to reparations is of great significance.

And so the micro-debates and the macro-arguments continue, about statements of intent, timetables for mass murder, precedents for evil, clouding the big issues and diverting attention from the two big questions. First, were the massacres of Armenians in 1915 and 1916 genocidal? The answer, by any conventional measure, has to be yes. Second, can Turks and Armenians be reconciled? And the answer is maybe, but only if the brand of Turkish nationalism that supports denial succumbs to internal and external pressure, the kind of internal pressure being applied by Turkey's liberal intelligentsia, in the face of, first, traditionalist Islamic thinking, which is still caught up with notions of Turkish honour and contempt for the infidel, and second, a more recent, bourgeois version of nationalist insularity, which is found in newly enriched, devout Turks. The latter development is, according to Orhan Pamuk, an international trend in developing nations:

> The drama we see unfolding [suppression of free speech in Turkey] is not, I think, a grotesque and inscrutable drama peculiar to

Turkey; rather, it is an expression of a new global phenomenon that we are only just coming to acknowledge and that we must now begin, however slowly, to address. In recent years, we have witnessed the astounding economic rise of China and India, and in both these countries we have also seen the rapid expansion of the middle class, though I do not think we shall truly understand the people who have been part of this transformation until we see their private lives reflected in novels. Whatever we call these new elites—the non-Western bourgeoisie or enriched bureaucracy—they, like the Westernizing elites in my own country, feel compelled to follow two separate and seemingly incompatible lines of action in order to legitimatise their newly acquired wealth and power... First they must justify the rapid rise in fortune by assuming the idiom and attitudes of the West... when the people berate them for ignoring tradition, they respond by brandishing a virulent and intolerant nationalism... On the one hand, there is the rush to join the global economy; on the other, the angry nationalism that sees true democracy and freedom of thought as Western inventions.

That rush to join the global economy has placed added strains on the traditional Turkish way of life, on its introspective nationalism and on its official interpretation of the Armenian question. During the past decade, the issue of Turkey's entry into the European Union has dogged domestic politics as much as it has exercised the foreign ministries of western European nations, including, in particular, France's Quai D'Orsay, where Turkey is regarded as Euro-impostor, with its predominantly Islamic population, its patchy record on human rights issues and its dog-in-the-manger attitude to the Armenian question. So hostile to Turkish interests have successive French governments been that, thanks to pressure from a large French Armenian population, Armenian genocide denial was, in October 2006, declared illegal in France, much to the fury of even moderate Turks. Germany too, caught between its progressive post-war attitude to human rights abuses, sensitivity to genocide issues and the voting power of its guestworker-descended Turkish minority, has come up with a conditional approach to Turkish entry, bearing in mind Germany's (and other nations') anxieties about the country, with its large and growing population, entering, cuckoo-like, into a European Union system already beset by migration controversies and euro-subsidy issues.

European Union membership is a large economic carrot constantly dangled and then pulled back by the major European powers, and, accordingly, its effect on Turkish domestic politics is at once positive and negative. The positives come out in small and transitory ways. For example, charges were dropped in an Article 301 trial of Orhan Pamuk in December 2005, shortly after the European Union parliament announced that it was sending a delegation to observe the trial and the Union's enlargement commissioner Olli Rehn declared that the trial would be a litmus test of Turkey's application for entry. On the other hand, the negatives continue and are mainly to do with Turkish isolationist anger at the presumption of western powers that they may interfere with internal Turkish affairs, both political and military. Meanwhile, the Turkish election of 2007, although producing large, predominantly urban demonstrations against any hint of state-enforced Islamisation, led only to a re-affirmation of Erdogan's government, splitting Turkish society in an old and dangerous way at the same time as the secularist army was distracted from internal politics by its anti-Kurdish campaign in Iraq.

The great irony in all of this is that Turkey's isolationist inclinations, for good and ill, have tended to flourish when the nation comes under the critical gaze of western eyes, as happened in the nineteenth century, as was the case in May 1915 when Turkey faced down the Entente ultimatum, and as it is in the early twenty-first century as the same western nations seem to be laying down the law yet again to the Turkish government about human rights and military behaviour.

2

FRAUDS AND FANATICS

The Pathology of Western Holocaust Denial

In the Berlin district of Kreuzberg, on Lindenstrasse, there stand two remarkable buildings. The older of the pair is imposingly handsome in the baroque style: yellow-walled and red-roofed. Its neighbour, in abrupt contrast, is a tall, gleaming, titanium-covered rectangular structure, uncompromisingly lacerated by dark, diagonal casements. The whole is the Jewish Museum, and the baroque façade is what remains of the *Kollegianhaus*, a former court building linked by an underground passage to the stark, rectangular blocks of Daniel Libeskind's ultra-modern museum design.

Libeskind, a US-based architect, devised a radical approach for the construction of the exhibition area of the museum. His idea was that the modern section, based on a broken Star of David, would have angular lines, stunning window shapes and a minimalist interior, with the spaces both functional, for exhibits, and metaphorical, as a comment on the history of the Jews in Germany.

One internal space that cuts through the museum is the Memory Void, a narrow, austere defile that reaches to a high ceiling, illuminated by natural light. The floor of the Memory Void is covered with the installation *Shaleket*, (*Fallen Leaves*), by Israeli artist Menashe Kadishman.

It consists of 10 000 heavy, circular iron discs, each about the size of a dinner plate, and each with human eyes, a nose and an open, pleading mouth. The installation represents 'painful recollections of the innocent victims of yesterday, today, and tomorrow'. Museum visitors are invited to walk on the fallen leaves. Few do. And those who try seem to be disconcerted by the experience of treading on beseeching, childlike faces that clank noisily underfoot; they quickly retreat to less disconcerting ground. The Memory Void itself was created by Libeskind to represent the cruelly diminished presence of Jews in German and in European society, a consequence of the Holocaust.

Both the Libeskind museum design and the Kadishman installation are dignified, striking and, ultimately, moving memorialisations, principally of the lost lives of Holocaust victims and of the damaged lives of Holocaust survivors and their families. They are precisely the kinds of collective remembrances that Holocaust deniers, in a second, political and psychological Holocaust, are trying to erase, in a hoped-for obliteration of the idea of Jewish suffering and a denial of the handiwork of the persecutors and the murderers of the Fallen Leaves.

Who Are the Deniers, and What Do They Say?

> I don't see any reason to be tasteful about Auschwitz. It's baloney. It's a legend. Once we admit the fact that it was a brutal slave labour camp and large numbers of people did die, as large numbers of innocent people died elsewhere in the war, why believe the rest of the baloney?
>
> David Irving, 1991

Unlike other denial stories, which are generally to do with defence of the deniers' national or political character, there seems to be no functional or pragmatic sense to Holocaust denial, except, perhaps, the internal logic of prejudice and delusion. When it comes to prejudice, there are people at large who simply hate Jews, in the same way that there are people who hate African-Americans, Africans, Muslims, Asians and Caucasians. Many anti-Semites do their hating in private, but others congregate, either physically, virtually or both, in small, fringe Holocaust denial groups. They are in the serious, if bizarre, business of hating Jews on behalf of a long-dead Nazi Germany, and, as far as they are concerned, the more the world takes notice of their business, the better. The delusional aspect of Holocaust denial attracts outlandish, if minuscular, networks and congregations of devotees whose dedication to the cause has turned Holocaust denial into a crackpot global industry, clinging, in parasitical fashion, to one of the twentieth century's major tragedies and trying to provide the larger anti-Semitic political groups with the kind of ammunition that they can use to denounce Jews, wherever they may be and whatever branch of Judaism or secular ideology they may follow.

The paradox of Holocaust denial is, of course, that if the Jews were quite as all-powerful as anti-Semitic prejudice attests, the deniers could not possibly allow Jews to be portrayed to the world at large as victims; if they did so, the world conspiracy and world domination thesis would implode, impaled on its own illogical argument that the omnipotent Jews connived at their own attempted destruction. Consequently, Holocaust denial tends to be based on a variety of false premises, with the Jews as non-victims, even perpetrators. A first argument of this kind is that the Holocaust simply did not happen—it was fabricated. Second, if it did happen, it has been greatly exaggerated to benefit Jews. Third, maybe it did happen in a small way, but the Jews brought it on themselves. Fourth, it did happen in a small way, but it was mainly the result of a combination of accidental deaths, poor organisation, poor hygiene and climatic conditions. Fifth, even if it did happen, worse things happened to non-Jews at the hands of Jewish-inspired Bolsheviks. Holocaust deniers therefore have no interest in searching for persuasive and authentic historical explanations. In an infantilistic way, by simply being, uttering and gaining attention, the deniers feel that they are winning a war, a war fought by any means. The consequence of denialist accusations is a counter-industry of refutation, which delights and gratifies the attention-seeking deniers, who love the publicity and who then claim, in a projectionist and paranoid way, that there is a worldwide Jewish conspiracy against Holocaust denial.

Countering the prejudices and delusions of a small minority would seem therefore to be an odd game for anybody with serious purpose, but, as US author and historian Anne Applebaum has pointed out, it still remains an important task:

> The near-destruction of the European Jews, in a very brief span of time, by a sophisticated European nation using the best technology available was, it seems, an event that requires constant reexplanation, not least because it really did shape subsequent European and world history in untold ways. For that reason alone it seems the archives, the photographs and the endless rebuttals will go on being necessary, long beyond the lifetime of the last survivor.

While most of these denialist self-publicists are more offensive than dangerous, they have harboured aspirations to provide ideological inspiration for two serious political groups that have the capacity to be very destructive indeed. The first group consists of revivalist Nazis, who, adopting a new persona, have resuscitated a European political version of Hitlerism in a way that, half a century ago, would have been almost inconceivable. Thanks to a racist response to large-scale immigration from eastern Europe, Africa and the Middle East, neo-Nazis are slowly gathering political momentum. Encouraging them, high-profile denialists attend neo-Nazi gatherings, give speeches and offer support to neo-Nazi racists and their leaders, who are happy to conflate anti-Semitism with anti-Arab prejudice and anti-African hatred, not to mention a loathing of Balkan refugees, Polish workers and Russian migrants. In a strange twist, the Russian racists involved in neo-Nazism, once abhorred by Hitler's Nazis as subhuman Slavs, now, in their turn, hate Jews and the dark-skinned or eastern ethnic minorities of their own motherland.

The second group of beneficiaries of Holocaust denial consists of extremist Islamist political and religious propagandists, who have seized on, and used, Holocaust denial to attack both Israel and all Jews. These groups and their associates have a vested interest in propagating myths of Jewish aspirations for world control and in giving support to the idea of generalised Jewish deviousness. The Islamic migrant populations of Europe and the established Islamic people of the Middle East and South Asia provide fertile ground for such denialist sentiments. That is why there exists, for example, no mention of the Holocaust in Palestinian history textbooks, why Abu Mazen, Yasser Arafat's successor, completed a soft-denial doctorate at Moscow's Oriental University, and why Iran's president Mahmoud Ahmadinejad convened a conference in December 2006 to discuss the mythic nature of the Holocaust. The Iranian conference was attended by several second-rate, if that distinction may be made, western deniers such as David Duke (formerly of the Ku Klux Klan), Georges Theil (French denier and author of *Heresy in 21st Century France: A Case of Insubmission to the 'Holocaust' Dogma*) and Fredrick Töben ('master' of the Adelaide Institute denial website), all no doubt pleased to find some kind of governmental recognition of their trade.

The loose, international coalition of Holocaust deniers contains individuals, political and terrorist groups and government figures who range in their beliefs from soft denial (arguing about figures and details) to hard denial (claiming that the Holocaust is a complete Jewish fabrication for gain). There are variations on the theme, for example the German ultra-nationalist position of 'enough is enough' combined with the counter-attack that the Holocaust was not as bad as were Allied war crimes. One noticeable trait of many of the English-language deniers is their connection with Germany, through birth or descent, or through a Teutonophile fondness for a bygone German culture and society, particularly for the 'accomplishments' of Nazi Germany. What they say, when added up in detail, is as follows:

The Jews and their henchmen, having long engaged in a policy of world domination, were responsible for backstabbing Germany in World War I, and for provoking World War II—perhaps even all modern wars—thus forcing the Nazis, quite justifiably, to lock up European and Russian Jewry in camps. These camps were admittedly harsh, but not genocidally so. In any case, the Jews, men, women and children, brought their fate, whatever it was (and it most certainly was not mass murder) on themselves by provoking the good German people, who were under the restrained leadership of a wise and benevolent Führer. The Führer himself was far too busy fighting, with unmatched brilliance, the evil Bolshevik Jewish regime in the east to pay close attention to what a few of his more zealous underlings were doing. If, indeed, they were doing anything. Those honourable men were not cruel, of course, and even if a small minority was cruel, the Jews deserved it. To cap it all, those ungrateful Jews and their supporters are still calumniating the Greater German Reich, which, as we all know, was a paragon of political and social virtue. And these calumniators, entirely in keeping with the Jewish track record for international conspiracy, have made up stories and faked evidence, mainly about millions being murdered in gas chambers, so that they can gain reparation and justify the illegal foundation of the State of Israel, which itself is still working on the Jewish campaign of world domination.

That is, more or less, what most of the deniers believe (there are variations), and all of the above is the logic, if it may be called such, of the fanatic obsessed with a grotesque set of beliefs.

This chapter will, in the first instance, consider Holocaust denial as expressed primarily through the work of the high-profile writer David Irving, a formerly reputable (in some circles) individual denier. It will then examine the work of the more bizarre deniers Willis Carto, David McCalden and Ernst Zündel, in truth mere stunt men, but closely associated with a group of quasi-academic deniers gathered around the US-based Institute for Historical Review. The final section of the chapter will discuss how fringe denialist ideology has opportunistically moved towards mainstream political opinion in Germany, focusing on the public controversy surrounding the Hamburg Institute's mid-1990s exhibition of 1940s Wehrmacht (German army) atrocities.

David Irving

> I don't accept that the gas chambers existed, and this is well known. I've seen no evidence at all that gas chambers existed.
>
> David Irving, 1992

> I made a mistake when I said there were no gas chambers at Auschwitz ... The Nazis did murder millions of Jews.
>
> David Irving, 2005

When it comes to grotesquery, the strange nature of Holocaust denial has achieved several apotheoses in its time, but few incidents have been stranger than the libel case of David Irving versus Deborah Lipstadt, which was fought in the Royal Court of Justice, London, in the European winter of early 2000. Long before that event, however, Irving, a prolific historical writer, had gained a reputation, to put it at its most euphemistic, as a suspiciously pro-Hitler author. His unusual backstory provides some clues about the origins of his beliefs.

Born in Britain, Irving's childhood followed a conventional middle-class progression, with attendance at a minor English public school before he commenced science studies at university. The only apparent variation from the norm was an absentee father, a naval officer and survivor of a wartime sinking who, after his maritime rescue, cut himself off from his family. According to his twin brother, Nicholas, from childhood David Irving has demonstrated several attributes that are immediately recognisable in David Irving the adult: a craving to shock and antagonise; an egotistical and fiercely competitive desire for the limelight; an obsession with the glories of Germany and Nazism; and a fixation with the iniquities of the Jews and Churchill, a disposition which in 1969 resulted in a visit to the USA to check on the Nuremberg trial process. While there, he met Robert Kempner, a former Nuremberg prosecutor, who was unimpressed by his visitor, describing him in a memo to J Edgar Hoover as a 'young man, who made a nervous and rather mentally-dilapidated impression' and who made 'anti-American and anti-Jewish remarks' in commenting that 'Sirhan Sirhan did the right thing in killing that "fat-faced" Kennedy'. If he, Irving, were an Arab, he said, 'he would have done the same thing, because of Robert Kennedy's alleged pro-Israel remarks'.

Prior to his visit to the USA, Irving had dropped out of university and left Britain to work in Germany, where he assuaged his Teutonophilia and became a fluent German speaker. More importantly, he became a proficient reader of German, particularly of *Fraktur*, the gothic script which is almost illegible to the untrained eye but which, until 1941, was the standard official font in Germany.

While abroad, Irving worked as a labourer to maintain himself as he commenced his work in the German official archives and among private papers, digging up documents that had been missed or not fully explored by other archivists and historians. It was through turning his discovery of these papers into controversial bestselling books that Irving made his early reputation. His sensational first book, *The Destruction of Dresden* (1963), was a historical groundbreaker, which argued that the bombing of the east-German city of Dresden in mid-February 1945 had produced massive casualties. Irving calculated 135 000 dead in his first edition, and upped the number to an enormous 250 000 in subsequent 1960s editions, the implication being that the bombing raid was a war crime against German civilians. This view has been adopted by neo-Nazis, who memorialise the bombing of Dresden as a surrogate celebration of Hitler's birthday (20 April), the latter date banned as a commemorative milestone in Germany. The legend of Dresden, whatever the morality of the bombing raids by the RAF and the USAF, has become a major part of contemporary German ultra-nationalist ideology, and Irving's book was a key contributor to the origin and continuation of an amended view of the Allies as unarraigned war criminals.

Irving's approach that there was a massive total of 250 000 civilian casualties (with the consequent claim that the Allies were war criminals on a par with the Nazis) was eventually demolished by historians Richard Evans, in *Telling Lies about Hitler*, and Frederick Taylor, in *Dresden: Tuesday 13 February 1945*, but not before it had become fixed in western popular cultural memory. The turning point in the refutation of Irving's Dresden argument was that he had disingenuously continued to use a forged document known as TB47, dated 22 March 1945, which Evans and Taylor were both able to discredit but which Irving persisted in using as supporting evidence for his inflated figures, notwithstanding consensual opinion among historians, from 1977 onwards, that it was indeed a forgery. Indeed, in the 1963 edition of *The Destruction of Dresden*, Irving had said it was a fake, recanting in later editions but maintaining the fiction until 1995. The generally accepted fatality figure now stands at about 25 000, still a terrible toll, but not so great as that caused by the horrific 1943 Hamburg firestorm.

There are other aspects of Irving's writing on Dresden that have been rebutted by serious historians but are too detailed to be reported here. However, Irving's part in the Dresden myth is characteristic of much of his post-1963 analysis of personalities and events to do with Nazi Germany, including, among other ideas, the view that Hitler was a relatively magnanimous leader, that Churchill was a war criminal in the sway of Jewish interests, and that the 20 July 1944 (anti-Hitler) plotters were traitors.

Irving's Day in Court

> Mr Irving: I have made a speech in 1992 and you take exception to my description of the Board of Deputies (of British Jews), and the words I use. Is any criticism of an organization like that permissible, do you think?
> Prof Evans: I do think it is rather over the top to describe the Board of Deputies of British Jews as cockroaches.
>
> *Irving vs Penguin & anr.* (2000)

When Irving took upon himself the task of suing Deborah Lipstadt for libel, he appeared confident that he would win, if only because England's relatively generous libel laws tended to favour the plaintiff. Lipstadt, at that time, was a relatively obscure but well-respected US historian, who had condemned Irving as a Holocaust denier in her 1993 book *Denying the Holocaust: The Growing Assault on Truth and Memory*, published by Penguin. Irving blamed her for poor sales of his biography, *Goebbels: Mastermind of the Third Reich*. With the standard denialist tactic of blaming the victim and the unsubtle insight so characteristic of deniers, he explained that it was Lipstadt herself who had forced him to attack her in court, and that was why he was suing for libel.

Serious event though it was, the libel trial took some odd, even absurd, turns. For example, towards the end of the second week, as Lipstadt was leaving the court, she discovered that an 'Australian reporter' with 'exceptionally blonde hair and gold wire-rimmed glasses' had been singing Irving's praises to a group of journalists, comparing him with Winston Churchill and announcing that he had been wronged by Lipstadt. This 'reporter' turned out to be Helen Darville-Demidenko, a young Queensland writer who, masquerading as a child of Ukrainian parents, had published, in 1994, the controversial, multi-prize-winning and highly lauded (by some, mainly littérateurs) novel *The Hand That Signed the Paper*. Why she was at the trial as correspondent for glossy magazine *Australian Style* (now defunct) is unclear. Nevertheless, in a March 2000 article for that magazine, the following remarkable paragraph appeared:

> Although some people would see a Hitler surrogate in this [Irving's] arrogance, I don't. I see Churchill instead. Except the enemy isn't Germany any more, it's the USA. Apart from the fact that the enmity between Churchill and Roosevelt was notorious, Lipstadt's emotive book is a little like the out-of-place gilded eagle overlooking the US Embassy on Grosvenor Square. It wears its heart on its sleeve and Irving—like many Englishmen of his class and age—loathes what he considers unnecessary displays of feeling.

Demidenko-Darville was clearly an Irving fan, and vice versa: Irving placed her article on his website.

Next in the long and peculiar story of the Irving–Lipstadt trial came one unforgettable moment which perhaps encapsulates so much of what the Holocaust denial movement is about. In the trial's final stages, Irving, having ignored legal common sense by choosing to represent himself throughout, was summing up. He spoke for five hours. At about the third hour of his disquisition, in explaining that he had objected to cries of '*Sieg Heil*' at a 1991 ultra-rightist rally in Germany, he unthinkingly turned to address the judge, Mr Justice Gray, as '*Mein Führer*'. There was a moment of shocked silence in the courtroom at this surreal 'Dr Strangelove' moment. Then, the spectators burst out laughing.

Notwithstanding the massive case built against him and despite his farcical but telling reference to the judge as '*Mein Führer*', Irving pressed on with his summing up, seemingly oblivious to his desperate position. It was all to no avail. Confounded by the weight of evidence submitted by the Penguin-Lipstadt team throughout the ten-week trial, his cause was eventually lost. The judge declared it 'incontrovertible that Irving qualifies as a Holocaust denier'. Justice Gray also found Irving seriously wanting as a disinterested historian: 'The content of his speeches and interviews often displays distinctly pro-Nazi and anti-Jewish bias. He makes surprising and often unfounded assertions about the Nazi regime which tend to exonerate the Nazis for the appalling atrocities which they inflicted on the Jews'. As for his misrepresentation of the past, Justice Gray said: 'Irving's treatment of the historical evidence is so perverse and egregious that it is difficult to accept that it is inadvertent on his part ... He has deliberately skewed the evidence to bring it in line with his political beliefs'.

As devastating and as financially ruinous as the legal decision was, Irving's publicity-hungry ego was such that the judgment was quickly seen by him as an opportunity to reiterate his views on Holocaust denial and the conspiracy against him. During a television interview with the formidable BBC current affairs presenter Jeremy Paxman, Irving was asked whether or not he would abandon his denialist position. 'Good Lord, no!' was his response, but when he realised that he was getting the worst of the discussion at the hands of the confrontational Paxman, he suddenly blurted out, 'You're not Jewish, are you?'

Thereafter, undeterred by his public humiliation, Irving appealed against the verdict, losing again. He blamed a Jewish-financed conspiracy and continued, in characteristically martyred style, to seek out publicity for his cause. In late 2005, for example, he arrived in Austria knowing that he would be arrested for a previous infringement of the Holocaust denial law. What an enraged Irving did not expect was a stiff prison sentence, and if further proof were required of his capacity for self-invented suffering, it was from his Austrian prison that he told an interviewer that 'they have burned my books', referring in typically grandiose and inaccurate terms to the simple pulping of some of his more legally offensive volumes.

Irving and Misrepresentation

> The legend was that Hitler ordered the killing of six million Jews in gas chambers in Auschwitz. This is roughly how history has had its way for the last forty or fifty years ... I think we are entitled to analyse the basic elements of the statement: Adolf Hitler ordered the killing of six million Jews in gas chambers at Auschwitz, and to ask, is any part of this statement open to doubt?
>
> David Irving, 1992

Prior to the trial, Irving's *modus operandi* had been carefully scrutinised by Richard Evans, who argued that it was based on the following techniques: there was a biased acceptance and propagation of suspect documents; Irving rejected authentic evidence that contradicted his position at the time; he mistranslated hard-to-access or difficult-to-read primary sources in a way that was favourable to his case; and he omitted mention of documents that he had seen but which worked against his argument. Evans found, in other words, that Irving, in the interests of his own political view, had been guilty of persistent misrepresentation throughout his entire career as a writer.

In this context of representations and misrepresentations, there is a generally accepted view that, from 1942 onwards, Hitler and the Nazi hierarchy intended to exterminate the Jews throughout the occupied lands and in Germany. The process had commenced prior to the war through dispossession, disenfranchisement and dehumanisation, and it continued at the outset of the war through regionally based purges. Finally, after the Wannsee Conference in 1942, the operation was implemented through a Reich-wide policy of systematic genocide. This was carried out under Himmler's command, with Himmler reporting directly to Hitler on the progress of the genocidal operations, a point often made clear to Nazi officials and officers by Himmler.

Many deniers, such as Irving, have insisted that Auschwitz was the sole site of the mass deaths of Jews and that Hitler's reputation as the instigator of mass murder is unfounded, since he was removed from these events, concentrating on the military aspects of waging war and leaving the anti-Jewish policy to be dealt with by allegedly over-zealous underlings. However, no reputable historian has made the claim that this policy was carried out in Auschwitz alone, and there is general consensus that the Nazi genocidal operation was carried out at Hitler's behest. The first proposition, the Auschwitz-alone claim, is a classic denialist tactic—a straw-man argument calculated to convince the credulous. The second denialist construction, of Hitler the warrior but not the mass murderer, shows that the deniers have an unreasoning attachment to the reputation of one of the twentieth-century's greatest criminals; it illustrates clearly and unequivocally the political sympathies of many, if not all, of the Holocaust deniers; and it is based on consistent distortion of the evidence, as Richard Evans was to discover when, preparing to be an expert witness, he examined Irving's work closely.

Evans found an example of this benign view of Hitler in Irving's *Goebbels*, in which the author, quoting a 1941 entry in Goebbels's diary, reported Hitler as remarking: 'Let nobody tell me . . . that despite that we can't park them [the Jews] in the marshier parts of Russia! . . . By the way . . . it's not a bad thing that public rumour attributes to us a plan to exterminate the Jews'. Evans, himself fluent in German and an assiduous archivist, went to the original document and translated the same section as: 'Nobody can tell me: But we can't send them into the morass! For who bothers about our people? It's good if the terror that we are exterminating Jewry goes before us'. With some deliberate looseness in his translation, Irving had changed 'we are exterminating' to 'attributes to us a plan to exterminate', changing the whole tenor of the remark in favour of the denialist viewpoint.

To Evans's increasing exasperation, Irving was proving to be an expert in misrepresentation through bending and breaking rules of evidence. Irving asserted, for example, that Hitler was benevolently disposed to the Jews of Berlin, a claim based on his interpretation of part of Himmler's phone log, regarding a purported conversation with Hitler on 30 November 1941, which Irving wrote up in his book *Hitler's War* as 'Jew transport from Berlin. No liquidation'. According to Irving, this was clear evidence that Hitler was prohibiting the generalised murder of Berlin Jews. But when Evans chased up the precise references, he found that the 'transport' was just one trainload of Berlin Jews sent to the Latvian capital, Riga, a city at that time used by the SS as a terminus for extermination of European and local Jews. As for the 'no liquidation' phrase, Evans discovered that its authorship was unclear and there was no evidence whatsoever that the phrase referred to anything other than the temporary halting of one transport. In Riga, according to SS records, the Berlin Jews of the postponed transport were machine-gunned on 30 November 1941, along with the Jews of Riga. Evans found no evidence corroborating Hitler's benevolence, a point that had already been made by other scholars in the 1970s. On the contrary, the evidence pointed the other way; but the professional scepticism of those same reliable historians, in whose company Irving wanted to be counted, failed to alter Irving's substantive position. In his hagiographical 1996 biography, *Goebbels*, Irving did trim his view slightly, but he persisted with the idea of Hitler's deliberate intervention to save a trainload of Berlin Jews.

Irving himself openly displayed yet another technique, that of biased surmise. For example, despite the fact that no document has yet been discovered that is signed by Hitler saying 'Kill all the Jews', Irving gave an eccentric, to say the least, account of his discovery in Argentina of a wartime memoir written by Adolf Eichmann that became of singular significance to the 'Führer order' debate. He stated that in the memoir there was a section regarding a meeting between Eichmann and Heydrich in the autumn of 1941, just a few weeks before Hitler's table talk remarks on extermination. Heydrich told Eichmann that he had been in conversation with Himmler: 'I come from the Reichführer [*sic*]. He has received orders from the Führer for the physical destruction of the Jews'. According to Irving, he found this passage difficult: it 'rocked me back on my heels frankly, because I thought "Ooops! . . . [the memoirs] show that Eichmann believed there was a Fuhrer order"'. Irving then rationalised Eichmann's evidence as follows: 'Eichmann must have had sleepless nights, wondering what he's going to do, what he's going to say to get off the hook (if he was brought to trial). And though he's not consciously doing it, I think his brain is probably rationalizing in the background, trying to find alibis'.

Irving was saying that Eichmann carefully invented a documented alibi, which was, according to Irving, fabricated to save Eichmann's own neck should he ever be brought to account. The false alibi was that the genocidal policy of the Nazis was based on Hitler's command and Eichmann was merely following orders. Eichmann was, according to Irving, attempting to demonstrate in a circuitous way that Hitler was not at all responsible. In any language, this is an incredible reading of a phrase that clearly suggests that Heydrich, one of Himmler's trusted lieutenants and a Hitler favourite, was simply telling Eichmann what he knew. In a totally unambiguous comment made at a time when the Nazis were seemingly invincible, Heydrich asserted that Hitler had assumed responsibility for the forthcoming Holocaust. But this is carefully, and without too much subtlety, transformed by Irving into a fantasised ruse. Even if an authentic written order signed by Hitler that said 'Kill all the Jews' were discovered, the Hitler hagiographers, through their convoluted reasoning and blind intransigence, would almost certainly denounce this hypothetically unimpeachable piece of evidence as a forgery or, conversely, would attack it as a self-serving attempt by a jealous Führer to claim the credit for Himmler and Heydrich's handiwork. Either way, in the denialist book Hitler always comes out as virtually the only major Nazi leader who had no reponsibility—direct or indirect—for the Holocaust.

Irving and the Historians

> No reasonable person would describe Sir John [Keegan] as a Nazi sympathizer. Yet it seemed to me that he was either unwilling or unable to rethink his earlier opinion that Irving was basically a sound historian who only had 'perverse' opinions on the single issue of whether or not Hitler knew about the extermination of the Jews.
>
> Richard Evans, 2002

The trial in 2000 effectively finished Irving as a contender for serious study as a historical writer, but it also cast an interesting light on the attitudes of more reputable historians who had, in the past, relied on Irving as a source. The behaviour and opinions of some mainstream historians were, to be charitable, very puzzling. Lipstadt once described her post-judgment meeting with Donald Cameron Watt, a major historian of international relations. As a subpoena witness (for the plaintiff), Watt had described Irving as a historian of repute and, according to Lipstadt, after the judgment he exclaimed, 'Penguin was after blood'. Astonished by this construction of Irving as victim, all Lipstadt could do was say 'Excuse me?' Later that day, Lipstadt was handed a copy of London's *Evening Standard* in which Watt had expanded on his theme of victimisation: 'Penguin was certainly out for blood. The firm has employed five historians, with two research assistants, for some considerable time to produce 750 pages of written testimony'. Watt added the astonishing comment 'Show me one historian who has not broken into a cold sweat at the thought of undergoing similar treatment', a point of view that seems to conflate a careful and professional examination of diligent scholarship with the process of detailed criticism of seemingly plausible fraudulence. John Keegan, a pioneering military historian and a national military correspondent for *The Daily Telegraph*, followed Watt's line by writing in that newspaper that the judgment would 'send a tremor through the community of twentieth-century historians' and that Irving's legally damned approach constituted merely 'a small but disabling element in his work'.

These two puzzling opinions, by *bona fide* British historians who should have known better, may be explained by an interesting set of circumstances. Watt had once prefaced an Irving book, and Keegan had publicly recommended Irving's *Hitler's War* as a primer on the Hitlerian view of World War II. These endorsements put them in the uncomfortable position of being seen by Irving as friendly witnesses, but they do not fully explain the pair's odd behaviour, and place each of them in the even more uncomfortable position of being regarded, by critical observers at least, almost as Irving sympathisers. This reputation came about notwithstanding Watt's and Keegan's having made qualifying remarks about Irving before, during and after the trial.

It is interesting to note that Irving has always had an ambivalent relationship with historians, at once regarding them with disdain and reverence, the former because they did not find the genuine documents that he himself has tracked down and the latter because they are members of an honoured profession which has effectively excluded him from its ranks. Irving's desire to cling to the coat tails of genuine historians, some of whom blithely (and freely) seemed to use him as an archival drudge, was evidenced when he proudly displayed on his website a statement made in 1978 by the doyen of German historians Hans Mommsen: 'It is our good fortune to have an Irving. At least he provides fresh stimuli for historians'. The quote stayed there until, two years after Irving filed his suit against Lipstadt, Mommsen wrote to him and asked for it to be removed.

It was a mere two years later that Irving's limited (see Mommsen's 'At least') reputation as an archivist and writer, at his own ego-driven behest, crashed and burned, whatever shred of credibility he may have had in mainstream opinion as a military specialist thoroughly compromised by his exposure at the trial.

Carto, McCalden and Zündel: Stunts and Scrapes

> Zündel has honed his public antics over many years. When NBC's *Holocaust* was screened in Canada in April 1978 he created an organization, 'Concerned Parent of German Descent', to protest the screenings. He declared the West German Government to be the 'West German Occupation Regime'. ... He has written to rabbis and synagogues throughout Canada offering to lecture on topics of common interest to Germans and Jews.
>
> Deborah Lipstadt, 2003

In 1978, Willis Carto, a US ultra-rightist associated with the Ku Klux Klan and Aryanist publications, founded the California-based faux-academic Institute for Historical Review (IHR). Initially, the IHR was generally regarded, by the few who knew about it, as an obscure gang of anti-Semitic eccentrics. However, in late 1979, the IHR had the brainwave of offering a publicity-attracting US$50 000 reward to anybody who could prove that Jews were gassed in a Nazi extermination campaign. The stunt had little success at first, but a year later a Northern Irish (by birth) member of the IHR, David McCalden (a former British fascist now known in the USA as Lewis Brandon), sent out challenging letters with application forms to Holocaust survivors, announcing that the 'contest' was to be decided at a forthcoming IHR 'Revisionist Convention', at which the IHR would set up a tribunal whose verdict would be final. The IHR targeted Long Beach resident Mel Mermelstein, an Auschwitz survivor who had written to the local *Los Angeles Times* and the *Jerusalem Post* about the IHR's gruesome challenge.

The upshot was that in early 1981 Mermelstein responded to the provocation, offering a sworn deposition about his family's experiences in Auschwitz; but his individual claim was pushed to one side for the time being when the high-profile Simon Wiesenthal Center accepted the test, a major public-relations triumph for the IHR. In March 1981, the Wiesenthal Center withdrew, however, when it became clear that the IHR would not budge on the issue of its acting as judge and jury in the process.

Resolute in the face of what appeared to be a combination of IHR intransigence and a stacked deck, Mermelstein took the organisation to civil court—a long process which resulted in the IHR being forced to pay Mermelstein the reward, plus costs, in October 1981. Following that decision, further legal skirmishes ensued, with the IHR claiming a victory but paying out a large amount of money. At the original pre-trial hearing, the judge, Thomas T Johnson, had cited the terms of California's Evidence Code regarding 'facts and propositions of generalized knowledge that are so universally known that they cannot reasonably be the subject of dispute', and confirmed that under that code, Jews were gassed to death at Auschwitz. From the IHR's point of view, the Mermelstein case had two disagreeable unintended consequences: they lost a great deal of money, and the Holocaust became an established fact in Californian law. The case was also followed by new debacles, including Carto's expulsion, debilitating internal factionalism and loss of patronage followed by a desperate search for new funding. The challenge-style outrageousness of the IHR was in abeyance, apart from a few flurries of half-hearted civil litigation.

When it comes to outrageous behaviour, Ernst Zündel, a German-born Canadian, has acquired a reputation as the denialists' expert in flagrant exploitation of the media. In his time, he has demonstrated in concentration camp stripes, turned up for trial in black face, dressed his bodyguards ('janitors') in SS-style uniforms and publicly worn a bulletproof vest to court. He excelled himself, however, when in the 1970s he produced a series of pamphlets and a book entitled *Hitler's Secret Antarctic Bases, Nazi Super-Weapons* which took advantage of the UFO craze by proclaiming that flying saucers were secret Axis weapons that were still being launched through a hole in the Antarctic ice. Of course, this linking of the Führer with flying saucers produced immediate interest in an electronic media unaware, apparently, that the Antarctic was a fairly solid mass of ice-covered rock with none too many hangar-sized holes. Nor had the media latched on to Zündel's real motives, as related in a later interview. He wanted to appear on television to talk about denial: 'The book was for fun . . . it was a chance to get on radio and TV talk shows . . . that was my chance to talk about what I wanted to talk about'.

Zündel's line of reasoning was that there is much to admire about national socialism and, unfortunately for the reputation of the German nation, the irritating myth of the Holocaust, perpetrated by self-absorbed Jews, had simply got in the way. In his quest for attention, Zündel displayed a shameless admiration for Hitler: 'I am an admirer of how this man took a country that was like a beaten child amongst nations and within six years made it into the marvel that National Socialist Germany was in 1938. He was a humble man with wonderful, intuitive gifts'. Admittedly, Zündel's paean was, in that interview, qualified by his saying that things went downhill after 1938, a characteristic denialist wriggle, but nevertheless, Zündel's neo-Nazism has been well established by such publications as *The Hitler We Loved and Why*, a White Power publication, which ended with the statement that Hitler's spirit was 'with us. WE LOVE YOU, ADOLF HITLER'.

After surviving two attempts at conviction in criminal trials in Canada (in 1985 and 1988), Zündel left his adopted country in 2000 for the USA but was expelled back to Canada in 2003 before being deported to his homeland by Canadian authorities. Arrested on his arrival in Germany, he was tried and convicted on several counts, including Holocaust denial (illegal in Germany). An appeal failed, thus ensuring his martyrdom in a small group of denialist *cognoscenti*.

Carto, McCalden and Zündel, with their unrepentant Hitler worship and unsubtle extremism, represented old-school denial, and it is the more recent emphasis on 'respectability' that has turned the deniers away from pamphleteering and stunts and towards developing a cosmetic professionalism. As far as the IHR was concerned, the lesson to be learned from the Mermelstein case and from Zündel's stunts was that such exploits detract from what became the IHR's new objective, to gain respectability as a quasi-academic organisation.

Mark Weber and the Institute for Historical Review

> In order to keep the IHR in the black they have to cater to the far right. I think if you were to look at their book sales you would see that some of the more complex, really solid historiographical works probably don't sell as well as Henry Ford's *International Jew* or the *Protocols of Zion*.
>
> David Cole, 1994

The prime mover in new-wave denialism has been Mark Weber. If there ever could be such a thing as the more acceptable face of Holocaust denial, this US propagandist tried to be it. He has a BA degree and a genuine master's degree in modern European history, both from reputable universities; he studied in Munich and (worryingly) has worked as a schoolteacher. Weber owns a small publishing house and was once news editor of the ultra-rightist *National Vanguard*. And yet, he has insisted that he is not a neo-Nazi.

Weber, described as 'bright and personable' as well as a 'likable antagonist' by authors Shermer and Grobman, has a track record in Aryanist, anti-Semitic and neo-Nazi activities going back to his 1988 appearance in a Canadian trial as defence witness for Ernst Zündel. In 1992, an article that he had written was circulated to colleges by his friend and co-denier Bradley Smith, arguing that the 'human soap' story (that Nazis made soap from the fat of concentration camp victims) was a lie perpetrated by Simon Wiesenthal and Zionist leader Stephen Wise. In 1993 Weber was caught out in a Simon Wiesenthal Center sting when a researcher from the centre, posing as a fellow ultra-rightist, met him and secretly filmed their discussion. It was clear that Weber had attended the meeting to gain information about European neo-Nazi groups. He denied this, of course. And in a speech at an IHR conference in Costa

Mesa, California, in 1998, Weber, in a wonderful piece of Freudian projection, spoke against Jews as the 'traditional enemy of truth'. All of his 130 listeners probably agreed with him.

Part of the IHR process of acquiring 'respectability' was to learn from denialist writer Arthur R Butz, author of the 1976 faux-academic *The Hoax of the Twentieth Century: The Case against the Presumed Extermination of European Jewry*. The IHR plan was to switch denialist tactics away from publishing books and pamphlets that merely strung together conspiracy-theory assertions about the Holocaust and towards producing monographs with footnotes and a quasi-academic gloss. IHR activities were also turned towards gaining support from 'technical experts', including the egregious Fred Leuchter (he pronounces his name 'Looshter'), a US self-styled engineer who produced, in 1989, *Auschwitz: The End of the Line. The Leuchter Report: The First Forensic Examination of Auschwitz*, published by Focal Point, David Irving's publishing company. Leuchter's 'report' was commissioned by Robert Faurisson, France's most prominent Holocaust denier, an IHR member and a supporter of Ernst Zündel in his second trial in Canada. (Leuchter's book was later published as *The Leuchter Report: An Engineering Report on the Alleged Execution Chambers at Auschwitz, Birkenau, and Majdanek, Poland*.) An amateur constructor and supplier of execution chambers to several US prisons, Leuchter met Faurisson and quickly became involved in the Holocaust denial movement as their expert witness on the non-lethal nature of Nazi gas chambers and the use of Zyklon B as merely an insecticide. These assertions were based on the analysis of some inadequate and unsuitable samples taken illegally from Auschwitz by Faurisson and on Leuchter's own 'expert' assessment of the inadequately homicidal capability of the surviving structures at the camps.

As an expert witness in the 1988 Zündel case, Leuchter was a dismal failure, the prosecution counsel quickly ripping up his supposed credentials as a specialist engineer. As it happened, Leuchter had only an arts degree with a history specialism and an obsession with death machines, hence his career. He had no engineering qualifications at all.

Accordingly, the judge ruled him out of court on the grounds that he had 'no expertise in this area'. The Zündel defence case collapsed, partially because the defendant was clearly an anti-Semite but also because Leuchter was seen for what he was—a fraud. He was also later exposed by US penal system authorities as an incompetent blackmailer.

Nevertheless, as Deborah Lipstadt has pointed out, some mainstream journalism outlets quickly latched on to Leuchter as a man with something to say, even if he was characterised in press reports as a creepy obsessive. In 1990, *Atlantic Monthly* published an article about Leuchter, describing him as a 'trained and accomplished engineer', giving rise to the IHR's publicising their *soi-disant* technical expert as a man 'certified by *Atlantic* as one of America's leading experts on gas chambers', yet another step on the road to seeming respectability.

As well as trying (and failing) to gather 'technical evidence', the IHR continued its search for credibility by publishing a seemingly scholarly periodical, the *Journal of Historical Review*, by sponsoring conferences and by conducting 'research'. Under Weber's leadership, in what is probably the organisation's most significant work, the IHR has also been instrumental in Holocaust deniers' attempting to appropriate the formerly genuine historical term *revisionism*.

Revisionism was once a legitimate expression applied by historians to scholars who re-worked existing interpretations of past events either by discovering new evidence or by re-interpreting old evidence. These revisions were generally expressed within an accepted framework of historical scholarship, which might include the statement of an informing paradigm (or approach) to the issue, a diligent, comprehensive and accurate review of the evidence and an authentic presentation of an explanation based on accepted practice. Indeed, there have been well-known and highly respected revisionists. In 1961, AJP Taylor, for example, the celebratedly quirky and productive English historian, wrote a highly controversial (at the time) book, *The Origins of the Second World War*. In it he suggested that Hitler was an opportunist who had been encouraged by western supineness, thus partially laying the blame for Hitler's early successes at the feet of the British and French leaders of the day. It is important to bear in mind, though, that, unlike Irving et al., genuine revisionists such as Taylor have a particular position that is explicitly stated in a commercial or academic publication; they generally follow accepted historical practice and each has published other books or articles which are more or less in the mainstream of historical scholarship. Holocaust deniers do revisionism differently. Their publications tend to be disseminated through small-scale, ultra-rightist online networks and private publishing enterprises, and their authors masquerade as 'researchers', while the work they have undertaken is generally a cobbling-together either of stale anti-Semitic propaganda or newer fantasies into which they add tales of the latest Israeli (that is Jewish) atrocities. They also stay within the boundaries of Holocaust denial and other ultra-rightist topics. In other words, they are the modern equivalent of the kinds of fanatics who used to operate out of back-street bookshops, peddling crank paperbacks that asked questions about UFOs, Roswell, Area 51, Small Greys (aliens) and whether or not six million Jews really did die. The upshot is that, notwithstanding attempts by Holocaust deniers to characterise themselves as serious players in an important social and political debate, time and time again they have proved themselves to be frauds and fakes who have confected a debate that has as much legitimacy as a fairytale.

And this is why Deborah Lipstadt refuses to debate Holocaust deniers in public. Her argument is that the debate starts from a false premise and any attempt to discuss Holocaust denial as a serious topic face to face is giving free publicity to a specious and offensive point of view. At the same time, however, Lipstadt and some other contra-denialists such as Michael Shermer are against deniers being silenced by criminal legislation, as was the case with Irving in Austria and Zündel in Canada. Their argument is that any suppression of ideas and free speech (within the law) in a democratic society, however offensive and misguided the ideas may be, militates against a more general and legitimate open debate in a free society. This is a crucial point, since the denialist position, when exposed to expert examination in civil courts, has collapsed, as was the case in the $50 000 challenge and in the Irving-instigated libel trial in

London. On a more pragmatic basis, when dragged before criminal courts, deniers make the most of their supposed martyrdom as well as gaining a foothold in the broader freedom-of-speech debates, a thoroughly unwelcome development for those who oppose their point of view.

That, however, is a complex argument between lawyers, scholars and political activists and one that is not immediately appealing to a mass, political audience. Indeed, it is an additional complication in the debates, in much the same way that micro-detail arguments put forward by deniers tend to block real discussion. It is that combination of intricate points of attack as well as the hit-and-run tactics employed by deniers that makes it hard for their opponents to pin them down, until, that is, they expose themselves, as did the IHR over Mermelstein and as did Irving over Lipstadt.

The Wehrmacht and Genocide

> At the center of the [first] exhibition was an installation in the shape of an iron cross, its sides hung with small photographs without captions or commentary under headings such as 'Tormenting Jews' or 'Gallows'. Museum educators and others predicted that the exhibition would be a failure because it included far too much text and photos that were too small and too unspectacular.
>
> Jan Philipp Reemtsma, 2005

Because of their marginalisation, it once seemed to be practically impossible for the fringe denialist movements to gain any serious political traction in western democracies. That was until a high-profile historical crisis affected Germany in the 1990s, when a well-meaning historical exhibition opened a veritable Pandora's box of political and even terrorist activity. The exhibition in question was a display of Wehrmacht atrocities during World War II.

The Prussian-German professional military tradition has never been particularly restrained when it comes to dealing with an unfriendly civilian population. In its African colonial war of 1904 to 1907, for example, the Kaiser's imperial army engaged in the destruction of the Herero and Nama peoples, acts of a military-institutional culture that was consumed with the notion of the 'annihilatory offensive'. These campaigns of extermination in Africa were followed by further atrocities in Belgium and northern France during World War I, including reprisals against civilians, the taking of hostages and the use of human shields, actions which were used for wildly exaggerated wartime propaganda by the Entente powers to the extent that the real atrocities eventually became discounted. The behaviour of the Wehrmacht during the World War II campaigns of 1941 to 1944 in the Soviet Union constituted about as brutal a military expedition as had occurred anywhere in recent history, with mass shootings of Jews, partisans and Communist Party members, as well as Slavs generally. And yet the myth arose that while the SS fought a dirty war in Russia (and in the west), the Wehrmacht came away with relatively clean hands.

That myth of Wehrmacht military integrity was destroyed in a very public way when, in 1995, the Hamburg Institute for Social Research staged the controversial exhibition *The War of Extermination: Crimes of the Wehrmacht 1941–44*, which contained more than 1000 photographs and documents clearly showing regular army troops engaged in wartime atrocities against civilians, both Jewish and non-Jewish. The exhibition, which moved beyond Hamburg as a travelling show, produced, as might be expected, a huge furore in Germany. The Hamburg Institute exhibition was not, of course, a surprise to those who already knew about Wehrmacht wartime behaviour, but these were mainly German historians (too scholarly for a general audience), elderly Wehrmacht veterans (too keen to keep quiet) and equally elderly survivors in Europe, Russia and overseas (too dispersed and possibly too hesitant to press any claims). The travelling show was based on the results of a serious German-language study of the same name and published in 1995 (in English). This weighty, multi-authored volume outlined how the Wehrmacht units had been fully complicit in the mass murder of civilians in central and eastern Europe, in the Balkans, in Soviet Russia and in Greece. But the study was an academic treatise and had a limited audience, which had been the case with much previous German scholarship on the issue. However this time, an exhibition inspired by the book was created, and it caused widespread astonishment in a public audience previously unaware of and unexposed to any refutation of the 'clean' Wehrmacht story.

The predominant German view is that, yes, the Nazis did commit genocidal crimes in the name of Germany: that is an admitted fact and responsibility for it has been accepted. But the Wehrmacht was a professional army with professional standards, and the documented Wehrmacht atrocities go beyond the admitted facts. The problem is that allegations of systematic Wehrmacht atrocities in the period from 1941 to 1944 take us closer to a truly testing question for Germans: can there be something that is consistently brutal about the German military character? This is an inquiry that incenses Holocaust deniers, of course, possibly even more than other, more established Nazi extermination policies or the memorialisation of Auschwitz, if only because it strikes at the heart of their Teutonophilia, their love of a mythically strong, pure and civilised Germany. That is why the deniers and their right-wing allies responded so violently to the Wehrmacht exhibition.

The original 1995 exhibition could scarcely have appeared at a worse political juncture for the German government. That year happened to be the fiftieth anniversary of the end of World War II, an event celebrated throughout Europe and Russia but more acknowledged than celebrated in Germany. Also, in 1995 German troops entered the Balkans for the first time since 1945, to set up a hospital in war-ravaged Croatia. And in December 1996, German combat troops returned to the Balkans, this time as peacekeepers in Bosnia-Herzegovina. In the light of national and international sensitivities about Wehrmacht atrocities in that region, the defence minister banned Bundeswehr members from taking part in any *Crimes of the Wehrmacht* exhibition activities or forums. This attempted circumscription of the exhibition intensified when Helmut Kohl, chancellor between 1982 and 1998, allegedly put pressure on the Poles to cancel the exhibition's proposed trip to Warsaw, and when the German government successfully put a similar kind of pressure on the Goethe Institute in New York. But these official responses, caused by the political and diplomatic sensitivities of the day, were less about denial than they were about diplomatic embarrassment. In contrast, the rightist political response was much more robust. Christian Democrat politicians took out advertisements in the press calling the exhibition an attack on 'love for the Fatherland', and, on a more serious note, former soldiers such as Alfred Dregger (Christian Democrat Party) and Erich Mende (Free Democratic Party) publicly attacked the exhibition for sullying the reputation of the Wehrmacht. They insisted that neither they nor their units had been involved in the kinds of atrocities described in the exhibition, which may well have been the case, since the Wehrmacht had drawn on a pool of eleven million conscripts and volunteers during World War II. However, Hannes Heer (the exhibition's first curator) and his researchers countered by confronting Dregger and Mende with evidence that their units had indeed been involved in war crimes.

The anti-exhibition campaign heated up in 1997 when ultra-conservative Peter Gauweiler (leader of the Bavarian branch of the Christian Social Union) attacked the work as a conspiracy of 'red cells' based in the Hamburg Institute and in the more progressive newspaper management boards. He and his Christian Social Union colleagues conducted a counter-demonstration by laying a wreath at the Munich Tomb of the Unknown Soldier, saying, 'We don't think it is right on the one hand to hold an exhibition about world war crimes and then only to present the half truth, for example, to completely ignore the crimes committed by the Russian Red Army'. Gauweiler's attack was followed by more extreme incidents, some of which involved the neofascist German National Party, and culminated in the bombing of the Saarbrücken venue of the travelling exhibition, which caused, according to Associated Press reports, millions of dollars' worth of damage, but did little harm to the exhibits. The police issued a statement blaming right-wing extremists.

In a development that heaped Pelion upon Ossa (and did so entirely coincidentally), the previous year, Daniel Goldhagen, a young

Jewish American scholar, had published his inflammatory book *Hitler's Willing Executioners: Ordinary Germans and the Holocaust*, the thesis of which was that ordinary Germans were willing perpetrators of anti-Semitic genocide and that it had not been the province just of fanatical Nazi murderers. The book caused a huge controversy and was greeted in Germany with a mixture of immense public curiosity, political fury and scholarly incredulity. According to Goldhagen, the post-war explanation that Nazi atrocities had been the work of 'culprits' (the so-called *Tätergeneration*—a generation of perpetrators) was now to be replaced with the view that there was something in the German character that disposed them towards mass murder—or eliminationist anti-Semitism. As Goldenhagen put it himself, 'the only appropriate proper name for Germans who perpetrated the Holocaust is Germans'.

The book became a bestseller in Germany, but its scholarly credentials were soon demolished through considered rebuttal by more established scholars in the field. However, there were two side effects from the book's publication, one positive and the other negative. The positive effect was that among many young Germans there was a huge arousal of interest in the issue of moral culpability; the negative effect was a reaction in centrist opinion against the continual resuscitation of German wartime behaviour, the latter response characterised by a speech given in 1998 by the playwright and novelist Martin Walser. When he accepted the Peace Prize of the German Book Trade, Walser, himself a wartime veteran and an outspoken political commentator with a pragmatic worldview, referred to the difficulties of dealing with his country's shame and, at the same time, commented in disapproving terms about the recurring memorialisation of the Holocaust, an activity which he considered to be an unnecessary monumentalisation of past disgrace ('*Monumentalisierung der Schande*'). His exact words were: 'No sane person denies Auschwitz; no person with an ounce of intelligence casts doubt on the horror of Auschwitz; but when I'm confronted daily in the media with this past, I notice that something inside me protests against being shown our shameful deeds without respite'.

A fierce debate erupted, and Walser then had to bear quite unjustified accusations of anti-Semitism from, among others, Ignatz Bubitz (sometimes Bubis), at that time the pugnacious leader of Germany's Jewish community.

All of this occurred at a time when rightists (mainly the National Democratic Party) and neo-Nazis demonstrated. Unfrightened, an engrossed, if shocked, public flocked to see the evidence of the Wehrmacht exhibition, notwithstanding the bombing in Saarbrücken. Events took an unexpected turn when the exhibition itself became part of the process of historical discovery, as visitors went home, poked around in trunks and cupboards and came up with further evidence of Wehrmacht barbarity. And, as the tour was wending its way around Germany, it became a controversial historical event in its own right as it became clear that a small number of the exhibits had been incorrectly labelled. Some photographs of 'German' atrocities turned out to be images of Soviet war crimes in the Ukraine. Neo-Nazis, conservatives and militarists were cockahoop with I told you so's. The exhibition closed temporarily in 1999, its director Hannes Heer was fired, and the Hamburg Institute revamped the whole show, re-opening in 2001.

The new exhibition put forward the same thesis as the old one, that the Wehrmacht had, contrary to popular opinion, engaged in large-scale atrocities against prisoners of war and non-combatants and had both actively and passively colluded in the Holocaust. This time, however, the curators had been more efficient in doing their homework. A team of sixteen historians had redesigned the show, now called *Crimes of the Wehrmacht: Dimensions of the War of Extermination 1941–1944*, doubling its size, and re-organising the exhibition in six topics: war and law; genocide; prisoners of war; deportation; the war for food; and partisan warfare. Interestingly, in one gallery, a case study was presented of the mass murder of Jews by a Wehrmacht battalion. One company officer had taken up the task without delay, another had requested a written order before taking on the mission, and another had refused, the consequence being that he was then labelled 'too soft' by his *confrères*. The supposed moral? That a measure of resistance had been possible.

During the lifetime of the two shows, from 1995 to 2004, the Wehrmacht exhibition aroused strong feelings, with demonstrations for and against, a bombing and some unsubtle ducking and diving by politicians. Gerhard Schröder, Social Democratic chancellor from 1998 to 2005, failed to visit the exhibition, commenting, in a wonderful moment of Nelsonian denial, that he found it 'impermissible to say that the bulk of the army was capable of committing such crimes'.

In summary, the Wehrmacht exhibition opened the eyes of many German citizens to an alternative construction of the wartime behaviour of their memorially respected army. At the same time, it produced a mushrooming of anti-exhibition feeling in right-wing extremist groups, who were given a huge free gift when the first exhibition got it wrong, admittedly in a minor way. But with denialist groups, there is no room for error. A classic denialist technique is to seize upon any small blemish as a vitiation of the whole. Furthermore, the combination of circumstances—the exhibition itself, the Goldhagen attack, the Walser controversy and the fiftieth celebration of the end of World War II—played into the hands of the ultra-rightists by edging more Germans towards what may be called Holocaust fatigue, in turn legitimising, on the face it, the hostility of the Christian Social Union, the German National Party and the minor rightist groups such as Die Republikaner (founded by an ex-SS officer). The ultra-rightists consider that their aggressively nationalist position is constantly undermined by external and internal attacks on the German national reputation; as one Republikaner supporter put it (using the nationalistic '*Vaterland*' instead of the more politically neutral '*Heimat*', or homeland):

> The most important goals and ideas [sic] is first of all, I say, to represent and to defend my fatherland; to defend ... to be allowed to be as a German to show my nationality, my national consciousness, my patriotism, and also to be allowed to live it. This is number one for me.

This point of view had already been brought to the fore in a more moderate fashion in the *Historikerstreit* (historians' quarrel), a fierce 1980s debate among German historians about an alleged attempt by conservative and nationalist historians to 'normalise' Germany's recent past. And, thanks to the controversy surrounding the Wehrmacht exhibitions and the Goldhagen debate, is not too far away from mainstream nationalist and conservative opinion in Germany today.

It may be argued that these historical crises of the 1990s presented the ultra-right side of German politics with an opportunity to build on the ideological groundwork of Irving and others, by moving the denialist debate more towards the centre. However, the shifting nature of ultra-right politics in Germany presents a more complex picture than the movement inspired in part by David Irving, Zündel and company. Part of a wider, European neo-Nazi movement, the German ultra-right is based on a disjunction between the more affluent western German *Länder* (provinces or states) and the far less prosperous *Länder* of the former East Germany, and on a tendency for political extremists to be drawn in any case to organisations that promise xenophobic militant violence against both traditional and new targets, but especially against immigrants. Meanwhile, keeping a misleadingly safe distance, the ultra-right leadership now clothes itself in the respectably dark designer suits of mainstream political players.

Still, the mythic personality of Hitler and the legend of a powerful, militaristic Nazi regime fighting against the might of colonial France, the British Empire, the USA and Russia still hangs like a shadow over modern German historical consciousness, and the Holocaust denial component of the legend continues to feed into ultra-right politics. But while it may be true that Irving and company contributed an initial ideological, anti-Semitic basis to incipient and receptive right-wing politics in Germany, the ultra-right, which includes the neo-Nazis, went on to develop its own, supplementary, more complex (and occasionally paradoxical) agendas. These included anti-migrant racism, anti-globalisation, anti-capitalism, anti-Israeli pro-Arab sentiment, hostility to the USA's 1990s interventions in the Balkans and even an equating of the September 11 attacks with the bombing of Dresden. This is precisely where western Holocaust deniers might once have made substantive political gains as the ideologues of neo-Nazism, were it not for the IHR's risible schemes, Irving's braggadocio and Zündel's stunts, all of which have ultimately meant that the deniers have gained microscopic political importance in North America and Germany. Indeed, the IHR is now in decline, unable to stage a major conference since its last significant event, in 2002, in Irvine, California. To reinforce the point, while it is the case that 100 or so friends of denial regularly attended IHR conferences up to and including the 2002 California gathering, these numbers contrast starkly with the estimated 35 000 UFO enthusiasts who turned up in July 2007 to commemorate the sixtieth anniversary of aliens landing across the state border at Roswell, Arizona.

Nevertheless, politically impotent, offensive and egotistical as they may be, the Irvings of this world, in Anne Applebaum's phrase, need ever to be the object of 'endless rebuttals', if only to commemorate the lives and the deaths of the Fallen Leaves.

3

A CULTURE OF DENIAL

Explaining the Politics of Remembrance in Modern Japan

Just before Christmas 2000, David McNeill, then a research fellow at the University of Tokyo, together with his wife, Keiko, began their weekly talk show on a local radio station. They mentioned, in passing, an affecting visit they had made earlier that year to Nanjing, to the museum commemorating the murderous behaviour of imperial Japanese forces in that Chinese city in 1937. David and Keiko suggested that those who denied Japanese culpability for the events in Nanjing should visit the museum and see for themselves. Half an hour later, a trio from a local 'political group' arrived at the radio station and demanded to speak to the talk show hosts and the management. A meeting was hastily convened in which the spokesman for the intruders told the McNeills that, since the Nanjing massacre had not been 'officially announced' by the Japanese government, it should not be mentioned at all. The station manager was then pointedly asked by the politely menacing ultra-nationalists (*uyoku*) if the station was communist. The meeting ended and the visitors were ushered out. Two days later, the station manager advised the talk show hosts not to discuss political issues and to apologise on air for their inappropriate comments.

He explained that he was frightened that the *uyoku* might park their intimidating black *gaisensha* (sound trucks) outside the premises of the local merchants who were the station's sponsors. Strident harassment would be certain. Violence could not be ruled out. And yet, buoyed by supportive fan mail, the McNeills dug in their heels. No apology was forthcoming. They continued with their policy of attempting to explore controversial issues, and there were continued counter-attempts at censorship.

Japan is a nation still striving to come to terms with the violent behaviour of its military forces in the 1930s and 1940s. The brief narrative above illustrates, in a nutshell, many of the elements of historical denial in Japan today. It contains a reference to Japanese atrocities against an Asian neighbour; a *gaijin* (foreigner) and a Japanese woman commenting on Japanese atrocities, which are especially provocative acts to many xenophobic and misogynistic nationalists; an ominous intervention by ultra-nationalists, when it is common knowledge in Japan that the ultra-nationalists have links with the *yakuza* criminal gangs; an allusion to the apparently blinkered approach of the government to Japanese war crimes; a reference to communist infiltration of the media, succeeded by a panicked management opting for self-censorship; and quiet support from a number of shocked Japanese listeners anxious to get the discussion of their controversial past out in the open. Indeed, one correspondent wrote, 'I was so surprised to hear the two of you discussing the Nanjing Massacre. I remember my own crazy uncle showing us photographs he brought back from the war of the bodies of the Chinese he said he had beheaded'. The messages from audience members were unanimous: the McNeills should press on. Their radio audience was keen to hear them tackle the issue of aggressive Japanese militarism in twentieth-century history.

The military brutality referred to by the McNeills is well documented, as are the countless atrocities (large- and small-scale) committed mainly by imperial Japanese land forces between 1931 and 1945. Victims included the soldiers and citizens of conquered Asian and Pacific territories, non-Asian prisoners of war and civilians. Of these offences, there are three war crimes that have, since the early 1980s, become an emblematic focus of Japanese and international controversy. They are the murderous rampage by Japanese troops after their capture of Nanjing in December 1937, the so-called 'comfort women' scandal, a policy of enforced prostitution of predominantly non-Japanese women before and during World War II, and the establishment of the infamous Unit 731, a Japanese chemical and biological warfare group stationed in Manchuria. Conflict between remembrance and denial of these atrocities has provoked serious heart-searching in Japan, strong official and unofficial protests in China and South Korea, and bewilderment in many western nations who are puzzled by what they see as Japan's effort to whitewash the more unpleasant parts of its recent history.

Explaining the denial of Japanese military atrocities in Asia during the period in question is a complex task. Although the three key events vary in scale, geography and character, they all have at least one thing in common that may explain their origins and Japanese nationalist reaction to their occurrence: part of the mentality that lay behind these officially approved crimes was a long history in Japan of blind submission to authority. Associated with that deference to authority was the rationale that the more sadistic the perpetrators were, the more closely they were following the wishes of their revered emperor. The US chaplain at Sugamo prison in Tokyo spoke about his post-war conversations with Japanese war criminals, who told him that the prisoners 'had the belief that any enemy of the emperor could not be right, so the more brutally they treated their prisoners, the more loyal to the emperor they were being'.

Nanjing

> There were about thirty-seven old men, women and children. We captured them and gathered them in a square. There was a woman holding a child on her right arm ... and another on her left. We stabbed and killed them, all three—like potatoes in a skewer.
>
> Shiro Azuma, Japanese soldier stationed in Nanjing from 1937 to 1938

In 1937, Nanjing, an ancient capital sited on the banks of the Yangtze river, was the chief city of the Chinese nationalists. Its fall, to the Japanese troops of the Central China Area Army, on 13 December 1937, came after a bitter but successful Japanese campaign to capture the downriver city of Shanghai, following which the leaderless Chinese nationalist forces in Nanjing were in disarray. There was brief resistance but, notwithstanding the relative ease with which the colonisers took the city, there then followed a six-week period in January and February 1938 during which the Japanese troops ran amok. Officially sanctioned acts of almost indescribable cruelty took place, and their occurrence is now more or less beyond dispute. Japanese troops, under the supervision of their officers, committed mass murder, engaged in rape and individual murder, embarked on massive arson attacks and looted on a grand scale.

Most of the killings were of men of military age, who were rounded up by Japanese soldiers and then killed by machine gun fire, used as live targets for bayonet practice or beheaded. Chinese eyewitnesses reported many other appalling incidents of savage and remorseless barbarism, including burning alive, nailing to trees and hanging by tongues. But not only the men were victims of murder; babies, young children, pregnant women and the elderly were also tortured and killed. Estimates vary on the number of rape victims, but conservative figures suggest the systematic rape of 20 000 women and young girls, many of whom were murdered and mutilated after being assaulted. There were reports of gang rapes and sexual slavery. Arson took the form of indiscriminate burning of official and residential areas; by the time the rampage was over, an estimated two-thirds of the old city had gone up in flames. When it came to looting and theft, Japanese soldiers were given carte blanche by their officers to rob, which they did enthusiastically, from rich and poor alike.

What happened at Nanjing scandalised world public opinion at the time, because of the reports of the savage behaviour of the Japanese troops as well as the scale of the atrocity. Casualty estimates at the low end suggest some 100 000 fatalities. There are much higher estimates, ranging from 200 000 to 300 000, but precise numbers are difficult to calculate. Nevertheless, the 'rape' of Nanjing is generally accepted, outside Japan, as a major atrocity. Within Japan, however, for several decades after the end of World War II, reports of atrocities at Nanjing were scarcely mentioned. The rape of Nanjing was buried history.

The Nanjing massacre of 1937 to 1938 would seem to be a candidate for sustained and universal post-war analysis and condemnation. To begin with, there were the proceedings of the International Military Tribunal for the Far East from 1946 to 1948, otherwise known as the Tokyo war crimes trial. Over the years that followed the tribunal, further evidence for events in Nanjing emerged from numerous Chinese and European eyewitness accounts, photographic sources, archived contemporary Japanese newspaper reports, diaries and burial records. But despite that growing weight of testimony, the Nanjing massacre did not become an international controversy until the early 1970s. This seems especially strange, since, during the late 1940s and the 1950s, anti-Japanese sentiment was strong in the western nations whose prisoners of war and internees had suffered cruelly at the hands of Japanese captors. Why the delay?

The answer seems to lie partly in a racist distinction between the western view of atrocities against Europeans, which were considered to be beyond the pale, and atrocities against Asians, thought perhaps to be part and parcel of life in the Orient. There was also the overwhelming influence of Cold War politics. Immediately China turned communist, in 1949, Japan was seen by the west as a bulwark against further communist infiltration of Asia, a development reinforced by Japan's role as a major staging post and supply depot for US forces involved in the Korean War. Japan was the USA's 'unsinkable aircraft carrier'. So mention of recent Japanese atrocities was not encouraged, particularly by the US authorities; after all, World War II was over, and communist China was now the new enemy in Asia. The character and location of denial took a strange turn in the early 1970s, however, when the Cold War thawed a little. Mainland China, under Mao, was attempting to foster a rapprochement with Japan, and mention of events in Nanjing was officially frowned upon in China itself, because of its provocative nature and the damage it might do to building Sino-Japanese relations.

Therefore, failure to acknowledge the severity of events in Nanjing from 1945 to the early 1970s was both an official Japanese *and* a (non-Japanese) international diplomatic phenomenon. While politicians and diplomats colluded in avoiding the topic, paradoxically, much of the post-war discussion about Nanjing during that period took place in Japan, mainly in relatively obscure academic circles in which Marxist historians had adopted a critical approach to Japanese behaviour at Nanjing. That remained more or less the case until 1971 when the left-liberal newspaper *Asahi Shimbun* moved the story into broader public debate by publishing a series of articles entitled 'Travels in China' by one of Japan's most celebrated journalists, Katsuichi Honda. While covering the war in Vietnam, Honda had been dismayed by what he considered to be the brutality of US forces. As an examination of US military behaviour in that war, his articles also considered Japanese actions in China during the 1930s and 1940s and included Honda's analysis of the Nanjing massacre. These exposés were later published as a book, *A Journey to China*, in 1981, provoking a response from prominent Japanese writers, including Masaaki Tanaka, a member of the *goyo gakusha* (a derisive leftist term loosely translated as 'official scholars'), a group of intellectuals who took upon themselves the role of defenders of Japan's reputation. Tanaka's riposte to Honda's book was his publication, in 1984, of *The Fabrication of the 'Nanjing Massacre'*, based largely on the diaries of a General Iwane Matsui, who had been in charge of the Japanese troops in Nanjing in 1937. The book denied that the events at Nanjing as described by Chinese survivors and by Honda took place. Yoshiaki Itakura, a historian and himself a defender of Japan's character, took Tanaka to task, demonstrating that the author had, in an ironically self-destructive fashion, fabricated parts of Matsui's testimony, simply altering the diary in hundreds of instances to favour the hard-denial point of view.

These revelations, counter-accusations and controversies slowly gathered pace in the 1980s as Japanese veterans began to make public statements about what had happened at Nanjing, first at the 1980s

Catholic-sponsored *Exhibition for War and Peace* held in Tokyo, and later, in 1987, when octogenarian ex-soldier Shiro Azuma spoke to the media about murder and rape in Nanjing, to the fury of ultra-nationalists, who immediately threatened his life. Thereafter, according to writer Ian Buruma, who visited the old soldier, Azuma kept brass knuckledusters in the glove compartment of his car.

The Japanese nationalist view of events at Nanjing began to change tack. The revisionist position of the 1970s and early 1980s was transformed from one of total denial to the more recent soft-denial argument that focused on the extent and character of the massacre. The pro-nationalist, or minimalist, line in the debate became (and still is) that casualties and behaviour had been exaggerated to support pro-Chinese propaganda and were part of a conspiracy by supposed victims and their supporters to seek reparation. Nevertheless, the Nanjing controversy remained a largely Japanese and Chinese squabble until Chinese-American author Iris Chang published *The Rape of Nanking* in 1997. It blew the whole debate wide open by adopting a maximalist line on both casualties and behaviour. The sudden storm of controversy was produced partly because the book was a tendentious summary of events but, more importantly, because it was a runaway bestseller, at first in the USA and later in the world market.

Chang's decision to write a vivid account of ghastly Japanese carnage and cover-up stemmed from her visit to a conference at Cupertino, California, in 1994. At that time she was a 26-year-old graduate of Johns Hopkins University with a background in creative writing and journalism, and she was a little-known non-fiction author. The Cupertino conference was organised by the Global Alliance for Preserving the History of World War II in Asia, a Chinese-American pressure group, and it contained graphic images of Japanese activities in Nanjing. Chang was traumatised by what she saw; indeed, she was so shocked that she told her publishers, Basic Books, that she would pay them to let her write a book about Nanjing. They demurred and gave her their standard contract. Chang then started her two-year Nanjing odyssey, which included visiting survivors in China. As she told it: 'I wrote *Rape of Nanking* out of a sense of rage. I didn't really care if I made a cent from it. It was important to me that the world knew what happened in Nanking back in 1937'. But her attitude to the Japanese atrocities seemed to alter as she pursued the project:

> After reading several file cabinets' worth of documents on Japanese war crimes as well as accounts of ancient atrocities from the pantheon of world history, I would have to conclude that Japan's behaviour during World War II was less a product of dangerous people than of a dangerous government, in a vulnerable culture, in dangerous times, able to sell a dangerous rationalization to those whose human instincts told them otherwise.

The Rape of Nanking provoked indignation in Japan, where it was regarded, even by many moderates, as pro-Chinese propaganda. The mainstream anti-Chang line, in Japan and elsewhere, was that she was no historian, and critics began to pick her evidence and her argument apart. There were indeed errors in the book that aided the cause of her opponents. A more typical nationalist response was to condemn Chang as a partisan and inaccurate writer who simply served up a Chinese communist line. The more rabid Chang haters set up a website, Iris Chang and Her Lies, and she was caricatured in ultra-nationalist papers as a bigmouthed Chinese. In the face of intense opposition from her critics, Chang took her views into the community and during 1997 and 1998 gave interviews, appeared on television and delivered talks in an astonishing sixty-five US cities. Throughout, she was adamant that Japanese attempts to object to her portrayal of the atrocities were based on lies, and she expressed exasperation at a continuing Japanese governmental failure to apologise for what had happened in Nanjing.

Comfort Women

> Whether it was morning or night, once one soldier left, the next soldier came. Twenty men would come in one day ... we would

try to talk each other out of committing suicide, but even with that, women still did it ... I told a colonel in the army, 'Do you think we are your maids and your prostitutes? How can you be a human being after making us do such things ... [He said,] 'It is the command of the army. The country's order is the Emperor's order. If you have something to say you can say it to the Emperor'.

Kumjoo Pak, a former Korean 'comfort woman'

The story of the *ianfu* ('comfort women') began when, between 1937 and 1939, the imperial Japanese army command became concerned about increasing military resistance in China. This was caused, in their view, by the Japanese troops' propensity for rape. The generals were also worried about the combat capability of their troops, who were experiencing a debilitating epidemic of venereal disease. In 1932, General Yasuji Okamura had ordered the opening of the first *ianjo* ('comfort station', or military brothel) in Shanghai, an initiative that spread throughout the occupied territories in the late 1930s and 1940s. The first groups of women enlisted for service in the brothels were Japanese prostitutes, but, as Japanese expansion continued, they were followed by impoverished Chinese and Korean women who were frequently forcibly 'recruited' to work in the militarily supervised sex industry. As the war spread further, women from the Philippines became dragooned into service, together with some Dutch internees, as well as women from Timor, Burma and the Pacific islands. The number of women involved remains contested, varying from a conservative 80 000 to a huge 200 000.

After the war, the topic of this mass sexual servitude was all but ignored, possibly because, and this is a charitable interpretation, the issue of sexual slavery was a delicate one for what were still fairly prudish times. Furthermore, many of the survivors were afflicted with shame and were reluctant to come forward. Lack of interest in the outrage may, more importantly, have been a consequence of Allied gender bias and racism, since the issue revolved around the enforced slavery of women, almost all of whom were non-European. To reinforce this point, the only recorded post-war sanction against the instigators of the Japanese sexual slavery took place in Batavia (now Jakarta), where twelve Japanese officers were convicted of forcing thirty-five Dutch women into military brothels. There is an additional, Japanese explanation for the failure of the Allied authorities to deal with this war crime: in his book *Japan's Comfort Women*, Toshiyuki Tanaka has suggested that because the colonising nations had a long tradition of running their own versions of military brothels, which also exploited the poverty of Asian women, they were reluctant to take on the issues. This *tu quoque* position was made all the more plausible by the Allies' own approach to prostitution in occupied Japan, which, Tanaka argues, in a controversial fashion mirrored that of the Japanese military authorities in pre-war China. More important than any of these factors, however, is the Allies' need for an eastern ally during the Cold War.

Whatever the case, there is little doubt that many of the comfort women were coerced, kidnapped or tricked into prolonged activity as sex slaves, sometimes 'servicing' between twenty and thirty soldiers a day. If they resisted they could be beaten or killed. And while the procurers and operators may have been private individuals or companies, it was the military that had overall management of the system and it was the soldiers who were the principal abusers of the women.

Despite a national silence on the issue, the comfort women controversy slowly gathered momentum in the 1970s. In 1973, Japanese writer Kako Senda published the results of his interviews with Japanese soldiers as well as with Japanese and Korean comfort women, which contradicted the prevailing sentimental, even romantic, view of the women in male-authored novels and wartime reminiscences. A decade passed before the next exploration of the topic occurred, in 1984, when Japanese feminist journalist Yayori Matsui published an article in *Asahi Shimbun* that was a damning portrait of the comfort women system. The article provoked little reaction in Japan at that time, but in the late 1980s, Professor Chung-Ok Yun of the Ehwa Womens' University in Korea met Matsui and, as a result of that meeting as well as her own interest in the issue, published reports that inflamed Korean public opinion against Japan. Yun set up a Korean activist movement and in 1990 the Korean women then established the Voluntary Service Corps Problem Resolution Council, demanding admission, apology and compensation from the Japanese government. This high-profile activity pushed a Japanese official into denying the Korean allegations at a Diet [parliament] session in June 1990. Outraged, the Korean women filed a class action suit against the Japanese government, and the issue then became an international controversy of both guilt and reparation, with Dutch, Chinese and Filipina survivors joining in. Their cause became an international feminist struggle, and feminist networks characterised Japanese intransigence as a discrimination issue.

Characteristically, the response of the Japanese government in the early 1990s was to continue to deny the existence of *forced* sexual slavery as military policy in World War II until it was obliged, in 1993, to accept that the imperial Japanese forces had been directly and indirectly involved in running the comfort stations and to admit that coercion had been used.

Unit 731

> Interviewer: What happened?
> Kurumizawa: She opened her eyes.
> Interviewer: And then?
> Kurumizawa: She hollered.
> Interviewer: What did she say?
> Kurumizawa: I don't want to think about it again ... (sobbing) ... She said, 'It's all right to kill me, but please spare my child's life'.
>
> Masakuni Kurumizawa, veteran of Unit 731, recounting an incident of human vivisection

In 1936, a small group of Chinese prisoners, still hobbled by their shackles, escaped from a forbidding scientific compound known as Zhongma fortress, situated 100 kilometres to the south of the occupied Manchurian city of Harbin. Almost all of the fugitives were captured and killed, but a few escaped to tell their tale. The secret was out: Zhongma was a clandestine biological warfare centre and the Chinese prisoners who were incarcerated there were being used as human guinea pigs. Japanese military authorities, alarmed by the security breach, closed down Zhongma and started all over again at Pingfan, closer to Harbin, where they built an extensive biological and chemical warfare research facility known as Unit 731. Officially it was an epidemic-prevention and water-supply plant, but in reality it was one in a network of secret biological warfare stations set up by the Kempeitai (military police) Political Department in occupied China and in Singapore. The station undertook experiments on a conservatively estimated 3000 men, women and children. The victims were mostly Chinese but included some Russians and Americans. There were very few survivors. To conceal their activities, Unit 731's buildings were deliberately burned down by defeated Japanese forces in the closing stages of the war.

The presiding officer of Unit 731 was the medically trained Lieutenant General Shiro Ishii, a notoriously bizarre egotist sometimes described as Japan's Dr Mengele. The 'experiments' for which he was responsible included human vivisection, deliberate inoculation with lethal bacilli, weapons testing, extreme (deadly) survival scenarios, irradiation and subjection to fatal sub-zero temperatures. Ishii was assisted by army officers, scientists and medical doctors, one of whom was a Dr Masaji Kitano, who appears later in this troubling account. The number of victims involved is difficult to pin down, but 3000 seems an over-cautious total for a death-dealing facility that covered 6 square kilometres, was divided into eight experimental divisions with 300 medical staff and 2700 support staff, and operated at Pingfan for almost a decade. One of the consequences of Pingfan's activities, according to Daniel Barenblatt, an expert on biological warfare, was a series of biological warfare attacks on Chinese civilians in the 1940s, resulting in approximately 400 000 deaths.

A CULTURE OF DENIAL

After the war, the activities of Unit 731 and its satellite facilities were suppressed by the Allies, because disclosure of Japanese atrocities in the area of biological and chemical warfare was hindered by Cold War politics, as with Nanjing and the comfort women, but in a much more active and specific form. This delay (or cover-up) began in 1945 when the US authorities made a deal with the scientists of Unit 731: an arrangement promising immunity from prosecution in return for information about biological warfare techniques. The US military authorities wanted the information in much the same way that they desired information about Nazi Germany's rocket technology. Accordingly, the information stored by Unit 731 was sent to the USA as 'medical research' data. In return, Ishii and his colleagues did not go on trial; far from it: many ex–Unit 731 staff forged respectable careers in post-war Japan's medical, scientific and academic communities. Dr Kitano, for example, who had taken over Unit 731 from Ishii towards the end of the war, went on to become director of Green Cross Corporation, a major Japanese pharmaceutical company and blood bank. Ishii kept a much lower profile (and his lieutenant-general's pension) and, in 1959, a year after he had attended a meeting of old comrades of Unit 731, he died, unrepentant and intransigently racist to the end.

Nevertheless, despite official attempts by the Allies and Japan to stifle immediate post-war broadcasting of information about the activities of Unit 731, stories did begin to leak out. For example, Soviet Russia had prosecuted its captured Unit 731 staff members in a war crimes trial in December 1949, at Khabarovsk, just north of Vladivostock, which had produced claims that Unit 731 had been engaged in war crimes of which the Allies were already aware. These revelations were dismissed in Japan and the USA as a communist propaganda stunt attacking alleged US inertia in bringing the members of Unit 731 to trial. There followed a hiatus in disclosures about Unit 731, and it was not until August 1955 that Hiroshi Akiyama, a former Unit 731 staff member, published an account of his experiments, purportedly to warn against any recurrence of the events at Pingfan. His confession came a few years after the end of the Korean War when the North Korean, Chinese and Russian governments accused the USA of using biological warfare, allegations that were rejected by the United Nations as communist propaganda. Condemnation of Unit 731 took a more official turn in 1982 when the Chinese government, in a politically calculated move, decided to commemorate the victims of the crimes committed at Pingfan and opened up a museum in Harbin. Nevertheless, despite the growing body of evidence about Unit 731, the Japanese government's official position, as late as the 1990s, remained steadfastly the same: there was no evidence for these Chinese accusations.

Forms of Denial

Current non-Japanese media representations of Japanese responses to their past war crimes tend to arouse indignation in some observers who ask, how it is possible for the Japanese so stubbornly to resist accepting responsibility for their past actions? There is some justice in this question. Many Japanese comments and reactions to the presentation of the evidence that Japanese troops behaved appallingly seem to be extraordinarily myopic and insensitive, and in some quarters this nationalistic position is seen as a sign of resurgent Japanese militarism.

At first glance, it is an open and shut case: Japan is out of step with the rest of the world. Accusations about the extent of Japanese denial are made all the more powerful by the common notion that Japanese people, as members of a disciplined society, conform largely to the denialist view.

If only it were that simple.

The New Nationalism

To begin with, it is quite clear that immediate post-war lack of concern about certain war crimes, for example Nanjing, the comfort women and Unit 731, was not solely a Japanese attempt at a cover-up. Allied indifference towards events in Nanjing and lack of western concern about comfort women were clearly not Japanese phenomena; nor was it the Japanese government that gave the staff of Unit 731 indemnity from prosecution for war crimes: General MacArthur's occupation administration, in cooperation with Washington, fixed the deal. In the 1970s, the temporarily and opportunistically pro-Japanese Maoist government further suppressed mention of Japanese war crimes. Conversely, the early 1980s saw a diplomatic reversal when Deng Xiao-Ping's opportunistically *anti*-Japanese government began to renew attacks on Japan's war record, making Chinese concerns about the war-guilt debate appear to be more of a *Realpolitik* strategy than a policy based on any form of humane concern. Add to that the history of war crime exposition by such Japanese journalists and writers as Katsuichi Honda and Yayori Matsui, the recent confessions of Japanese veterans and the continuing criticism of Japanese feminist researchers and leftist historians, and it is quite clear that acceptance and acknowledgement of Japanese responsibility for its troops' behaviour between the years of 1931 and 1945 have hardly been low-profile activities in Japan itself.

On the other hand, in certain political groups in Japan there is a strong culture of obstruction and denial, which stems from a variety of factors but which finds its most vociferous, most emotional and most extreme representation in the activities of the ultra-nationalists. According to David McNeill, there are approximately 100 000 ultra-nationalists in Japan, who belong to an estimated 1000 rightist factions often beset by bickering and ideological divisions. Of these, some 800 groups are associated with the organisation *Zen-nipon Aikokusha Dantai Kaigi* (National Conference of Patriotic Associations). The more militant of these societies are responsible for the sound trucks, paramilitary marches and physical intimidation of left-liberal opponents, notably the targeting of *Asahi Shimbun*. In 1987, an ultra-nationalist murdered the newspaper's reporter Tomohiro Kojiro, and in 1993, another rightist, Shusuke Nomura, committed suicide spectacularly in *Asahi Shimbun*'s office. Precisely how many extremists there are is difficult to calculate, because they are tied in with various nationalistic cults as well as the *yakuza* gangs that suddenly became attached to nationalist politics in the 1960s when the Political Fund Regulations allowed 'political' groups to raise money and claim tax benefits.

The ultra-nationalists are emperor-worshipping, intolerantly chauvinistic, anti-communist racists who are committed to a return of Japanese militarism. One of their major targets is the abolition of Article 9 of the Japanese constitution, which renounces war and forbids the maintenance of 'land, sea and air forces', a clause that modern Japan has chipped away at by setting up land, sea and air *self-defence* forces. The ultra-nationalists operate, however, on the bigoted fringe of the more conventional and much more influential broad nationalist movement. The position of the 'respectable' nationalists is known as *shin-minzokushugi*, or 'new nationalism', suggesting a modern, non-violent approach, but even so, some nationalists are quite happy to use the flamboyant and confrontational ultra-nationalists as street activists. Many of the *new* nationalists espouse a seemingly reasonable version of patriotism, which criticises the Tokyo war crimes trial as an unjust kangaroo court. This position argues against notions of 'imperial Japan the aggressor' in the 1930s and 1940s. Attacks on imperial Japanese military honour are regarded as largely communist lies, and, in line with ultra-nationalist ideology, the continuation of Article 9 in the constitution is seen as an emasculating obstacle to Japan's ability to define itself as a complete nation.

As part of a renewed 1990s emphasis on the new nationalism, and shortly after a brief period of mid-1990s Liberal Democratic Party–socialist coalition rule in Japan, during which nationalists were infuriated by what they considered to be the over-apologetic attitude of the government for Japan's wartime activities, Nobakazu Fujioka, a Tokyo University education professor who had been visiting Rutgers University in the USA at the time of the first Gulf War and had been overcome by chagrin at Japan's apparent marginalisation in such an important global event. On his return to Japan, together with a group of like-minded allies, he founded two nationalist pressure groups: the 'Liberal View of History Study Group' and the better known 'Society for the Making of New School Textbooks in History' (the Society for short). The Society auspiced the writing and publishing of the notorious *New History Textbook*, approved as one of eight middle-school history texts in April 2001. The textbook's government endorsement caused a national and an international sensation. It was denounced for, among other matters, presenting the myths of Japan's foundation as historical fact, characterising the 1931–1945 conflict as a war of liberation from colonial oppression, representing the invasion of China as an 'advance', omitting the activities of Unit 731 and comfort women, and describing Nanjing as an 'incident'.

It is clear from the activities of the Society at least that while the other major Axis nation, Germany, may have come to terms with its responsibility for an aggressive and destructive war policy, this is not the case for the new Japanese nationalists, particularly the Liberal Democratic Party (LDP) politicians who attract national and international opprobrium for their periodic public eruptions in the Diet. In the 1980s and 1990s, for example, there was a stream of provocative statements, including such outbursts as LDP junior minister Masahiro Morioka's attack in May 2005 on the Tokyo war crimes trial and defence of Japan's Class A war criminals, a controversial position supported publicly by former LDP trade minister Takeo Hiranuma. The governor of Tokyo Shintaro Ishihara has also joined in from time to time, describing US failure to apologise for the wartime bombing campaign against Japan as 'racist'.

The overt and covert activities of these less rabid right-wing groups cause national and international controversy because the groups' adherents are not the easily discounted street thugs who make up the visible presence of ultra-nationalism. The new nationalists include approximately 100 politicians from the dominant conservative LDP, an unknown number of officials and leaders of industry and commerce (including the chair of the Keidanren, Japan's largest business federation, and the mass-circulation daily newspaper *Sankei Shimbun*), a small but vocal group of academics and an even smaller group of high-profile artists, in particular the graphic-book artist Kobayashi Yoshinori.

The line taken by the Society and its supporters is that Japan's behaviour before and during World War II was simply a variation on the behaviour exhibited by many modern nation states. In a peculiar twist on postmodernism, as part of their relativist approach they point to colonial oppression and more recent US foreign policy as cases in point. This places Nanjing, comfort women and Unit 731 on a kind of moral continuum where Hiroshima, Nagasaki and the firebombing of Japanese cities can also be found. They consider any modern attempt to interpret Japanese actions in a negative light as 'masochistic', since, in their view, Japan, as the proud creator of the world's second most important economy, has a natural right to lead Asia both morally and politically. At the same time, they carefully attempt to separate imperial Japanese acts from the systematically genocidal activity of their wartime allies, the Nazis: what happened in Asia between the years 1931 and 1945 was nothing more than expected military behaviour when Japan was fighting a tough war of liberation against superior foes. They also assert that US failure to apologise for its own war crimes is hypocritical. This position is reflected in the new nationalists' attitude to comfort women: they allege that the women were in it for the money, and that comfort women survivors claiming compensation are still in it for the money. Furthermore, events in Nanjing were not an atrocity, new nationalists claim, and Unit 731 is a Chinese fabrication. Fujioka and his colleagues work hard to spread these messages; below is a sample nationalist assertion, from Fujioka's speech to the Foreign Correspondents' Club of Japan on 25 February 1999:

> The masochistic slant in Japanese history education has reached the point to include a completely ungrounded, actually false story, that it is included in all the middle-school history textbooks authorized by the Ministry of Education. I would like to explain to you why a description of so-called 'military comfort women', should not be included in middle-school textbooks . . . The term 'military comfort women', or jugun ianfu, has come to mean an absolute distortion of historical fact, that the Japanese military transported women, against their will, to war zones. People all over the world now seem to believe that these women then became 'sex slaves' to satisfy the sexual needs of Japanese soldiers.

The Textbook Controversy

Of all the campaigners involved in the denial debate, left-leaning Professor Saburo Ienaga fought longest and hardest for an accurate and non-nationalistic depiction of Japanese history. Ienega's crusade received widespread publicity in Japan and gained worldwide recognition and respect for his almost half-century of struggle against institutionalised Japanese nationalism.

Ienaga graduated from Tokyo Imperial University in 1937, avoiding customary military conscription because of his ill-health. He became a schoolteacher, entering a system dominated by a militaristic and colonialist ethos founded on the 'historical' myth of imperial divinity. Ienaga was opposed to Japan's aggressive involvement in World War II, but because of the political circumstances at the time he kept quiet until after 1945. That was when he began to write.

In 1947, by which time he was a professor at the newly established Tokyo University of Education, Ienaga published a well-received history of Japan. Following this success, he was asked by publishers Sanseido to write his first textbook for high schools, and in 1953, he submitted the manuscript to the Ministry of Education certification process. To Ienega's astonishment, his textbook failed the test. The rejection was based on his 'malice towards the Japanese family system', his 'treatment of peasant uprisings [which] seemed to legitimize illegal activity', and the book's focus on 'historical facts about the Pacific War and the postwar era ... these were things the pupils had all experienced, so it would be better to delete them all'. Ienaga then found himself engaged in a series of running battles with the ministry's screening committee, as subsequent re-submissions of drafts provoked similarly negative responses, including the comment that the book 'veers from the goals of teaching history: "through academic activities to recognize the efforts of ancestors, to heighten one's consciousness of being Japanese, to instil a rich love of the race"'.

Meanwhile, disturbed by what he considered to be the reactionary policies of the 1960s Kishi government, Ienega became a leading figure in the pro–democratic reform movement in Japan. He supported, in particular, reform of the university system and defence of Japanese teachers against what he considered to be oppressive governmental interference in their employment conditions. These activities did not endear him to authority.

In 1965, after more than a decade of criticism and rejection of his earlier textbooks, Ienaga took his case against the Ministry of Education to the Tokyo District Court. So began a long and bitter legal fight against state censorship of the hidden side of Japanese history, a campaign which ended only with Ienaga's death, in 2002. In 1968, Ienaga encountered an additional rebuff by the ministry when he published his book *The Pacific War*, which detailed Japanese war atrocities such as the Nanjing massacre, the conscription of Korean comfort women, the inhumane activities of Unit 731 and the forced suicides of Okinawan civilians in 1945. As part of the official screening process, Ienaga was asked to make 200 'corrections' and to excise all references to Unit 731. Ienaga's fight against these acts of censorship by the ministry produced three successive lawsuits. These were increasingly successful in drawing public attention to the alleged iniquities of the screening policy, which was altered after foreign pressure in 1982 and again in 1990; but to this day the process remains in place, albeit in a modified fashion. Every four years, the Japanese Ministry of Education (which now also looks after culture, sports, science and technology) nominates seven or eight commercially published but 'authorised' history textbooks that have been 'screened' by ministry committees. Schools in the prefectures may choose one of the authorised books from which to teach their school students.

Japanese history textbooks are notably dull: the range of texts is narrow, and, apart from a few illustrations to liven up the stodgy, evenly measured prose and a tediously steady narrative, the books generally have little to recommend them as a good read. Mercifully, there is no compulsion at school level to choose any one particular textbook, and most school authorities at prefecture level have consistently rejected the nationalist *New History Textbook*, the cause of so much rancour in the rest of Asia. Indeed, the Japanese anti-nationalist campaign against the book has been so successful that only an estimated ten schools used it in 2001, its first year of publication, and, even though it was revised to meet some of the criticisms levelled against it, the textbook is still used in very few Japanese middle schools.

So, if the book is a dud in the school system, where does the real problem lie? The controversy about the *New History Textbook* centres essentially on the ministry's sanctioning of such a brazenly nationalistic volume, an accusation that has been exaggerated by anti-nationalists, who exaggerate the harm and point out the pernicious effects that the book may have on the generality of Japanese students in schools. Another problem concerns the commercial publishing market: although the book may be losing out as an official text, it is making solid ground as a commercial venture and as a school giveaway: an estimated 750 000 copies were sold in bookshops between 2001 and 2004, and a further 700 000 were distributed free to schools during that time, in a program subsidised by nationalist business interests and managed by the Society. At the same time, Fujioka's partisan *History Not Taught in Textbooks*, first published in 1997, is a runaway bestseller. And so the nationalist deniers, while dismal failures in the education system, are making solid gains in the public arena.

Manga and Denial

The phenomenon of the nationalist public success is exemplified by *mangaka* Yoshinori Kobayashi. His manga series *Senso Ron* (*On War*), first published in 1998, has plugged in to another phenomenon: the mass cultural Japanese obsession with comics. *The Japan Times* estimated in 2003 that the Japanese spent 520 billion yen a year on manga, compared with a mere 4.7 billion yen spent on comics in the USA, a nation with two and a half times the population of Japan. Manga reach approximately 80 per cent of the highly literate Japanese population, cutting across social barriers by appealing to different audiences, both young and old. For example, there are child-rearing manga, working men's manga, romance manga, pornographic manga and even manga that come close to paedophilia (*lolicon manga*, as in 'Lolita').

Manga frequently feature brilliant and highly stylised graphics and racy tales. Part of their marketing technique is to increase sales by emphasising their scandalous nature. In the 1990s, there were official attempts to ban them, but that shot at censorship came to nothing: sales continued to rise. And it is the massive sales of manga that make Kobayashi's work so important a feature in the denial debate. With a copy of *On War* retailing for approximately 1500 yen, less than twenty Australian dollars, a revisionist manga makes for much more interesting reading than a school textbook.

Kobayashi makes no secret of his ideological stance, which he writes explicitly and forcefully into his manga. He has strong links with the Society, appears frequently on television and sponsors a rightist political magazine, *Washizumu* (*My Own Principle*). He believes that Japan is overwhelmed by corrupt individualism and materialism, that it has lost its spirit by tagging along with the USA, and that, in attempting to appease Chinese and South Korean governments, it has lost its way. Kobayashi also asserts that Japanese involvement in World War II was a just attempt to remove western imperialism from Asia and that the Tokyo war crimes tribunal was a conscious attempt by the victorious Allies to make the Japanese feel bad about themselves. 'If you really want to look at falsifications of history during the Tokyo International Tribunal [sic], look how they treated the Nanking incident ... They [the Allies] needed a crime that would balance the 300 000 Japanese dead in Hiroshima and Nagasaki', he has remarked. And Kobayashi's manga reflect that point of view, from his *On War* series through to the more recent *Taiwan Ron* (*On Taiwan*), published in 2000, in which he claimed that 'becoming comfort women was a step up for them, because they preferred military brothels to civilian brothels'. In his long-running *Gomanism Sengen* series (loosely translated as *Manifesto for a New Pride*), he presented his personal ideology of *gomanism* ('pride', or 'philosophy of insolence'), with which he tackled race issues, AIDS and Japanese relations with the USA. *Yasukuni Ron* (*On the Yasukuni Question*), published in 2005, reflected his iconoclastic position by attacking as spineless Prime Minister Koizumi, who was the darling of the new nationalists and generally regarded as a charismatic reformer. Koizumi's regular and controversial visits to the Yasukuni shrine, which commemorates Japanese war dead, may have appeased nationalistic sentiment, but, as far as Kobayashi was concerned, Koizumi did not go far enough down the nationalist road.

Kobayashi's importance in the denial debate cannot be underestimated. Rebecca Clifford, a Canadian scholar of war remembrance, has pointed out one reason for his success: 'Part of [*On War*'s] appeal lies in the pseudo-academic style: Kobayashi uses complex and archaic Chinese characters in his text, and does not include the phonetic readings usually found in Japanese comic books, giving the text an air of scholarly credibility'. And, as we have seen, mangas such as *On War* sell in huge numbers: more than 1.5 million, all told, for the three-volume series *On War*, including twenty-nine editions alone in its first year of printing; the first print run of *On the Yasukuni Question* was 200 000 copies.

Kobayashi's vividly nationalistic interpretation of the war is countered by those largely insipid and unimaginative school textbooks: the manga are filling the vacuum of historical understanding in succeeding generations of Japanese school students. Kobayashi himself has pointed out where he thinks the real debate is centred; in a reported comment, he announced, with some grandiosity, that 'even the Chinese Communist Party doesn't care about [Japanese] leftists anymore. It's me they want to talk to'.

Conclusion

Imagine that a conference of Japanese scholars has recently been convened. It is in Kyoto. The topic of the conference is 'Overcoming the Modern', a reference to the west. One scholar announces that westernism is like a disease that has tainted the Japanese spirit; modernism is a 'European thing', suggests another; a Japanese film critic attacks Hollywood for its decadence. There is discussion about the differences between oriental and occidental thought processes. Conference members conclude that, in the west, ideas are splintered and over-specialised, and this foreign approach has infected the holistic approach of Japanese thinking. There is common agreement that Japanese culture is, at heart, spiritual and deep, in contrast with US and European culture, which is materialistic and shallow. There is only one way forward: Asia must be united under Japanese moral leadership and regain its spiritual centre.

Interestingly, such a conference did take place in Kyoto. But it happened in July 1942, just seven months after the attack on Pearl Harbor and five months after the fall of Singapore. The film critic who attacked Hollywood, Hideo Tsumura, preferred the work of Leni Riefenstahl, and, in Tsuruma's view, the war against the west was a war against a poisonous materialist civilisation founded on Jewish capital. This Kyoto conference took place in the heart of wartime imperial Japan and at a time when it appeared that the proposed moral leadership of Asia by a spiritual Japan was a certainty.

Apart from the obsession with Leni Riefenstahl and international Jewish conspiracies, the 1942 Kyoto conference could have taken place yesterday. If this is the case, what does it tell us about the currently bitter debates about Japanese denial? Can this modern form of denial be explained away as a totally Japanese phenomenon that goes all the way back to an unrepentant imperialist mindset? As we have seen, the answer is yes and no. To begin with, the origins of Japanese denial have to be laid partly at the door of Douglas MacArthur and his occupation administration, or SCAP. As was not the case for Nazi Germany's leadership, the post-war settlement exculpated the emperor from any responsibility for the war, allowing what was then a narrow thread of residual nationalism and emperor worship to remain unbroken. From a Japanese nationalist perspective, the emperor was more than just a figurehead during wartime; as a divine person, he could not have been responsible for atrocities; therefore, atrocities did not happen. To be fair to MacArthur, his occupation administration did not have much choice over this part of the settlement, and at the time it seemed the best possible outcome.

But Japanese denial did not come about simply through SCAP's decisions; the seeds of incipient nationalist revival had already been sown when the victorious Allies arrived in Tokyo to accept surrender. Indeed, in August 1945, when Emperor Hirohito announced Japan's capitulation in an unprecedented radio broadcast, he made no mention of either defeat or surrender. What had happened, according to Hirohito's speech, was that the war for the 'stabilisation' of East Asia had not been successful. The direct quote is that 'it being far from our thought either to infringe upon the sovereignty of other nations or to embark upon territorial aggrandizement ... [the war] has developed not necessarily to Japan's advantage, while the general trends of the world have all turned against her interest', phrases that still resonate in nationalist propaganda. Then there is the problem of the Tokyo war crimes trial. Of the major figures accused of war crimes, seven were executed; eighteen were jailed, later to be released, many of them going on to become senior figures in Japanese politics and business. This produced two consequences as far as denial is concerned. First, the almost speedy release of Class A war criminals eventually reduced whatever moral authority the trial might have had. The criminals' careers ran parallel with the professional paths of the ex–Unit 731 experimenters, thus vitiating, in the eyes of the nationalist deniers, any suggestion that members of Unit 731 were engaged in proven war crimes. Second, the trial came shortly after the atom bomb attacks on Hiroshima and Nagasaki, two horrendous events which were widely publicised and universally acknowledged at the time as tragedies. The Allied governments claimed that they were necessary tragedies because of the intransigence of the Japanese war cabinet; the past and current nationalist position, in the face of accusations that imperial Japan committed war crimes, is that any US denial that the atom bombings were at least an equivalent act of turpitude is hypocritical. The nationalists could, and do, argue that the surprise attack on Pearl Harbor in December 1941 was a response to US intransigence over supplying raw materials to Japan. This opens the door to contemporary moral relativism and endlessly irreconcilable arguments about responsibility and culpability.

Having said all that, the next question is: why? Why are the nationalists still pursuing their denial agenda? And why has overt nationalism become so visible in the past twenty years? Part of the answer may indeed be that there is something distinctive about Japanese culture that allows this special brand of nationalism to thrive. During the period of the Tokugawa shogunate (1603–1867), the outside world was cut off from Japan, and Japanese ideas about racial and cultural superiority were allowed to develop without contradiction. During the modern period, Japan absorbed what it needed from the western nations and turned itself into a powerful, aggressive and highly nationalistic state. It was serviced by an obedient population and ruled through divine right, a position exemplified by the political slogan of the 1930s and 1940s—'a wealthy nation, a strong army'—and by the Japanese Ministry of Education's 1937 pamphlet *Kokutai no Hongi* (*Fundamentals of National Polity*), which required that the Japanese should discard individualism and look to the emperor as the foundation of their existence and asserted that the Japanese were superior to all other nations and 'completely different . . . from the so-called citizens of the West'. *Kokutai*-ism then became the basis for a sense of uniqueness that was consciously developed prior to World War II. There are still nationalistic elements in Japanese society that profess Japanese racial, intellectual and moral superiority.

The 'why' question may also be answered in part by the continuing cultural and racial tensions in relations with China, as exemplified perhaps in the Japanese label for their giant neighbour. In Japanese, China can either be *Choguka*, meaning 'centre of the world', or *Shina*, meaning 'oppressed'. The first term reflects Japanese ambivalence to an overseas culture which, annoyingly if you are a Japanese racist, gave Japan the basis of Confucianist belief, the essence of that artificially constructed and politicised state religion Shintoism, and the fundamentals of the Japanese written language. The term *Shina*, on the other hand, exemplifies the racist strand in Japanese nationalism, for there is a Japanese stereotypical view of the Chinese as members of an undeveloped society, inefficient and grasping. In return, some Chinese see the Japanese as crude and greedy, and vulnerable to being brow-beaten over their lamentable war record, about which the Chinese are only too happy to remind the Japanese and their Asian neighbours. So, the arguments persist and the new Japanese nationalism continues to thrive on them.

That this cultural context of Japanese denial helps to explain its survival is a point made by Ian Buruma in his 1994 book, *Wages of Guilt*.

A CULTURE OF DENIAL

In looking for a starting point for allocation of fault and of culpability, Buruma refers to Ruth Benedict's book *The Chrysanthemum and the Sword* (1964), in which she separates cultural attitudes: Japanese (Confucian) shame from German (Christian) guilt. Each dynamic supposedly produces a different response in today's Japanese and German approaches to atrocities such as Nanjing and Auschwitz. Benedict's approach is initially attractive because it seems to explain modern Japanese denial (producing ignorance) and contemporary German philo-Semitism (producing agonised self-examination). It also helps to explain the contrast between German acceptance of past wrongdoings and a continuing toleration in Japanese academic and political quarters of modern right-wing nationalist denial of the shame of World War II. Although Buruma sees some merit in the cultural approach, he views Benedict's idea as a mechanistic over-simplification, since many of today's Japanese citizens, including politicians, have been publicly apologetic (two-dozen government apologies at the last count) and many Germans remain far from philo-Semitic. Buruma prefers to combine the cultural explanation with a political view that both Japan and Germany, as nation states, were diplomatically and militarily aggressive, and that this disposition invariably led to 'criminal' and 'cruel' acts. Buruma also differentiates between the horrific individual and mass carnage carried out by Japanese (and some Korean) soldiers and guards and Nazi concentration camp atrocities. The former, he argues, were appalling activities carried out during and after military campaigns, unlike the systematic campaign of genocide that produced the Holocaust. This echoes the Japanese nationalist argument but takes it in a different direction, in allowing that Japanese military behaviour was appallingly immoral, which the nationalists still refuse to admit. Buruma's approach is useful because it combines an acknowledgement of the cultural with a focus on the political.

It is the political aspect of modern Japanese denial that explains its longevity. This is because Japanese nationalists appear to be playing a long game, a political game based on cultural foundations and on political foundations. The cultural foundations are that sense of superior worth; the political foundations go back to August and September 1945 and the failure to deal with the origins of denial at the outset.

Having said that, the reason for a new emphasis in conservative Japanese concern about the nation's war record relates directly to the events of the past decade or so. The end of the Cold War, the demise of the Soviet Union and the rise of a market economy approach in China have all changed the balance of politics of east Asia. Japan is faced by a resurgent China, and, although still tied to the USA militarily and diplomatically, Japan is looking for more diplomatic and military autonomy, as befits a nation with a record of being one of the major leaders in the global economy. This issue of Japanese autonomy and national identity has recently become much more acute because, until the first decade of the new century, Japan was inarguably the world's second major economy, just behind the USA. But Japan is now being overhauled by China and India as an economic and financial force, and both of these nations are already taken seriously as major players in world affairs, but not just because they are huge economically: China and India have substantial military forces and they also have nuclear weapons. If we go back to Fujioka's epiphany at Rutgers in the early 1990s, we can see what the problem is: Japan may be a great nation in economic, financial and technological terms, but, unlike China and India, it has no featured role in world politics because it has little or no international authority.

Nationalists such as Fujioka and Kobayashi cannot cope with the idea that their nation is still seen simply as a client state of the USA. Even moderate Japanese opinion has a problem with US relations. A symptom of this cross-political desire to shake off US paternalism is the recent increase in the criticism of the presence and behaviour of US armed forces in Okinawa, long a sore point with leftists in Japan but now a focus of conservative as well as socialist condemnation; in 2006 an agreement was reached which allowed US withdrawal from Okinawa. The nationalist argument is that the USA takes Japan for granted as its tame and toothless tiger, and the nationalists can see their traditional opponent, China, with its huge military resources and its rapidly developing technological and financial capacity, overtaking them as the major power in the region. At the same time, an ambitious China, while expanding probably slightly too hurriedly, is playing a diplomatic spoiling game to keep Japan on the back foot. It is no simple coincidence that renewed and violent Chinese objections to the *New History Textbook* in 2005 coincided with Japanese efforts to become a permanent member of the United Nations Security Council, where it could join the other big players, including China. 'Look!' the Chinese were saying. 'Japan hasn't learned the lessons of the past, so it has to be kept on a leash.'

Stung by what they see as continuing Chinese provocation, the new nationalists argue that Article 9 must be abolished so that Japan can resume its former position as a major power. However, in Japanese opinion polls, there has been a consistent strain between acceptance of the need for constitutional reform and rejection of changes to Article 9. And so, whatever the rest of the world may think, the only way in which the article's removal from the constitution can be justified in internal Japanese politics is to reconstruct Japan's past as a progressive, liberationist narrative in which, admittedly, a few individual mistakes may have been made, but they were no more worthy of blame than similar Allied atrocities such as the firebombing campaign against Japan, the two atom bombs and the alleged exploitation of Japan as a helplessly occupied nation. The consistent and unrelenting nationalist campaign of denial prepares the way for the end goal: a change in public opinion leading to a change in the constitution and 'a wealthy nation, a strong army'. By the time this takes place, the Nanjing massacre, the comfort women scandal and the activities of Unit 731 will perhaps have become distant, hazy and rosy memories, part of a dominant myth of the imperial Japanese liberation of Asia.

Epilogue

In his January 2006 speech to the Diet, reformist prime minister Junichiro Koizumi outlined his government's plans for what was his final term in office before he retired later in the year. In his concluding remarks, just after a crucial section in which he announced the introduction of a Bill that would allow female succession to the imperial throne, he had this to say:

> Now that more than sixty years have passed since the end of the Second World War, debate is continuing within each political party concerning the amendment of the Constitution. I believe that the time is now ripe to actively engage in discussion with the people of Japan on the modalities of the Constitution for the new era . . . We must construct a system that allows us to respond to a new era and the rapidly changing environment at home and overseas while solidifying the foundations of prosperity that were created by our ancestors.

Koizumi, an unrepentant and highly controversial annual pilgrim to the contentious Yasukuni shrine, was clearly referring to a 'new era' in which Japan, once serenely confident about its economic clout, is faced with continuing internal domestic problems and growing external threats. His reference to constitutional change was arguably the second step on a road towards constitutional adjustment that will see Japan eventually re-establish its armed forces as part of a process of re-joining the ranks of the great powers. This means that Japan will regain its place, to quote an earlier nationalist phrase, as 'an ordinary Japan', that is a fully armed Japan. Koizumi, the first Japanese prime minister to declare the Japanese Self Defence Forces (SDF) a military organisation, had already said that the Ground Self Defence Force 'should be identified as the nation's army' and, on several occasions, advocated revising Article 9. Even the former leader of the centrist Democratic Party of Japan Seiji Maehara advocated a revision of Article 9 to allow protection of crucial sea lanes beyond the current 1000-kilometre limit, a clear nod at the possibility of rising military tensions with North Korea and China. Japan's US ally has also hinted that Article 9 is a serious hindrance to the country's being recognised as a world power.

Koizumi's work was taken up by his short-lived successor as prime minister, Shinzo Abe, who, while more circumspect about visits to the

A CULTURE OF DENIAL

Yasukuni shrine, began an announced six-year constitutional reform plan in 2006 with replacement of the 1947 pacifist 'Fundamental Law of Education' with a more traditionalist law. Originally drafted to espouse the 'teaching of patriotism', the new law was modified to teach 'civic-mindedness'. Also, before his forced resignation, in 2007, Abe, already tagged as a strong denier of the forced recruitment of comfort women, gathered a 'Cabinet of [ultra-nationalist] Pals' around him, promising (and enacting) an upgrading of the Japanese SDF to be administered by a fully fledged Ministry of Defence (its former status was as an agency within the prime minister's office). In 2007, the SDF was freed from the need for special case-by-case legislation allowing it to operate overseas.

Not everybody in Japan supports the moves towards opening up the military options. John Junkerman reported in *Japan Focus* that only one-third of surveyed Japanese citizens support a revision of Article 9. Understanding this, Mizuho Fukushima, one of Japan's few women members of parliament and leader of the leftish Social Democratic Party, has spotted where Japan is headed and expressed her reservations in an article in *Asahi Shimbun* published on 14 January 2006:

> Peace that has supported Japan's prosperity is also starting to waver. Article 9 of the Japanese Constitution bans the maintenance of war potential and renounces war. The article came into being at the cost of more than twenty million lives in World War II in Asia alone ... The Constitution is Japan's public pledge not only to ourselves but to the people who died in the war and to the people of Asia and the world.

Perhaps Fukushima had been re-reading, with some alarm, page 284 of Kobayashi's first *On War* manga, in which the artist explained that it was the duty of the Japanese to once again commit themselves to their nation and 'respect our grandfathers and what they wanted to protect in the war'.

4

BRITISH COMMUNISM AND TWO DECADES OF DENIAL

From Moscow 1936 to Budapest 1956

On Monday 29 October 1956, employees of the communist newspaper the *Daily Worker* gathered for their regular weekly staff meeting in the paper's Farringdon Road offices in Clerkenwell, east London. The meeting was normally a routine collective event attended by editorial staff, journalists and administrators. On this occasion, however, it was a crisis meeting. Alison Mcleod, the paper's television correspondent, listened with growing horror as a senior colleague outlined why it was important to report the dominant story of the previous week, the bloody anti-Soviet uprising in Hungary, as a counter-revolution by fascist reactionaries and not as a genuine revolt of workers and students against Stalinist repression. Mick Bennet, the acting editor, explained the paper's line: 'We can't allow ourselves to join an anti-Soviet camp', he said, but not everybody agreed with him. Frank Patterson, the copytaster [sifter of the day's stories] and a dyed-in-the-wool Scottish communist, told the meeting that 'Stalin's personal apparatus [of terror] was working in all these [eastern European] countries'. He was joined in his dissent by Malcolm MacEwen, the features editor, who said that 'there are members of this staff begging and pleading for a more realistic line'. Sub-editor George McDougall agreed: 'We are still in the cult of the one nation, the USSR'. The meeting ended with only one firm conclusion: that the staff of the *Daily Worker* were now irrevocably split over events in Hungary.

What happened at that meeting was a microcosm of future events in the Communist Party of Great Britain (referred to hereafter as 'the Party') as its leaders and many of its members struggled to deal with the rapidly fading illusion of Soviet political integrity, an integrity that had been the very cornerstone of their beliefs since the 1917 Bolshevik revolution and a credo largely maintained through almost unwavering denial, until the year of the Hungarian revolt, at least.

This denialist approach eventually reached a point of rupture in 1956, with that Soviet suppression of the Hungarian uprising. The contortions of the Party and its press outlet the *Daily Worker* at that time almost beggar belief, the whole fiasco leading to a later widely held misconception that the 1956 schism had been a sudden turning point in Party denial. As is so often the case in the historical analysis of causation, these kinds of arguments tend to fall into two broad camps: the continuum approach characterised by a rejection of sudden turning points, and the catastrophic view that courses of action are, in certain cases, precipitated mainly by short-term causes. It was not, however, the latter circumstance that occurred in the Party in 1956. While it is indeed the case that an end point in denial was reached in that year, with Khrushchev's earlier, traumatic denunciation of Stalinism, the convolutions of 1956 and thereafter had their origins as far back as the 1930s, when the Party began to face unfolding evidence of large-scale, lethal Soviet hypocrisy beginning with the 1930s Moscow show trials.

That is why, in this chapter, as part of the continuum view of communist denial, a fairly detailed analysis will be undertaken of the two decades that preceded the crisis of 1956, starting with the Moscow trials. These farcically and murderously unjust hearings were followed by the completely unexpected Nazi–Soviet pact (August 1939); the fully anticipated outbreak of a major European war, with the consequent partition of Poland (September 1939); the sideshow Soviet invasion of Finland

(November 1939); and the long-anticipated Nazi invasion of Russia (June 1941), an event not, however, expected by a flabbergasted Stalin, who, caught up in his own version of denial, was still waiting and hoping for an invasion in the following year. The official Party response to that series of events was a constant twisting of political logic, a defence of indefensible fictions and a denial of reality, all of which gave many Party members a continuing and growing sense of uncertainty as to what they would be expected to believe next. As we shall see, the psychological dynamic in operation was not straightforward denial in the Freudian sense, that is the mere inability to cope with an unpleasant reality and a consequent construction of a false actuality; it was more a dysfunctional capacity to maintain one firmly established and overwhelming set of beliefs in the face of a contradictory body of evidence which was growing both in credibility and in intensity over a period of two decades. Members of the Party were destined to suffer from cognitive dissonance, the condition in which the individual or the group suffers from a growing discomfort by believing one thing but knowing another. This feeling of dissonance produces increasing distress, and the options are either to find comfort in re-intensifying the existing belief, with a consequent denying and discrediting of any belief-threatening phenomena, or to retreat from the growing source of discomfort. In the 1950s, some Party members chose the former course, and a substantial number chose the latter.

The Show Trials

> Who fights for Communism must be able to fight and not to fight, to say the truth and not to speak the truth, to render and to deny a service, to keep a promise and to break a promise, to go into danger and to avoid danger, to be known and to be unknown. Who fights for Communism has of all the virtues only one: that he fights for Communism.
>
> Bertolt Brecht, 1960

BRITISH COMMUNISM AND TWO DECADES OF DENIAL

That the Communist Party of the Soviet Union (CPSU) would purge supposed and real internal opponents in the 1930s is explicable because of the callous political culture of a regime that had ruthlessly clawed itself into power and which, with some justification, believed itself still surrounded by enemies. As far as Stalin and the members of the CPSU Politburo were concerned, drastic problems required drastic solutions. Furthermore, the morality underpinning the British Communist Party's eventual support for the 1930s' show trials had been evinced in as early as 1924 with the announcement that 'in a Revolutionary State there can be nothing legal, but that which is in the interests of the revolution, and further that it is the body which is charged with the direction of the revolution that must be responsible for deciding what is and what is not legal'. Revolutionary ruthlessness and iron discipline were the prevailing maxims in the British Party, supported by the Leninist notion of democratic centralism (in theory, an unquestioning support for democratically arrived at decisions), a dynamic which, over time, became far less democratic and all too centralist.

The Soviet trials and purges began after the assassination of respected Politburo member Sergei Kirov, in late 1934, an event probably orchestrated by a paranoid Stalin anxious to implement his minimalist 'socialism in one country' policy and prepared to brook no hindrance from 'oppositionists' such as Kirov. During those turbulent times, any political or personal disagreement with Stalin was labelled 'counter-revolutionary' and 'oppositionist', terms frequently used to describe Trotskyism, the maximalist 'world revolution now' ideology of Leon Trotsky, Stalin's greatest rival. So intent was Stalin on destroying any potential challengers that, in 1936, he even replaced the pitiless Genrikh Yagoda as head of the People's Commissariat for Internal Affairs (NKVD), or secret police, because the Soviet dictator thought Yagoda was soft on the Trotskyite conspiracy theory. Yagoda was later shot. His successor was the even more venomous Nikolai Yezhov (also eventually shot), and it was at that point that the Stalinist purges of peasants, workers, intellectuals and the military, later known as the Great Terror, began in earnest, with a series of Moscow-based show trials.

The major figures on trial, from 1936 onwards, included Leon Trotsky (tried *in absentia* and assassinated in Mexico in 1940), Grigory Zinoviev (shot in 1936), Lev Kamenev (executed in 1936), and Nikolai Bukharin (executed in 1938). Behind the façade of these supposedly *bona fide* public trials lay a vast, hidden campaign of persecution of millions of Russians and an untold number of foreigners (including well-known British Party members resident in Russia), many of whom were rounded up, some were tried and almost all were despatched either to the next world or to the Gulags. The final figures are unclear, but Anne Applebaum has suggested that 2.7 million died in the Gulags between 1929 and 1953, with more than 786 000 killed outside the camp system. In the Soviet Union, eligibility for denunciation, imprisonment and execution was almost universal, with the only legal exemption from the death penalty applying to children under twelve years of age.

As a contextual rationalisation for the British Party members' acceptance of Soviet harshness in 1936, it was made clear to many British communists that, in Stalinist terms, the 1934 assassination of Sergei Kirov had been a counter-revolutionary provocation and that the utmost solidarity was now required. This was partly because the mid-1930s was not a good time for the international socialist movement. German socialism had collapsed following Hitler's 1933 accession to power, and in Britain the home-grown Mosleyite fascists were being seen by some as a mainstream rightist alternative to socialism. Furthermore, in the year that the show trials began, Hitler re-entered the Rhineland without opposition, Mussolini subdued Ethiopia, and Franco began his march on Madrid. The British Party, now under orders from Moscow to form a broad, anti-fascist popular front with the previously despised centrist bourgeois political forces, lay divided between those who favoured that new, opportunistic popular front movement and those who retained a loyalty to the discarded, hard-nosed 'class-against-class' approach. Party officials and the rank-and-file hardliners, faced with so much domestic and foreign danger as well as with internal division, were obliged to advocate unity in the face of adversity and support for Moscow despite capitalist criticism of the show trials.

What was puzzling to many Party members, especially to the workers, was the idea that former Bolshevik comrades in Russia should be accused of unspecified counter-revolutionary activities in these trials, which were, uncharacteristically for the Soviet Union, given massive publicity by the propaganda machine of the Comintern, the Soviet agency set up to foment revolution outside the USSR. According to a worried Harry Pollitt, the normally compliant general secretary of the Party and a popular and persuasive Mancunian, 'the workers don't worry about counter-revolutionaries being shot, they want to know the actual concrete crimes they have committed'. Some questioned the disappearance of Party members who had been sent to the Soviet Union either as youthful recruits for ideological training at the Lenin School, for re-education (after ideological lapses) or to assist at the headquarters of the class struggle. For example, Rose Cohen, a well-known London activist who had once been close to Pollitt, was arrested in Moscow in August 1937, her detention, on trumped-up charges, occurring on the very day that Pollitt arrived in the Soviet capital with a Party delegation. Pollitt, who had inscribed a 1920s group photo: 'Rose Cohen, who I am in love with and who has rejected me fourteen times', knew in his heart that she was innocent of any counter-revolutionary activities and took her case to the Comintern, but his protests had no effect and he backed off. In presenting his case, Pollitt was only doing what he thought was reasonable, as was Scottish member of parliament Willie Gallagher, who also made representations to the Comintern about Cohen, as well as about other vanished foreigners. Georgi Dimitrov, head of the Comintern, responded ominously and unambiguously: 'Comrade Gallagher, it is best you do not pursue these matters'. Taking Dimitrov's advice, Gallagher retreated and Rose Cohen was shot three months after her arrest. Pollitt may have realised that he had gone too far (it seems to be the case that his colleagues were sounded out on his 'reliability'), so some inkling of Comintern dissatisfaction may have reached him. Whether or not he knew of his vulnerability upon his return from that

Moscow trip in 1937, Pollitt never again publicly questioned Soviet policy. On the other hand, he did raise private doubts about Soviet actions. However, his qualms did not prevent his involvement with recruiting Party members as NKVD agents, standard procedure for the Party's leadership at that time.

In Britain, Party iron discipline promulgated from its King Street, London, headquarters was resumed, for the time being at least. To make known the mid-1930s official line, prominent members published pro-Stalin articles in Party organs such as *Discussion*, the *Daily Worker*, *Inprecor*, *Left Book News* and *Labour Monthly*. John Strachey, a rising communist ideologue, announced in one article that the show trials were 'the greatest anti-fascist victory which we have yet recorded'. Other members were even more fervid in their support for the trials: Dorothy Diamond and Kathleen O'Shaughnessy, two firebrand London socialists, were perfectly happy to advocate the merciless rooting-out of distant traitors, an attitude which supported the official declaration that the British Party supported 'the measures against the Trotsky-Zinoviev terrorists, whose treacherous activities against the Workers' State have met with well-merited sentences of death'. In the Party at large, with members protected from Soviet reality by this kind of spin, the trials were largely regarded, allowing for minor grumbles by some, as a justifiable response to the threat of counter-revolutionary terrorism carried out principally by Trotskyite 'oppositionists'. However, in the offices of the *Daily Worker*, where Party members were a little closer to events, there was a sense of disquiet that all was not well in the socialist paradise. Notwithstanding these anxieties, the newspaper, in responding to a 1938 *Daily Herald* campaign of protest against Rose Cohen's arrest, maintained its correct journalistic stance when it castigated the Labour *Herald* for daring to 'attack Anglo-Soviet relations ... they are using the case of a former British subject on a charge of espionage ... This is not the first time that the *Daily Herald* has lent itself to the most poisonous attacks on the Soviet Union'.

While it is true that behind-the-scenes activities in the Soviet Union were difficult to fathom, Francis Beckett, in his book *Enemy*

Within, makes the reasonable point that Party members who visited Moscow on regular visits could not have failed to pick up emanations of the increasing levels of terror, as they either tried to rescue British-born relations and friends or responded to the disappearances of old Russian friends with passive silence, anxious that questions might lead to further denunciations. This was particularly the case with Pollitt and Johnny Campbell (Party representative to the Comintern and 1950s editor of the *Daily Worker*):

> They did not know everything. They probably had no idea of the appalling scale of the terror ... Campbell, like Pollitt a decently motivated and able man, told [Marxist historian] Monty Johnstone of negotiating with someone who simply disappeared the next day. He [Campbell] was told in a hushed voice: 'He was one of them'. It was harder for Campbell, says Johnstone, because 'he did not have Pollitt's capacity for self deception ... They knew enough to know that Stalin was a monster, but did not allow themselves to acknowledge it'.

Before he died, Campbell told Party colleagues that he had, at that time, informed Pollitt about the Stalinist campaign of extermination against political enemies—real and imagined—but that he had told no-one else. In the decade of the Great Terror, it was clear that the Party leadership knew that something was up.

In summary, the Party membership's official position in the 1930s over the Stalinist purges and show trials was a devoted or a puzzled (or both) conformity to the stated orthodoxy, inspiring an eventual obedient belief of a kind that smacks of devout religiosity. Indeed, the Party of that period was ascribed a quasi-religious character by more than one member. For example, wartime recruit Peter Cadogan, in commenting on the Party of the 1940s, remarked: 'One has to appreciate that the Party was really a church. You belonged to it ... It was a great fraternity, a bit like the Catholic Church, only secular and up-to-date'. Cadogan's characterisation of the Party as a welcoming but orthodox religious entity rings true, and it is that combination of almost metaphysical dogma (the CPSU and Stalin as the true interpreters of revolutionary socialism) and emotional blackmail (treacherous and counter-revolutionary criticism of the official Party line leading to a capitalist victory) that reinforces the view that 1930s Marxism was more about blind faith than it was about scientific materialism. In the words of Harry Pollitt, 'The fundamental facts give rise to the simple historical truth that whatever the policy of the Soviet Union it is always in the interest of its people and the working people of every other country in the world'. Party membership was about unquestioning loyalty, family, companionship and, possibly, as Eric Hobsbawm explained, even about sex:

> Next to sex, the activity combining bodily experience and intense emotion to the highest degree is the participation in a mass demonstration at a time of great public exaltation. Unlike sex, which is essentially individual, it is by nature collective, and unlike the sexual climax, at any rate for men, it can be prolonged for hours. On the other hand, like sex it implies some physical action—marching, chanting slogans, singing—through which the merger of the individual in the mass, which is the essence of collective experience ... The occasion has remained unforgettable.

To be a communist in the pre- and post-war period was to be an outsider, and the Party offered emotional shelter in an extended, international family of soulmates. Beset by anti-communist sentiment and propaganda but committed to a lifetime of sacrifice for their ideology, many Party members developed affectionate relationships (bearing in mind the puritanical nature of the British branch) with fellow British communists, with cosmopolitan western-European communists, with exotic eastern-European and Balkan communists and, last but not least, with exalted comrades from the socialist motherland.

This search for security particularly applied to the rootless Eric Hobsbawm, born into an Anglo-Austrian Jewish family perforcedly resident in Egypt during World War I. He was subsequently removed to Vienna with his family, orphaned by the age of fourteen, sent to visit relations in England, returned to Vienna, and then fostered out in Berlin, finally, as a young adult, ending up in London and then Cambridge. As a youth, he initially sought comfort and stability in a Viennese Boy Scout troop and later in the Berlin Socialist School Organisation. There, when looking for emotional satisfaction, the benefits of socialism could be taken one step further than mere social satisfaction, even, as we have seen, equating moments of an active membership of a radical movement with ectstatic, sexual pleasure. However, after moving from Berlin to London in 1933, Hobsbawm joined a morally austere communist organisation undistracted by such private thoughts of mass sexual gratification. The Party was much more exercised by some awkward questions being asked within the socialist church and family regarding what was going on in the Soviet Union, the incipient misgivings of a Party heading for crisis point and an eventual schism.

But it was early days yet. Overriding all considerations and every querulous thought at that time was the Party's blind trust in the infallibility of the CPSU and Stalin. This submissive response to the purges of the 1930s represented the first plunge in the downward spiral towards the events of 1956 and the eventual destruction of the Communist Party as a meaningful political force.

The Nazi–Soviet Pact

> The Soviet–Nazi [sic] pact had the effect of breaking up the alliances we had in Sheffield. A lot of people were horrified. The alliances we had built up around disarmament were developed by Aid to Spain, which was massive, strengthened by the campaigns around Munich and Czechoslovakia. Up to August 1939 the alliances we had built not only held but were strengthened. Then suddenly the Nazi-Soviet pact ... instead of being allied to us, those people became hostile.
>
> Bill Moore, 1939

There was no doubt about it: the international communist movement of the 1930s was the only consistently active anti-fascist party in Britain, and the Soviet Union was the only nation that was unambiguously anti-fascist and pro–working class. At this distance, and as members of a more or less comfortable and politically stable consumer society, it is difficult for us to imagine the hardships caused by class divisions in Britain in the first half of the twentieth century, and the bitterness that these divisions caused between Right and Left, particularly during the Depression years. To Pollitt and the other class warriors who had, for example, grown up in the harsh and punishing slum environs of Manchester, Liverpool, Clydeside, Lanarkshire, the West Riding of Yorkshire, the north-east of England and South Wales, the bosses stood unequivocally and utterly condemned, at worst, as the eternal enemy of working-class aspirations, and, at best, as patronising appropriators of proletarian labour. There were also Party members, such as Johnny Campbell, who had been celebrated for their part in World War I but had been sickened by the conflict and were committed to fighting against what they saw as the use of war as capitalist exploitation of the workers. As for the warmongering fascists, they were unreservedly loathed as rivals in the battle for revolutionary control. Jimmy Friell, the *Daily Worker*'s cartoonist 'Gabriel' (as in the last trumpet), later explained the views of many of his generation: 'I still can't understand anyone who grew up in the 1930s not being political', a comment on the struggle against the bourgeois capitalist class enemy and against Mosley's fascists, the political enemy.

Crucially, in the late 1930s, the Party had become firmly anti-Nazi, having recently moved away from the class struggle and from the hard-line argument that Nazism was just another form of capitalism to the view that Nazism was the major threat to world socialism. That is why, for the world at large but more especially for Communist Party members worldwide, the Nazi–Soviet pact of August 1939 was such a jaw-dropper. British Party members, having recently switched from socialist pacifism to socialist support for a broadly based anti-fascist military build-up, were suddenly faced with a Soviet leadership that was prepared to cosy up to the Hitlerite regime, socialism's most powerful rival. Yet seasoned Party members seemed to have little difficulty with the change of direction. Their sanguine approach was based on the view that, however strange the deal, Stalin, the CPSU and the Comintern, as navigators of the class struggle, knew what they were doing. Jimmy Friell remembered that the pact was 'a shock to everybody. Nobody liked it, but if you examined it, you could see why it was necessary to Russia'. Douglas Hyde, who shortly thereafter left the Party for the Catholic Church, explained the official line of the day in his anti-Party memoirs: 'The Soviet leaders had a responsibility to the working class of the world and could, if necessary, for this reason make an alliance with the devil himself'. Since the Party had already committed itself to Pollitt's 1938 line of unquestioning loyalty and had come through the turbulence of the trials of the counter-revolutionaries, the Nazi–Soviet pact now made perfect sense, albeit within the internal logic of dedication to the Moscow line. As with the Party's response to the show trials, this sudden transformation was based on an ideological rationalisation arrived at in the absence of any other reliable (that is Comintern-provided) information. It was simple belief all over again, a belief that Stalin knew what he was doing, notwithstanding the compelling evidence that he, as a leader, was unprepared for the later German onslaught in 1941. That is how the myth of the all-wise 'Stalin the Delayer' was perpetuated by Stalinist revisionists: what the great leader had really been up to by agreeing to the pact was gaining time for the Soviet Union in the lead-up to the inevitable battle with the fascist enemy.

Stalin, of course, never had any intention of keeping to the pact. If he had a consistent reasoning about his position in 1939, it was that he would watch Germany battling it out to the point of mutual destruction with France and Great Britain, and then the Soviet Union could step over the recumbent corpses of its fascist and capitalist opponents. In the meantime, both he and Hitler could slice up central and eastern Europe between them and create a mutually beneficial, if temporary, buffer zone. But the official Party reason remained the same: the Soviet

Union had been obliged to sign an agreement with the Nazis because the western powers were trying to force Stalin into a debilitating conflict with Hitler—more or less a reasonable proposition, considering the circumstances. Furthermore, Party reasoning went, capitalist press horror at a deal struck between the Nazis and the Soviets that left Poland isolated, eastern Europe vulnerable and western Europe exposed was just so much propaganda. None of this took into account Hitler's real intentions, which were to gain a quick victory over Poland, neutralise France and Britain and then defeat and annexe Bolshevik Russia.

A week after the signing of the pact, Nazi forces invaded Poland, with Britain and France declaring war on Germany, thus presenting the Party with yet another psychological challenge. After vigorously opposing fascism in Germany for half a decade, British communists were now in the uncomfortable position of vicariously supporting Nazi Germany, a state at war with their own country. Harry Pollitt had been a vigorous supporter of the need for military re-armament against the Nazi threat; indeed, the *Daily Worker*, following Pollitt's line, had declared that 'the war CAN and MUST be won'. To emphasise the point, Pollitt quickly wrote and published a pamphlet, *How to Win the War*, and on 2 September 1939, the day before the war began, the Party had issued a manifesto urging a struggle on two fronts for a victory over fascism, little knowing that the Comintern was about to pull the rug from underneath their collective feet.

Four days after the start of World War II, Stalin informed Comintern boss Dimitrov that foreign communist parties must follow the new line and cut out their anti-Nazi propaganda. The war was now an imperialist war, a communist regression to the old revolutionary defeatism approach, a strategy which argued that working-class interests were best served by their assisting in the collapse of capitalist warmongers.

An 'Imperialist War'

> The victory of imperialism, whether of one or the other camp, in this war—either of the German-Italian-Japanese combination

or of the Anglo-American combination—would mean the victory of capitalism over the aspirations of the people.

Palme Dutt, c. September 1939

A clarification of the latest Comintern line was personally delivered to the Party in late September by its central committee member Dave Springhall, newly returned from Moscow. Pollitt was working at home, trimming his hedges in suburban Colindale, when he saw Springhall walking along the street, bringing the fateful message to him as a memorised set of Comintern theses. Several days later, confirming the incredible news, the official document arrived from Moscow. Pollitt was immediately sacked as general secretary because of his pro-war stance. His mother, on hearing of her son's dismissal, wrote consolingly to him: 'Don't lose your pride, you can always go back to your [boilermaker] trade. I've kept your tools greased'. That is precisely what he did, while still retaining a seat on the Party's Central Executive Committee.

The Party's theorist Palme Dutt, an arrogant, intense and ruthless (in a theoretical way) intellectual, slavishly followed the new Moscow line. This new world war was declared by Dutt to be a fight between capitalist and fascist forces for political supremacy, at the expense, of course, of an exploited proletariat. To justify this line, the Party then came up with the wonderfully demented slogan 'No Unity with the Chamberlain Socialists'. As a result, in early October 1939 a depressed Pollitt became involved in a fierce central committee debate (official notes of which were sent to Moscow, and an unofficial transcript to MI5) in which Dutt, now leader of a central committee 'troika', wanted the Moscow line enforced as Party gospel. Non-troika members, including Pollitt, Gallagher and Campbell, could see the hypocrisy and the impending political fallout; they vehemently opposed what they considered to be Dutt's Muscovite fanaticism. The irrepressible Campbell put it succinctly: 'We started by saying we had an interest in the defeat of the Nazis, [and] we must now recognize that our prime interest is in the defeat of France and Great Britain . . . We have to eat everything we have said'. Notwithstanding these heated exchanges, the official line went through. Campbell's view was marginalised and the new editorial policy was to criticise Chamberlain for not caving in to Hitler's peace terms, the substance of later Party fulminations against the war effort until the Nazi invasion of Russia in June 1941. This latest twist in communist policy allowed anti-communist labourite Herbert Morrison, home secretary in the Churchill war cabinet, to close down the *Daily Worker* in January 1941, suspending its permission to publish until the following year.

A 'War against Fascism'

Smash the fascist bastards once and for all.

Harry Pollitt, 1939

When the Nazi armies, in pursuit of Lebensraum and of the extermination of 'Jewish Bolshevism', invaded Russia in June 1941, the Party immediately, and emphatically, stood on its head, declaring its solidarity with the communist homeland. Pollitt, vindicated, returned from ideological exile in Colindale and was given back his old job. What had recently (quite clearly) been an imperialist war was now (quite clearly) a justifiable fight against fascism. This was a much more comfortable position for the Party, as well as for Pollitt. Furthermore, during his exile, the suspended general secretary, having resumed his trade as boilermaker, had been pragmatically extending his political connections in directions that would not have been approved of by Dutt, sharing drinks in pubs with leftist journalist Michael Foot (who later went on to become a Labour member of parliament and accident-prone leader of the Labour Party from 1980 to 1983) and calling in on the *Evening Standard*'s conservative editor Frank Owen. Even after his reinstatement, Pollitt held clandestine meetings with Ernest Bevin (a Labour minister whom Pollitt disliked) and with Lord Beaverbrook (then minister of Aircraft Production, whom Pollitt regarded as a congenial sort of class enemy). These new contacts had their purpose:

they allowed the Party to operate during the war more or less with tacit government support, on the basis that Pollitt, as reinstated Party leader, was the least worst option, as far as the wartime government was concerned. But the Party was not prepared simply to fall in line with the new prime minister Winston Churchill's stated war policy. The major point of difference between the two sides during the period following the 1941 German invasion of Russia was (genuine class enemy) Churchill's alleged lack of support for the Soviet war effort, with the Party adopting a reckless 'Second Front Now' slogan as the basis of its war platform. This satisfied Moscow and British comrades and brothers, but exasperated a war government already committed to providing Stalin's forces with war supplies along the hazardous Arctic convoy route.

Meanwhile, the Party's renewed anti-Nazi policy, a growing awareness of domestic social injustice, and the British public's support of and admiration for the struggles of the Soviet people against their German invaders resulted in a sharp rise in Party membership, from a 1939 figure of 17 750 to a mid-war peak of 56 000. By 1942, the Party was even on the verge of affiliation with Labour, a move blocked by its baleful nemesis Herbert Morrison, first in 1942 and again in 1945. However, as the war ended and when a briefly triumphant Churchill was replaced by moderate socialist Clement Attlee, the Party, by now progressivist rather than revolutionary, had passed its prime, retaining a powerful presence only in the trade union movement. Its support for a strong social policy combined with ideological indecisiveness resulted in a poor electoral showing in 1945, pushing it into the fairly supine role of a critical friend of Attlee's Labour government.

The Cold War and Stalin's Death

> The enemies of Communism accuse the Communist Party of aiming to introduce Soviet power in Britain and abolish Parliament. This is a slanderous misrepresentation of our policy.
>
> Harry Pollitt, 1951

The Cold War all but killed off the Party's chances of becoming an effective political force. In the late 1940s, seizing on the class-based problems of a devastated post-war Britain beset by a war-damage housing crisis, food shortages and labour problems, the Party had regressed almost to where it had been in the 1920s, a small sectarian group of mistrustful, hardline ideologues propped up by union support. In the Cold War climate, this retro approach just did not work. By the early 1950s the Party was largely regarded as an instrument of Stalin's propaganda machine, an agency of the Bolshevik bogeyman, perceptions not helped by Red Threat spy scandals, internal Party conflict and an anti-communist hot war in Korea. Moreover, Britain, in the 1950s, was run by successive Conservative Party governments basking in the reflected glow of an economic boom, thus reducing the electoral potential of socialism of whatever stripe. Any associated attempts at effectiveness by the Party were blocked by the new prosperity, forcing it (in the Pollitt-inspired document *The British Road to Socialism* of 1951) away from a narrowly purist ideology and towards a broad electoral approach, even assisting Labour candidates in their campaigns. It was all to little effect. By the early 1950s, Party membership had plunged from its wartime peak of 56 000 to a trough of 35 000, and it was repeatedly humiliated in successive post-war elections.

As if this slide in Party fortunes were not bad enough, the communist world was rocked to its foundations when Stalin died, in March 1953. Stalin's death led to what was later a well-documented struggle for control in the Moscow Politburo, which Nikita Khrushchev, a wily, pragmatic political operator, eventually won. Stalin's demise was greeted with obsequious tributes to his steely genius and his iron will but, within three years, communist parties worldwide were thrown into turmoil as his successor, to bury once and for all the memory of Stalin as revolutionary hero and war supremo, revealed what had actually been going on in the Soviet Union under the Great Teacher. In February 1956, Khrushchev launched his famous attack on the personality cult surrounding the dead dictator in a six-hour secret speech to the twentieth USSR party congress. Stalin was no longer to be regarded as a hero of communism; instead, he was officially declared a dead tyrant, publicly excoriated in coded fashion by Anastas Mikoyan, the Soviet foreign minister, 'The principle of collective leadership is elementary for a party of the Lenin type. Yet for twenty years we did not have collective leadership but the cult of the individual. This had a harmful effect'.

In a well-worn story, at the precise time of Khrushchev's speech, Harry Pollitt and George Matthews (assistant secretary of the Party) were being shown around a Moscow contraceptive factory. Dutt, however, was missing from the visiting party, and the suspicion is that he was either in the closed session or being briefed by Politburo officials. Whatever the case, the British delegation was handed a copy of Khrushchev's speech to be taken back to Britain. Somewhere between Moscow and London, that crucial copy disappeared. In Britain, Party members, hearing rumours about Khrushchev's denunciation of Stalin, were confused yet again. Dutt, ever the Moscow loyalist, was now caught in a trap from which he tried to extricate himself. In a badly judged *Labour Monthly* article in May 1956, he used a typically hagiographical metaphor, arguing that any attacks on Stalin were like mere 'spots on the sun'. Dutt was howled down, literally in one case, and the Party turned on its leadership. After members caught sight of a full transcript of Khrushchev's speech, published on 10 June in the mainstream Sunday newspaper *The Observer*, tumult followed and resignations began to ravage the Party's already faltering recruitment strategy.

Unwell, and unable to cope with his new job as a detractor of Stalin, his hero, revolutionary inspiration and former drinking companion, Pollitt resigned. Meanwhile, in that crisis-torn summer of 1956, two leading Party intellectuals, historians Edward Thompson and John Saville, set up what was virtually a *samizdat*, hand-produced by supporters including *Daily Worker* staff on a Roneo machine. It was called *The Reasoner* and the first edition impudently took the Party leadership to task by quoting the Bolshevik Alexander Fadeyev ('by our excesses and our stiffness we have made [ideology] a cross-grained shrew') and by borrowing its attitude from the iconoclastic US *Daily Worker*, which had already set off on an anti-Stalinist tack. As if that were not enough for the Party leaders and members, the situation grew steadily worse.

Doubt and Denial at the *Daily Worker*

What happened in the *Daily Worker* offices during 1956 only reflected what was happening to the Party that lay beyond the newspaper's splendidly modernist Farringdon Road offices. The key to it all was a growing sense of unease about the history of the various CPSU and British lines, starting slowly in the spring of 1956, with increasingly angry denunciations of Soviet anti-Semitism and dismay at the announcements of the 'rehabilitations' of former Russian and eastern-European comrades culminating in an autumnal rage at the suppression of crucial despatches from Budapest, a city then being ravaged by Soviet military intervention.

The shocking news of long-term Stalinist anti-Semitism initially came through Polish-Jewish sources. In April 1956, a Warsaw-based Jewish community newspaper, *Folks-sztyme*, published a Yiddish-language account of Stalin's anti-Jewish purges. Translated by Alec Waterman, a *Daily Worker* staff member, it came as a huge shock to those who read the story. In summary, it suggested that between 1948 and 1953, Stalin had pursued a vigorous and lethal anti-Semitic campaign, starting with the shooting of every member of the Jewish Anti-Fascist Committee and ending with the notorious 1953 Jewish 'doctors plot', Stalin's paranoid belief that Jewish doctors were planning to poison the Soviet leadership, a fantasy brought to an end only by the dictator's death. Both the Party leadership and the *Daily Worker* editorial team suppressed the Polish report, but in New York, the dissident US *Daily Worker* published the story, producing a furore among Jewish and non-Jewish Party members in the USA. In Britain, a similar row erupted when the anti-Semitism story was published in the *Jewish Clarion*, the Party's 'Jewish' newspaper. Leading members of the Party's influential and numerous Jewish community were dismayed at this turn of events, and the staff of the *Daily Worker* soon found themselves embroiled in a debilitating public debate about the Party's attitude to Soviet anti-Semitism. In the

Daily Worker office, the official line was explained, with no hint of irony, by the assistant editor Mick Bennet: 'You mustn't say that Stalin stifled Jewish culture. Stalin stifled *all* culture'.

Party members were also encountering further horrific details of past Stalinist purges: various Soviet bloc countries had started to announce 'rehabilitations' of members who had formerly been declared heretics. The word 'rehabilitation' meant, in most cases, a posthumous recognition that the Soviet regime and its allies had erred in murdering quite so many of its leaders, functionaries and members. Two of the most prominent of these had been the former Hungarian Interior minister Laszlo Rajk (a ruthless Stalinist himself, but nonetheless tried and executed in 1949) and Rudolf Slansky, the Czech-Jewish Party general secretary (tried and executed in 1952). Such revelations were a further blow to many Party members, who began to dread news of these rehabilitations, which were, in most cases, *de facto* death notices of former Party friends and acquaintances in their great, if murderous, family and church.

The Hungarian Revolution

Meanwhile, in eastern Europe, the news of Stalin's debasement together with the law of rising expectations produced a summer of protests in Poland, Czechoslovakia and East Germany. Before events got out of hand, the dissenters were quickly accommodated in Poland, but suppressed elsewhere by the Soviet regime. While this was happening, the twists and turns of British communism agonising yet again over the contrast between the Party line and events on the ground were being rehearsed in, for example, the *Daily Worker*'s attitude to the anti-Soviet rebellion in the Polish industrial city of Poznan. On 3 July, the paper's first edition splash headline read: 'Poznan Rioters Had Been Drilled in Murder', but the second edition re-write was headed: 'Poznan Workers Speak Out on Grievances'.

The eastern-European uprisings and the Soviet concessions in Poland inspired revolutionary-style demonstrations in Budapest in October, which were immediately put down by Soviet troops on 24 October in the first of their Hungarian military interventions of 1956. A post-intervention revolt alarmed the recently installed but out-of-touch prime minister Imre Nagy [pronounced 'Nodge'], a mildly reformist and popular politician and a more pragmatic premier than his immediate predecessor, the hardline but ineffectual Erno Gero. Nagy had initially been recruited as prime minister by Moscow in 1953, only to be forced out by the detested, egotistical Stalinist prime minister Matyas Rakosi in April 1955 and thereafter reinstated by an anxious Kremlin on 23 October, the very eve of the first Soviet intercession. Nagy, still a loyal communist, was indecisive and slow to react to the palpably anti-Soviet atmosphere in Hungary, but by 28 October he had accepted the genuinely reformist character of the uprising, whereupon he announced a progressive agenda, negotiated an armistice with the Soviet authorities and, on 2 November, declared that Hungary was withdrawing from the recently formed Warsaw pact.

With the western-European nations distracted by the unfolding Suez crisis, Soviet, Czech and Romanian troops poured in to Budapest in a second intervention, allegedly invited by the Hungarian people to suppress the counter-revolutionaries. Over the next few days, Russian tanks turned low-lying Pest, heart of the government district and commercial centre, into a war zone; by the morning of 4 November, it was all but over. Nagy, most of his government and several Hungarian army officers were placed under arrest, with the recently installed prime minister and several of his ministers then 'disappearing'.

During the twelve-day struggle against Soviet-style government, an estimated 2652 Hungarian fighters and 720 Soviet soldiers were lost (both dead and missing). An estimated 289 AVH (secret police) officers had also been killed in the fighting and a further 100 or so had been murdered: taken out of their headquarters and publicly shot, beaten to death or hanged. As a consequence of the collapse of the revolt, 200 000 Hungarians fled over the border to Austria and to the world beyond.

With the rebellion crushed, there were now Soviet scores to be settled. Stalin might have been dead for three years, but Budapest had fallen to old-style Stalinist repression, notwithstanding some internal divisions within the Politburo and the Red Army about how the Hungarian uprising should have been handled. Nagy was replaced by Janos Kadar, a Soviet puppet, and the reprisals began against those who remained. The AVH was transmogrified into the Karhatalom, a similar organisation with similar personnel. Arrests, abductions and imprisonments followed, with some 330 Hungarians executed under the Kadar regime. Nagy was hanged on 16 June 1958.

The Party, the *Daily Worker* and Hungary

The conflict in Hungary was matched by a parallel struggle in British Party circles, a commotion nowhere more tumultuous than in the offices of the *Daily Worker*. The Party's initial position had been that the eastern-European uprisings had been counter-revolutionary fascist plots to attack innocent communist regimes, all part of the international capitalist strategy to bring about the downfall of socialism by weakening the Soviet bloc. Hungarian workers had been obliged to request Soviet intervention to suppress the putschists. The *Daily Worker* initially followed the Party line; but that was to change.

In Farringdon Road, Hungary's plight provoked a strong and agonised response among half of the thirty or so staff, who had growing doubts about the Party's stance. After hearing of the news of Stalinist anti-Semitism, they had become increasingly unhappy about more generalised past and present Soviet acts of despotism, cruelties which might once have been discounted as a series of mistakes but which were now beginning to form a perceptible pattern of longstanding CPSU oppression. The *Daily Worker* staff were also horrified at the news of the severity of the Soviet intervention in Budapest, brought to them, admittedly, by a bourgeois reactionary capitalist media, but vividly portrayed in radio broadcasts, photographs and smuggled, grainy newsreel film. In a more immediate way, they were disillusioned by the *Daily Worker*'s approach to Peter Fryer, its newly commissioned special correspondent in Budapest, who reported both what he saw and what he felt, a style that was strictly against the official Party line. Fryer had spent time in Hungary before, and had even reported the Rajk show trial back in 1949, then spinning the official line that Rajk had been working for the imperialists. Rajk's subsequent 'rehabilitation' in 1956 and his reburial on 6 October were among the precipitating events that sparked the Hungarian uprising and led to further dismay and confusion at the *Daily Worker*. Rajk's reburial had taken place in front of a huge Budapest crowd—estimated to be 200 000 strong—on the very day that commemorated the 1848 executions of thirteen Hungarian generals of the anti-Habsburg revolutionary army. This was ironic really, since Rajk had been no angel—far from it—but his symbolic funeral acted as a focus for a rapidly increasing anti-Soviet hatred combined with hope that there could be change. Moreover, the Rajk business produced in Fryer a feeling of profound remorse: regret that he had been so closely involved in the denigration and death of a man, ruthlessly unpleasant as he may have been, who had at least been innocent of the show trial charges. Fryer's experiences were vividly and emotionally documented in his 79-page book *Hungarian Tragedy*, first published in December 1956, just a few months after his return to London.

But it was not only Fryer who was beginning to turn. Alison Mcleod, at that time the *Daily Worker*'s television critic, kept a journal of the discussions that took place during the autumn of 1956, which she published much later in book form as *The Death of Uncle Joe*. Her commentary is a detailed memoir, combining humour with growing exasperation and showing increasing scepticism about the Party line. While Mcleod may not necessarily have been an impartial witness (she could not stand Dutt and she thoroughly disliked Pollitt), in sections, the book amounts to a verbatim record of the regular Monday staff meetings consumed with agonised and heated debate about Hungarian revolt and the consequent Soviet repression. Mcleod's account is more or less backed up by journalist Francis Beckett, whose book about the Party, *Enemy Within*, is a compilation of a wide range of documentary and oral history sources, with both Mcleod and Beckett appalled at the Party's treatment of colleague Peter Fryer.

The energetic and talented Fryer, sent to Budapest by editor Johnny Campbell to cover the conflict and to come up with a conventional

Party-approved report, had wandered off-message as soon as he reached Hungary. When the first student-led revolt broke out, on 23 October, at the commencement of the new academic year, Fryer headed for Budapest, via Vienna. He reached the Hungarian industrial border town of Magyarovar and then the regional centre of Gyor. In both places, he was surprised to discover a genuine people's rebellion at work, not a fascist counter-revolution at all. His despatch from Magyarovar on 31 October, detailing a massacre of unarmed demonstrators by the local AVH, infuriated Mick Bennet (the paper's then acting editor), because it contained an account of innocent civilian casualties at the hands of heavily armed secret police and failed to follow the Party line. The story contained the following heretical commentary:

> This was no counter-revolution, organized by fascists and reactionaries. It was the upsurge of the whole people . . . I am the first Communist journalist from abroad to visit Hungary since the revolution started. And I have no hesitation in placing the blame for these terrible events squarely on the shoulders of those who led the Hungarian Communist party for eleven years.

At that time, Campbell was inconveniently absent in Moscow, accompanying a pre-arranged delegation seeking an official Soviet briefing on alleged Soviet anti-Semitism, so Fryer's inflammatory words, pro-dissent in tone and content, were blocked at the London end by Campbell's deputy. This initial despatch had been hurriedly transferred to Bennet's office without being circulated to editorial staff in the normal way. Those few staff members who were allowed to see the Fryer despatches over the period of the insurgency (three stories in all) were sworn to secrecy. This embargo did not stop the word getting around.

Accordingly, and paying absolutely no public attention to any contradictory dissenting evidence, the *Daily Worker* continued to explain that when Soviet tanks withdrew from their first intervention in Budapest, 'gangs of reactionaries began beating Communists to death in the streets'. This was the kind of reportage that resonated only too well with the generation of left-leaning readers who were familiar with the violent activities of Hungary's pre-war fascist movement, the Arrow Cross. Indeed, the rebel capture of Budapest's Communist Party headquarters on 30 October, in which twenty-three AVH secret policemen were publicly lynched as western news cameras clicked and flashed, horrified not only Moscow but also a worldwide audience of Communist Party members.

A few days later, on 4 November, as Soviet tanks were mopping up the resistance, the socialist Sunday newspaper *Reynolds News* carried a version of a speech (probably sourced from TASS, the Soviet news agency) by the recently freed Cardinal Mindszenty. The cardinal, a prickly and feudally inclined cleric, had in his time taken on the Nazis, the Arrow Cross, the Communist Party and the Vatican, all with equal mulishness. His speech constituted a reactionary and pro-capitalist diatribe. The *Daily Worker* continued the anti-Church theme, carrying a report of Mindszenty's allegedly reactionary rant in the same edition (5 November), splashing the headline 'Hungarian Anti-Fascist Government in Action' with the sub-head 'Soviet Troops Called In to Stop White Terror'. These counter-revolutionary allegations, later established as fabrications, were not reassuring for comrades familiar with Mindszenty's long association with an aristocratic and reactionary Catholic Hungary and still mindful of white attempts to overthrow a shaky Bolshevik regime during the Russian Civil War, a mere thirty years before.

On that very day, John Gollan, Pollitt's popular but low-key successor as general secretary, was sent by the Party Politburo (the King Street inner executive) across town to Farringdon Road to outline the official view to the wavering journalists and other staff. His explanation was much as before: the Hungarian uprising was a long-planned, capitalist-backed, right-wing counter-revolution. Gollan referred to Hungary's fascist past and accused the Hungarian counter-revolutionaries of indiscriminately murdering Party members. But Peter Fryer, the *Daily Worker*'s eyewitness in Hungary, was about to confound that view and pile on the agony for the paper's staff. Fryer had eventually arrived in the capital, Budapest, on 31 October, where he witnessed the brutal, second Soviet suppression at first hand and met many of the thousands of recently released and badly brutalised prisoners of the AVH, including Edith Bone, a British citizen. She had been imprisoned by the AVH at the age of sixty, in 1949, when she had been acting as an unpaid correspondent for the *Daily Worker*. Hungarian-born and an abrasively indomitable character, Bone had been abducted by the AVH as she was leaving the country and was accused of being a foreign spy. She had then spent seven years in solitary confinement, harassing and tormenting her jailers in a way that was all too familiar to her British comrades, who had always regarded her as a bit of a thorn in their, and the Party's, side. Nevertheless, the Party had made representations to the Rakosi regime on her behalf in the 1950s, to be told flatly that she was no longer in Hungary. When she eventually showed up in Hungary in early November 1956, wandering through the streets of Budapest, the news filtered back to Farringdon Road. To those who knew her and knew of the Hungarian response to inquiries about her whereabouts, Bone's reappearance, combined with a now apparent history of Hungarian official mendacity, threw up further milestones on the road to disillusionment and dissent.

Eventually, with the Soviet suppression in Hungary complete by 10 November, Fryer ended his time in Budapest by filing his third and final story on 11 November, prior to leaving the country in a car laden with fleeing US journalists. In part, Fryer's final despatch aimed a barb at the heart of pro-Soviet propaganda by turning the class war argument back on its believers:

> If the Soviet intervention was necessary to put down counter-revolution, how is it to be explained that some of the fiercest resistance of all last week was in the working class district of Ujpest, in the north of Budapest, and Csepel, in the south, both pre-war strongholds of the Communist Party? Or how is the

declaration of the workers of the famous steel town of Sztalinvaros to be explained: that they would defend their Socialist town, the plant and houses they had built with their own hands, against the Soviet invasion?

When Fryer reached Vienna, on his way back to London, he phoned his wife. 'What about my story?' he asked. 'The editor won't even let the staff see it', she replied.

By this time, disillusionment had really set in at Farringdon Road. The *Daily Worker*'s staff were split between hardline Moscow loyalists on the one hand and argumentative 'realists' on the other. The latter group wanted a more questioning approach to events in Hungary, along the lines of the US *Daily Worker*'s heretical campaign against Soviet intervention. Sixteen of the British newspaper's workers, organised by Malcolm MacEwen (the features editor), signed a petition against the editorial treatment of the Hungarian uprising, referring specifically to the Edith Bone case. MacEwen was brave enough to take the petition to a hostile Party executive on 3 November. They reacted predictably, by rejecting both it and him. Thereafter, journalists began to resign in protest against the Soviet crackdown or Party denial, or both.

Most prominent among the fugitives was Fryer, who resigned from the paper and even from the Party. He did not go quietly, joining the Club, a Trotskyite faction led by detested Party enemy Gerry Healy. Fryer, livid at his treatment by the Party, also gave interviews to the hated capitalist press and publicly spilled the beans to Beaverbrook's *Daily Express*. MacEwen, after a humiliating interrogation at the hands of the *Daily Worker*'s leadership, was eventually thrown out, mainly for organising the anti-editorial petition. After much soul-searching, the *Daily Worker*'s cartoonist Jimmy Friell also resigned from the paper, later finding work with the Beaverbrook press. Leon Griffiths, a journalist and later a successful screenwriter, resigned from the paper, as did Llew Gardner, a promising young reporter who had little patience for the old-time class warriors who dominated the Party. Gardner took his journalistic talent with him, going on to become a political correspondent for a major independent British television channel.

All of this occurred amid office and Party rumours that Peter Fryer, by now an official outcast, had been submitting hysterical accounts from Hungary and was receiving psychiatric counselling. Moreover, there were whispers that his wife, who had worked in the Farringdon Road accounts section, had been caught with her hand in the till. None of it was true, of course. The source of the classic Party dirty-tricks campaign is not too difficult to fathom. It could only have been the work of someone in an editorial group; that included general manager David Ainley, editor Johnny Campbell (unlikely, as he was still in Moscow) and adjunct editorial member, Party deputy general secretary George Matthews. Palme Dutt, too, may have been involved; he was still the Party's chief ideologue and viewed the *Daily Worker* staff as a gang of unreliable mavericks, some of whom had, in the past, demonstrated a most undeveloped political consciousness by slashing and cutting his turgid sermons. (The term 'maverick' could not, of course, be applied to the *Daily Worker*'s Party line apologias on Hungary.)

Faced by the contorted rationalisations of Party-loyal Farringdon Road staff and of the Party generally, the *Reasoners*, Edward Thompson, John Saville and many of the Party's Historians' group and Writers' group resigned, as did thousands of others who had been sickened by the duplicity and hypocrisy of their formerly beloved Party. At a more organisational level, between the 1956 Budapest suppression and the pre-Christmas meeting of the Central Executive Committee, 219 resolutions were sent to King Street headquarters on the Hungarian issue, almost all critical of a Party leadership that had left members feeling duped and dismayed, their belief systems shattered.

The iron discipline of former years had been replaced, in 1956, by bitterness and confusion. From King Street, the predominant view, metaphorically, was of retreating backs, as members began to desert the Party in droves. The consequence was catastrophic. In a two-year period, from February 1956 to February 1958, a time that saw increased disillusionment with both Soviet and King Street leadership, the Party lost one-third of an already modest membership, and many of the refugees were influential trade union leaders, key rank-and-file workers and leading intellectuals. In 2006, even four decades after the event, memories were still strong of the last group for author and Nobel Laureate Doris Lessing, who commented briefly and bitterly on her one-time affiliation with a Party that had so strongly supported Stalinist and post-Stalinist atrocities. 'What fools we were', she said, simply and sadly.

Unlike Lessing and other intellectuals, however, Eric Hobsbawm did not resign.

The Hobsbawm Answer

It was a single word, tersely uttered by the doyen of British Marxist historians, Eric Hobsbawm, during a notorious BBC television interview in October 1994 that provided ammunition for a decade of Hobsbawm baiting and renewed communist hating at the hands of right-wing authors such as Martin Amis and Robert Conquest, and conservative commentators Oliver Kamm and David Pryce-Jones. The interviewer was Michael Ignatieff, Canadian historian and cultural commentator; the occasion was the publication of Hobsbawm's *Age of Extremes*; and the question was aimed at eliciting Hobsbawm's summary analysis of the morality of the Stalinist Great Terror. Hobsbawm, former leading light of the Communist Party's Historians' Group (which ran, broadly, between 1946 and 1956), carefully circled around any moral assessment of the impact of the Stalinist regime by asking Ignatieff a diversionary question: 'Do people now say we shouldn't have had World War II because more people died in World War II than in Stalin's Terror?' Brushing aside the facile comparison, Ignatieff pursued him. And this is the crucial section of the interview: Ignatieff asked, 'What [your belief] comes down to is saying that had a socialist "radiant tomorrow" actually been created, the loss of fifteen, twenty million people might have been justified?' Hobsbawm's reply was the monosyllabic affirmative 'Yes'.

BRITISH COMMUNISM AND TWO DECADES OF DENIAL

To be fair to Hobsbawm, allowing for some enduring equivocations about Stalinism, his book *Age of Extremes* does contain the admission that 'it does not much matter whether we opt for a "conservative" estimate nearer to ten than to twenty millions or a larger figure: none can be anything but shameful and beyond palliation, let alone justification'. Since Hobsbawm has made such a moderating acknowledgement, why is there a continuing focus on this prolific and highly regarded historian as the leading *bête noire* of the Right? The answer lies in the 1980s when the British Labour Party and the communist movement were searching for a new post-Thatcher direction. Hobsbawm, together with fellow historian Edward Thompson and the editor of *Marxism Today* Martin Jaques, began to play an active part in developing what was known as 'realistic Marxism' to the extent that Hobsbawm became known as the Labour Party's favourite communist. Having modified his revolutionary views to accommodate changing times, Hobsbawm helped to defeat the hard (or traditionalist) Left in the 1980s Communist Party with his reformist agenda; indeed, Party supporters have made much of this approach, seeing it as a prelude to Tony Blair's centrist Third Way. However, while a reformed, if very small, Party did experience circumstances parallel to New Labour (a move towards a unified reform platform), it was still running on a very different track from the mainline Labour Party. If Tony Blair was in charge of a sleek, inter-city express, the reformed British Communist Party was effectively puffing along on a branch line.

Nevertheless, by the late 1990s, Hobsbawm's ideas had become acceptable in the New Labour camp and were acknowledged even in some conservative circles as part of the agreeable face of reformed communism, to the extent that Robert Conquest—a former communist himself, and the vindicated anti-Stalinist author of the book *The Great Terror* (1968)—could not resist refreshing his readers' memories of that BBC television interview in his memoir *Reflections on a Ravaged Century* (1999), providing a reminder to the world at large of the New Labourite guru's earlier acceptance of Stalinist policies. This kind of criticism did not, however, prevent Blair from nominating the former apologist for

Stalinism as Companion of Honour in 2004, a move that enraged the more excitable rightists such as Pryce-Jones.

Leaving aside Hobsbawm's incongruous and ironic elevation to royal comradeship, his philosophical position in the period prior to 'realistic Marxism' represents a special kind of rationalisation, as expressed in the Ignatieff interview. In 1994, Hobsbawm explained just how things were in the 1930s: 'You didn't have the option. You see, either there was going to be a future or there wasn't going to be a future and this [Soviet communism] was the only thing that offered an acceptable future'. Simply put, loyalty to the communist cause was a matter of steadfast hope and belief. This was precisely the kind of thinking that underpinned all the tortured logic of denial when the Party was eventually faced with evidence that Stalin was a mass murderer who instigated slaughter out of mistrust, whose underlings killed for communism and whose colonised eastern-European allies were little better than slave states. In the face of these slowly unfolding revelations, Party logic, actually a form of Marxist utilitarianism, attempted to retain its belief, its faith in the greater good. What Stalin did for Russia and the international proletariat *in its totality*, so the argument ran, was better than *any* non-communist alternative.

The Hobsbawm Question

The months in Berlin made me a lifelong communist.

Eric Hobsbawm, 2002

The Soviet intervention in the Hungarian Revolution moved several of us [Communist Party's Historians' Group] to a second and even more flagrant breach of Party discipline, technically punishable by expulsion, a collective letter of protest signed by most of the better known historians ... rejected by the *Daily Worker* and demonstratively published by the non-party press.

Eric Hobsbawm, 2002

> Contemporary history is useless unless it allows emotion to be recollected in tranquillity.
>
> Eric Hobsbawm, 2006

The first question is, why did Hobsbawm, committed and dedicated socialist that he was, remain in a Party whose leadership stood condemned as accomplices in mass murder? In addition, can he justifiably be accused of condoning Soviet excesses knowing his immense reputation as an ethically rigorous historian and his genuine commitment to a utopian future for the working classes? To answer these questions, and to understand his position more clearly, it is important to see his decision in the specific terms he outlined in an important 2002 newspaper interview:

> Why I stayed is not a political question about communism, it's a one-off biographical question. It wasn't out of idealisation of the October Revolution. I'm not an idealiser. One should not delude oneself about the people or things one cares most about in one's life. Communism is one of these things and I've done my best not to delude myself about it even though I was loyal to it and to its memory. The phenomenon of communism and the passion it aroused is specific to the twentieth century. It was a combination of the great hopes which were brought with progress and the belief in human improvement during the nineteenth century along with the discovery that bourgeois society in which we live (however great and successful) did not work and at certain stages looked as though it was on the verge of collapse. And it did collapse and generated awful nightmares.

What Hobsbawm seems to be saying is that his loyalty to the idea of communism transcended his loyalty to Party structure and to the Party leadership. In other words, he was under no illusions about the failings of Party leading lights, as eventually demonstrated, for example, in the revealed activities of the CPSU and the British Party during the pre- and post-war years. He did not shrink from the consequences of malign human character as evinced in the activities of Stalin and his stooges. However, in Hobsbawm's writing, wry and ironic as it is, while the masses are important, individuals are not; for, when it comes to scholarship and ideology, he is the very apostle of professional and personal detachment.

Indeed, in his autobiography, while he acknowledges the agonies of 1956, he recounts his own rebellious part as a narrative that focuses on his assistance in drafting a letter of protest to the Party executive combined with his request for the Party to commission an after-the-event history of its own doings, a vivid confirmation of his post-1945 disposition—that of cerebral commentator deliberately distancing himself from past and present events. In his historical writings, for example, there is no empathetic description of the situation of political prisoners incarcerated in the depths of places such as 23 Nikolskaya Ulitsa, nicknamed by local Muscovites 'The Shooting House' and home of the Military Collegium of the Supreme Court of the Soviet Union. Here, an estimated 40 000 prisoners were sentenced to death during the 1930s. The Shooting House was part of an NKVD complex of large premises close to the Kremlin and to Lubyanka prison. The NKVD, preferring not to murder their Muscovite prisoners in Lubyanka, would temporarily imprison them in these requisitioned villas, and eventually there would be a placing of a suppressed Nagant revolver against the back of a prisoner's head, followed by a shot . . . and then oblivion. Events such as these occurred hundreds of thousands of times—in cells, torture chambers, prison courtyards, camps—and they are described in the literature of the Gulags. Sometimes it was the noose, sometimes the Nagant, sometimes the firing squad, sometimes death under torture. But if you read Hobsbawm, none of these real and individual excesses appear to have reached him. There is no cognitive dissonance, no sense of growing discomfort. The voices of the real casualties of Stalinism do not appear, for it was the *idea* of communism, not its people and certainly not its practice, that kept him going in 1956. He maintained his utopian vision, a view that was not to be diverted by low emotionality.

Hobsbawm's writing displays an intellectual removal from what he sees as an unnecessary and distracting disturbance to the psyche that may be caused by over-involvement in the stories of individual people. Indeed, a careful reading of *Age of Extremes* reveals a wonderful, synoptic account of the 'short' twentieth century, but it is a secluded narrative without the intrusion of too many people. Ideas, movements, parties and principles are Hobsbawm's *forte*. On balance, as far as Hobsbawm is concerned, communism was a good idea, if of its time and in its time, and Party ideology took precedence over the people.

That being the case, when Ignatieff asked him that crucial question—'What [your belief] comes down to is saying that had the radiant tomorrow actually been created, the loss of fifteen, twenty million people might have been justified?'—we can almost see Hobsbawm's mind quickly at work, a mind that readily toys with counter-factual history:

The Bolshevik revolution required forceful implementation—Lenin himself helped to set up the CHEKA to deal with counter-revolutionary forces—Lenin's death produced a leadership hiatus—Stalin's accession was not inevitable but if it hadn't been Stalin, it would have been another more or less tyrannical leader—without strong central leadership, the Soviet Union might have collapsed—many Russians would have died whatever the case—the continuation of the spirit of the October revolution inspired anti-fascist resistance and the defeat of the Axis—more Russians died in the (worthy) fight against Nazism than in the (nightmarish and bad) Gulags—after the war socialism spread to Asia, Africa and Latin America . . .

'Yes.'

5

TALES OF HEARTLESS DENIAL FROM THE BALKANS

Serbian Victimhood and Marxist Conspiracy Theories

There is an old Serbian fairytale and this is how it goes:

Once upon a time there was an emperor called Trojan. Unfortunately for the emperor, he had been born with goat's ears. Every day a barber would be summoned to shave Trojan, and the emperor would ask the barber if he saw anything unusual. If the barber said yes, Trojan would have him executed. Before long, Trojan had run out of barbers and a young apprentice was called upon to do the job. The emperor asked his novice barber the fateful question and the apprentice, realising that he was on the spot, lied, saying that he saw nothing unusual. The young man returned again and again to shave the emperor and was handsomely rewarded. But one day, the apprentice could stand the stress of lying no longer and dug a hole into the ground into which he whispered, 'The emperor Trojan has goat's ears'. Magically, from that hole, an elder tree grew. Some passing shepherds, seeing the magic tree, made a flute from its wood but all the flute would do was say 'The emperor Trojan has goat's ears'. Trojan, on hearing the story, confronted the apprentice, who told him all. They both hurried to the elder tree, together with the emperor's attendants, and, once there, Trojan ordered a flute to be made from the wood, telling his chamberlain, the best flautist in the land, to play a tune. But all the flute would do was say 'The emperor Trojan has goat's ears'. It was at that point that Trojan realised that, whatever he did, the earth would always give up its secrets.

Finding the Secrets

In 2006, Eric Stover wrote about the excavations of the mass graves containing Bosniak victims of the notorious Srebrenica massacre that took place in July 1995. Stover is a US lawyer and director of the Human Rights Center at the University of California, and since the 1980s he has conducted research into human rights abuses in Argentina, Brazil, the Balkans and Rwanda. In 1996, he accompanied an investigative forensic team at work in the former Yugoslavia.

> The Srebrenica graves were unlike most sites the scientists had worked on in their own countries. To begin with, they were larger and contained more bodies. Many of the bodies, especially toward the bottom of the graves, were fairly well preserved. A body can decompose quickly if it is lying on the surface or buried just below it. But the deeper it is buried (and if the soil conditions are right), the more likely it will remain preserved for a longer period of time. This is especially true if the burial is near or below the water table, as was the case at Srebrenica. . . . So far, more than 2000 bodies have been exhumed from the Srebrenica graves, and most of them have been positively identified, largely by DNA testing, and returned to relatives. . . . Yet, eleven years after the fall of Srebrenica, the two men who bear the greatest responsibility for the massacre—Radovan Karadzic and Ratko Mladic—remain free. 'What troubles me', one of the forensic investigators told me in 1996, 'is that these people may have died in vain. Without justice, all of this will end up being a mockery of the dead and of all that we've accomplished'.

The Bosniaks who were massacred at Srebrenica were the victims of the largest single atrocity in the bitter inter-communal war in the Balkans in the 1990s, which consumed the region, as well as troubling the world, and which produced the new and misleadingly euphemistic term 'ethnic cleansing'. During a succession of conflicts that erupted, died down and erupted yet again during the first half of that decade, an estimated 97 000 people were killed in Bosnia alone. Of those casualties, 65 per cent were Bosniak, 25 per cent were Bosnian Serb and 8 per cent were Bosnian Croat. Of the war missing, 85 per cent are Bosniak, 12 per cent are Serbs and 3 per cent are Croatians. Notwithstanding the stark nature of these figures, Serbian nationalist mythology continues to perpetuate the fairytale that the Serbs were the victims of Bosnian, Croatian and western aggression during the war. This Balkan conflict (the last of several in the twentieth century) was a result of the disintegration of the former Yugoslavian republic in the early 1990s. Although there were atrocities committed by all forces participating, it was the behaviour of Serb irregular and regular forces that attracted the most international criticism. This is because, in most cases, the Serb irregulars, with the support of the Serbian paramilitary police and the Yugoslav national army (JNA), were directly involved or complicit in the worst example of mass murder and genocide that Europe had seen since the end of World War II.

Despite overwhelming evidence of the appalling events that took place between 1991 and 1995, all sides (Serbs, Croats and Bosniaks) have strenuously denied misdeeds and have asserted that the real atrocities were committed by the others and that they were either guilt-free or provoked into justifiable reprisals. Beyond the Balkans, there is a disparate group of politically motivated denialists who argue that the Serb case is either much misunderstood or deliberately misrepresented. There are, therefore, two schools of Serb denial. The first is based, not unexpectedly, on blind, nationalistic refusal to believe that Serbs, either from Serbia itself or from the other regions of the former Yugoslavia, were capable of mass brutality and murder, in Bosnia or elsewhere. The second, less easily anticipated point of view, is a radical assertion from outside Serbia that the Serbs have been the victims of a western conspiracy to excite opinion against a much-traduced Serbian government and people.

Before we move into a more detailed discussion of Serbian denial, it is important to remember that there was, and still is, a strong body of opinion within the Serbian community that was opposed to the war. Furthermore, some Serbians emigrated or deserted the JNA, either out of disgust with their government or through apprehension about the conflict. Other dissidents remained in Serbia, bravely opposing the war as it took place and subsequently resisting any post-conflict cover-up. We should bear in mind that the denial within Serbia itself originates from a small, fanatical Serbian nationalist faction goaded by ruthless politicians and a hysterical Belgrade media. Nevertheless, in Serb culture as a whole, there was, and there remains, a defensive and strongly held view that the Serbs have consistently been the injured party in a long series of events that have adversely affected their legitimate national aspirations. As Dobrica Cosic, nationalist writer and one-time president of the former republic of Yugoslavia, once put it (with wild inaccuracy): Serbians tend to win the war but lose the peace.

The Serbian Mythology of Victimhood

> [Serb nationalist] historical revisionism, thus, cast Serbs as victims and Serbs' neighbours—especially Croats and Albanians—as Serbs' oppressors. The demonization of antagonists serves the function of casting them as permanent foes ... This historical revisionism, in turn, fed a certain kind of nationalism, indeed a most dangerous kind, in which the solution to present difficulties could only be sought in the arrival of a Serbian messiah. Needless to say it was Slobodan Milosevic.
>
> Sabrina Ramet

Leaving aside long cultural folk memories of betrayal and victimisation by enemies and neighbours, for Serbs, the crucial symbol of detestation in the post-Tito era was the 1974 constitution, an arrangement which tried to continue to balance the competing interests and identities of the Yugoslav republics and provinces, all eight of them, under the Titoist banner of 'brotherhood and unity'. When Tito died, in 1980, fraternal relations in the south rapidly disintegrated as Kosovo Serbs turned up the heat over exaggerated claims of maltreatment at the hands of the Muslim majority. At the same time, two of the northern republics, Slovenia and Croatia, began to agitate for autonomy.

The crisis of Yugoslavian unity reached a turning point in September 1986 when a group of Serbian academics combined to draft a manifesto, unabashedly expansionist and Greater Serbian in character, which was subsequently leaked to a major Belgrade newspaper. This sensational document, outlining a list of Serb grievances at the hands of its foes, caused consternation among the Serb people and within the Yugoslav government. The latter, however, initially maintaining its post-Titoist unity stance, criticised the memorandum as a danger to the federation, with Slobodan Milosevic, the opportunistic and wily leader of the Serbian Communist Party, publicly denouncing it as overtly nationalistic, that is anti-Titoist.

Yet, a mere seven months after the memorandum's publication, in April 1987, Milosevic himself fractured the federalist model. He visited Kosovo on two fateful missions that marked a transition in the Serbian political agenda from pragmatic inter-ethnic communism to ardent Serb patriotism, disguised, in the early years of the ensuing conflict at least, as an attempt to preserve the Titoist spirit of cooperative federalism. Milosevic had been despatched to Kosovo by his mentor, Serbia's president Ivan Stambolic, to calm down the Serb minority there, which had been agitated by a largely mendacious propaganda campaign against alleged violence by the Kosovars (ethnic-majority Albanians). Milosevic, at first nervous but later growing in confidence, gave an impromptu but significant speech during his second appearance, in the town of Kosovo Polje. Hemmed in by an angry crowd that had been carefully organised and provocatively incited into anti-Muslim hatred, he spontaneously bellowed, 'No-one should dare to beat you', all but telling the Kosovo Serbs that the province was their land and that they should stay there 'for the sake of your ancestors and descendants'.

In this one brief and localised explosion of Serb sentiment, broadcast by the nationalistic Belgrade television station RTS, Milosevic was changed from an obscure but politically powerful party hack to a charismatic political leader, an outcome that, for him, proved too seductive to resist. Stambolic later remarked that his protégé 'was transformed, set afire by Kosovo'. From that time on, during a remarkable rise to power in the rapidly fragmenting republic of Yugoslavia, Milosevic played the twin cards of Serbian nationalism and Serbian victimhood. In a thoroughly deceptive piece of opportunistic politics, as he asserted that Yugoslavia needed to stay united and using the slogans of brotherhood and unity, he wielded the federal military and police apparatus to manoeuvre for Serb expansionism at the expense of the other ethnic minorities. In a characteristic act of duplicity, one of his first steps in consolidating his power was to depose his friend and guide, the more conciliatory Stambolic, taking over the position of president of Serbia in 1989.

The Rise of Serbian Nationalism and the Wars of 1991–95

> Milosevic told me, as he did throughout the conflict, that he didn't have any control over the Bosnian Serbs, but he would try to use his moral authority ... His official position was that if Bosnia was independent, then the Federal Army would move out. Obviously what he didn't tell me ... was that a great part of the command of the Federal Army was going to stay in Bosnia as a Bosnian army. At that moment this wasn't as clear as it was later in retrospect.
>
> Jose Maria Mendiluce, Head of United Nations High Commission for Refugees in Yugoslavia, 1995

After Milosevic's visits to Kosovo, the Kosovar community was subjected to a campaign of suppression by Belgrade in a move that alarmed other non-Serb leaders, including Milan Kucan, the Slovenian party boss. Keen to break away before the anticipated imposition of a

Belgrade-dominated 'Serbo-slavia' and anxious about resurgent Serb nationalism and the suppression of the non-Serb population of Kosovo, Kucan began to initiate secessionist moves. Slovenia, Yugoslavia's northernmost and richest republic, contained the federation's proportionally smallest Serb population and was seen by Milosevic, by this time the major player in the renaissance of Serb nationalism, as relatively dispensable. After some political manoeuvring reminiscent of the Stalin era, there followed a Slovenian declaration of independence, and a brief, almost bloodless war, with Kucan becoming the first president of a sovereign Slovenia, a move that had already encouraged Croatia to take the same path.

While Serbia had let Slovenia go almost willingly, it now had to reckon with the much larger and more troublesome Croatia, bent on its own breakaway course. The relatively effortless Slovenian transition to independence was not about to be paralleled in Croatia. With its largely Roman Catholic population, Croatia retained strong ties with neighbouring Hungary (Magyar and mainly Catholic) and was under the sway of the devious, egotistical, arch-nationalist and anti-Semitic politician Franjo Tudjman, whose arrogance and vehemence reminded Serbs that, in the narrative of Serb suffering, Croatia still occupied a justifiably major role.

Croatia's pre-Tito relations with Serbia included its Ustase fascists' enthusiastic siding with the Nazis during World War II, to the extent that an estimated 500 000 Serbs (as well as 500 000 Jews, gypsies, homosexuals and political opponents of the Ustase) were either brutally killed in local campaigns of almost unimaginable terror or died in Croat concentration camps, the largest of which was at Jasenovac. Of the many incidents of Ustase cruelty, one episode stands out as a precursor to the Balkan atrocities half a century later. In July 1941, Ustase forces gathered about 500 Croatian Serbs at the small town of Glina, and murdered them all, men, women and children. Peasants who had been quick enough to escape to the woods prior to the round-up were lured back by the Ustase, ostensibly for the purpose of conversion from their orthodox religion to Roman Catholicism. The 250 or so who decided to trust their captors were herded into the local Serbian orthodox church, where, one by one, they were murdered with spiked clubs.

Memories in the Balkans are very long, and in the Serbian capital, Belgrade, as well as throughout modern Yugolavia, many Serbs were unable to shake off old grudges, still referring to Croatians as the 'Ustase' and fascists. They were fearful, therefore, for the safety of their Slav cousins, who might find themselves residents in a newly independent Croatian republic. By the same token, Croatians (and Bosniaks) called the Serb nationalists and their paramilitaries 'Chetniks', a reference to the brutal Serb monarchist partisans of World War II. This epithet was not undeserved, since some reservists and Serb paramilitaries later gloried in wearing the distinctive Chetnik forage cap, a version of which was later adopted by the Bosnian Serb Army (BSA) as their uniform headwear. In turn, the Serbs disparagingly referred to Bosniaks as '*balijas*' (a racist term to do with Hindus) and 'Turks', even though they are of the same racial background.

The modern tensions between Belgrade and the Croat capital, Zagreb, stemmed from the existence of sizeable Serb-minority populations in Croatia, to the east in Krajina and to the west in Slavonia, that could not, from Milosevic's point of view, be abandoned to Croatia's resurgent nationalists. Milosevic adopted an aggressive strategy. His aim was that Serbs of Croatia would form part of Greater Serbia, with the Croatians expelled from the crucial border areas in both east and west Croatia and the Bosniaks evicted from eastern and southern Bosnia. Milosevic's newly espoused brand of Serb expansionism led to Croatian retaliation, while at the same time Croatian nationalists relished the provocation as an opportunity to drive out its own Serbs. This strain in relations led to a war between Belgrade and Zagreb that produced horrors on both sides not too dissimilar to the atrocities of the Ustase period. By the end of the conflict, in 1995, an estimated 200 000 Serbs had been driven out of their homes by an increasingly effective Croat army assisted by accompanying Ustase-style irregulars, but not before the Serb forces had created havoc in Croatian territory.

Tudjman and Milosevic were greedy for additional territory in Bosnia, with its more freely mixed population of Bosniaks, Serbs and Croatians, and both had designs on the mountainous republic, designs that did not include a role for the Muslim majority. As part of the move towards a Greater Serbia, from 1992 onwards, Milosevic condoned a campaign of ethnic cleansing by Belgrade's surrogates, the Bosnian Serbs, which was intended to drive the Muslims out of the east and south. Meanwhile, Tudjman, by this time president of an independent Croatia, was moving troops and irregulars into northern and western Bosnia, intending to annexe large portions of the republic for the new Croatian state. In the ensuing war for territory, the Serb campaign in Bosnia tended to follow a consistent pattern. First, Bosnian Serb reservists and irregulars would move into an ethnically mixed area, terrorising and murdering the non-Serbian inhabitants, often with the assistance of the local Serbs; then would come the heavily armed JNA, still under Belgrade's control and purportedly acting to stabilise the local conflict. In effect, the JNA elements in Bosnia, manned largely by Bosnian Serb soldiery, merely consolidated Serb territorial gains. From 1992 to 1995, the conflict ebbed and flowed, with the heavily armed BSA, covertly supported by the JNA, able to take territory but not able to establish total victory over the lightly armed but resilient Muslim regular and irregular forces. Indeed, the generality of BSA forces gained a reputation among their enemies as half-hearted infantrymen who preferred to let the artillery do the hard work. When the United Nations Protection Force (UNPROFOR) became involved, in 1992, a similar and parallel process began to occur, with BSA and JNA forces initially occupying new territory by terrorising the non-Serb inhabitants, and UNPROFOR called in to separate the combatants, but in reality consolidating Serb gains.

The Croatian campaign in Bosnia was fought differently. Zagreb's troops, with the help of military assistance from friendly nations to the north and military training from the west, became increasingly well organised and well armed. As the fighting progressed, the Croats eventually gained the upper hand against the Bosnian Serbs in the north and, allowing for a mid-war opportunistic change of alliance, against the Bosniaks.

During the fighting, atrocities were perpetrated by all participants. Bosniak forces were supplemented by several hundred foreign Islamic fighters, many of whom were gathered into the irregular 'El Mujahed' unit in 1993. It was later acerbically remarked that these foreigners 'differed considerably' in their 'fighting methods'; they were responsible for the torture, rape and murder of Serb captives in central Bosnia, notably in their 'detention' camp at Orasac. The Croats also carried out atrocities, mainly during a campaign to retake Krajina from separatist Serbs, although, compared with the deliberate and sustained campaign of terror instigated by Serb nationalists in 1992, Croatian atrocities were relatively sporadic and small-scale. Nevertheless, they did occur, with the massacre of approximately 120 civilian Serbs in Gospic late in September 1991 the most significant. Also, in 1993, at an army barracks near Mostar, the Croatians incarcerated Muslim prisoners, their former allies, in half-buried fuel tanks in the heat of summer and in appalling conditions, clearly a criminal act and later recognised as such by the local Croat leadership. It was the Serbs, however, in particular the Bosnian Serbs, who gained a special kind of notoriety during the fighting of 1992 to 1995, for large-scale acts of obscene and grisly violence, mutilation, rape and murder. And it is Serbian denial, as well as that of their supporters, that remains an unresolved element in Balkan and international politics. An examination of three major atrocities will demonstrate how the denial operates.

Omarska and Trnopolje Camps

> There is nothing quite like the sight of the prisoner desperate to talk and to convey some terrible truth that is so near yet so far, but who dares not. Their stares burn, they speak only with their terrified silence, and eyes inflamed with the articulation of stark, undiluted, desolate fear-without-hope.
>
> Ed Vulliamy, on Serb detention camps, 1994

In the summer of 1992, a Bosniak community leader implored Roy Guttman, the Belgrade correspondent for New York's *Daily News*, to visit Serb detention camps in northern Bosnia, where the BSA had been making inroads into Bosniak territory. What he found there—Bosniak men imprisoned in apparently brutal, even fatal, conditions—caused a media sensation, temporarily distracting the western press from the ghastly spectator sport of the Serb siege of Sarajevo. At that very time, Radovan Karadzic, the Bosnian Serb leader, was in London for talks, and his media advisers counselled him to allow journalistic access to other camps, presumably to show that the Bosnian Serbs had nothing to hide. Unfortunately for Karadzic, and for the imprisoned Bosniaks and Croats, the Bosnian Serbs had plenty to hide.

The International Red Cross had already been trying, without success, to gain access to Omarska camp, situated in a former mining complex near Prijedor. There, some 1000 Bosniak and Croatian prisoners, including the administrative, social and political Bosniak elite of Prijedor, were being held in horrific conditions. Following Guttman's initial scoop, further horrors were revealed by an intrepid ITN crew fronted by reporters Penny Marshall and Ian Williams, and by *Guardian* reporter Ed Vulliamy in August 1992. The most vivid image of their visit to Omarska and Trnopolje was that of Fikret Alic, a Bosniak prisoner in Trnopolje. Alic had wasted away to skin and bone, much like the victims of the Nazi concentration camps shown in films of the liberation of Europe in 1945. The combination of the ITN footage, the news photo stills taken from the film and Vulliamy's report led to a sensation worldwide and, together with the prior shelling of Dubrovnik and the siege of Sarajevo, did irreparable harm to Serb credibility and to any nascent Bosnian Serb public relations campaign, not that public relations were uppermost in Bosnian Serb thinking in July 1992, since they had already seized 70 per cent of Bosnia, creating an exodus of more than one million refugees.

Investigations later revealed that there were four large detention camps: terminal camps at Omarska and Keraterm, and transit camps at Trnopolje and Manjaca. At the terminal camps, prisoners were categorised as A class (Muslim leaders and volunteer combatants), B class (drafted combatants) and C class (the rest). A class prisoners were, as a rule, murdered. The others were generally held in inhuman conditions, awaiting death through maltreatment, or an exchange. Prisoner mortality rates in the Bosnian Serb camps are unknown, but the overall impression created by the discovery of the Omarska and Trnopolje camps, together with evidence of the ethnic cleansing of the occupied territory, was that the Bosnian Serbs were possibly engaged in genocidal activities against their former neighbours.

The Market Place Massacre

> A walk down any side street in Sarajevo provides visible evidence that nowhere was safe from the random mortar: the city's streets are pockmarked everywhere with the distinctive splatter of mortar impact points. The local people call these imprints 'Sarajevo roses'—the colour of blood.
>
> Laura Silber and Allan Little, 1997

On 5 February 1994, during a lull in the shelling, hundreds of the besieged inhabitants of Sarajevo hurried out of their houses, apartments and shelters to buy, to trade and to gather at in an improvised market place in front of the Catholic cathedral, the steps of which had traditionally been a hang-out for young Sarajevans. Two years into the siege of the city, the cramped space in front of the cathedral had been turned into a shabby place of barter with stalls displaying selections of used electrical equipment and second-hand clothes. Shortly after noon, and without warning, a large mortar shell plummeted into the packed market, killing sixty-eight civilians and wounding more than 200.

Television footage and news photos of the massacre were carried by agencies around the world. Bosnian president Alija Izetbegovic announced that the Bosnians of Sarajevo felt 'condemned to death'. Peter Jennings, veteran American Broadcasting Corporation reporter and anchorman, interviewed the Bosnian prime minister Haris Silajdzic, who was similarly indignant. Radovan Karadzic, by this time the president of the secessionist (Bosnian) republic of Serbia, in yet another public relations disaster denied Serb responsibility and blocked aid convoys into Sarajevo until his community was absolved of all blame. He then adopted another tack, alleging first that a bomb had been planted by the Muslims and second that bodies had been brought over from the Sarajevo mortuary to inflate the death rate.

The market place massacre was reminiscent of a previous incident, on 27 May 1992, portrayed in Michael Winterbottom's film *Welcome to Sarajevo* (1997), in which a bread queue was shelled, killing twenty-two civilians. On that occasion, a whispering campaign started that alleged that the Muslim Bosnian forces, desperate to gain western sympathy, were shelling their own people, a view egregiously supported by Canadian UNPROFOR general Lewis Mackenzie, who had been in distant Belgrade at the time of the explosion. Subsequent to the queue shelling, on 30 August 1992, further Serb shelling killed fifteen Sarajevans gathered at a food market in the outer suburbs; on 12 July 1993, a Serb shell landed among Bosniaks queueing for water in the suburb of Dobrinje; and on the day before the February 1994 market place massacre, nine Sarajevans were killed in yet another shelling, this time of a food queue in Dobrinje. Following the 1994 market place killings, a United Nations Military Observer spokesman, Major Jose Labandeira, announced that almost all the shelling during that week had been by Serb forces and that on the day preceding the massacre all shells fired had come from Serb positions. The military observers had recorded no artillery fire from Bosniak positions.

A later United Nations (UN) investigation revealed that in the 1994 market place massacre, the mortar shell had probably originated from the city's north-east, where both Bosniak and Serb forces were situated. Any conclusion about who did what has to be tempered by the knowledge that mortar bombs normally need ranging before they are fired for effect, so an aimed first-time hit on a smallish target hidden by tall, surrounding buildings is highly improbable. Indeed, as anyone who has been to Sarajevo knows, the city centre consists mainly of a tangle of narrow streets overlooked by apartment buildings and offices that are three, four and even five storeys high. The most likely scenario is that in each of the cases cited the casualties were caused by a round, or rounds, lobbed speculatively by one of the many Serb mortar crews besieging the city.

Apart from the horror of the casualty figures, the more significant consequence of the market place massacre was its impact on western political and public opinion, which pushed the USA closer to anti-Serb intervention through air strikes. In the interim, the Serbs were told to pull their artillery back, and they did comply, but more draconian tactics against the BSA now had strong domestic public support in the USA, since the Bosnian Serbs had, in February 1994, quite clearly moved into the territory of the irredeemably wicked. Accordingly, in August 1995, a similar shelling attack produced NATO air strikes against the Serbs under the operational title of 'Deliberate Force', a move that coerced the Serbs to the negotiating table and into signing the December 1995 Dayton Peace Accord.

Srebrenica

> Near the center of the town, a Muslim man who looked to be about thirty years old surrendered to the [BSA] group. He was of military age and could have been a soldier.... [BSA Lieutenant Milorad] Pelemis eyed the Muslim. 'Slaughter him', he said to Zoran, a new man in the unit. In one swift motion, Zoran stepped behind the terrified man, pulled his head backward and slashed his throat.
>
> Drazen Erdemovic, BSA sergeant, 1996

> Get on with it. There is nothing anyone can do to us now.
>
> Milan Jolovic, BSA Drina Wolves brigade commander, 1995

> The bullet strikes that you see here on this wall opposite the door ... and the bullet strikes outside are multiple gunshot strikes straight throughout the building.... [The Bosnian Serb forces]

stood outside these windows ... and threw grenades in through the windows.... Some of the material on the wall here is human flesh and blood splattered from the bodies [of Bosniak prisoners]. This is not filth, it's people.

                    Dean Manning, Australian federal police officer, c. 2003

In the autumn of 1992, as Bosnian Serb forces advanced into Muslim and ethnically mixed areas, terrorising and driving out their adversaries, three eastern enclaves remained under Bosniak control: Zepa, Gorazde and Srebrenica. The last of these is situated within a loop of the Drina river as it courses its way along the border with Serbia proper, protruding provocatively, from a Serb perspective, into the republic of Serbia itself. For the Bosnian Serb forces, each of these recalcitrant islands of Bosniak settlement remained an annoyance since, in an eastern Bosnia that was now largely abandoned by Bosniaks, they contained residual Bosnian government forces and Muslim refugees. An additional exasperation was that Srebrenica was situated not far from the mountain retreat of Pale, Radovan Karadzic's 'capital'. All three towns were next on the BSA's list for 'cleansing'.

    Of the three Bosniak enclaves, Srebrenica was probably the most symbolically challenging, because its relatively few, lightly armed defenders had repulsed the largely unenthusiastic Serb infantry in the initial 1992 attack. By early 1993, Srebrenica was besieged, its estimated 40 000 mix of troops, townspeople and refugees surrounded by the BSA, led by former JNA officer General Ratko Mladic. In mid-April, after a bitter winter of starvation and with the Srebrenica defenders running out of ammunition, Mladic was ready to move. The Bosnian Serb forces advanced directly into Srebrenica. Anxious to avoid a bloodbath, and after intense UNPROFOR negotiations with Mladic, the UN Security Council declared Srebrenica a 'safe area'. A ceasefire was agreed and arrangements were made for disarming the remnant BSA troops and for the repatriation of the wounded.

TALES OF HEARTLESS DENIAL FROM THE BALKANS

The safe area concept was an improvisation intended to appease international opinion (already outraged at the possibility of further Serb atrocities) and to block Mladic's campaign. As it happened, the compromise was a cosmetic exercise. In the face of an unclear but highly public UN mandate, Mladic backed off, but only temporarily, since the BSA strategy to develop a Greater Serbian, Bosniak-free corridor in the Srebrenica–Upper Drina region remained in place.

Within Srebrenica itself, the disarmament process was not complete. Although UNPROFOR took charge of some Bosniak heavy weapons and occasionally acted against blatant, individual weapons infringements, there remained a considerable force of lightly armed defenders, some of whom were under the direction of their aggressive warlord-style commander Naser Oric, who over the next two years waged a guerilla war, a campaign that included several atrocities against surrounding Serb settlements.

In June 1995, however, Oric was mysteriously recalled to Sarajevo by the Bosnian government, together with several of his senior officers. While he was absent, some of his remaining forces broke out of the siege and sacked two local Serb villages. Mladic, purportedly infuriated by these attacks and having finally decided to implement his BSA strategy, ignored Srebrenica's negligible UN protection and began to bombard it. On 6 July, taking the campaign a step further, the BSA issued an ultimatum to evacuate the town. By this time, the Bosnian government had clearly all but given up on the enclave, and UNPROFOR was unwilling to take decisive action against Mladic's forces. This was partly because the BSA had taken a contingent of Dutch UN troops hostage but also because Srebrenica, a straggling valley community surrounded by heavily forested mountains and hills, was virtually indefensible: sniping and mortar strikes into the heart of the town were a simple and deadly matter. UNPROFOR did, after much delay, send in a token air strike by two Dutch warplanes on 11 July, but, in the face of the advancing Serbs, the Dutch ground troops, together with approximately 25 000 refugees, retreated to the nearby UNPROFOR camp, 7 kilometres north at Potocari, a small industrial settlement. The trek to the camp and the arrival at Poticari produced scenes of utter chaos, the refugees quickly discovering that the camp could house only about a fifth of their number at most. The rest clustered outside the camp.

Meanwhile, the BSA advanced into the undefended Srebrenica, led by a triumphant Mladic. As his men and tanks poured through the main street, Mladic spoke to video: 'Here we are on 11 July 1995, in Serb Srebrenica, the day before one of the greatest Serbian holidays. We give this town to the Serbian people. The time has finally come, after the rebellion of the Dahijas, to take revenge against the Turks in this place'. Later, Mladic sent for Lieutenant Colonel Karremans, the hapless commander of the Dutch contingent, and offered him a glass of plum brandy as they watched a Serb soldier slaughter a pig with a knife. 'That is how we deal with our enemies', Mladic remarked. Next morning, Mladic headed off to Potocari to talk to the Dutch and to supervise the arrangements for the remaining refugees. There, in a scene staged for the BSA video crew, an event occurred that, in retrospect, is almost as unsettling as the Omarska and Trjnopolje camps film clip. Mladic, mingling with the apprehensive refugees, announced that those who wanted to leave could do so. 'Don't be afraid of anything. Easy. Let the women and the children go first. Thirty buses will be there. We will transport you to Kladanj. Don't be afraid. Nobody will do anything to you.' He patted the heads of Bosniak children reassuringly. One of the boys, aged about twelve, anxiously clutched a large, white pet rabbit to his chest.

Prior to Mladic's outwardly affable and reassuring walkabout, Lieutenant Colonel Vujadin Popovic (Mladic's chief of security in the BSA Drina corps) had spoken with Momir Nikolic, the BSA Bratunac brigade's chief of intelligence and security:

> At that time Lt. Colonel Popovic told me that the thousands of Muslim women and children in Potocari would be transported out of Potocari toward Muslim-held territory near Kladanj and

that the able-bodied Muslim men within the crowd of Muslim civilians would be separated from the crowd, detained temporarily in Bratunac, and killed shortly thereafter.

What happened next is a matter of great controversy, but the best estimate is that over the next week, close to 8000 Bosniak males between the ages of about thirteen and seventy were either corralled for execution or hunted down like animals in the Srebrenica and Bratunak area and the surrounding hills. The task was undertaken by BSA troops, Serb irregulars and Serbian police formations. Some victims were tortured and murdered singly while others were shot in groups. Many others died of their wounds or from exhaustion, starvation or dehydration after fleeing in small clusters over the mountains to supposed safety in Bosniak-held Tuzla, 55 kilometres to the north. To avoid an assured fate, others committed suicide. One whole column, made up partly of armed men, broke out and headed for Tuzla, but they were harassed along the way by Serb ambushes and affected by heat and exhaustion, and many died on the journey.

All of this came as a direct consequence of an orchestrated campaign of Bosnian Serb brutality. The perpetrators of the massacres, Mladic's forces, took six days to complete their ghastly work, even gloatingly recording video footage of haggard Bosniaks climbing steep hillside tracks under guard and on their way to an almost certain death. Srebrenica was the worst post-1945 mass murder to take place in Europe.

Nationalist Denial

> One thousand prisoners of war were executed [at Srebrenica]. It is an atrocious crime, but it is not genocide.
>
> Vojislav Seselj, Serb paramilitary leader, 2007

Serb nationalist denial takes several forms: there is the 'we did not commit genocide' tactic—the outright lie; the approach that says 'they got what they deserved'—the justifiable reprisal; the 'what is this flawed evidence?' tack; and the 'they did it to themselves to gain sympathy' gambit.

Radovan Karadzic, the Bosnian Serb leader, was the master of the outright lie. After an ominous and accurate announcement to the Bosniaks in a pre-war parliamentary debate—'I warn you. You'll drag Bosnia down to hell. You Muslims aren't ready for war—you could face extinction'—he orchestrated, together with Belgrade's help, a policy of attempted mass expulsion and extermination that was the fulfilment of his threat. And yet, when attending the London talks at the time of the detention camp revelations, he blandly assured reporters (in English) that 'we give full guarantees according to Geneva Convention for civilians', a theme taken up by Milosevic himself during his post-war trial at the Hague, at which he asserted (also in English) that 'in the Serbian tradition and in the tradition of the Serbian army, a prisoner of war and an unarmed man are holy. Everyone who infringes that holiness must answer for his actions, but neither the army nor the police did so'. His final phrase was meant to indicate Serb innocence but unintentionally gave the game away in an unguarded Freudian slip. Finally, as late as 2007, Vojislav Seselj, former commander of Serb paramilitaries and a self-confessed participant in the unholy and murderous 'cleansing' of the city of Zvornik in 1992, still clung to a denialist position. Defiant, he angrily informed the ICTY that the court was anti-Serbian and had falsified modern Serbian history.

A distinct lack of Serb holiness is also evident in the justifiable reprisal approach, based on the morality that two wrongs make a right and seen at its worst in the Srebrenica massacre. Here, murderous but admittedly quite localised attacks on Serb villagers by marauding members of the Srebrenica resistance were, justifiably in some Serb eyes, responded to by the massacre of thousands of Muslim men and boys. The victims of Srebrenica were murdered as after-the-event hostages, a war crime in its own right, but the Serb rationale for the deaths served only as a cover-up for their previous and continuing policy of genocide against Muslim males. The justifiable reprisal ethos, begun in Kosovo back in 1987 with those false claims of rapes and beatings by Muslims, was continued by the Serbs in Bosnia in the mid-1990s. Even after the Bosnian war had been brought to a close by the 1995 Dayton agreement, the Serbs were at it again: in the Kosovo conflict of 1999, General Nebojsa Pavkovic, the Serbian commander, described the Serbian paramilitary police's reprisals against the inhabitants of the Kosovar village of Prekaj as a 'standard police operation'. Questioned about accusations of atrocities, he replied calmly, 'I don't remember the other details'. The 'other details' included the summary shooting of fifty-three members of one Kosovar family alone.

The young Serbian lawyer Dragoslav Ognjanovic, who advised Slobodan Milosevic during his war crimes trial, provided a politically characteristic response to anti-Milosevic accusations at the trial and a useful illustration of the Serb 'flawed evidence' argument. While giving evidence, Milan Babic, former mayor of the rebellious Serb town of Knin, had turned against his former boss Milosevic, outlining the strategy devised by the Serbian president and by the Knin Serbs to outwit the Croats. In response, Ognjanovic rejected outright the evidence of the key former ultra-nationalist commander, dismissing it not on the facts but on Babic's statement—credible, detailed and important as it had been—as a betrayal of Serb values, which, according to Ognjanovic, are based on a Balkan version of the Mafia's *omuerta*: 'Mr Milan Babic, they [the prosecution team] said is a most important insider. I have to laugh on that. His testimony was against his own people, against his grandfathers, against his child, or kids, and grandchild. It was against past times and it is against future of Serbian people'. Serb *omuerta* had not, however, prevented Vojislav Seselj, the ultra-nationalist paramilitary leader, from boasting of the Belgrade connection during the vicious ethnic cleansing of the Muslim-majority city of Zvornik, the first major attempt to clear Bosnia of Muslim locals:

> The Zvornik [ethnic cleansing] operation was planned in Belgrade. . . . The Bosnian Serb forces took part in it. But the special units and the best combat units came from Serbia. These were police units—the so-called Red Berets—special units of the

Serbian Interior Ministry of Belgrade.... The operation had been planned for a long time.

The 'they did it to themselves' denialist argument is attached particularly to the bread queue attack of 1992 and the market massacres of 1994, and it circulated widely within the community of UN observers in Sarajevo, particularly among the French. This was because during the siege of Sarajevo there were several incidents involving Bosniak fighters who, it was argued (probably with some legitimacy), had acted provocatively in order to broaden the conflict. The aim was to draw the reliably and predictably explosive Serbs into more noticeably disproportionate responses to Bosniak pinprick attacks, the hoped-for consequence being international intervention that would favour the Bosniaks. The upshot was that small-scale Bosniak infringements of the rules of war were seen by Serb nationalists as part of a larger Bosniak policy of deliberate escalation (of which the 1992 and 1994 massacres in Sarajevo were a part). This argument has been backed by a pattern of gratuitous, absurd and obfuscatory Serbian accusations; for example, when Tudjman's palace was rocketed in 1991, Belgrade announced that the Croats had done it themselves. These kinds of suspicions were amplified by Serb leaders, including Karadzic, and became part of the post-war mythology, based solely on selective perception which ignored any firm evidence that the shells used were indeed Bosniak, or any sign of a causal relationship between the firing of a few shots at UN observers by Muslim defenders and the lobbing of mortar shells into the city centre.

All in all, there remains a continuing Serb suspicion of all accusations that Serbs initiated atrocities, based on a long-established perception of outside hostility to their cause. The suspicion was fomented originally by the Milosevic camp, by the Karadzic faction and by bigoted nationalist propaganda in the Serbian media during the 1990s, particularly in RTS, the main government-linked Belgrade television station; it remains entrenched in some sections of Serb society. This residual bias towards the Serbs can be seen, for example, in a 2006 survey of Serbia by the

Organization for Security and Co-operation in Europe, which showed that while 71 per cent of Serbian respondents had heard that a large number of Bosniak civilians had been killed at Srebrenica, only 50 per cent of these believed that the claim was true. Forty-three per cent of these respondents believed that the massacre was a crime, while 28 per cent acknowledged the occurrence of the massacre but held the view that it was not a crime. On the other hand, 78 per cent of respondents had heard that Croatian forces had committed war crimes against Serbs in western Slavonia in 1995, with 75 per cent of these believing the accusations to be true and 70 per cent thinking that the Croatian behaviour constituted a crime. This clearly demonstrated a more credulous approach to anti-Croatian propaganda. Overall, the denialist tendencies in the survey came from supporters of the radical nationalist and more mainstream nationalist parties: the Democratic Party of Serbia, the New Serbia Party and the Serbian Radical Party. Supporters of what may be called the acceptance position tended to come from the more moderate Democratic Party.

The survey did at least show that majority public opinion in Serbia, concerned primarily with the economy, unemployment and judicial corruption, was looking forward to the new constitution and wanted simply to move on. This is not the case, however with western denialists who are still fighting a bitter and mainly internet-based war of words.

'A Curious Bunch'

> Hungry for controversy, a sizeable portion of London's intelligentsia lined up to support Living Marxism. They rallied round those who had named me and others as liars in the name of free speech—so why not name them too, the great, the good and the up-and-coming? Fay Weldon, Doris Lessing, Harold Evans, Toby Young ... a diverse coterie, eager to sip Living Marxism's apparently excellent claret at the ICA, to eat their canapés and run alongside the rotten bandwagon of revisionism.
>
> Ed Vulliamy, 2000

In 1997, in a sardonic feature piece called 'Second Front: A Shot That's Still Ringing', *Guardian* writer Luke Harding characterised the pro-Serb (and anti-western intervention) denialists as a 'curious bunch'. At a Church House (London) rally in March 1997, Harding encountered what he described as the trendy bourgeois British Marxists of the Revolutionary Communist Party splinter group. He also came across an 'odd' German journalist, an ex-US State department official called George and a gang of 'beautifully-coiffured Serbian ladies with fascistic leanings'. A few days later, the circus moved to Bonn, and, after hearing a talk by Thomas Deichmann, the very same 'odd' German, Harding wandered into the bar of the Press Club, where he asked a fellow drinker, one of the British Marxists, about interventionism generally. Should Britain and France have intervened over Poland and Czechoslovakia back in the 1930s? 'No', the Marxist reportedly announced. 'That would have been fighting for the British ruling classes.'

Forgetting nothing and learning nothing, the Marxists of the Revolutionary Communist Party were apparently in an ideological time warp: it was 1939 and Palme Dutt all over again, but this time the imperialist war theory was being applied to Yugoslavia, with the assistance of what Ed Vulliamy called a diverse coterie of revisionists. This included the staff of a glossy, small-circulation British Trotskyite journal entitled *Living Marxism*, ex-trainee engineer and aspirant journalist Thomas Deichmann, Noam Chomsky's former co-author Edward S Herman, onetime 1960s student and Maoist radical Jared Israel and, most quixotic of them all, prominent activist, journalist and US émigrée Diana Johnstone, author of *Fools' Crusade: Yugoslavia, NATO and Western Delusions*, a book that reads as an anti-western, pro-Serbian tirade. If the miscellaneous makeup of this varied array of polemical talent looks familiar to students of other forms of denial, it is because the supporters of what may be called the Living Marxism school of thought on Yugoslavia is the mirror image of assorted far-right dissenters. When it comes to denial in history, form appears to follow function, with widely varied agendas coming together for an ideological purpose—in this case, the discrediting of western intervention.

Living Marxism and 'The Picture That Fooled the World'

> One night, while I was going through the pictures again at home, my wife pointed out an odd little detail. If Fikret Alic and the other Bosnian Muslims were imprisoned inside a barbed wire fence, why was the wire fixed to the poles on the side of the fence on which they were standing? As any gardener knows, fences are, as a rule, fixed to the poles from the outside, so that the area to be enclosed is fenced in. It occurred to me then that perhaps it was not the people in the camp who were fenced in behind the barbed wire, but the team of British journalists.
>
> Thomas Deichmann, 1997

The connection between *Living Marxism* and Thomas Deichmann began in February 1997, when the journal re-published Deichmann's article 'The Picture That Fooled the World' in a translation from the original German. The article professed to be an analysis of the ITN crew's 1992 trek to the Omarska and Trnopolje camps. Deichmann had visited Bosnia as a self-styled 'media expert' following his appearance at the ICTY trial of Serb war criminal Dusko Tadic in 1996. (Notwithstanding Deichmann's evidence, Tadic was convicted.) In his criticism of ITN's filming of the camps, Deichmann suggested that the image of the emaciated and incarcerated Fikrit Alic that had so shocked pubic opinion was staged by the television crew. The purpose of the fabrication, he alleged, was to create the false impression that the Serb detention centres were Belsen-like concentration camps. Using his newly acquired gardening knowledge (see extract above), Deichmann argued that the ITN crew filmed Alic from *inside* a barbed-wire enclosure, and that the Muslim prisoners were at liberty, *outside* the enclosure. According to Deichmann, the prisoners were voluntarily gathered in a collection centre.

In the eyes of many who saw them, the resulting pictures left the false impression that the Bosnian Muslims were caged behind barbed wire ... It was not a prison, and certainly not a 'concentration camp', but a collection centre for refugees, many of whom went there seeking safety and could leave again if they wished.

As it happened, Deichmann and *Living Marxism*'s case was eventually demolished in court. In an uncanny coincidence, and in an inversion of the Irving versus Penguin trial (see Chapter 2), the magazine was sued by ITN for libel in 1997, and the case commenced in February 2000 (coincidentally, just over a month after the Irving suit had begun). ITN won the verdict on 14 March, and, a month later, on 11 April, the Penguin-Lipstadt team won their case as well. The barbed-wire assertions, based as they were on Deichmann's interviews, which had taken place only with local Serbs, were refuted at trial by Dr Idriz Merdzanic, a Bosnian medic who had been imprisoned at Trnopolje and who had witnessed the atrocities and had treated abused inmates. At the libel trial it became quite clear: Trnopolje might not have been a Belsen, but it certainly had been a place in which Bosniak prisoners were tortured, beaten, starved and murdered.

ITN's legal victory imposed a huge £375 000 judgment against *Living Marxism*, plus an estimated £600 000 costs, bankrupting the journal. One would have expected the Deichmann thesis to have been destroyed as well, but not so: supporters of the *Living Marxism* case, such as it was, condemned the legal judgment as an example of corporate bullying and legal bias and pressed on with their portrayal of Alic as a stooge of western capitalist media manipulation. Deichmann's 'picture that fooled the world', after being adopted by the alternative leftist *Project Censored* program in the late 1990s, popped up next on Jared Israel's US-based 'Emperor's Clothes' website. This same Jared Israel produced a pro-Serb video, *Judgment*, a cooperative endeavour with Deichmann and Belgrade's RTS. The resilience of the deniers of Serb atrocities at the camps recognised no obstacles, not even Alic's own testimony about Penny Marshall's visit:

I remember when Penny Marshall arrived about midday. She was the only one who tried to help people in the camp. The Serb translator Igor who translated for ITN was the son of the Serb doctor in the camp. The Muslims had to say on camera it was a gathering centre. They had no choice. I only said my name. The Serbs were standing behind the camera. They said 'Write down the names so we can kill the Muslims'.

According to Alic, the beatings and killings continued after the ITN crew left.

The Follies of *Fools' Crusade*

Part of a plan of genocide? For this there is no evidence whatsoever.

Diana Johnstone, 2001

A Serb commission's final report on the 1995 Srebrenica massacre acknowledged that the mass murder of more than 7800 men and boys was planned.

The New York Times, 9 November 2004

Last month the government of Serb-run Republika Srpska (RS) was said to have accepted an official report that over 7000 Muslims were killed in the [Srebrenica] massacre.

Agence France Presse, 8 November 2004

The International Court of Justice ... found [Serbia] guilty of failing to prevent genocide in the massacre of more than 7000 Bosnian Muslims in the town of Srebrenica.

United Nations News Centre, 26 February 2007

The accumulation of evidence from survivors and guards that the camps were far from collection centres did not deter Diana Johnstone from sticking to the Deichmann position two years after the *Living Marxism* case had been settled. In her book *Fools' Crusade*, published in 2002, she reiterated the barbed-wire fence diversionary argument as if nothing new had been discovered in the previous decade, nor even since 2000. Readers of *Fools' Crusade* may have more than a few qualms about Johnstone's fanciful style of investigation. She blithely attributed the formation of the (allegedly anti-Serb) ICTY to the stir caused by the 'fake' Fikret Alic photo. In what was at best a disingenuous act of reportage in keeping with her style of analysis, she completely ignored the ITN libel case and sourced the Deichmann article not from the notorious *Living Marxism* issue but from a 1998 piece in *Covert Action Quarterly*, an obscure radical publication. Her claim of unconscionable anti-Serb bias was further supported, in her own view, by her allegation that the ICTY was prejudiced in focusing on naming the Serb big fish—Milosevic, Karadzic and Mladic—while only naming minor Croat and Bosniak players. As far as Johnstone was concerned, the ICTY's bias was politically motivated. Serb crimes were judged, even before the evidence was given, to be part of a deliberate policy. Here we have more insincerity, with a question-begging assertion that a deliberate policy of widespread expulsion and extermination by politicians and senior army officials is somehow the same as localised acts of brutality by individual thugs and psychopaths.

Johnstone's approach, a combination of conspiracy theory, selective perception and fanciful supposition, also applies to her analysis of the Sarajevo bread queue massacre of 1992, the market square massacre of 1994 and an additional city centre shelling in 1995. For Johnstone, each of these has to be placed in a causal relationship with larger, global events: the UN sanctions against Belgrade in 1992, the threat of NATO air strikes against Serb artillery positions around Sarajevo in 1994 and the actual air strikes against Serb positions in 1995. The politically based premise of *Fools' Crusade* is a variation of the Chomskyan view that the (mainly US) mass media are in cahoots with big business and the US government to create a climate of opinion favourable to whatever the exploitative, globalised, imperialist capitalist activity of the moment may be. Johnstone has inserted the 1990s Balkans conflict as a case study into this framework; it is attention-grabbing, but it means that the theory comes first and the carefully selected theory-backing evidence comes second.

Johnstone's book has become a talisman for deniers of Serb-instigated Bosnian suffering. It is, however, a travesty of historical methodology. It commences with an ideologically based premise and continues by cherry-picking the evidence to suit Johnstone's case, all the while stoutly ignoring inconvenient facts that either contradict or fail to support her contentions and relying throughout on supposition, unsubstantiated claims and the misrepresentation of opposing views. In a list of suppositional statements, Johnstone targets the Bosniaks as the beneficiaries of these sinister connections, she asserts that, *ergo*, they carried out the massacres themselves. One of her wilder claims is that 'veterans of the war in Afghanistan and Algerian Islamic terrorists, for whom Sarajevo's fun-loving, often hard drinking inhabitants were not exactly their own people ... *might* [emphasis added] have few qualms about killing a number of Sarajevo citizens'.

Johnstone takes a Chomskyan view towards the evidence itself, a view which can be briefly summarised as follows: there are three characterisations of atrocities in media reporting: 'our' (US or western) atrocities, which are explained away or discounted by western media; 'benign' atrocities, which go unreported or under-reported because they don't concern us; and 'their' (the notional enemy's) atrocities, which are given massively unfavourable coverage. Chomsky's broad point, and it is a valid one if adopted in a balanced fashion, is that 'our' atrocities deserve the same kind of analysis as 'their' atrocities; but Johnstone does not follow this precept, failing to examine diligently Serb atrocities while amplifying Muslim atrocities. She also alleges that there are Muslim conspiracies but dismisses the well-documented policy of Serbian expansionism. She castigates the western media for fomenting anti-Serbian opinion but fails to comment on the crucial role of the Serbian media in maliciously whipping up Serb nationalism. Indeed, at the heart of the Johnstone argument is the view that Serbia, the last European socialist republic, has been the victim of a western-led conspiracy abetted by the Bosniaks and Croats. According to *Fools' Crusade*, the Serbs have been tricked and coerced by US-led diplomacy and 'globalisation' (untrammelled capitalist exploitation), misrepresented to a duped western audience by a capitalist press and consequently attacked by gung ho and overwhelmingly powerful armed forces (NATO).

One of the key demonstrations of the tendentious nature of Johnstone's approach in *Fools' Crusade* is the nine-page analysis of events at Srebrenica in July 1995. Johnstone's opening remarks immediately cloud the issue of what happened in that stricken Bosnian town: 'The difficulty in knowing the truth about Srebrenica began with the fact that before any solid information was available, Srebrenica had already become an important symbol and overwhelmingly political weapon'. Implicit in this loaded statement is the view that we will never be able to get to the bottom of what happened during a Serb atrocity, a conveniently relativistic approach. The next phase of Johnstone's argument concerns the 'safe area' status of Srebrenica, which she claims was not demilitarised (Srebrenica, as we have seen, was not *fully* demilitarised). She alleges that the Bosniaks attacked Serbs, and that is essentially as far as her discussion of the 'safe area' goes. She sanguinely ignores the international arms embargo that heavily favoured the JNA and the BSA, and the Serb siege of Srebrenica between 1993 and 1995, in which the BSA used sniping and heavy weapons against the town; she also expediently overlooks Serb harassment of UNPROFOR staff and UNPROFOR-guarded humanitarian aid convoys, remarking instead that the convoys were used to smuggle weapons, a claim based solely on an unsourced German foreign ministry statement.

Johnstone asserts that the Bosniak commander Naser Oric led murderous raids and that these were, together with other atrocities against the Serbs, ignored by western media, as if, somehow, there were a causal connection between, on the one hand, the sins of Oric and the exaggerations of the western media and, on the other hand, the outlook of the generality of the inhabitants of Srebrenica. Johnstone maintains that to end these Bosniak raids, the BSA's regional command planned to take over only the area surrounding Srebrenica—again, an incorrect assertion that has no precise source or real weight, considering later events. Johnstone's next proposition is that the Bosnian government pulled Oric out of Srebrenica as part of an (unproven) conspiracy to divide contested territory between Bosniaks and Serbs, which, Johnstone asserts, 'has aroused the strong suspicion of a calculated sacrifice'. In other words, Sarajevo was happy to hand over the inhabitants of Srebrenica to an army that had a track record of rapine and murder in order to make gains elsewhere and to instigate sympathetic NATO intervention. Again, no substantive, corroborated evidence is offered for these claims, except for an off-the-cuff remark to disgruntled Srebrenicans by Alija Izetbegovic, the cagily noncommittal president of Bosnia. The more likely explanation, and that is all it is, is that Oric and his officers were pulled out because Sarajevo calculated that Mladic would move in on the indefensible Srebrenica and that a captured Oric would be bad for the Bosniak cause, for whatever reason.

Johnstone moves on to assert that the USA (presumably the Clinton government) used the failure of the 'safe area' concept to push the pre-eminence of NATO's later role over that of the UN. This is a *non sequitur.* Johnstone's point may, or may not, be the case, but it is not germane to what actually occurred in and around Srebrenica in July 1995.

We come then to the body count minimalisation tactic common to many denialists. Johnstone states that 'the number of Muslims killed or missing after the fall of Srebrenica is uncertain, and more effort has been made to inflate the figures than to identify and count the real victims'. This is an astonishingly inaccurate but ideologically unsurprising statement, and Johnstone actually contradicts herself a few paragraphs later when dealing with victim identification efforts. Of course the numbers are uncertain, but we do know that many thousands were killed. By 2002 (Johnstone's date of publication), there was a solidly confirmed 2000 dead. (At the time of writing, it is almost certain that the number killed was well over 7000.) Serious internationally backed efforts to identify the dead and missing began in 1996, and while exaggerated Bosniak claims may have been made, Serb assertions of not many dead have also appeared, leading to the question of how these claims actually relate to the large numbers of identified Bosniak bodies in real, primary and secondary mass graves. The denialist logic here is that if some Bosniak and western claims are proven to be overstated, this minor fact completely nullifies the entire moral effect of the realistic sets of casualty figures. When some doubt exists regarding the details, an overwhelming doubt is cast on the totality of the original accusations. This is a completely nonsensical position: Bosniak exaggeration may be a fault but it cannot be blamed for mass murder.

After this, Johnstone makes the arbitrary claim that the Clinton administration used Srebrenica to distract attention from a US-friendly (but very nasty) form of Croatian expansionism and its ethnic cleansing of Serbs in Krajina: another red herring. What Clinton may or may not have been up to and what the Croats were doing in Krajina (and it was not good) have not the faintest bearing on the killing of thousands of Bosniak men and boys on the other side of the former republic, in Srebrenica. While there may have been a relationship between events in Srebrenica and an alleged subsequent Clinton–Croatian connection, there can be no reverse causal relationship between a Clinton–Croatian nexus and events at Srebrenica. This is such an elementary methodological error that it beggars belief.

Finally, Johnstone asserts that the 'executed' Muslims were victims of spontaneous acts of Serb revenge, as if this were some kind of excuse. She actually writes: 'Part of a plan of genocide? For this there is no evidence whatsoever', a claim contradicted by the discovery of thousands of bodies, by the longstanding BSA plan to 'cleanse' the Upper Drina area, by survivor testimony prior to the release of her book and by Momir Nikolic's testimony, made publicly available in the year before Johnstone's book was published.

Johnstone simply refuses to believe that the Serbs deliberately committed genocidal acts in Srebrenica, a belief based on the view that the atrocity does not fit the theory. For Johnstone's thesis to work, she has had to bend the facts to suit her purpose and to inject assumptions galore into her politically inspired narrative.

Nothing in Johnstone's argument changes in the slightest degree the generally accepted analysis. What did actually happen in the Srebrenica region in July 1995 was mass murder on a huge scale, systematically perpetrated by Serb forces, the very Serbs inaccurately described by Johnstone as victims of western deviousness and of a media-inspired fictional saga. It is perfectly legitimate to argue, first, that the USA has had a deplorable foreign policy track record when it comes to dictatorial regimes; second, that the world has seen a post-Soviet growth in exploitative globalisation; third, that the western media can be sensationalist and one-eyed; and fourth, that the US military, at that time, seemed to be over-eager to try out new military tactics and gadgets. But none of these allegations successfully rebuts the contention that expansionist and nationalist Serb policies in Bosnia led to the break-up of Yugoslavia, to a brutal and widespread oppression of Bosnian Muslims and to mass torture, rape and murder in Bosnia. What happened on the ground in Bosnia actually did happen, however hard Johnstone may argue, using both *post-hoc* and straw-man reasoning, about what the politicians, diplomats, press barons and generals were saying, doing or plotting at the time, before or after.

The Chomsky Matter

> History doesn't offer true controlled experiments but it often comes pretty close. So one can find atrocities or abuses of one sort or another that on the one hand are committed by the official enemies and on the other hand are committed by friends and allies or by the favourite state itself. And the question is whether the media accept the government framework or whether they use the same agenda, the same set of questions, the same criteria for dealing with the two cases as any honest outside observer would do.
>
> Noam Chomsky, 2005

Fools' Crusade, while attacking the motes of chaotic and pusillanimous US-European self-interest as well as Bosnian governmental irresolution, is dismissive of the beams of aggressive, vigorous and remorselessly genocidal Serbian behaviour at Srebrenica and the Belgrade-supported ethnic cleansing throughout the former Yugoslavia. Nowhere is this disingenuous, myth-creating approach more evident than in Johnstone's analysis of what happened in eastern Bosnia in July 1995, not that the partiality and the polemical nature of her tract has prevented her point of view from being supported by such radical veteran luminaries as Tariq Ali and John Pilger. The strength of support for Johnstone's view has a direct relationship to the contrarian force of her argument: the more extreme her opinion, the more support she has gathered from knee-jerk, anti-western crusaders, as was the case when Noam Chomsky, unhappy at criticism of Johnstone, offered his public backing to the contentious author.

The Chomsky matter began with a newspaper interview with *Guardian* writer Emma Brockes. Chomsky had already been in hot water many times, particularly in the 1980s for his support for French Holocaust denier Robert Faurisson. Criticism of Chomsky's position at that time was largely based on the false assumption that Chomsky, as a Jew, had given credence to Faurisson, when what Chomsky actually supported was Faurisson's right to express an opinion, however loopy. (Interestingly, this is not so far from Deborah Lipstadt's view that Holocaust denial should not be criminalised, because the repression of free speech through the criminal law system is, in a democratic society, a step in the wrong direction.) Brockes's interview with Chomsky was published on 31 October 2005. Emma Brockes, not generally known for her hard-hitting journalism, began her article in conventional style with some harmless colourful scene-setting on the subjects of Chomsky's office, his liking for fig rolls and his 'nubbly old jumper'. Brockes then got down to business and, as a preface to the core of the article, dropped in the telltale comment: 'There remain suspicions over how [Chomsky] has managed to become an expert, seemingly, on every conflict since the second world war: it is assumed by his critics that he plugs the gaps in his knowledge with ideology'. The interview moved on to what Brockes described as 'ratty exchanges about Bosnia', during which the journalist raised *Living Marxism* and Johnstone's interpretation of the Bosnian conflict. When asked whether or not he regretted his prior published support for Johnstone, Chomsky replied, 'No. [*Fools' Crusade*] is outstanding. My only regret is that I didn't do it strongly enough'. He followed this angry comment with the puzzling statement that *Fools' Crusade* 'may be wrong; but it is very careful and outstanding work'. Brockes wondered aloud how it could be both wrong and outstanding. Chomsky's reply stuck closely to his propaganda model approach:

> Look, there was a hysterical fanaticism about Bosnia in western culture which was very much like a passionate religious conviction. It was like old-fashioned Stalinism: if you depart a couple of millimetres from the party line you're a traitor, you're destroyed. It's totally irrational. And Diane [sic] Johnstone, whether you like it or not, has done serious, honest work. And in the case of Living Marxism, for a big corporation to put a small newspaper out of business because they think something they [ITN] reported was false is outrageous.

Chomsky continued in similar vein, saying that *Living Marxism* was 'probably correct', and, puzzlingly again, adding that the *Living Marxism* case 'had nothing to do with whether LM or Diane [sic] Johnstone were right or wrong ... And if they were wrong, sure; but don't just scream well, if you say you're in favour of that [presumably the *Living Marxism* case] you're in favour of putting Jews in gas chambers'.

The exchanges between Brockes and Chomsky, as Brockes told it, became more strained, with Chomsky announcing that *Guardian* journalist Ed Vulliamy, who was present with the ITN crew at the Serb camps, was 'caught up in a story which is probably not true', later 'exploding' when pushed on the corroborating accounts of Bosniak survivors:

That's such a Western European position. We are used to having our jackboots on people's necks, so we don't see our victims. I've seen them: go to Laos, go to Haiti, go to El Salvador. You'll see people who are really suffering brutally. This does not give us the right to lie about that suffering.

Following the description of this peculiar outburst, Brockes added, in an editorial aside to her readers: 'Which is, I imagine, why ITN went to court in the first place'.

It seems that Chomsky, the radical guru prone to expounding freely on a wide variety of issues but uncertain of his Bosnian details, when confronted on his support for Johnstone's position, floundered. He stuck to his generalised free speech tactic and capitalist media line, loading his response with emotive *non sequiturs* ('gas chambers' and 'jackboots'), ambiguous guesswork ('probably correct' and 'probably not true') and what can only be described as a revealing instance of Freudian projection ('Stalinism'). The article, headlined as 'Chomsky the Denier', caused immediate uproar, with Chomsky incorrectly under attack from gleeful opponents for supporting a denialist position on Srebrenica. There followed an in-house investigation at *The Guardian*, which culminated in Brockes's article being removed from the paper's online archive, with the agreement of both interviewer and interviewee.

All in all, it was something of a storm in a teacup, perhaps, compared with other features of the Bosnian conflict. To his credit, Chomsky kept the Brockes article on his website, defending her right to free (if incorrect, in his view) speech. The more significant event in the Chomsky–Brockes story occurred a month after the original furore, when Diana Johnstone wrote to *The Guardian*, reiterating many of her earlier views. The long (500-word) letter contained a key statement: 'My book', she commented baldly, 'does not attempt to recount what happened at Srebrenica'. To a large extent, this cast further doubt on the authenticity of her reportage. Contrary to Johnstone's claim, *Fools' Crusade* quite clearly does endeavour to give an account of the Srebrenica events, since the section on the massacre begins with the indelible and important comment that 'in trying to understand what happened at Srebrenica, a number of factors should be taken into consideration'. There then follow eight and a half pages, or approximately 4500 words, of 'factors', including, as we have seen, a detailed discussion and topic-based analysis of events. This gives Johnstone's use of the word 'recount' an unusual kind of novelty. The most charitable, but unlikely, interpretation of this construction is that Johnstone had not recently re-read her own work. A less generous view is that her approach to accuracy in reporting is nothing if not consistent. When it comes to explanation, the only consistency required, it seems, is that politics should always trump the evidence—a characteristic denialist trait.

Notwithstanding the post-Srebrenica investigations and revelations and the consequent confirmation of the brutal nature of Serb expansionism in the 1990s, and despite the 2004 admission by the Bosnian Serb authorities themselves that what happened in Bosnia was genocidal, and the remorseless gathering-up of Serb, Croatian and Bosnian indicted war criminals by the ICTY, deniers such as Johnstone remain adamantly convinced that the Bosnian war was a western capitalist plot to destroy the last genuine, but economically struggling, socialist state in Europe. In their more recent updated and unrepentantly tendentious version of the Johnstone thesis, 'The Dismantling of Yugoslavia', Edward S Herman and David Peterson assert, in part, that

> by encouraging the secession of republics, but flatly ruling out some comparable form of self-determination or secession for the Serb minorities who feared for their security in the newly independent state of Croatia and Bosnia-Herzegovina, Western powers ensured that the conflicts would become open wars with all their brutality and ugliness.

The conclusion is simple, therefore, if you believe Herman and Peterson. The Serb people, anxious about their scattered minorities, were forced by the western powers into attacking Croatia and Bosnia. In doing so, they unfortunately found themselves caught up as hapless participants in a brutal and ugly war, a conflict in which Serb behaviour was unfairly characterised in demonic terms by a corrupt and ideologically motivated western media. In this latter-day Marxist analysis, there is no genuine assessment of the idea of a Greater Serbia, discussion of proven Serb war crimes, examination of Serb genocidal behaviour, ethnic cleansing or territorial ambitions; instead, these are constantly presented as little other than western propagandist claims.

In the case of denial over the Bosnian conflict, as it currently stands, the overall impression is that a tiny cabal of European and US leftist radicals, supported by US libertarians, have re-constructed the myth of Serbian victimhood, which ties in nicely with existing nationalistic Serb paranoia. To foster this fairytale, the alleged vilification of Milosevic, Karadzic and Mladic is undermined by, among other things, the portrayal of the ICTY as a partisan tool of western imperialism. In order to relieve guilty Serbs of any feelings of remorse for what happened in the 1990s, Bosniak casualty figures are minimalised and trivialised, while Serb casualties are inflated and given enhanced significance. To justify this pro-Serb position, a global conspiracy is cited.

Finally, to explain all of this, a breathtakingly half-baked analysis is offered, which, in showing a complete lack of respect for the sensibilities of all Balkan moderates as well as for the testimony of Balkan survivors and witnesses, demonstrate little or no humanity on the part either of the unholy crew of Serb extremists or the curious bunch of befuddled intellectuals who continue to perpetrate the lie of virtuous Serb ultra-nationalism.

The continuing campaign of denial about the major atrocities of the Balkan war comes in three disparate forms. The first of these is the Serb nationalist view, either genuinely believed or disingenuously held, that Serbian forces could not and did not commit crimes of this nature; indeed, the Serbs are victims of a huge conspiracy to defame both their nation and their ethnicity. As Milos Milanovic, an ex-paramilitary and ultra-nationalist Serb councillor in modern Serb-dominated Srebrenica, pointed out to *Guardian* writer Ed Vulliamy, in a characteristic rant: 'The [Srebrenica] massacre is a lie. It is propaganda in order to make a bad picture of the Serbian people. The Muslims are lying, they are manipulating the numbers, they are exaggerating what happened. Far more Serbs died at Srebrenica than Muslims'. The second argument is more complex. It consists of a latter-day socialist attack on the alleged western myth of a fiendish Serbia; this ideological position is combined with a Chomskyan analysis of western media bias and US-based libertarianism, all bound together in an unusual alliance. The third argument is wholly predictable and largely inconsequential; it consists of crackpot right-wing hostility to anything Islamic, the kind of neo-Nazi denial already dealt with in the chapter on the Holocaust.

What happened to the Muslims of Bosnia during the 1990s constituted the worst series of political and military outrages in Europe since World War II. The scale and character of these outrages cannot be diminished by denialist counter accusations designed, among other things, to take attention away from the kinds of crimes that Eriz Weitz outlined in his book *A Century of Genocide*, including 'the murder, often in front of their eyes, of loved ones and compatriots; the rapes of family members; the [forced impregnation of] "little Cetniks", the fetuses Muslim victims of rape carried to term or had aborted'. For, as Weitz has pointed out, when it came to atrocities and the ability to carry out atrocities, it was the 'Serb nationalists [who] were the pacesetters, and Serbia, the largest and most populous of the republics of the former Yugoslavia, [that] had the greatest power at its disposal', a conclusion that stands up in the face of some lingering Serbian denialism and notwithstanding any harebrained, latter-day Marxist conspiracy theories.

6

FAILING THE SCHOLARLY TEST

Australian Denial and the Art of Pseudohistory

There are two alternative stories when it comes to Australian denial. This is the short, counter-factual version:

While researching in the Tasmanian archives, writer and critic Keith Windschuttle discovered several apparent discrepancies in the works of historians Henry Reynolds, Lyndall Ryan and Lloyd Robson. Excited by his findings and keen to put the record straight, he wrote to Reynolds and Ryan (Robson died in 1990), pointing out his discoveries. They replied, thanking him for his efforts and agreeing that they might, in some cases, need to revise their views. They told Windschuttle that, although some of his points were arguable, they would either ask their publishers to make appropriate factual corrections in the next editions of their current publications or they would modify the text in question in any new books or articles. Windschuttle, who found some aspects of their scholarship troubling, published a neat, carefully researched and refereed article in *History Australia* that summarised his views, and everybody was much the wiser. The interests of dispassionate scholarship had truly been served, and historical denial remained something that happens in other countries.

Then there is the second, longer story. It begins in 2000, in Sydney. Bob Gould's Book Arcade in King Street, Newtown, is an unlikely Sydney institution. In a city known more these days for its self-promoting glitz than for the seriousness of its scholarly argument, the Book Arcade is a throwback to earlier times when Sydney was a more dynamic centre of intellectual debate. The Arcade itself is a Dickensian, two-storey, book-crammed cavern, squeezed between the more conventional shops and trendy espresso cafés of its grunge suburb. Presided over by the zealously Marxist Gould, who perches behind a high wooden desk in the manner of a counting house overseer, the Arcade is jammed, floor to ceiling, with hundreds of thousands of volumes, some soft porn, some more general reading and a great deal of politics. The books and magazines spill out onto tables and into milk crates, the last creating floor-based obstacles for the engrossed book lover.

It is difficult to imagine how 300 or so eager Sydneysiders packed themselves into Gould's already over-crowded lair on Sunday 12 November 2000 to join in a public debate about history, but this was no commonplace academic discussion. The crowd was there to witness combat between two writers. In the red corner was historian Henry Reynolds, the imposing, calm and sonorous champion of past victimisation of Indigenous Australians. In the blue corner stood Keith Windschuttle, a more staccato, intensely focused speaker, an opponent of what he has called the 'fabrication' of Indigenous Australian history. The gathering at Gould's Arcade, serviced by a hired public address system and moderated by mutually acceptable chairman Hall Greenland, was one of the first of many unabashed head-to-head confrontations between Windschuttle and his opponents, confrontations that became a major part of the rancorous Australian 'History Wars' debates of the early 2000s. Over a period of six years, from around the time of the 2000 Sydney meeting until his controversial mid-2006 appointment to the board of the Australian Broadcasting Corporation, an unrepentant and unyielding Windschuttle cut a belligerent, no-holds-barred swathe through the ideas and attitudes of an astonished and infuriated community of academics (and others), much to the delight and excitement of many mainstream conservative commentators. More disturbingly, his activities also provoked unrestrained glee among anti–Indigenous Australians bigots and racists, for whom Windschuttle, unintentionally, became something of an icon.

The angry debates saw Windschuttle, together with the more vocal of his supporters, accused of a larger, race-based campaign of historical denial, which involved rejection of the view that Tasmanian and mainland Indigenous Australians had been massacred in significant numbers, denunciation of the 'stolen generation' narrative that there had been large numbers of ill-intentioned removals of Indigenous Australian children from their families and disagreement with the idea that there needed to be a national apology to Indigenous Australians. Windschuttle has rejected any denialist or racist labels, arguing that his complaint is only with sloppy and tendentious scholarship. His dispute, as he has explained it, is with the character of historical discussion in Australia, which is supposedly dominated by a masochistic, anti-colonial consensus. The propagators of this smug accord, he has maintained, belong to a cabal of left-leaning and politically correct historians, mainly of European descent, who are, in Windschuttle's eyes, renegades all too eager to denounce an allegedly brutal colonisation of Australia.

At first glance, Windschuttle's interpretation of Australian settlement by European colonists, the main focus of his early writing, appears to be supported by the mainstream view of settler brutality during the early colonial period, as summarised in archaeologist Josephine Flood's highly regarded book *The Original Australians.* Flood argues that there were indeed hideously brutal massacres of Indigenous Australians and that they took place in many locations and over more than a century. The numbers killed in the massacres were, at the lowest, in the tens and, at the highest, probably around the 100 mark. Furthermore, a critical examination of several incidents shows that frontier clashes cannot be classified as undifferentiated massacres. Of a group of four notorious mass killings selected by Flood, one (Pinjarra, Western Australia, 1834) was almost certainly a battle; another (Waterloo Creek, New South Wales, 1838) was a genuine massacre; a third (Forrest River, Western Australia, 1926) was probably a myth; and the fourth (Coniston, Northern Territory, 1928) was a sadistic punitive expedition that murdered an admitted thirty-one (but possibly more) Indigenous desert-dwellers. The more serious killers, as pointed out by Flood and by pioneering authority in the field Richard Broome, included disease, internecine conflict, European-instigated black-on-black violence, infanticide and starvation. The main challenge to Windschuttle's worldview can be found within the community of Australian historians itself, where there have been longstanding and sharp differences of opinion about what universally respected historian John Hirst calls the 'liberal fantasy' of overwhelmingly violent dispossession, widespread mass murder and conscienceless state abduction. Here we have reasoned sceptics such as Hirst to the right and what Flood calls 'passionate advocates' such as Reynolds to the left, leaving, for example, Flood and Broome somewhere in the middle. In consequence, while Windschuttle's case may have some overblown merit when it comes to the massacres, it has little merit when it comes to his fiction of a politically correct consensus among scholars of Australian history.

There are three questions here. What turned Keith Windschuttle into such a scourge of Australian historians? Is he the genuinely disinterested and systematic scholar that he claims? Or is he just a crass, self-publicising denier on the make, as his enemies have suggested?

Keith Windschuttle: A Case of Weak Views Strongly Held

> Since 1985, the dissidents have expanded their territory enormously. Although they still like to portray themselves as embattled outsiders, they are today the ones making all the running—devising the new courses, contracting the publishers, filling the new jobs, attracting the postgraduate students.
>
> Keith Windschuttle, 1994

The bespectacled and balding Windschuttle seems an unlikely contender for the role of pugnacious champion of the Right, unlikely in both appearance and background. To begin with, as a public speaker, he has the uncharismatic demeanour of a nervously determined schoolteacher addressing a resentful morning assembly. And, if we retrace Windschuttle's career in politics, his eventual destination as right-wing guru seems improbable, even incredible, if only because he started off, according to his own view, as a young, superficial, anti-war socialist who was carried away by the spirit of the times. Windschuttle remembers his initial period of political activism in the 1960s as part of a misspent youth, carefully denying that he was in any way an unbending radical, a label later attached to him by infuriated ex-friends and exasperated opponents in an attempt to categorise him as an extremist, first of the Left, then of the Right.

Windschuttle's transition from radical leftism to hardline conservatism is seen as crucial to understanding his *modus operandi* by his adversaries, and even by his supporters, who present a familiar narrative: that of the fundamentalist who moves from one form of extremism to another, the old 'from Catholicism to communism' journey, or, in this case, perhaps, the more recent 'from socialism to neo-conservatism' phenomenon. The process by which Windschuttle became a conservative, however, is less clichéd than that. His 1960s shallow but highly dogmatic leftism was subsequently directed into a campaign against the right-wing misrepresentations of dole bludgers in a 1979 paperback, *Unemployment*. His socialist credentials were further strengthened in his next book, *The Media*, published in 1984, in which he attacked conservative bias in the press. During the next decade, Windschuttle wrote, co-edited or co-authored a series of publications (including Labor government reports) on media influence, employment policy and communication techniques, all standard stuff and nothing out of the ordinary. He had a rather sentimental opinion of himself in this period as a 'civilised Whitlamite'. It was in 1994, in his book *The Killing of History*, that it became clear that a Damascene change had taken place in Windschuttle's thinking. In a 2006 article, 'Why I Left the Left', Windschuttle's own chronology of his slow conversion from Left to

Right places his epiphany at around 1988. Apparently, horrified at the activities of the genocidal regime in Cambodia, he gradually realised that he was on the wrong side: 'The [1970s Pol Pot revelations] were for my generation what the Moscow trials of the 1930s had been for the Depression generation. ... Call me a slow learner, but it took another decade for me to realise that the traditional Labor response of state intervention was not the solution but the problem'.

In 1988, however, when the third edition of *Media*, his readable and mildly socialist treatise, was published, Windschuttle's targets remained much the same as they had been in 1984, including the New Right, globalisation, Rupert Murdoch, Althusserian structuralism and out-of-touch academics. It must have been something in the years after 1988, therefore, that influenced Windschuttle's thinking, pushing him from that soft-left position to the hard-right. One of the first signs of change (spotted by Bob Gould himself) came in the next edition of *Media*, in which Windschuttle revisited globalisation of the media, formerly a bad thing, but now, according to Windschuttle, a good thing, but with no explanation as to how or why he had come to this conclusion. Windschuttle's post-1988 transition went beyond a mere fondness for globalised media; he converted from a mainstream, secular socialist analyst to a believer in an amalgam of historical positivism, economic rationalism and the benefits of right-minded Christianity. Working in a university environment in which, at the time (late 1980s and early 1990s), humanities faculties and media studies departments were teeming with mainly youngish, postmodernist zealots, Windschuttle, a mature age fringe figure, swapped ideological targets by finding a new source of displeasure, in this case the overweening claims of postmodernism in all its forms. In 2005, Windschuttle explained this change to *Financial Times* journalist Virginia Marsh:

> Academia didn't live up to my expectations ... I got tired of left-wing theories and very tired of leftwing people, quite frankly, and, at the same time, the universities filled up with leftwing people.

By the 1980s, to teach humanities you had to be on the leftwing or no one would even consider you. People say the politics of academia are the worst in the world apart from the church. People literally hate each other. I thought, why am I wasting my time?

This was an understandable reaction, perhaps, but in his newly acquired persona as the modern Savonarola, Windschuttle displayed incipient signs of the type of behaviour that later made him, depending on your point of view, one of the most loathed or one of the most fêted public commentators in Australian public life.

After her interview with Windschuttle at the prize-winning Rose Bay Pier restaurant overlooking Sydney Harbour, Virginia Marsh neatly summarised his reasoning and aspirations:

> So, in the early 1990s, he left [university teaching] and set up a printing house, Macleay Press, to publish his own work and those of fellow conservatives. The American market was an obvious target: 'Conservatism is much more institutionalised and a lot richer in the US than in Australia', he says.... 'Most of my guests are American. I like bringing them here to give them the impression that we live like this all the time.'

The Killing of History

> Keith Windschuttle argues with energy and bite, that history as a discipline is in mortal danger of disappearing under a concerted attack from literary critics, social theorists, and historians who have allowed themselves to be seduced by popular social theory. His thesis is complex and he advances it with a dozen or more examples from around the globe. He castigates his targets for starting with a theory and forcing historical data to fit the premise, ignoring or distorting the facts where they fail to fit into the author's preconceptions.
>
> Roberta Sykes, 1994

FAILING THE SCHOLARLY TEST

Windschuttle's 1994 self-published diatribe against postmodernism, *The Killing of History*, inspired by his personal detestation of the changing nature of cultural studies, was greeted with acclaim by conservative commentators, mainly for its denunciation of fashionable Gallic philosophers and their allegedly dangerous influence on historical studies. The book was something of a hit, both domestically and internationally, selling as many as 25 000 copies in the USA, which was at the time embroiled in its own history wars. Windschuttle's timing was perfect, since in the USA's conservative community any anti–politically correct point of view was grabbed with gusto by the customarily anti-intellectual neo-conservatives. The sales figures were all the more remarkable since the Australian version was published by Windschuttle's small publishing outfit, Macleay Press, and since the book was a home-grown work of non-fiction written by an obscure media lecturer who, until 1994, had been invisible on the radar of historical scholarship.

After the publication of *The Killing of History*, however, Windschuttle was no longer obscure. From 1994 onwards, he became a talismanic figure of reactionary opinion, subsequently taking his strongly positivistic beliefs into journalistic practice with the assertion that media students ran an 'incomprehensible and odious gauntlet' of postmodernism. His new-found polemical approach worked beautifully, in history and in media, and it is possible that, as far as Windschuttle was concerned, there was a lesson to be learned from the success of *The Killing of History*. This lesson was that what really worked were exaggerated language—'killing'; exaggerated argument—lumping together such 'killers' as post-positivist thinker Karl Popper, post-structuralist philosopher Michel Foucault, Marxist historian Perry Anderson, Marxist littérateur Terry Eagleton and new-wave narrative historian Simon Schama; and exaggerated external threat—'murdered by literary critics'. This Procrustean synthesising technique certainly got people's attention, leading to books sold, speaking engagements arranged and articles commissioned. Playing intellectual games in these types of Australian forums was unlikely to turn anyone into a millionaire, however; the US market was the better bet for serious riches. The initial benefit of the sensationalist tabloidisation and over-simplification of complex debate cannot have been lost on the ambitious Windschuttle. Relishing the friendly glow of the limelight, he successfully altered his line of rhetoric from history under fire to the pernicious effect of postmodernism on media studies. In attacking the enemies of scholarly history and of rigorous journalism, by the end of the decade he had transformed himself from a tetchy media critic to an ambitious media tart. That was when, to keep the momentum going, it was time to change targets again.

The Fabrication of Aboriginal History

> No one who disagrees with them need now apply for any position teaching history at an Australian university. No graduate student seeking to write a dissenting thesis should waste his time applying to any of our academic schools of history. The ruling intellectual environment that has long controlled Aboriginal history has warned off book publishers.
>
> Keith Windschuttle, 2002

The three rules of Windschuttleism—relentless frontal assault using exaggerated language, exaggerated argument and exaggerated external threat—were now applied to Indigenous Australian history. Some additional tactics were thrown in for good measure, including personalised attacks, selective quoting, straw-man arguments and misrepresentation of opponents' arguments. However, Windschuttle's latest change of direction created a problem: although his impromptu sally into Indigenous Australian history, once again motivated by personal contempt and ideological conviction, proved to be a publicity success, it turned into a financial dead end. Virginia Marsh wrote:

> It is not the friends he has lost or the hatred he has aroused that seem to bother him most. It is that he has been sucked into what

he says is a relatively parochial, Australian issue when he would much rather be writing about the history of western civilisation and the Enlightenment.

Before his book *The Fabrication of Aboriginal History* appeared, Windschuttle was a little-known publisher and historian who planned to write books for the US market from Sydney. In 2000, the year prior to the celebration of the centenary of Australian federation, Windschuttle published a provocative series of articles on Indigenous Australian history that were inspired by a book he had been asked to review which argued that a massacre in Western Australia was a myth, not a historical reality, confirming everything that he had known (since 1994 at least) that leftist 'postmodernist' historians just made it up. The outlets for his research were *Quadrant*, a small-circulation but relatively influential (with conservatives at least) Australian magazine that later convened agenda-laden conferences on Indigenous Australian history, and *Quadrant*'s US equivalent, *New Criterion*. Both journals used the standard political magazine practice of accepting or commissioning contributions without vetting them through peer review. In late 2002, Windschuttle's articles, controversial in tone and content, were turned into a substantial Macleay Press book, *The Fabrication of Aboriginal History* (hereafter shortened to *Fabrication*), weighing more than 2 kilograms and with 472 pages of argumentation (barring references and index). The whole book totalled approximately 250 000 words of text, twice the length of a large PhD thesis. As Windschuttle later said, 'The trouble is this damned Aboriginal issue came up ... I thought, "I'll write a couple of articles on this", but it's taken control of my life. The last thing I wanted to do was spend what's going to be six to ten years writing four huge volumes'.

The gist of Windschuttle's argument, as expressed in his book, was that a school of leftist Australian historians, influenced by what he referred to as an admiration for anti-colonial struggles in south-east Asia, had conspired to concoct the view that ill-intentioned European invaders had exterminated the hapless Indigenous Australian people. These historians had created this myth of victimhood by fabricating the evidence. As if that were not enough, one of them, Henry Reynolds, had crossed the boundaries of historical practice by supporting Indigenous Australian claims for land rights. Windschuttle reached this point having watched, with some exasperation, the success of Indigenous Australian plaintiffs in the celebrated Mabo and Wik land rights cases of 1992 and 1996. His claims of fabrication (fraudulence, really, although the word itself is ambiguous) were based on his examination of the Tasmanian archives. He insisted that, whereas his opponents were motivated by political bias, he based his work on disinterested and unassailably scholarly objectivity. In the introduction to *Fabrication*, he explained:

> This series has been written in the belief that the factual details are matters not to be waived [*sic*] aside but to be critically examined. ... This series is also an excursion into the methodology of history. It examines how we can know about the past, the kinds of evidence we can regard as reliable, and how to detect false claims when they are made.

The book created a huge controversy in some sections of Australian society, shoring up diehard right-wing opinion by pandering, as it did, to scarcely concealed, ultra-conservative, bourgeois bigotry. While it is important to deal with the issues raised by the book as a whole, it is huge, and a page-by-page test would be beyond the scope of this chapter; therefore, we will focus on three of the work's characteristic aspects. First, the ten-page introduction will be tested against Windschuttle's insistent assertion of his own scholarly thoroughness and detachment. Second, we will look at the book as a whole by analysing the post-publication debate known as the 'Battle of the Footnotes', as expressed in *Whitewash*, a 2003 collection of essays edited by prominent public intellectual and politics professor Robert Manne, a volume that responded in detail to the claims contained in *Fabrication*. Third, we will look at whether or not Windschuttle may be considered a denialist.

Testing the Windschuttle Technique

> But historians should report the facts accurately and cite their sources honestly. To pretend these things don't matter and that acceptable interpretations can be drawn from false or non-existent evidence is to abandon the pursuit of historical truth.
>
> Keith Windschuttle, 2003

Windschuttle claims that *Fabrication* is a dispassionate and learned analysis of a deliberately ideologised school of historical study. Taking him at his word, this section of the chapter will review his technique, as displayed in *Fabrication*'s introduction. Why examine the introduction in this way? There are two very good reasons. The introduction to any scholarly work lays out the methodology used and provides a map showing where the research is heading: in an empirical-historical approach, it should pose a question, stake a claim and offer an evidence-based hypothesis, with a glimpse of a resolution (or resolutions). By Windschuttle's own forcefully positivist rules and by any other conventional measure, the introduction ought to be the key to the whole. Accordingly, *bona fide* scholarly researchers will, as a rule, write the introduction extremely carefully.

We will therefore examine Windschuttle's introduction as if it were a genuine research report prepared as a PhD, the basic, entry-level research qualification in the field of history. The question is, does his introduction measure up to his own standards, as expressed in his justification for writing *Fabrication*?

To begin with, the title of the introduction, 'The Final Solution Down Under', is an exaggeratedly phrased term, making the extreme point of a purported Holocaust connection to Indigenous Australian history by academic historians. Remembering that Windschuttle's critique is aimed at contemporary academic historians (working in the past twenty years), the hyperbole implied in the title stems solely (in *Fabrication*, at least) from his reference to an article written in 1972 by passing English essayist, travel writer and historian Jan Morris. A historian using the exact words of another in this way would normally insert them in quote marks, but to embellish his point, Windschuttle appears to have eschewed the convention here, while on page 7 he gives the appropriate quote marks to former governor-general Paul Hasluck's comment on the 'colossal fictions' of history, which is used in a heading, is not a promising opening. Were this a dissertation, an examiner would require the candidate to correct the contextual and methodological errors.

The opening lines of *Fabrication*'s introduction present an odd state of affairs, since the first two sentences form a schoolboy syntactical howler. Here is the ungrammatical text: 'The centenary of Federation in 2001 was ostensibly to celebrate 100 years of independent, democratic Australian government. Given the very few other societies that have recorded such an achievement, the event should have been an occasion to focus on national virtues'. Given that most good researchers and authors hone and polish their opening lines in an attempt to capture the reader's attention, and allowing for Windschuttle's background in media and in writing, his oddly expressed assertion that 'few other societies' have recorded 100 years of 'democratic Australian government' comes as a surprise. More astonishingly, it remains uncorrected in the revised 2003 volume: a minor point, but, once again, not a good beginning.

Moving on, Windschuttle attacks what he calls 'the politicisation of academic history', a phenomenon that, he asserts, was a consequence of 1960s radicalism surviving and spreading into historical writing. He quotes a well-known Marxist commentator, Humphrey McQueen, and (non-Marxist) Henry Reynolds as examples, carefully ignoring the long tradition in historical scholarship of divergent, often partisan, political views, with Geoffrey Blainey, one of Windschuttle's heroes, as a perfect example. Clearly, for Windschuttle, as for many of his supporters, the politicisation of debate lies in the eye of the beholder. In this context, Windschuttle argues that history should be a politics-free environment. He commits a scholarly error in supposing that historical explanation, a highly contentious area of study that is both about politics and infused with politically based commentary, can be free of personal, political involvement and moral judgment. This simplistic position, if expressed in a thesis, would almost certainly provoke an examiner into sending Windschuttle back for a further detailed study of historiography and the philosophy of history, the intention being for the candidate to set out a consistent and persuasive scholarly paradigm in a revised dissertation, a paradigm that took into account the varying positions that exist in the current world of historical scholarship.

Let us look next at Windschuttle's commentary on the views of others. In *Fabrication*, it is clear that his main target for revisionist critique is high-profile academic Henry Reynolds, and in his introduction Windschuttle specifically comments on Reynolds's position on Geoffrey Blainey.

Blainey is one of the most stimulating and prolific historians at work in Australia today. His research and depth of knowledge are marvellous, and his narrative style is engaging. In person, he is a courteous and amiable scholar whose inspirational teaching is well remembered by generations of students from the University of Melbourne. He has, however, held some very odd, populist views in his time. Famously, it was Blainey who made the comment about 'black armband' (apologetic) historians that was picked up by the national press and became a major controversy. Blainey's remark was disparaged by many of his university colleagues but was adopted with relish by several conservatives, including politician (and later prime minister) John Howard. The Blainey story seemed to turn sour when, in 1987, he failed to be re-elected for an unprecedented third term as Melbourne's dean of arts, in a vote perhaps influenced by hostile student electors. In the following year, Blainey retired early (at a time when thirty-three other university staff retired on salary packages), saying he wanted to write and pointing out that politics played only a minor part in his decision. Blainey's retirement, constructed by the Right as a coerced resignation, became a conservative *cause célèbre*, based on the view (shared by John Howard) that he was pushed out by leftist Melbourne historians led by prominent labour historian Stuart Macintyre.

Quite what part Henry Reynolds, at that time in Tasmania, played in these University of Melbourne proceedings is, at best, unclear, but Windschuttle has no doubt. In one of the key passages in the introduction to *Fabrication*, Windschuttle remarks: 'It was time for a new generation of historians to pull down [Blainey's] "edifice", Reynolds asserted, so "a whole team got together with jackhammers" to criticize Blainey's views'. Then follows a brief, edited comment made by Reynolds in 1985:

> What you've got to expect if you engage in that sort of public controversy is that you are going to be shot at ... if you are going to get down there and engage in the crossfire you have got to expect to be clobbered and people will really jump on you.

This is followed immediately by: 'Although widely recognized as one of this country's greatest historians, Blainey eventually resigned from his chair at the University of Melbourne'. Windschuttle's assertion combines a *non sequitur* with the implication that an activist Reynolds was somehow responsible for ousting a blameless and passive Blainey, but the connection between the two events, Reynolds's 1985 call for strong debate and Blainey's 1988 retirement, is unevidenced and therefore unproven. Where is the causal relationship, an examiner would ask? The Reynolds–Blainey allegation is, accordingly, unscholarly and represents another case for sending Windschuttle back to the methodological drawing board.

As for misrepresentation and straw men, Windschuttle's introduction persists with earlier attacks on the design of Canberra's National Museum of Australia (NMA) as a commemoration of Indigenous Australian genocide, alleging that it borrows a design feature from the Jewish Museum in Berlin. Windschuttle's claim is that the NMA was consciously designed in this way as part of a national left-wing plot. The director of the museum at the time, Dawn Casey, who happens to be an Indigenous Australian, denied, on behalf of the NMA council (apparently contentedly led at that time by a John Howard confidant,

Tony Staley), that any conscious decision had been made to compare Indigenous Australian experiences with the Holocaust. Nevertheless, in *Fabrication*, Windschuttle's accusation reads:

> Architect Howard Raggatt borrowed its central construction— shaped as a lightning bolt striking the ground—from the Jewish Museum in Berlin, signifying that the Aborigines suffered the equivalent of the Holocaust. The Museum housed its 'First Australian' of Aboriginal collection within this zigzag structure ... yet apart from a handful of conservative objectors, the country accepted it without demur.

There is so much that is incorrect about this statement that it is difficult to know where to begin; however, as putative examiners, we do need to start somewhere. We know that Raggatt was no friend of the Howard government, even going to the extraordinary length of creating hidden anti-colonisation braille messages in the museum walls, but the lightning bolt, or zigzag, is not the NMA's 'central construction'; it is actually to one side of the main entrance. Furthermore, in 2001, the gallery that visitors arrived at first was the 'European' gallery; this layout was a design statement that provoked some controversy among left-leaning commentators who wanted a more chronological approach. There are substantial differences too in the structural symbolism of the Australian and the German zigzags, since the Berlin zigzag explicitly represents a broken Star of David, while the NMA lightning flash, at its very strongest, may symbolise the thunderbolt of European colonisation but there is no clear connection with genocide. As far as protests about the museum was concerned, there were architectural objectors (on plagiarism grounds) and left-wing objectors including historian and broadcaster Michael McKernan, as well as a (left-wing) special edition of *Meanjin* on museums, published in 2001. Windschuttle's incorrect and partial representation of a controversial and high-profile debate would cause dissertation examiners to scratch their heads, since, although the NMA's design relationship with the Holocaust may have, at most, contained a cryptic and surreptitious anti-colonial statement, neither the NMA council nor its curatorial staff made or approved of any Holocaust connection.

Finally, in this consideration of *Fabrication*'s introduction, there is a small but crucial detail that presages Windschuttle's style in the following 'Battle of the Footnotes' discussion. Coincidentally, and ironically, it is in a footnote.

Footnotes, often derided by non-historians, are vital to historical scholarship, since they present the more detailed and substantive evidence that may otherwise slow down a narrative in a quagmire of minutiae. In this context, there are three large and damaging accusations in Windschuttle's introductory narrative: first, that Henry Reynolds and his supporters control university appointments procedures; second, that all graduate students with 'dissenting' theses (supposedly propositions rather than hard-copy dissertations) are excluded from academic circles; and, third, that publishers are too frightened to take on dissenting points of view, intimidated as they are by the unnamed 'ruling intellectual elite'. These potentially injurious assertions are supported by a solitary footnote, which reads: 'See Chapter Seven, pp. 199–200'.

On arrival at those pages, Windschuttle tells us, in an unsourced micro-narrative, that in 1984, contracted author Vivienne Rae-Ellis submitted an allegedly controversial typescript to a minor academic publisher (the Australian Institute of Aboriginal and Torres Strait Islander Studies), by whom it was turned down. (According to Windschuttle, Rae-Ellis's book, titled *Black Robinson*, was subsequently published in 1988 by the more prestigious Melbourne University Press, at that time run by Peter Ryan, a Blainey supporter in the alleged retirement–resignation imbroglio.) In a curious piece of reversed causality and chronology, Windschuttle blames the rejection on historian Lyndall Ryan's subsequent criticism (in 1996) of Rae-Ellis's 1984 draft, citing no evidence except that Ryan did not agree with Rae-Ellis's point of view. *On that foundation alone*, Windschuttle builds his own fabrication, in which he alleges that university appointments Australia-wide are corrupted by ideology, graduate studies are politicised and dissenting authors are persecuted.

While it is perfectly possible, in the scheme of things, that some of these allegations may be correct at any given time, one solitary footnote linked to a further, blighted set of assertions and an over-generalised false extrapolation do not a proof make. Again, examiners would ask Windschuttle to go back to the drawing board, pointing out to him his later assertion that 'footnotes are one of the principal reasons why those who practise scholarly history can be trusted' and suggesting that he abide by his own conventions.

As we have seen, in *Fabrication*'s introduction, Windschuttle indulges in a form of pseudohistory—politicised historical explanation, usually of a controversial nature, masquerading as the genuine article but substantially based on seriously flawed methodology.

That was just the introduction: now for the main text.

The 'Battle of the Footnotes'

> Scholarly history distinguishes itself from popular works by providing references to its sources. It does this through the device of footnotes. . . . The role of the footnote is to make historians publicly accountable.
>
> Keith Windschuttle, 2002

Having established that the introduction to *Fabrication* is a poorly expressed piece of polemics that fails the test as competent scholarly analysis, we will now consider what has become almost a small-scale Windschuttle industry in Australia, an industry based on ideological divisions, personality clashes, city rivalries and microscopic analyses of the written work of the protagonists, a conflict that came to be known, slightly derisively, as the 'battle of the footnotes'.

On the one hand in this conflict, there are the friends of Windschuttle. They are mainly Sydney-based conservative commentators, some with their vanity websites, their newspaper columns, their litigiousness and their humourless denunciations of any insult, imagined or otherwise, aimed at the soul or the ethics of conservative politics. In that tally are some senior politicians of note, a major journalistic connection and the regular contributors to *Quadrant*: a small coterie of about twenty or so friends of Windschuttle who delight in the discomfiture that their champion creates among what they see as trendy, chardonnay-drinking, bleeding-heart, black armband urban socialists. By and large, the conservative commentators earn some, or all, of their income through writing and speaking, have no attachment to a university position and despise tenured academic life as a feather-bedded form of public service. In contrast, they are out there in the wide world, living by their wits. Indeed, one such has proudly described himself as a 'small businessman'. This conservative group's view is that the (state-subsidised) Left's advocacy of Indigenous Australian nobility and victimhood is an unrealistic and self-hating form of inverted racism by inner-city trendoids who would not survive for a day in the world of freelance writing or business.

On the other hand, there is a (much larger) array of Windschuttle opponents, mainly academics, who write sometimes measured, sometimes intemperate, occasionally self-righteous denunciations of Windschuttleism and who attempt to tear apart his major and minor propositions, as outlined in *Fabrication* and elsewhere. The most authoritative and considered of these opponents are Robert Manne, Bain Attwood and Stuart Macintyre, all Melbourne-based academics. These diverse critics are gathered together, in Windschuttle's mind, and in line with his technique in *The Killing of History*, at least, as advocates of the 'orthodox' view, notwithstanding their professional and precise disagreements on the historiography of Indigenous Australian history.

Although there have been many public debates in halls and in the media following the publication of Windschuttle's original *Quadrant* articles, there remains no common ground between the two opposing camps. For Windschuttle, the debate meant war, and he was out to win, knowing that, in the world of mass media confrontation, where complex counter-argument frequently loses out, he had gained some authority in the popular consciousness, if only because he had the slogans that operated at both the major and the minor propositional levels, while his opponents had merely the arguments.

What are the major Windschuttleist slogans? The first, as we have seen, is that that Henry Reynolds and others have connived at a 'fabricated' view of genocidal activity in Australia that is based on ideology, poor scholarship and self-delusion. A second proposition is that Indigenous Tasmanians did not wage a systematic guerilla war against white settlement but were indeed simply robbers and murderers attacking largely defenceless, well-intentioned settlers whose casualties outnumbered Indigenous victims. The third proposition, associated with the second, is that European settlement of Tasmania (and, by implication, the whole of Australia) was influenced by the benevolent nature of Christianity and the essentially honourable nature of the British empire; that being the case, atrocities described by Reynolds, Ryan and others simply could not have happened, or, if they did, they were not atrocities. The fourth proposition is that the Indigenous Tasmanians did not deserve to survive anyway, because they were brutes who had neither compassion nor functionality, and were eventually 'rescued' by enlightened European intervention.

How do these propositions survive in the battle of the footnotes? In other words, does Windschuttle make his points or not? Since much of the footnotes debate is of a specific and highly detailed kind that can easily stultify interest in the argument, in this section of the chapter, a series of representative and illustrative examples will be discussed.

Windschuttle displays an element of accuracy in at least one of his allegations. In some of their earlier work, Henry Reynolds and Lyndall Ryan did indeed err in presenting their cases. (Ryan's blithe and catastrophic announcement on a national television show that 'historians are always making up figures' did not help.) In the chapters 'Historical Scholarship and Invention of Massacre Stories' and 'Death Toll and Demise of the Aboriginal Population', Windschuttle analyses, in great detail, the evidence for violent deaths of Indigenous Australians, and arrives at the conclusion that the 'orthodox school' (Reynolds, Ryan and company) exaggerated the numbers; he suggests that there is no 'hard evidence' regarding Indigenous casualties consequent to European settlement. What he means is that there is no official list of corpses. Windschuttle was, prior to *Fabrication*, correct in another respect, as we have seen: Henry Reynolds had already admitted that his original, pre-*Fabrication* calculation of 20 000 Indigenous Australian deaths across the continent at the hands of the colonists was possibly flawed, and later he also admitted that he had included a misquote in his work. Lyndall Ryan also accepted that her figures needed revision. Both accordingly put their hands up and amended their thinking.

However, while Windschuttle may be right in places, he is also wrong in places. His *corpus delicti* criterion for measuring deaths—essentially every body tagged and named, and every death witnessed by a 'reliable' observer—is so unrealistically reductive that, if applied universally, for example to deaths in the Aztec empire caused by war and human sacrifices, to Native American deaths caused by official and unofficial nineteenth-century wars and purges, to violent Armenian deaths in Anatolia in 1915, to Russian excess deaths under Stalin (deaths caused by internal state actions, not by war) and to violent deaths in Bosnia in the 1990s, the mortality rates would have to be scaled down to perhaps one-tenth of the generally accepted totals.

In his attack on Ryan and others, Windschuttle resorts to unsubstantiated supposition and conjecture, the very sins for which he castigates his opponents. For example, in criticising a discussion of District Chief Constable Robertson, an observer of the 1828 Pittwater massacre, in Ryan's 1975 PhD, Windschuttle asserts that 'as demonstrated below Robertson was a notoriously unreliable witness, prone to exaggerating rumours about violence done to blacks'. However, when it comes to 'below', all that Windschuttle provides is: '*It appears* [italics added] that this was how Robertson's peers regarded his evidence in 1830'. This piece of guesswork is offered as a question-begging assertion to back up the previous claim, a tactic reminiscent of the dangling footnote technique in *Fabrication*'s introduction.

There is more: Windschuttle accuses Ryan of wilful distortion, for example regarding deaths of Indigenous Tasmanians in early colonial conflicts with kangaroo hunters. Ryan claims that probably 100 Indigenous Australians were killed. Windschuttle says: 'To support her death toll above, Ryan cites pages 128, 140 and 146 of [Reverend Robert Knopwood's] diary'. He goes on to argue strongly that Knopwood's diaries do not support Ryan's argument and that only four Indigenous deaths occurred overall in the area and period specified. Ryan's riposte is that Windschuttle's analysis has conflated two paragraphs in her text as if they were one and has ignored her placing of the Knopwood reference as a source only for the existence of kangaroo hunting. She argues that he has ignored a crucial footnote reference to two accounts by a John Oxley which suggest that about twenty kangaroo hunters were active in the area in question at the time and that there had been 'considerable loss of life among the natives'—hence her 'guesstimate' of about 100 deaths.

There are two points here. First, from a scholarly point of view, Ryan's estimate of Indigenous casualties, even based on the two sets of references, remains open to question. Second, and this is an equally important point, Windschuttle has omitted the small amount of evidence from Oxley that may help to refute his vehement argument against Ryan's figures. Ryan should have cited both Knopwood and Oxley more clearly, the first as a witness to kangaroo hunting and the second as a specific witness to deaths. She should have either found more evidence for her estimate or given the number of deaths a much more conditional term than 'probably', maybe even re-classifying it as 'a considerable number', to bring it in line with the available evidence. As for Windschuttle, in a critique of this kind, he should have included the Oxley references. His conflation of the paragraphs and omission of a key footnote break the rules. While Ryan's case is thin to the point of invisibility, Windschuttle's poor methodology is both inarguable and inexcusable. Two wrongs do not make a right.

Unfortunately, this kind of tendentious and careless work by Windschuttle permeates *Fabrication* in a manner too frequent and too detailed to be examined further in this chapter. However, while Windschuttle may not be well regarded in Australia's community of historians, his criticism has at least engendered one important, if unintended (and probably unwanted), consequence: forcing historians to check their footnotes. On the face of it, Windschuttle's unrestrained attack on historical methodology has meant that Australian historians, already highly professional, have had to lift their game, albeit slightly. Windschuttle was not interested in such a positive outcome, however; he simply wanted to win the war. He still does.

Fabrication versus *Whitewash*

> For almost twenty years certainly since the Bicentenary of 1988, Australian intellectuals have been part of a worldwide movement to disparage the nation-state and transfer its key functions to international organizations. This movement is based on two premises: that the nation-state is a racist warlike institution that is now an impediment to world harmony, and that economic globalisation has already rendered much of the role of the traditional state redundant.
>
> Keith Windschuttle, 2007

In keeping with Windschuttle's own number-crunching style, the next step is to lay out a final tally in the footnotes contest. As a case in point and using solely the responses of the specialist authors in *Whitewash*, there are eighty-five substantive allegations against Windschuttle of egregious error, methodological blunders, economy with the truth, misrepresentations of the opposing point of view, convenient elisions and significant factual errors. These claims, made by respected representatives from the fields of history, sociology, law and archaeology, average out at one major blemish in every fifth page of Windschuttle's book.

Windschuttle's failings, as outlined in *Whitewash* (for details see the Appendix), include: unsupported, politicised assertions; over-reliance on government (particularly post-1827) sources, on newspaper accounts and on sources that favour his interpretation; dismissing or ignoring uncooperative primary and secondary sources and evidence that may either contradict or not support his point of view; exaggeration of the influence of factors that support his opinion; supposition; creation of a highly questionable set of categories and numbers regarding Indigenous deaths; failing to contextualise evidence and to understand the Indigenous–Australian way of life, cultural practices and vocabulary; using, as supposedly disinterested, vindicatory sources for his anthropological views (writers whose work is, at best, controversial and, at worst, seriously flawed or hostile to Indigenous Australian culture); attacking testimony that is hostile to his own point of view without applying the same level of scrutiny to witnesses who favour his opinion; using either outdated research or ignoring the latest research; failing to correct factual errors; persistent inconsistency in his use of evidence; making causal links that are just not there; using ahistorical generalisations when it suits him; misrepresenting the views of others; and adopting simplistic analysis in a highly complex debate. Add in the five major concerns identified above about the introduction and we have ninety substantive claims regarding Windschuttle's inadequate scholarship in *Fabrication*. Even though the authors in *Whitewash* are not sympathetically disposed towards Windschuttle, their claims may be regarded as persuasive by many neutral observers. This would be quite a list for a whole body of work, but in this case we are talking about just one book.

Looking at it from the other side, Windschuttle claims that he has found, in Ryan's key publications, 'at least seventeen cases where she either invented atrocities and other incidents or provided false footnotes, plus another seven cases where the number of Indigenous Australians she claims were killed or captured is either outright false or exaggerated beyond belief'. Windschuttle may be correct, and on the evidence we have seen regarding the Knopwood and Oxley sources, Ryan certainly needs to sharpen up her technique. When it comes to Robson, Windschuttle is less precise, alleging that 'Robson committed a similar degree of fabrication'. But what of the alleged errors by

Windschuttle's prime target, Henry Reynolds? Windschuttle does not specify the number of Reynolds's errors, but the index in *Fabrication* makes twenty-four clear references to Reynolds's work (that is citing a named issue), some of them doubling up. Windschuttle is, therefore, more circumspect in his attack on Reynolds than he is on the more methodologically vulnerable Ryan, although he categorises Reynolds as the highly politicised leader of the pack and a historical apologist. In other words, while publicly holding up a piece of paper with Reynolds's name on it, Windschuttle finds it difficult to nail him down when it comes to detail. The spurious nature of this tactic becomes clear when we look at the sum total of his accusations against Reynolds as outlined in *Fabrication*: Windschuttle cannot find any clearly substantiated, dead-set errors in Reynolds's work. Indeed, his major criticisms are Reynolds's political attitude; his role in both the 'myth' of the 'Great Australian Silence' and the Blainey business; his belief that there should be an Indigenous Australian war memorial; and his support for Lyndall Ryan: contentions so open to disputation and so politicised in themselves that they can be regarded only as a case of playing the man, not the ball.

Windschuttle also disagrees with Reynolds over points of interpretation. Principally, this concerns the enclosure of land; the myth and the efficacy of the Black Line; death claims (both black and white); the starvation thesis; Indigenous population numbers; events at Cape Grim; the disease or settler bullets argument for Indigenous deaths; guerilla war or not; the disposition of the 40th regiment; fears of extermination by Tasmanian colonists; and the role of Robinson as a protector of Indigenous Australians. Oddly, Windschuttle also criticises Reynolds for changing his mind over time, as if historians are not permitted, in the light of new evidence or a reworking of existing evidence, to modify their views. Instances cited include frontier killings and extermination policy. Finally, and more seriously, Windschuttle takes Reynolds to task on methodological grounds. His complaints are that Reynolds relies on only one contemporary source (and one after-the-event source) for his enclosures argument; that he has omitted white deaths from his black deaths argument; that he is critical of the 1830 Aboriginal Committee (Broughton) report because of a key phrase; that he inaccurately uses the colonial press and settler statements to back his extermination thesis; and that he is over-reliant on a petition to Queen Victoria as his source of a possible verbal treaty with Indigenous Australians. Again, these are interpretative points, a 'more or less' type of debate with nothing absolute.

That is it. That is why Windschuttle has labelled Henry Reynolds a histrionic historical fabricator, an accusation to which Reynolds has responded coolly and in detail. What is fascinating here, and this is an important point, is that by emphasising Ryan's imperfections while finding little in Reynolds's work that he can nail down, Windschuttle has used the more exposed Ryan to get at the more redoubtable Reynolds, lumping them both together in that characteristic technique first employed in *The Killing of History*.

Having reached this position, at which we have competing claims, a comparison of the two sets of assertions and the context in which the claims are made would be salutary. If the accusations in *Whitewash* remain uncontested in precise detail, as opposed to being ignored or rejected, Windschuttle is clearly shown up for what he is— a politically motivated tabloid writer who, adopting a pseudohistorical approach, props up his extreme and harsh assertions with a mass of footnotes. So far, however, Windschuttle's reply has been based on denial, additional straw-man reasoning and counter-attack. He simply reiterates his point of view, denounces specific criticisms as minor points of detail and refocuses, over and over again, on the already established errors, avoiding any serious effort to deal with criticism of his own work.

Home-grown Denier, or Just Keith Windschuttle?

> I bin born la bush. I never bin go school. We got own language, Gija, Miriwoong, Worla ... Now people like this Windschuttle try to say nobody bin get killed because gardiya [white people] never write 'em down what they bin do. He make out I stupid

because he can't understand my word. He reckon I gota put my word in high English myself. He reckon he good one telling true story proper way. He say other people should make sure they got true story. He can't take notice when people tell him he make mistake himself.

Peggy Patrick, 2003

As scholarly works go, *Fabrication* is a disaster area. It is activity dressed up as accomplishment. But that is the verdict on his book as a contribution to historical understanding. It would require a big leap from here to argue that Windschuttle may be a denialist. He could be that, or he could be just a politically motivated propagandist grabbing a convenient cause and masquerading as a historian. Most tabloid-style, neo-conservative rhetoric contains some or all of the following Windschuttleist features: the assertion that, solely on behalf of the common good, the author is an ideologically disinterested observer fighting against overwhelming leftist odds in an effort to correct an injustice; the author's resorting to misrepresentation of the opposing point of view in order to reach this goal; the tendency to allege conspiracy and guilt by association; the use of unsupported assertion with the diversionary red herrings; the selective use of evidence; and (most barefaced of all) the tendency not to abide by the rules demanded of others. But these techniques do not of themselves constitute denial. So, is Windschuttle a denier?

Windschuttle and Irving

If a source doesn't fit, then argue it out of existence if you can't ignore it altogether. If you want to alter a few words in a document in order to make it support your argument, then either do so ... or argue that the author would have done so had he been telling the truth.

Richard Evans on David Irving, 2002

> I don't have any kind of political agenda, and really it's kind of defamatory for people to suggest that I do have an agenda to present. The agenda I have, I suppose, is, all right, I admit it, I like seeing the other historians with egg on their face. And they're getting a lot of egg on their face now, because I'm challenging them to produce the evidence for what they've been saying for fifty years.
>
> David Irving, 1993

Initially, the answer seems to be that yes, Windschuttle is a denier, especially if we compare him with that doyen of individual deniers, David Irving. The point to be made here, however, is that Irving-style denial is several steps further on from neo-conservative bombast. The consequent question is does Windschuttle follow Irving towards fully fledged Holocaust-style denial, or is he a different kind of denier altogether?

There are many interesting similarities between Windschuttle and Irving. Both writers, with breathtaking insincerity, claim political neutrality, arguing that, as a consequence of their unprecedented diligence, either they have found detailed evidence in the archives that supports their particular case or they have failed to find evidence that supports the opposing point of view. Irving and Windschuttle love to dwell on the idea that they are not professional historians and that they are able to upset the conventional historical applecart. As inverted narcissists, they seem to enjoy publicity, to claim victimisation and to thrive on public appearances in which they can flaunt their notoriety. Each has been accused of fudging interpretations, bending the facts and concealing inconvenient evidence. They both work hard to diminish the scale of any atrocity by reducing the body count, although the numbers involved differ massively. They publish privately. Irving and Windschuttle both claim that there is a conspiracy at work to conceal unpalatable truths. Irving has a racial element in his line of attack and Windschuttle uses race as an issue to launch a campaign and get publicity. Both blame the victims for their downfall—supposed Jewish dominance of German life in the one case and alleged Indigenous dysfunctionality in the other.

And yet Irving, as a Holocaust denier, is in a special category. He and his cohorts have adopted and propagated an extremist form of denial that, in content, is substantially beyond the accepted boundaries of historical debate by starting with a palpably false premise. Holocaust denial is especially obnoxious in attempting to conceal from present and future generations a huge, well-documented horror that cannot, in any way, be justified as an accident or as a benevolent act. This category of denial is much less comprehensible and far more wicked than the denialism of nationalist rejectionists such as Windschuttle who find it difficult to come to terms with the past wrongdoings of their own people, so to speak, and who attempt to rewrite their national history as a benign narrative. While Irving starts from a baseline that is manifestly absurd and works via denialist methodology to conclusions that remain absurd, in contrast, Windschuttle's starting point lies *within the boundaries* of accepted historical debate while using denialist techniques to arrive at his inflated and fanciful pseudo-historical conclusions.

Windschuttle, who shows no evidence of anti-Semitism and who, as far as we know, has never spoken at a racist rally, is, in short, merely an inconsequential Australian polemicist who feels uncomfortable with the idea that the foundation of his modern nation was based on anything other than a largely compassionate and progressive intervention by an enlightened European culture. In other words, Windschuttle has created a new category of lesser denialism, combining the benign myth with hardcore ideology as well as throwing in more than just a touch of racial obsession. In arguing for his case, Windschuttle has traduced academic writers, made brutally offensive racial assertions and, as far as *Fabrication* is concerned, declined to modify his views, notwithstanding a growing body of criticism that refutes his hypotheses. Indeed, the only changes he has made between the first and the revised editions of *Fabrication* are some minor footnote references. Trapped within the character of his own intractability, Windschuttle the pseudohistorian seems incapable of reasoned scholarly behaviour.

Irving, in contrast, generally treats historians with respect but has been much more offensive racially than Windschuttle. He has also modified his position, though usually when it suits him. These are differences that seem to draw the two men apart. The key to the comparison, however, is that while they are different personalities engaged in different forms of denial, there is a structural-functionalist element to their work which necessarily draws them together. To make their case, they have to fudge, to misrepresent and to diminish casualties; to publicise their point of view, they have to tackle the perceived enemy with relentless venom. There will be some, those who regard Irving as beyond the pale, who are uncomfortable with this comparison of Windschuttle with Irving (and with Johnstone), but, in essence, placing Windschuttle in the category of denier is about methodology rather than a measurement of iniquity.

The Friends of Windschuttle

> It is not difficult to see that the politicization of history is self-defeating for the aims of these interest groups themselves. By abandoning truth and objectivity, they unwittingly validate political positions they might find less congenial.
>
> Keith Windschuttle, 2002

How, in a progressive and democratic society, did Windschuttle's aggressive, denialist behaviour get as far as it did? To begin with, Windschuttle's political stance was seized upon and encouraged by a small group of Sydney commentators who are grouped in and around *Quadrant* and the Murdoch News Limited broadsheet *The Australian*.

That *Quadrant* would be involved in supporting Windschuttle is not unexpected. It is a small-circulation political magazine that has a strong neo-conservative ethos, and Windschuttle's translation from Left to Right falls into that gratifying category of political conversion; better yet, not only was he converted, but he became a renegade activist against the Left. However, *Quadrant* is merely an echo-chamber publication, preaching to the already converted. This is small pond stuff.

In the bigger pond, Windschuttle's public flaying of an out-of-touch leftist elite that apparently controls the scholarly culture of the nation suits *The Australian*'s anti-intellectualism, hostility to socialism and contempt for postmodernism, crusades which intensified after the appointment of editor Chris Mitchell in 2002. During the 'History Wars' period, *The Australian* employed gung ho culture warriors Janet Albrechtsen, Christopher Pearson (a former John Howard speechwriter) and Kevin Donnelly (a former Liberal staffer), as well as giving regular space to *Quadrant* writer Frank Devine. To be fair to Mitchell, he still employs the newspaper's token socialist, Phillip Adams, and the paper has taken part in an occasional well-reported campaign that would not have pleased the Howard side of politics. Nevertheless, when it comes to a consistent political position, *The Australian*, under Mitchell, has acquired a reputation for standing so close to *Quadrant* that the separation is almost invisible.

Part of the campaign technique adopted by *The Australian* is the established media tactic of setting up 'debate' by encouraging head-to-head arguments in the newspaper's pages. It is a simple enough ploy and not one that is unique to *The Australian*. The editor organises a splash news story or feature written either by a staff writer or by a commissioned controversialist. The article, in tabloid fashion, duly slams the target for that particular day. Predictably, the target's supporters demand right of reply. The newspaper, claiming that it is fair-minded and independent, may publish a reply, usually an ingenuously complex and convoluted piece that only confirms initial prejudices. The reply is then pilloried in the letters column, the opinion columns and even the editorial. There are variations on this theme, including the editorial-friendly expert who is wheeled out for commissioned philippics, and the ambush interview in which the unwitting interviewee may be publicly ridiculed by inserting or topping and tailing the interview with damning or embarrassing quotes from other sources. All in all, this bully pulpit technique, justified by sanctimonious editorial claims of righteousness, is a no-win arrangement for any designated target suckered into a one-sided media quarrel. Even better, if the 'debate' is taken up by radio and television, it becomes good publicity for the instigating newspaper. Whatever the particular issue of the day may be, it is rarely taken up by rival newspapers, on the grounds that they do not use their competition as a news source (unless it is bad news about their rivals), and they can spot the gambit a mile away. This invariably leaves the battlefield victory to the campaigning editor.

Between September 2000, the date of Windschuttle's first significant foray into the public arena, and December 2005, the month of the Cronulla riots, *The Australian* published 142 articles or substantial comments featuring Windschuttle on history, politics and race, this number leaving aside letters to the editor, articles in which Windschuttle was named but played a relatively insignificant part, and front-page teasers. To be fair, the articles included a selection of critical responses from opponents of Windschuttle, but a sceptic may suggest that this was partly a device to stoke up the fires of controversy.

The general thrust of many of the pro-Windschuttle articles can be inferred from the labels and accusations that appeared in them: fashion statement, deception, dishonest, misleading, Windschuttle versus the professors, bluster, systematic fraud, false, accusations beggared belief, charlatan, nerds, false history, lying, self-loathing, fanatics, fundamentalism, sovietisation, paedophile priests, brutality, comrade, poisonous, fudge, stupid, bloody myth, pathetic, heresy, history airbrush, well-heeled, ganging up, pack-attack, shut down debate and queuing up to bash. Windschuttle's critics defended themselves with such expressions as: misrepresented, undermine, fabricate, crude and politicised, political motivation, baseless, heart-sinking, sanitise, not new and mishandling the truth. The conclusion? While the Windschuttle supporters were playing dirty pool, the historians were playing a gentlemanly game of snooker. There was, as it happens, an accusation of plagiarism against Windschuttle by Robert Manne that was quickly dismissed by *The Australian*, which took the trouble to persuade the object of the alleged offence to deny that the supposed copying was really an issue. A possibly traumatised Lyndall Ryan also made the hyperbolic accusation that historians had been 'raped by a voracious media'; her comment was characterised by *The Australian* headline 'Historians Cry "Media Rape"', a characteristic piece of wild, journalistic over-generalisation. All in all, however, those seem to have been the only examples of exaggeration from the other side in the five-year war of words.

If we compare this record with *The Australian*'s main New South Wales rival, *The Sydney Morning Herald*, bearing in mind Windschuttle's Sydneysider background and the parochialism of the major city newspapers in reporting local identities, we find that *The Sydney Morning Herald* carried sixty-four equivalent articles during the same period as *The Australian*'s 142. The arithmetic is simple: every month during the period under review, *The Australian* published on average 2.7 articles on Windschuttle, while the *The Sydney Morning Herald* published less than half that, on average 1.3 articles. The conclusion is clear: one of the reasons why the Windschuttle debate continued to maintain its head of steam, notwithstanding the deficient nature of Windschuttle's scholarship, was that his campaigns were sustained at a national level by his unofficial public relations department, *The Australian*, a newspaper that also happens to be John Howard's required morning reading.

Windschuttle and Howard

> Howard, who is reading Keith Windschuttle's controversial *The Fabrication of Aboriginal History* (Macleay Press), takes satisfaction that he has contributed to a changed Australia, has reversed 'the tide of political correctness'.
>
> 'Australia is more self-confident, it doesn't feel the need to explain itself, we don't have perpetual self-identity seminars any more', he says.
>
> Howard identifies the rejection of much political correctness by ordinary people showing self-confidence as the single biggest

change to Australia during his years as Prime Minister and predicts 'it is a lasting confidence'.

The Sydney Morning Herald, 2004

The mutual admiration that existed between Keith Windschuttle and John Howard was based on three fundamental elements. First, they were both exasperated with what they saw as an Australian foundation myth based on original sin. Second, Howard, always the politician and never the statesman, was happy with the polling on the 'Culture Wars' issues. That is why he could, with an apparently clear conscience, associate himself with the more callous, close-to-redneck inferences that may be drawn from Windschuttle's work. Third, Windschuttle had the ability to kick populist goals for the conservatives at a time when the party rhetoric painted a picture of beleaguerment by leftist radicals in the universities and in the media and by radical activists in divisive special interest groups such as advocates of multiculturalism and of Indigenous causes. This context is important, because when Howard finally became prime minister, in 1996, after a long and tiresome apprenticeship, it was at a time when the conservative side of politics had been forced to endure thirteen years of parliamentary suffering at the hands of the Labor Party's master of unrestrained political invective, Paul Keating. With Keating gone, it was the conservatives' turn. They had been waiting, and, after a hesitant start, the Howard government was ready for a bit of pain creation of its own. Windschuttle was their man.

The conservative supporters of Windschuttle, including Howard, blinded by their desire for revenge and oblivious to the manifest faults in Windschuttle's book, cheered him on against those molly-coddling 'elites' who, it was alleged (in a wonderful piece of projection), would try any dirty trick to bring down the conservatives' iconoclastic champion. Having re-framed the obviously political black armband historical debate as high-ground scholarly revisionism, the conservatives then used the convenient tactic of arguing that any criticism of

Windschuttle's work was mere politics, with Reynolds's and Ryan's defence of their position characterised as 'told you so' shiftiness and Manne's careful and persistent dissections of Windschuttle's technique set up as sour grapes from a discredited ex-rightie. The more the historians squealed, the more the conservatives loved it, and the more they loved their man.

That is why Howard could say with some satisfaction, at *Quadrant*'s fiftieth anniversary dinner, held on 3 October 2006, that 'of the causes that *Quadrant* has taken up that are close to my heart none is more important than the role it has played as counterforce to the black armband view of Australian history'. Even if Howard had not started reading *Fabrication* until late 2004, it was still the political value of Windschuttle's work between 2000 and 2004, and its impact beyond those years, that had always been the real interest to Howard in his role as prime minister. Invective dressed up as scholarship is more politically valuable than the genuine article, since, in the world of partisan politics, tabloid historical journalism backed by sloganeering and a slew of impressive-looking footnotes is easier to sell to the punters than complex historical debate.

How Will Windschuttle Be Remembered?

> The responsibility of the historian is not to be compassionate; it is to be dispassionate. It's to stand above current political squabbles and aims.
>
> Keith Windschuttle, 2003

Fabrication is a genuinely atrocious book. It is atrocious not because of its politics but because of its hypocrisy about its politics; not because it criticises historical accounts but because of its shrill, denunciatory condemnation of historians and its tendentious and unreasoning and dismissal of Indigenous Australian testimony; not because its methodology is seriously flawed—which it is—but because of its false claims to quasi-scientific correctness. Even more, it is a book that lacks humanity. To

Windschuttle, history is not about empathy; it is about numbers, technicalities, absolute proof, settling scores and winning. To Windschuttle, history is certainly not about explaining the lives of the living, breathing people of the past. In time, because of these flaws, Windschuttle's book will be relegated to a minor footnote in historiography, regarded as an ill-advised oddity, like *Hitler's Willing Executioners*, Daniel Goldhagen's huge, carefully documented but thoroughly unsound book on the Holocaust, and as an ill-conceived notoriety, like Hugh Trevor-Roper's 1983 endorsement of the fake Hitler diaries.

Debates about Indigenous Australian history have, in the past, been pervaded by prejudice, by condescension, by moralism and by emotionalism; Windschuttle's point that, in this context, historians need to be both detached and methodologically careful was a good one—at first blush. *Fabrication*, however, is about an author on the warpath with such ideological zeal and such flagrant insincerity that he completely lost his credibility, joining the eccentric ranks of fringe pseudohistorians. Indeed, his own words have come back to haunt him: 'By abandoning truth and objectivity, [authors] unwittingly validate political positions they might find less congenial'.

CODA

Denial persists. In Zimbabwe in the 1980s, Robert Mugabe's regime denied that it was responsible for the mass murder of an estimated 20 000 tribal opponents in Matabeleland in what was then called, in classic denialist language, the *Gukurahundi*, or 'washing away the chaff'. The regime has continued its campaign of denial into the twenty-first century, blaming the outside world for, and thereby externalising, its own felonies. Indeed, Britain and its 'white' allies have been accused by the grandiose Mugabe, in a fit of denialist paranoia, of undermining the manifestly brutal Zimbabwean regime, which has been systematically looting, torturing and killing its own people for more than two decades. And in April 2008, as an already devastated Zimbabwe was racked by post-election violence and agitation, Thabo Mbeki flew into Harare, the country's capital, and announced, in line with his former HIV-AIDS approach to political problems, that there was 'no crisis in Zimbabwe'.

It is not only Mugabe and Mbeki who continue to deny. In Burma (Myanmar), the junta, propped up by a military whose sole purpose seems to be repression of the Burmese people, was badly caught out by the devastating cyclone of May 2008. It refused western help on the grounds that everything was under control. In other words, its repressive and supposedly all-powerful regime could not be seen to be helpless in the face of a natural disaster, whatever the needs of the cyclone's survivors.

It is interesting, at this stage, to reflect on how contemporary self-deception in Zimbabwe and Burma may be remembered in post-colonial historical writing. Will present and future generations of historians tell it as it was, or will some of the more radical purveyors of the unalloyed merits of post-imperial regimes fall into the trap of presenting bad governance in a good light, thus adding a new variety to the catalogue of denialist histories?

Returning to those histories discussed in this book, state-supported denial of the Turkish or Japanese variety remains a seemingly dysfunctional form of national defensiveness characterised by commonality of aims and tactics. For example, Turkish and Japanese nationalist deniers have much in common in their denialist behaviour, since the foundation of their historical defiance is based on each nation having passed through the self-inflicted punishment of a harrowing war. In Turkey's case it was World War I, and in Japan's case it was World War II. As it happened, notwithstanding the traumatic impact of wartime casualties, both nations then managed to escape the full consequences of Allied retribution.

Turkey, taking advantage of political circumstances at the time, was the only Entente power allowed to renegotiate its settlement (at the 1923 Treaty of Lausanne), thus avoiding being dismantled and being made to pay massive and crippling reparations, as had been the case with Germany and Austria-Hungary.

Japan, again because of political circumstances, escaped the kinds of demands made on the defeated Nazi Germany, which included partition, multi-national occupation and de-Nazification followed by diligent democratisation and a high-profile war crimes tribunal that attached blame to the Nazi party, its leaders and its civil and military functionaries. In contrast, Japan's relatively light post-war burden was a benign US occupation, not much in the way of ideological decontamination, a move towards parliamentary democracy and a war crimes tribunal that was seriously flawed in several ways, one of which was its maintenance of the authority of Emperor Hirohito, by the diversion of blame onto the 5000 accused war criminals. The consequence was, in the cases of Turkey and Japan, an intact and continuing narrative thread of national honour that provides the basis for modern denial.

With the Turks and the Armenians, as matters stand at the time of writing, the best the Armenians and their supporters may be able to get from Turkey is an equivocal acknowledgement along the lines of Turkish foreign minister (later president) Abdullah Gul's note to the participants at the 2005 Bilgi University conference. In his message, Gul pointed out that, while the Armenians had suffered, so too had the Turks. This remains the stock 'soft' official answer on the Armenian question, and it is not one that is likely to change. If a straightforward national apology from Turkey is unlikely, the sought-after reparations for the Armenians are an impossibility, if only because of the lag in time, the complexity of apportioning responsibility and the likelihood that any move by a Turkish government to compensate the Armenians would be political suicide. For example, in the eastern Turkish town of Erzincan, once the site of terrible bloodshed in 1915 but now a prosperous rural centre with more than 100 000 inhabitants, it would simply be an unfeasible task to disentangle property ownership, culpability for violence and the effects of the wartime massacres, knowing that probably most of the villagers and townspeople of Erzincan who were involved in the events at Kemakh in 1915 may themselves have been murdered shortly afterwards by advancing Russian and Armenian soldiers and irregulars. There is also the knowledge that any externally pressured apology and settlement in eastern Turkey, or anywhere in Turkey for that matter, would almost certainly lead to violent protest from the Turks, who are increasingly resentful of the perceived hypocrisy of European moral censure. Indeed, they may argue, and with some justice, that if they are good enough for NATO, why are they not good enough for the European Union?

In Japan's case, the picture is mixed and much more ambiguous. Since 1945, there have been more than a score of apologies that have then been contradicted by politically motivated anti-apology rebuttals in parliament and in the media, high-profile symbolic gestures of solidarity with the fallen dead, including war criminals, and governmental refusals to pay reparations to the surviving victims of forced prostitution. In these circumstances, a cynical observer may be forgiven for thinking that successive Japanese governments are waiting for the last 'comfort women' to die, thus clearing the decks for renewed attacks on Article 9 of the constitution, revival of an unbroken, unsullied Japanese military tradition and preparations for a renewal of traditional rivalries with China, all on the back of tacit western approval. As dysfunctional as Japanese denial may at first seem, thanks to global *Realpolitik*, dysfunctional it may not be in actuality: shades of the 1950s and the unsinkable aircraft carrier all over again.

Serbia, conversely, has, through its 2004 commission of inquiry, admitted partial liability for wartime guilt and has shown some willingness to move on, although the situation in 'ethnically cleansed' eastern Bosnia remains tense. However, the expected Serbian convulsions over the unilateral declaration of independence by Kosovo on 17 February 2008 failed to eventuate, with the subsequent Serbian general elections of 11 May showing the Serbian nationalism of the Slavic, eastward-turning variety apparently being replaced by a war-weary desire to be counted as a member of the western camp. As with Turkey, the attraction of membership of the European Union has given many Serbs pause for thought; but, unlike the Turks, the Serbs, in admitting just a little, appear willing to put their inglorious past behind them, but with, perhaps, that admission soon to be forgotten.

In contrast to Turkey, Japan and Serbia, modern Germany (in reality the old West Germany) has provided a model example of how a nation should behave well after having behaved appallingly. Apologies have been promulgated and reparations have been paid in full. Furthermore, in Germany and in Austria, the law has been altered in an attempt to combat Holocaust denial. Compare that move, contentious as it is, with the pro-denial provisions of Turkey's legal code and the struggle that Saburo Ienaga had with the pro-denialist Japanese legal system. Moreover, in the former capital of Nazi Germany itself, there are two striking monuments to the Holocaust. The first is the Jewish Museum in Lindenstrasse and, sited close to the Brandenburger Tor, the second is the Holocaust memorial. Set that German approach to memorialising an uncomfortable past against the mealy-mouthed behaviour of successive Turkish and Japanese governments when it comes to their acknowledgement of historic wrongs. Where in Ankara or Istanbul, for example, are the official Turkish monuments to the Armenian dead? Where in Tokyo are the permanent exhibitions that commemorate the civilian dead of imperial Japan's occupied territories, the casualties of Unit 731 or the comfort women?

Having said that, Germany, as we have seen, is beset with resurgent neo-Nazism, which, while changing the focus of its xenophobic attacks, proudly wears its anti-Semitism on its sleeve like a death's head badge left over from the Hitler era. The only good news from that direction is the apparent decline of the prominent individual Holocaust deniers such as Ernst Zündel and David Irving, whose blatant and unremitting reverence for a ghastly regime has pushed them out beyond the edge of effectiveness.

When it comes to effectiveness, the minor-key Australian version of denial, Keith Windschuttle's *The Fabrication of Aboriginal History*, has all but vanished from the historical and political landscape now that Labor prime minister Kevin Rudd has issued a national apology (on 13 February 2008) to the 'stolen generations'. The key question here is just how effective was Windschuttle's campaign in the first place, knowing that the failings of *Fabrication* were masked in the public arena by a four-year pro-Windschuttle media blitz in *The Australian*? Combine that *Australian* masquerade with sporadic interest in the electronic media and slim book sales, and you have what in Australia is referred to as a 'beat-up' story, an artificially confected issue, suggesting a very low level of impact on popular historical consciousness. Interestingly, and in that context, the Nielsen Bookscan figures for *Fabrication* are about the same as the estimated subscription and sales figures for *Quadrant*. As a case in point, therefore, *Fabrication* was a nine-day historical wonder but is also a wonderful case study of a combination of ideology, opportunism and grandiose intellectual pretension, for, as James Boyce pointed out in *Whitewash*, with some prescience:

> The number of elementary errors in *Fabrication* will soon exclude it from serious historical debate. The political and cultural impact of the book, however, is more complex, given the appeal of its claim to be upholding the truth in the face of politically-motivated intellectuals who are setting us up for an unwarranted guilt trip.

'Offensive rather than effective' may, therefore, be *Fabrication*'s epitaph.

Finally we come to the Communist Party of Great Britain, a once-influential organisation that represented the genuine aspirations of a sizeable proportion of the British working class. In an increasingly acute state of denial from the mid-1930s onwards, the Party lost its utopian way and became progressively more dysfunctional by bending over backwards while simultaneously standing on its head and doing occasional somersaults. These contortions eventually led to its fragmentation and marginalisation and, after the 1968 'Prague Spring', Party splitters derisively referred to their former colleagues, now opponents, as 'tankies', a comment on the Party's track record of supporting regimes that had reflexively called in Soviet military support whenever the aspirations of its workers were seen to be too ambitious.

It is a sad and ironic footnote to the decline of the Party and to the disillusionment of its idealists that the former *Daily Worker* offices in Farringdon Road currently stand empty: they were, most recently, a 'cash and carry' store. Straight across the road from the handsome *Daily Worker* entrance once used by Johnny Campbell, Peter Fryer and Alison Mcleod is an impressively luxurious suite of offices, the Lincoln Place branch of Merrill Lynch, globally prominent financial managers and the apotheosis of international capitalism.

As for the 16 King Street Party headquarters in cross-town Covent Garden, the former Party corner office is now a branch of the HSBC banking conglomerate. Right next door, at 15 King Street, is a trendy and expensive clothes boutique called, of all things, TZAR.

APPENDIX

Below is a summary of the largely unanswered claims against Keith Windschuttle's *The Fabrication of Aboriginal History* that are contained in Robert Manne's *Whitewash*. A few of the claims (for example, McFarlane's Brown Bess argument) appear thin, but most appear to be substantive. Some of the issues are discussed in detail elsewhere—Flood deals with mortality through disease in detail—but, to date, the comprehensive rebuttal promised by Windschuttle has not been delivered.

The page numbers are references to the relevant pages in *Whitewash*. Indigenous Australian author Greg Lehmann's chapter, which is more a rumination than an analysis, is not included in this section; nor is Neville Green's chapter, which was about the earlier *Quadrant* articles. Dirk Moses wrote a final, summary chapter on Windschuttle as a denier, which is interesting but does not make the same specific claims against the scholarly merit of *Fabrication* as do most of the others.

The brief biographies are taken directly from the 2003 publication and refer to the status of the authors at that time, although some have been productive since; for example, Martin Krygier has produced *Civil Passions: Selected Essays* (Black Inc., Melbourne, 2005), Marilyn Lake and Henry Reynolds have published *Drawing the Global Colour Line* (Melbourne University Press, Melbourne, 2008), and James Bryce has published *Van Diemen's Land: A History* (Black Inc., Melbourne, 2008). There are additional claims against Windschuttle's work in Attwood, but that is a different story.

As in the rest of this book, to avoid confusion for readers who are not familiar with Australian history, 'Tasmania' is used to describe the colony under its original title, Van Diemen's Land, and its later title.

James Boyce

(Boyce was a researcher at the University of Tasmania.)

Windschuttle relies mainly on government documents regarding
    Indigenous Australians that 'hardly began to appear until 1827' (p. 17).

Windschuttle ignores the influential 1852 history of Reverend John West
    (p. 18).

APPENDIX

Windschuttle excludes 'almost all primary source material from the period in question, 1803 to 1847' (p. 20).

Windschuttle places French explorer Baudin's visit as 1807–16, which are the dates of the publication of French author Perron's account of the actual 1801–03 expedition (p. 21).

Windschuttle ignores Labillardière's account of the significant landing in Tasmania of d'Entrecasteaux in 1793 (p. 21).

Windschuttle ignores accounts of contemporary eyewitnesses David Burns and James Ross (p. 21).

With the exception of George Hobler's diaries, Windschuttle completely ignores crucial private diaries and letters that contradict his thesis. Either the evidence in the diaries is ignored or Windschuttle's claim to have consulted them would appear to be untrue (pp. 23–4).

Other diaries from that period contradict Windschuttle's low body count claims (pp. 24–6).

Windschuttle ignores published accounts that contradict his claims, for example Rosalie Hare's reporting of massacres (pp. 25–6).

Windschuttle is over-reliant on non-existing or patchy official government records prior to 1827 that paint an inadequate picture of early Indigenous Australian–settler relations (p. 27).

Windschuttle has relied too much on author NJB Plomley's research for his low body count claims, when Plomley has admitted himself that his sources are not complete enough to paint a comprehensive picture on this issue (pp. 29–30).

Windschuttle has omitted the published account by John Batman (Tasmanian and founder of Melbourne) of a roving party that killed fifteen Indigenous Australians in September 1829 (pp. 30–2).

Windschuttle grossly exaggerates the influence of evangelicals and the government on British colonial policy and on attitudes and activities in Tasmania (pp. 32–4).

Windschuttle exaggerates government control over the convicts and settlers (p. 38).

It is unclear why orders forbidding the killing of Indigenous Australians were issued in 1810 and 1813 if, as Windschuttle claims, there were no killings carried out by whites between 1808 and 1813 (p. 38).

Windschuttle over-emphasises the policing role of the peripherally useful 40th Regiment (p. 39).

Windschuttle's representation of the 1804 Risdon cove massacre is faulty, as it is suppositional and dismissive of the only eyewitness evidence to the inquiry, which, as it happens, contradicts Windschuttle's categorical point of view (pp. 40–2).

The evidence suggests that Windschuttle's claim that disease was the 'major cause of depopulation' cannot be substantiated (pp. 42–4).

Windschuttle's application of various forms of the term 'plausible' when it comes to Indigenous Australian deaths lacks credibility as it relates to the evidential conventions of historical scholarship (pp. 44–5).

Windschuttle's contention that kangaroo hunting, one source of Indigenous Australian–settler conflict, had largely died out by 1811 is not borne out by the available evidence (pp. 46–8).

The inaccurate claim that Indigenous Australian coastal food sources were not depleted by settler depredations is dependent on one source and is not fully contextualised (pp. 51–2).

Windschuttle fails to realise that, regarding competition for territory, settler land ownership was not the same as land occupation for pasture. Of the latter, there was significantly more than stated in the official 'ownership' statistics, and this pastoral occupation was extensive and produced Indigenous Australian–settler conflict (pp. 51–7).

Windschuttle contends that Indigenous Australian resistance was sporadic, was based on criminal intent, and was exacerbated by the failure of Indigenous Australians to negotiate. However, there was actually continuing negotiation culminating in a period of peace, as demonstrated in George Robinson's journals (pp. 61–2).

Windschuttle's claim that there is 'abundant' evidence that Indigenous Tasmanian society was dysfunctional and doomed is based on the work of Robert Edgerton, a US author who theorises about the island's Indigenous society using hostile and flawed sources. In this matter, Windschuttle ignores, misreads or dismisses the more favourable evidence (pp. 63–8).

Martin Krygier and Robert van Krieken

(Krygier was a professor of law and Krieken was an associate professor of sociology, both at the University of Sydney.)

Settler testimony that supports Windschuttle is not scrutinised for meaning, while settler testimony that contradicts Windschuttle is 'mercilessly cross-examined' (p. 93).

Windschuttle selectively uses John Gascoigne's research on the influence of the Enlightenment in Australian society (pp. 98–9).

Henry Reynolds

(Reynolds was an Australian Research Council senior research fellow at the University of Tasmania.)

Windschuttle says (without evidence) that Indigenous Tasmanians did not have the concept of 'ownership' and did not use 'property', in the face of twentieth-century scholarly consensus that the nineteenth-century linguistic picture used by Windschuttle is incomplete. He did not, for example, refer to Plomley's *A Word List of the Tasmanian Aboriginal Languages* (1976), which explains that Indigenous Australians refer to country, not property (pp. 109–13).

Windschuttle ignores the written evidence that suggests that Indigenous Australians lived and hunted within territorial boundaries (pp. 113–15).

Windschuttle ignores or dismisses the written evidence that Indigenous Australians resented settler expansion and retaliated violently in the 'Black Wars' (pp. 115–20).

Arguing that the 'Black War' was an anachronistic term about a non-war, Windschuttle ignores Tasmanian Lieutenant Governor Arthur's 1825 instructions to treat Indigenous Tasmanians 'as if they proceeded from subjects of an accredited state' and other evidence that this was considered at the time to be a guerrilla war (pp. 121–7).

When discussing the death toll, Windschuttle does not take into account the activities of 'borderers' (edge-of-society settlers such as sealers and mounted stockmen), which are unrecorded but are generally accepted as having taken place (pp. 128–9).

Windschuttle fails to quote fully the relevant 1830 evidence of the Tasmanian Aborigines Committee when it contradicts his assertions (p. 132).

Shayne Breen

(Breen taught at the University of Tasmania.)

Windschuttle displays little understanding of the impact of social evolutionism as a nineteenth-century concept as it applies to his own loaded terminology (p. 141).

Windschuttle ignores the view that his major Tasmanian source for anthropological comments, H Ling Roth, occupies a controversial position as a social evolutionist (p. 142).

Windschuttle relies too much on the now contentious 1960s work of archaeologist Rhys Jones regarding degeneration of Indigenous Tasmanians and ignores later research (pp. 142–3).

Windschuttle argues that Indigenous Tasmanians had no sacred sites, but there is one at Cox Bight (p. 144).

Windschuttle argues that Indigenous Australian survival depended on 'good fortune'—for 35 000 years (pp. 144–5).

Windschuttle claims that Indigenous Australians' primitivism meant that they were incapable of military action, but this is countered by Breen's analysis of tactical skills (pp. 146–8).

Windschuttle's arguments about Indigenous Australian brutality, the selling of women into sexual slavery and the significance of venereal disease are not supported by the evidence. This is still a highly contentious issue (pp. 148–50).

APPENDIX

Marilyn Lake

(Lake was a professor of history at La Trobe University.)

Windschuttle is not familiar with 1970s scholarly work on gender relations within Indigenous Australian societies (p. 168) or with Catherine Hall's post-colonial work on racialisation of English identity, for example in *Civilising Subjects: Metropole and Colony in the English Imagination, 1830–1867*, Polity Press, Cambridge, 2002.

Cathie Clement

(Clement was a Western Australian professional and heritage historian.)

Windschuttle made several errors over Governor General Dean's speech and 'apology' in 2001 (pp. 205–14).

Windschuttle created, with the help of the media, a myth of his own (pp. 205–14).

Peggy Patrick

(Patrick was a Mirawoong-Gija woman of the east Kimberly region in Western Australia.)

Regarding a mistake made by Windschuttle over Indigenous Australian eyewitness accounts, Patrick said: 'He reckon I bin say "my mum" when I bin really talk "ganggayi", or "my mum mum", not "my mum"' (pp. 216–17).

Philip Tardif

(Tardif was a writer on Tasmanian history.)

Regarding the 1804 Risdon cove massacre, Windschuttle accepts uncritically the views of self-interested contemporary eyewitnesses Moore and Mountgarret, who agree with his hypothesis about few casualties, notwithstanding their individual reputations at the time, as a 'rascal' (Moore) and a man who acquired 'eternal disgrace and infamy' (Mountgarret). But Windschuttle discounts the contradictory evidence of White, the more reliable witness (pp. 219–22).

David Hansen

(Hansen was a senior curator of art at the Tasmanian Museum and Art Gallery.)

Windschuttle makes several basic mistakes in his captioning of the John Glover painting of Mount Wellington, Hobart (p. 228).

Lyndall Ryan

(Ryan was a professor of Australian studies at the University of Newcastle, New South Wales.)

Windschuttle's accusations that Ryan's seven references regarding the 1827 Meander Rover skirmishes are technically correct in two instances but incorrect in the remaining five (pp. 236–9).

Windschuttle is dismissive of the naming of North Tasmanian people on no evidence (p. 240).

Windschuttle is unable to discredit the testimony of Hellyer, key witness to the 1830 massacre at the Retreat (p. 241).

Windschuttle dismisses the evidence of Punch, a witness, because he was an ex-convict, living with an Indigenous Australian woman and illiterate (pp. 241–2).

Windschuttle ignores casualty figures supplied by Plomley and 'other evidence' (pp. 242–3).

Windschuttle says he cannot find a reference to the 1828 Pittwater massacre (which was inconvenient to his case) in the Tasmanian archive, but Ryan says it is there (pp. 244–5).

Ryan admits incorrectly sourcing some references that are actually elsewhere but argues that this is not 'fabrication' (p. 246).

Windschuttle claims that an uncorroborated massacre at Tooms Lake took place in 1828, basing his assertion on the type of evidential framework that he attacks in others (pp. 246–8).

Windschuttle accuses Ryan of uncritical use of George Robinson, but uses Robinson himself when it suits him (p. 249).

APPENDIX

Windschuttle's definition of 'roving parties', or posses, is narrow and debatable (pp. 250–1).

Windschuttle reads the Tasmanian archives and newspaper accounts uncritically regarding (low) body count (p. 254).

Windschuttle naively assumes that the same level of recording took place for Indigenous Australian deaths as for white deaths (p. 254).

Windschuttle's evidence for Indigenous Australian population figures is highly contentious (p. 253).

Windschuttle's population thesis is based on outdated research (pp. 253–4).

Cassandra Pybus

(Pybus was an Australian Research Council professorial fellow at the University of Tasmania.)

Windschuttle's account of the Rae-Ellis incident does not take into account the 'lurid' and 'absurd' approach of the author's book on George Robinson, with its accusations of cannibalism and the consequent highly critical response by established scholars (pp. 258–9).

Windschuttle seems unaware that Plomley and Ryan were critical of Robinson prior to the Rae-Ellis book or that Reynolds had actually written a more benign interpretation of Robinson, against Windschuttle's thesis (p. 259).

Windschuttle's motivation in attacking Robinson is to discount him as a witness (p. 260).

Windschuttle does not apply the same standard of scrutiny to Rae-Ellis's work as he does to that of Reynolds and Ryan (p. 260–2).

Using H Ling Roth, Windschuttle claims that Indigenous Australians cannot make fire, an assertion contradicted by other sources (p. 268).

Windschuttle discredits as 'notoriously unreliable' (that is contradictory to Windschuttle's point of view) the respectable but argumentative Robertson as a witness in the 1830 Aboriginal Committee but offers no evidence (p. 268).

In his analysis, Windschuttle fails to take into account Robertson's racial origins (part–West Indian), which meant that his peers saw him as reliable and compulsively frank but beneath them (p. 274).

Ian McFarlane

(McFarlane was a doctoral graduate at the University of Tasmania.)

Windschuttle asserts that interest in the 1828 Cape Grim massacre is a post-1960s leftist construct, whereas McFarlane says that the initial records were not available until the late 1950s and slowly increased in accessibility over the following decade or so (p. 277).

Windschuttle claims, inaccurately, that 'academic historians' take a view in opposition to the more localised authorities (p. 278).

Windschuttle inaccurately accuses Lloyd Robson of mislocating a site associated with the 1828 Cape Grim massacre (pp. 278–9).

Windschuttle dismisses or overlooks eyewitness accounts that might contradict his view that the massacre was not inspired by the Van Diemen's Land Company, that it caused few casualties and that it has been misrepresented by academic historians (pp. 281–5, 289).

Windschuttle supports evidence by Curr and Robinson that props up his view (pp. 285–6, 290–1, 294, 296).

Windschuttle's claim that massacre numbers would have been low because of the use of Brown Bess muskets by the killers is dubious (pp. 285–8).

Ahistorically, Windschuttle outlines contact experience in Tasmania as an undifferentiated set of encounters (pp. 292–3).

Mark Finnane

(Finnane was a professor of history at Griffith University.)

In asserting that the settling of Australia was 'the least violent of all Europe's encounters with the New World', Windschuttle does not take into account the population base (pp. 300–4).

Windschuttle disguises the scale of Indigenous Australian deaths while exaggerating white deaths, using a 'hopelessly wrong' methodology and tendentious point of view (pp. 304–8).

APPENDIX

Tim Murray and Christine Williamson

(Murray was a professor of archaeology at La Trobe University, and Williamson worked in the archaeology program at La Trobe University.)

Generally, Windschuttle's archaeological and ethno-historical Chapter 10 shows poor knowledge and poor understanding of the research (p. 312).

Windschuttle's comments are based on a point of view that uses small glimpses of Indigenous Australian society by white settlers (p. 313).

Windschuttle's base population calculation is no more or less accurate than the ones he criticises (pp. 314–15).

In a key paragraph, Windschuttle conflates the view of Rhys Jones, an authority, with his own opinions, giving the false impression that Windschuttle's (incorrect) views on Indigenous Australian societal regression are actually Jones's views (p. 315).

Windschuttle does not take into account more recent research on the supposedly 'maladaptive' nature of Indigenous Tasmanian society (pp. 316–18).

The assertion, based on a suggestion in Jones's 1971 PhD, that Indigenous Tasmanians had regressed is more complex than Windschuttle states (pp. 320–1).

Recent archaeological data from the first forty-five years of European occupation 'strengthens the argument against regression' (pp. 320–3).

Excavation of the Burghley Van Diemen's Land Company site in the 1990s counters Windschuttle's claims about the post-contact adaptability of Indigenous Tasmanian society (pp. 323–8).

Windschuttle's 'negative assessment' of Indigenous Tasmanian society 'owes at least as much to such [*a priori*] assumptions as it does to lack of knowledge about, or understanding of, more than 35 000 years of Tasmanian history' (p. 328).

NOTES

INTRODUCTION

Page vii, Mbeki's HIV-AIDS denial: Meldrum.

Page vii, Bush's Iraq denial: 'Testing Two Leaders: George Bush, in Denial'.

Page vii, Deng's Tiananmen Square denial: Suettinger, esp. pp. 81–2.

Page x, From 1899 onwards: This section allows for the 1864 Geneva Convention, the subsequent creation of the International Red Cross and the 1868 St Petersburg Convention as valuable nineteenth-century initiatives hampered by having no internationally accepted backing organisations such as the twentieth century's largely ineffective League of Nations and the more variably effective United Nations.

Page xi, Denial and prejudice: See Allport; Dovidio, Glick & Rudman; and Sherif & Hovland. See also Cohen for a social scientist's perspective on the normality of denial and how and why people deny manifest atrocities.

Page xi, beyond a merely psychodynamic definition: Prior to Allport's work, the psychological-psychoanalytical view of prejudice was based on the Freudian notion of frustration leading to aggression, or unconscious and irrational impulse expressed as hostility (usually racism) against an outgroup. This approach assumed that such behaviour was relatively normal, but, after 1945, post-genocidal anti-Semitism could no longer be construed as normal, and a more individualistic approach was taken. This led to the view in the early 1950s that (prejudiced) authoritarian personality traits sprang from poor child-rearing practices, producing a need for regulation and rigid social structures. See, for example, Adorno et al.

Page xi, 'faulty and inflexible generalization': Allport, pp. 395–408.

Page xii, cognitive dissonance: See Cooper; and Festinger, *When Prophecy Fails*, *A Theory of Cognitive Dissonance* and *Conflict, Decision & Dissonance*.

NOTES

Pages xii–xv, Freud and denial: See Sandler, esp. pp. 311–54.

Page xvii, Definition of genocide: See Weitz, esp. pp. 8–15.

1 UNDER WESTERN EYES

Full chapter: The intense historical debate about the Armenian massacres stretches back to 1916 and the publication in Britain of J Bryce and A Toynbee's *The Treatment of Armenians in the Ottoman Empire 1915–1916*, a compilation of harrowing and largely authentic individual pieces of evidence presented to the British foreign secretary Lord Grey. The report was, and has been since, discounted by Turkish authorities because of its origins (wartime), its authorship (pro-Armenian Bryce) and its sources (largely Christian missionaries and western diplomatic staff). Because of the similar ideological commitment of several more recent scholars engaged in this controversial topic (see, for example, Suny), this chapter is largely based on the work of four of the more reliable modern authors: Akcam (*A Shameful Act*), Bloxham (*The Great Game of Genocide*), Hovannisian (*The Armenian Genocide*) and Lewy (*The Armenian Massacres in Ottoman Turkey*). Akcam is a Turkish sociologist-cum-historian who at the time of writing was working in the USA at the University of Minnesota; Bloxham was teaching and researching at the University of Edinburgh; Hovannisian was professor of Armenian and near-eastern history at the University of California, Los Angeles; and Lewy was professor emeritus of political science at the University of Massachusetts. There are dozens of other writers and editors in the field, but all too frequently their emotional or ideological position is so transparent that their value as witnesses is accordingly diminished, notwithstanding their commitment to researching the issue. At the same time, there has been a recent growth in Turkish scholarly interest that transcends the politics of nationalism. See, for example, Gocek, in Hovannisian, *The Armenian Genocide*; and the account given below of the proposed conference at Bogazici University in 2005.

    In this chapter, Turkish language accents are not used. Some Turkish and Armenian proper names and place names vary in their spelling, for example, Hnchak / Hunchak and Vahakn / Vahakan; therefore, an internally consistent approach has been adopted.

The title of this chapter is a reference to J Conrad's novel *Under Western Eyes* (1911), a political account of 'eastern' Russia observed by a western narrator.

Pages 1–3, Dink's assassination: The incidents described and the quotes relating to the death of Dink are taken from news accounts of the time, mainly in January 2007, including BBC News Online, CNN, *Guardian International*, *International Herald Tribune*, *Journal of Turkish Weekly*, *The New York Times* and *Turkish Daily News*. See, for example, Birch, 'Outspoken Armenian Editor' and 'Seven Held Over Killing'; and Harvey. According to *The Guardian*, a newspaper unsympathetic to the Turkish denial case, eighteen other Turkish journalists had been killed since 1992. (Leader, *The Guardian*, 23 January 2007.) The assassination of Dink was one significant event that led to the uncovering of an alleged 'Deep State' conspiracy of Turkish ultra-nationalists. (Burke.)

Page 1, Erdogan's announcement: Arsu. Erdogan's Islamist Justice and Development Party (AKP) came to power in 2002 with the support of traditionally inclined regional and rural Islamists together with a burgeoning electorate of metropolitan bourgeois and working-class Islamists. Erdogan had been initially banned from office because of a 1998 pro-Islamist conviction for incitement, an obstacle that was quickly dispensed with through legislation. Generally regarded as a charismatic and principled nationalist leader whose Islamist convictions are strongly held, he more or less accepted that hard-line Islamic politics might wreck Turkey's fragile stability and its chances of membership of the European Union. After gaining power, however, his government gradually whittled away some of the symbols of secularism, including abolishing the headscarves ban at universities, leading to a Supreme Court challenge in March 2008 over the legitimacy of the AKP, a potentially divisive and destabilising move by the secularists.

Page 2, Pamuk crossing swords: Pamuk, 'On Trial'.

NOTES

Page 3, more than one in three Turkish Armenians: Lewy (pp. 234–41) provides carefully worked figures.

Page 4, French descendants as an influential anti-Turkish minority: Chrisafis. Dink had opposed the French Bill on free speech grounds. A precise total of French Armenians is hard to calculate because of French government tradition that statistical information should be neither ethnically nor racially categorised. The figures vary, with Bloxham estimating the French Armenian population at 500 000.

Pages 4–5, Anyone who espouses the Armenian cause is an enemy: The Turkish Ministry of Culture and Tourism website, among pages that deal with culture and tourism, promotional films of Turkey and tourism development regions, has a genocide section that combats 'Armenian Allegations'. (Look under 'History' at www.kultur.gov.tr/EN) The former Soviet republic of Armenia has its own official governmental counter-page at www.armeniaforeignministry.com/fr/genocide/main.html

Page 5, 'The propaganda work necessary . . .': A Refik, Turkish army officer and historian, in his short book *Iki Komite Iki Kotal*, 1919 (republished 1994), cited in Akcam, *A Shameful Act*, p. 125. Exiled Turkish sociologist-historian Akcam's scrupulously researched book provides a useful analysis, as does its 2004 predecessor *From Empire to Republic*. Both of these works have made Akcam unpopular with Turkish government authorities and nationalists, who regard him as a leftist renegade. He was granted political asylum in Germany after being arrested in 1976 and sentenced to imprisonment for student journalism activism. His role in the story of Turkish–Armenian relations is crucial, since authors in this field tend to be passionate supporters of their own ethnic groups and detractors of the opposing point of view.

Page 7, 'Talat said that . . .': H Morgenthau, *United States Diplomacy on the Bosphorus: The Diaries of Ambassador Morgenthau 1913–1916*, compiled by A Sarafian, 2004, cited in Akcam, *A Shameful Act*, p. 155. Morgenthau, a Jew, is reviled by Turkish anti-genocidists as a pro-Armenian witness, as are the Christian missionaries who testified to Turkish atrocities.

Page 8, Djemal's role: Lewy, pp. 196–7. In the conventional retellings of the Armenian persecution it is Talat Pasha who comes out worst, mainly as a lying anti-Armenian egotist—probably a justifiable summary. Talat was assassinated in Germany in 1921 by a young Armenian, Soghomon Tehlirian, who pleaded guilty and was acquitted of the murder, which says something about popular feeling in Berlin at the time.

Page 8, anti-Armenian feeling was almost palpable: Pre-war tension in regional Anatolia was exacerbated by growing numbers of Islamic refugees (*mujahirs*) from the Balkans and Tsarist Russia.

Page 9, The CUP Central Committee: Enver Pasha was the prime mover in the proposed mass-deportation policy. Talat Pasha and Sakir Bey were responsible for the operational details.

Page 11, Vehip's allegation: Kevorkian (pp. 119–20) says:

> Among the documents collected by the Mazhar Commission [a commission of inquiry set up by the sultan in 1918 and chaired by Hasan Mazhar Bey], the most sensational is indubitably the written testimony sent on December 5th 1918 to Hasan Mazhar by General Vehip Pasha, a high-ranking military member of the CUP and former commander-in-chief of the 3rd Army, in whose province the most systematic massacres occurred, especially in the slaughter houses of the Kemah gorges, close to Golcuk Lake and in the Kanli Dere mountains, close to Malatya. The General concluded in his Summary of Convictions as follows:
>> The deportations of the Armenians took place in complete contradiction with humanity, civilisation and the Government's honour. The massacre and extermination of the Armenians and the sacking and looting of their properties are the result of decisions taken by the Central Committee of the CUP; it was Dr Bahaettin Sakir Bey who trained gangs of butchers to slaughter human beings and he too urged them to carry it out. The administrative authorities [that is the *valis* and the *mutesarifs*]

obeyed Bahaettin Sakir's directives. As a matter of fact, all the disorders and troubles in the Third Army were set off by Bahaettin Sakir Bey's underhand dealings. Driven in a special car he moved from one centre to another, delivering decisions taken and the directives to the various local sections of the Union and Progress Party and the local authorities in the same place by word of mouth ... The atrocities were committed according to a scheme conceived in advance and were organised absolutely intentionally. First they were directed by the delegates of the Union and Progress Party, and secondly, they were implemented by local government officials who had become submissive tools of this lawless and unscrupulous organisation's desires and aspirations ... All these instructions were dictated by oral instruction and not one document remains. The Army and the Turkish element have nothing in common with these crimes and atrocities and did not take part in them.

After the war ended, the CUP was disbanded and the Turks held their own courts-martial of the Triumvirate and others. (The Triumvirate members were sentenced to death in absentia.) At the same time, the Allies insisted that those involved in the massacres be held accountable. Accordingly, 145 Turkish civil and military officials were held in exile on Malta from 1919 but were gradually released by 1922 because there were irresolvable procedural and evidential issues as well as problems with political and military expediency, including prisoner exchange. There were other circumstances that favoured dropping the prosecutions, including British anxiety about Lenin's Bolshevik government teaming up with the Kemalist regime to dominate the eastern Mediterranean and access to India, a dynamic repeated later in the century with US and British policy trying to balance importunate Armenians against Turkey's vital NATO membership.

Page 11, The plot thickened: Sabit: Akcam, *A Shameful Act*, p. 150; Bey: Akcam, *A Shameful Act*, pp. 153–4. For a good summary of this crucial series of events, see Akcam, *A Shameful Act*, pp. 149–204. The overwhelming impression is one of intentional mass removal by any means, which would inevitably lead to the obliteration of the Armenian communities in the east.

Page 12, Russian troops arrived in Van: Bloxham, p. 84. McCarthy (seen by the Armenian side as pro-Turkish) argues that the mythologised Armenian rag-tag hero-victims of Van were actually well armed and well organised (notwithstanding their lack of artillery).

Page 12, on 24 May the Russians asked: Bloxham, pp. 85–6.

Page 12, 'be brought to an end . . .': Turkish Ministry of Interior statement, in M Demirel, *Birinci Demirei, Birinci Dunya Harbinde Erzurum ve Cercevesinde Ermeni Hareketleri 1914–1918*, 1996, cited in Akcam, *A Shameful Act*, pp. 155–6.

Page 12, the Turkish High Command ordered: Lewy, p. 152.

Page 13, massacring Armenians as they went: Bloxham, p. 85.

Page 13, 'resisters and escapees' and **'killed while attempting to escape':** Bloxham, p. 86.

Page 13, Because of exigent circumstances: This radicalisation standpoint is close to the argument discussed in Hovannisian's chapter 'Wartime Radicalisation or Premeditated Continuum?', in *The Armenian Genocide*, pp. 3–17. The other (continuum) view is that Turkish genocidal activity began in the late nineteenth century.

Page 14, small minority, punished: Akcam, *A Shameful Act*, pp. 164, 166–7.

Page 14, 'The authorities talk of . . .': Einstein, *Inside Constantinople*, pp. 183, 230, 231.

Pages 15–16, Lewy's calculation: Lewy, pp. 233–41.

Page 16, 'Due to famine, epidemics, and warfare . . .': Lewy, p. 241.

Page 16, 'Until the main court martial . . .': Lewy, p. 87.

Page 18, two divergent points of view: For a detailed discussion of the SO's role, see Akcam, *A Shameful Act*, pp. 123–39; for the SO's origins, remarks on the role of the SO and criticism of Dadrian's view, see Lewy, pp. 82–7.

Pages 19–24, A Case Study: Akcam, *A Shameful Act*, pp. 158, 160–1, 175, 181, 328; Lewy, pp. 119, 162–5; Walker, pp. 213–14. For details of unreliable eyewitness accounts of other, similar incidents in 'Trebizond' (Trabzan), see Lewy, p. 145. On the whole, the weight of evidence suggests that Kemakh gorge saw an atrocity in the early summer of 1915, but it was not on the scale suggested by Armenian propaganda. In the west, the technique of dispersal differed, with a few Armenians left alone but with many sent south by train to be crowded into inadequately supplied internment camps. In the north-east coastal region, boats were sometimes used for mass drownings of Armenians.

Page 19, 'The first convoy set off . . .': Walker, p. 213.

Pages 21–2, 'The whole surface of the river . . .': Hovannisian, *The Armenian Genocide*, pp. 146–7, cited in Bloxham, p. 87. The account appears to be based on hearsay evidence from a Greek villager who apparently witnessed the events in Erzincan but only heard accounts of what happened between Erzincan and Kemakh. A Greek eyewitness would not normally favour the official Turkish position and might be considered an unreliable, even hostile, witness, but other corroborating evidence regarding the massacres at Kemakh gorge along with the details of the account lend credibility to a massacre of some kind there.

Page 23, two Danish Red Cross nurses: Hovannisian, *Remembrance and Denial*, p. 52; Lewy, pp. 133–5.

Page 24, 'Since both the Turkish government . . .': I Inonu, Treaty of Lausanne, 1923, regarding a post-war settlement between the Allies and Turkey, cited in Akcam, *A Shameful Act*, p. 366. Inonu was the Turkish negotiator during the Lausanne treaty discussions. The 1923 treaty proclaimed amnesty for all Turkish political and war crimes committed between 1914 and 1922.

Page 26, 'All we can rely on are cold, hard FACTS . . .': Tall Armenian Tale website.

Page 28, Turk Telecom was ordered: 'Turkey Pulls Plug on YouTube'.

Page 28, On 4 May 2007, a Bill was passed: 'Bill Censoring Online Content'. One of the more restrained Armenian genocidist websites is Armeniapedia, which collects and collates items supporting the Armenian point of view. Pro-Turkish websites include the interestingly named Tall Armenian Tale, which bills its contribution as 'The Other Side of the FALSIFIED GENOCIDE'.

Page 29, 'The Armenian Genocide . . .': Look under 'Our Mission', Armenian Genocide Information & Recognition website, one of the more moderate Armenian sites.

Page 30, 'Lewis Einstein, . . .': Oren, p. 39.

Page 30, 'The murder of Armenians . . .': Einstein, 'The Armenian Massacres', p. 231.

Page 30, 'This year, Congress . . .': Sokatch & Myers.

Pages 31–5, Hitler's quote: For further details on the military and political background to this controversial quote, see Kershaw, *Hitler*, pp. 206–11; and Lewy, pp. 264–5. Although still regarded as authentic by many Armenians (see, for example, a line by Raffi in A Egoyan's 2002 film *Ararat*), the 'Hitler quote' is now largely disregarded by mainstream authorities as playing any part in the rationale for the Holocaust. In the German, the quote reads: '*Wer redet heute noch von der Vernichtung der Armenier?*'

Page 33, Melson's arguments: Melson has been criticised for seeing the 1915 events as a new phenomenon, whereas other scholars view them as part of a continuum. See Horowitz.

Page 34, Bogazici University conference: Labi; 'Turkish Court's Ban of Armenian Conference is Circumvented'.

Page 35, 'This conference proves that . . .': B Oran, cited in Soylemez.

Pages 35–6, 'The drama we see unfolding . . .': Pamuk, 'On Trial'.

Page 37, European Union membership is a large economic carrot: Steele; 'The Battle for Turkey's Soul'.

NOTES

2 FRAUDS AND FANATICS

Full chapter: Authentic literature on the Holocaust is huge, varied and detailed. Recent scholarship has tended to focus on the big issue of the split between the intentionalist view, that the Nazis planned the total extermination of the Jews from the start, and the mid-war radicalisation view, that the Nazis weren't fully sure how to deal with the ever-increasing captive Jewish populations, that the process was made more urgent because of wartime circumstances and that they eventually made up their minds in January 1942. Current debate has seen the two sides moving together. Meanwhile, dozens of other debates rage furiously outside the bigger intentionalist–radicalist issue. Probably the best single introduction to the scholarly side of the topic is Bartov's *The Holocaust: Origins, Implementation, Aftermath*. Bartov is a prolific and generally well regarded scholar in the field of German wartime history. Gilbert is arguably the best known English-language scholar in the general field of Holocaust studies and his *The Holocaust: A History of the Jews of Europe during the Second World War* is also a good introduction to the topic. The 900-page book, which contains much vivid personal testimony, has had ten British paperback printings and eighteen US printings since it was first published in 1986. Rees's *Auschwitz: The Nazis & the Final Solution* is a comprehensive, authoritative and accessible book, in which neither Irving nor Leuchter is mentioned.

Page 38, Jewish Museum: Details of the building are based on two personal visits in 2007 and the museum's guide, *Stories of an Exhibition*.

Page 39, 'painful recollections ...': *Shaleket*, wall plaque, Jewish Museum, Berlin, viewed 2007.

Page 39, 'I don't see any reason ...': D Irving, speech at Holocaust denial meeting, Calgary, 1991, cited in Lipstadt, *History on Trial*, p. 84.

Page 39, no functional or pragmatic sense to Holocaust denial: The Holocaust and its denial are the subjects of an extensive literature. For the most significant publications to date, see Shermer & Grobman; and Lipstadt.

Page 41, 'The near-destruction of the European Jews . . .': Applebaum, 'Tehran's Holocaust Lesson'.

Page 41, revivalist Nazis: In 1995, Human Rights Watch produced a report which detailed an alarming rise in violent racist incidents (including anti-Turkish and anti-Semitic attacks) in a post-unification Germany (a 400 per cent rise between 1990 and 1994). (Fullerton.) The situation was not helped by an identified poor response from authorities. A decade later, *Spiegel Online* reported:

> Right-wing Violence on the Rise. This year has seen 20 percent more attacks by right-wing extremists than the same period last year—and more of those incidents were violent. Political pressure is growing to address right-wing extremism as a dangerous trend rather than isolated incidents . . . following major gains by the neo-Nazi National Democratic Party (NPD) in Mecklenburg West Pomerania's recent parliamentary elections where they carried 7.3 percent of the vote. Right wing parties now hold seats in three of Germany's state parliaments with the NPD having entered the Saxony parliament in 2004 and the German People's Union holding six seats in Brandenburg, the state which surrounds Berlin. Rampant unemployment and socio-economic dislocation is commonly blamed for the NPD's success, but there is growing pressure not to dismiss the right-wing political advances as isolated flukes or protest votes. Charlotte Knobloch, leader of the Central Council of Jews in Germany, on Tuesday accused the country's politicians of having 'a weak position' on how to address the problem. ('Neo-Nazis in Germany', *Spiegel Online*, 17 October 2006.)

Page 42, Palestinian history textbooks: Firer & Adwan throughout, especially p. 152.

Page 42, Mazen's soft-denial doctorate: Hale; 'New PA "Prime Minister" Denies Holocaust':

> The Memri Institute for monitoring media in the mid-east reports that Arafat's newly appointed 'prime minister' for the PA, Mahmud Abbas [Abu Mazen's real name] completed a doctoral

NOTES

thesis in 1982 titled 'The Secret Connection between the Nazis and the Leaders of the Zionist Movement'. In his thesis, Abbas wrote that the estimated number of Jews killed during World War II was 'less than one million'. Abbas stated that the Zionist leadership collaborated with the Nazi regime to 'facilitate the wide-spread destruction' of Jews. Abbas' 'research' was later printed by a publisher located in Amman, Jordan.

Mazen's current reputation is as a moderate.

Page 42, Ahmadinejad convened a conference: The Iranian government organised the conference as a response to the Danish cartoons incident in which, on 30 September 2005, a Danish newspaper published twelve cartoons of Mohammed considered by many Islamists to be at best offensive and at worst sacrilegious. Demonstrations against the cartoonists, the paper and Denmark broke out in many Islamic countries, with some turning into riots, followed by anti-Danish boycotts and death threats. As reported in *The Boston Globe*, an Arab scholar, Khaled Mahameed, who wished to attend the post-cartoon conference to argue that the Holocaust did happen, was refused a visa. (Barnard.) Interestingly, in Berlin, the Federal Agency for Civic Education sponsored a less well publicised counter-denial conference, as did Yad Vashem, the Israeli Holocaust memorial.

Page 42, individuals, political and terrorist groups and government figures: Shermer & Grobman, pp. 39–74; Lipstadt, *Denying the Holocaust*, throughout. Any close examination of the world of Holocaust denial reveals a mosaic of weird beliefs and strange characters with one thing in common: their anti-Semitism.

Page 44, 'I don't accept . . .': D Irving, IHR audiocassette 114, 11 October 1992, cited in Evans, p. 131.

Page 44, 'I made a mistake . . .': D Irving, in court in Austria, 2005, cited in Shermer.

Page 44, Irving versus Lipstadt: The official name is *Irving v. Penguin & anr.* (2000). For a carefully arranged transcript of the trial, see www.holocaustdenialontrial.com/trial/transcripts

Page 44, According to his twin brother: Craig.

Page 44, 1969 USA visit: Lipstadt, *Denying the Holocaust*, pp. 294–5.

Pages 44–5, Kempner comments: R Kempner, memo to JE Hoover, US National Archives, 1969, cited in Lipstadt, *History on Trial*, pp. 294–5.

Page 45, *Fraktur*: In 1941, Martin Bormann ordered that the script be eventually replaced, because it had originated in a section of the print industry dominated by Jews. Most handwriting at that time was in the almost equally illegible *Sütterlin* script.

Page 46, TB47: Evans, pp. 160–75. The document's brief title is *Tagesbefehl 47* (*Order of the Day 47*).

Page 46, Evans and Taylor: Evans refuted Irving's claims in preparing the main dossier for *Irving v. Penguin & anr.* (2000) and in his *Telling Lies about Hitler*, pp. 157–92. Taylor's *Dresden* focuses just on the bombing. He devotes a special section (pp. 503–9) to what he terms 'the macabre argument' about the casualties, in which he points out that Irving, in a letter to *The Times* on 7 July 1966, admitted that TB47 was 'probably' a fake. See also Evans, p. 177. Nevertheless, Taylor points out that 'Irving has never let go of the Voigt [135 000] figures altogether'; he wrote this in 2004.

Page 46, Irving's Day in Court: For the best summaries of the case, see Lipstadt, *History on Trial*; and Evans. Irving also has comments on the website of Focal Point Publications (Irving's own publishing house).

Page 46, 'Mr Irving: . . .': *Irving v. Penguin & anr.* (2000), cited in Evans, p. 228.

Page 47, 'Australian reporter' and 'exceptionally blonde hair . . .': Lipstadt, *History on Trial*, p. 229. *The Hand That Signed the Paper*, supposedly based on an exotic Ukrainian background and family reminiscences, kicked up a huge storm in Australia, because it repeated the blood libel that wartime Ukrainian involvement in the Holocaust had been all but legitimised by supposed KGB and Jewish persecution of Ukrainians in the 1930s. The novelist's credibility as a source fell apart when 'Demidenko' was subsequently exposed as an impostor. Her real name was Helen Darville; she had no Ukrainian

NOTES

connections and, indeed, was of English descent, her parents coming from the singularly unexotic town of Scunthorpe. Following further accusations, this time of plagiarism, Darville-Demidenko's authorial career took an even deeper plunge. In the excellent *The Culture of Forgetting*, Manne makes the salient point, among others, that Demidenko-Darville managed to get away with her pretence because her literary supporters were ignorant of the historical background of the events and of the anti-Semitic motivations she described. Darville later trained as a lawyer.

Page 47, 'Although some people would see . . .': Darville.

Page 48, '*Mein Führer*': D Irving, *Irving v. Penguin & anr.* (2000), cited in Lipstadt, *History on Trial*, p. 263.

Page 48, 'incontrovertible that Irving . . .': Justice Gray, *Irving v. Penguin & anr.* (2000), cited in Lipstadt, *History on Trial*, p. 274.

Page 48, 'The content of his speeches . . .': Justice Gray, *Irving v. Penguin & anr.* (2000), cited in Evans, p. 236.

Page 48, 'Irving's treatment . . .': Justice Gray, *Irving v. Penguin & anr.* (2000), cited in Lipstadt, *History on Trial*, p. 275.

Pages 48 and 49, Paxman interview quotes: 'Irving Defiant over Libel Defeat', BBC News, 12 April 2000, cited in Lipstadt, *History on Trial*, p. 280.

Page 49, 'they have burned my books': D Irving, 2006, cited in Herwig. The article provides information about the background to Irving's Austrian adventure. Herwig describes Irving as a 'master of the insinuating bluff'.

Page 49, 'The legend was that Hitler . . .': D Irving, speech, Primrose Hotel, Toronto, November 1992, cited in Evans, p. 127.

Page 49, Irving's *modus operandi*: Evans, chapters 2–5, and p. 192:

> Irving's manipulations and exaggerations merely got in the way of proper discussion of these events . . . since dealing with his falsifications took up time and effort . . . Perhaps the best way of dealing with his version of the destruction of Dresden was found

in 1985 by his German publishers, who appended to the title page of his book the description, 'a novel'.

Page 50, Goebbels's diary entry: Evans, pp. 78–9.

Page 51, Hitler's supposedly benevolent disposition to the Berlin Jews: Evans, pp. 84–8.

Page 52, Eichmann's memoir: For the memoir quotes and Irving's misrepresentation of their significance, see Shermer & Grobman, pp. 53–4. Himmler's SS title was Reichsführer, not Reichfürher, almost certainly a Shermer & Grobman typographical error, since it is unlikely, in this instance, to be an Irving mistake.

Page 53, 'No reasonable person would describe ...': Evans, p. 249.

Page 53, Irving as a historian of repute: Evans, p. 251.

Page 53, 'Penguin was after blood': DC Watt, 11 April 2000, cited in Lipstadt, *History on Trial*, pp. 278–9.

Pages 53–5, Irving and historians: For an interesting discussion of the uneasy relationship that existed between legitimate professional historians and Irving, and about the debate over free speech that preceded the trial, in which Irving was mistakenly seen as the object of a Lipstadt libel suit, see Evans, pp. 21–32.

Page 54, Mommsen wrote to him: Shermer & Grobman, p. 49. By and large, German historians held Irving in low regard. (Evans, p. 251.)

Page 55, 'Zündel has honed his public antics ...': Lipstadt, *History on Trial*, pp. 158–9.

Page 55, IHR's US$50 000 reward: It was later admitted that the offer was a publicity stunt, and that at the time there had been no intention of paying the reward. For details of the Mermelstein case, see Lipstadt, *Denying the Holocaust*, pp. 139–41.

Page 56, 'facts and propositions of generalized knowledge ...': *California Evidence Code 1967*, Section 451f, www.leginfo.ca.gov/cgi-bin/calawquery?codesection=evid&codebody=&hits=20

NOTES

Page 57, 'The book was for fun ...': E Zündel, cited in F Miele, 'Giving the Devil His Due: Holocaust Revisionism as a Test Case for Free Speech and the Skeptical Ethic', *Skeptic*, vol. 2, no. 4, 1994, pp. 58–70. Interestingly, in 1977, Zündel had set up his own publishing house, Samisdat Publishers. Private publishing is a common initiative among deniers.

Page 57, 'I am an admirer ...': E Zündel, interview with authors, cited in Shermer & Grobman, p. 67.

Page 57, 'WE LOVE YOU, ADOLF HITLER': E Zündel, in C Friedrich & E Thomson, *The Hitler We Loved and Why*, 1977, cited in Lipstadt, *Denying the Holocaust*, p. 158.

Page 58, 'In order to keep the IHR ...': D Cole, interview, in Shermer & Grobman, p. 45. Cole is a denier who claims Jewish descent.

Page 58, 'bright and personable ...' and 'likable antagonist': Shermer & Grobman, pp. 47–8, part of a useful section on Weber.

Pages 59–60, Leuchter: For probably the best introduction to Leuchter's work, see *Mr Death*, which contains a guest appearance by Zündel. Leuchter does not come out of the movie too well. In 1991, after much publicity about Leuchter's spurious credentials and his appearance in Canada in defence of Zündel, the Commonwealth of Massachusetts obliged him to sign a document stating that he agreed to desist from presenting himself as an engineer and publishing 'engineering' reports. This undertaking came two weeks before he was to go to trial on charges of practising without a licence. See also Shermer & Grobman, pp. 129–33; and Lipstadt, *Denying the Holocaust*, pp. 162–73, 177–82.

Page 60, as Deborah Lipstadt has pointed out: Lipstadt, *Denying the Holocaust*, p. 177.

Page 60, 'trained and accomplished engineer': Lehman.

Page 60, 'certified by *Atlantic* ...': IHR newsletter, cited in Lipstadt, *Denying the Holocaust*, p. 177.

Page 62, 'At the center . . .': Reemtsma.

Page 63, 'annihilatory offensive': Eley. Of Hull's view, Eley says that 'this prevailing military mindset placed a premium on rapid and unrestrained action against an enemy, without distinction of civilians or soldiers. This "absolute destruction" meant not just a decisive battlefield outcome, but a larger repertoire of justified savagery—of laying waste, reprisals, summary justice, mass killings and even genocide'. There is a sizeable scholarly literature on the continuum nature of aggressive German military culture in modern times: see, for example, the various works of M Messerschmidt and J Förster; and Shepherd.

Page 63, That myth of Wehrmacht military integrity was destroyed: The revisionist view of the Wehrmacht's operation of 1941 to 1944 (there was some criticism that the 1939 Polish campaign had been excluded) came in the decade following the *Historikerstreit* (historians' quarrel), a period of fierce debate among German historians about an alleged attempt by conservative and nationalist historians to 'normalise' Germany's recent past. For example, Bartov had already questioned the myth of the 'clean' Wehrmacht in *Hitler's Army*, but his version was based on the view that Wehrmacht discipline broke down under the pressures of the campaign in the east, which is a different position from the more damning continuum point of view.

Page 63, *The War of Extermination* exhibition: Heer et al. For a counter-view, see Bundeswehr academic F Seidler's *Fahnenflucht: Der Soldat Zwischen Eid und Gewissen* (Herbig, Munich, 1993), cited in Welch. Seidler's book, championed by several ultra-right German websites, does not yet appear to have been translated into English.

Page 63, *The War of Extermination* book: The German edition of Heer and Naumann's *The War of Extermination* was originally published in 1995; a revised and abbreviated edition was published in English in 2000 (Berghahn Books, Oxford). For an academically framed account of both exhibitions' travels and travails, see Heer et al. For a useful and accessible narrative of events by Reemtsma, curator of the second exhibition, see the Hamburg Institute's website. See also Fulbrook.

NOTES

Most of the news reporting in this section of the chapter is based on BBC, CNN and *Guardian* accounts of the events, although for a useful if politically tendentious summary, see W Weber's account on the Trotskyite World Socialist Web Site, www.wsws.org/articles/2001/sep2001/wehr-s19.shtml and www.wsws.org/articles/2001/sep2001/wehr-s20.shtml

Page 64, banned Bundeswehr members: During the *Historikerstreit*, Bundeswehr soldiers had participated in several televised panels.

Page 65, Dregger: For an outline of Dregger's background and position, see Childs.

Page 65, The anti-exhibition campaign heated up: Kuderna; Underwood.

Page 65, 'We don't think it is right …': P Gauweiler, cited in Underwood, 1997.

Pages 65–6, Goldhagen controversy: Kershaw, *The Nazi Dictatorship*, pp. 253–62; Finkelstein & Birn, no pagination. The latter is a slim book but controversial in its own right, consisting of two essays originally published separately in journals. Finkelstein's essay is dismissive of Goldhagen's work, referring to Goldhagen as an author of 'Holocaust literature' (as opposed to Holocaust scholarship—a contestable distinction). Birn's essay is on safer ground, with a precise demolition of Goldhagen's use of sources.

Page 66, 'the only appropriate proper name …': Goldhagen, p. 5.

Page 66, Walser's speech: Waine; Kemenetzky.

Page 67, The new exhibition: For the exhibition's origins, opening and response, see Broomby; and Jahnke & Kallinich.

Page 68, 'impermissible to say …': G Schröder, cited in Wise.

Page 68, Ultra-rightist opinion and **'The most important goals …':** Klein & Simon.

Page 70, 'endless rebuttals': Applebaum, 'Tehran's Holocaust Lesson'.

3 A CULTURE OF DENIAL

Page 71, McNeill narrative: McNeill, 'Media Intimidation in Japan'. In the article, McNeill makes the point that there are close connections between *uyoku* (ultra-nationalist) and *yakuza* (gangster) groups. The *yakuza* have infiltrated ultra-nationalist associations, partly to gain political power and financial advantage but also because of characteristic *yakuza* ultra-nationalist leanings. The sinister *gaisensha* (sound trucks) are a familiar part of ultra-nationalist intimidation in Japan and, in appearance and the manner in which they are used, are not dissimilar from the propaganda trucks used by the SA Brownshirts in 1930s Germany. At the time of the radio program, McNeill was foreign research fellow at the University of Tokyo. He subsequently taught at Tokyo's Sophia University and wrote feature articles for *The Independent* (UK), going on to become coordinator of *Japan Focus*, a well-regarded online journal. For a useful grid outlining *uyoku* versus left-wing attitudes, see Wakisaka, p. 6.

Page 73, Nanjing: Also known as 'Nanking'. The more current 'Nanjing' form is used throughout this chapter unless quoted in the alternative form from another source.

Page 73, 'had the belief that any enemy of the emperor ...': Buruma, *Wages of Guilt*, p. 173.

Pages 73–5, Nanjing massacre: This account of the massacre and its aftermath is drawn from a variety of sources. Prior to the publication of Chang's book, in 1997, most general histories or commentaries carried a page or two about Nanjing. See, for example, Buruma, *Wages of Guilt*, pp. 32–3 and *Inventing Japan*, pp. 83–6; Ienaga, *The Pacific War 1931–1945*, pp. 186–7; and Andressen, p. 106. Although Chang's book has been criticised for exaggeration, it remains a useful source.

Page 73, 'There were about thirty-seven old men ...': S Azuma, in a post-war public statement, n.d. but probably c. 1987, in one of a series of media appearances, cited in 'Scarred by History'. Azuma died in January 2006, aged ninety-three. Various Chinese news agencies reported his death as well as his record as a contrite veteran of the

Nanjing massacre. Azuma's full confession was published in 1987 in his controversial diary *My Nanking Platoon*, following which a Japanese soldier identified in the diary successfully sued the author for libel. The case was won on the basis that Azuma's statements about the plaintiff's actions were based on 'opinion'. ('Funeral Held for Japan Veteran'.) Buruma met and talked to Azuma in 1992; for a detailed account of the interview, see *Wages of Guilt*, pp. 129–35. Azuma was only one of many veterans who began to recount horrific tales of events in China in the late 1980s; for a discussion of the impact of these confessions, see T Yoshida's chapter in Fogel, pp. 70–132.

Page 75, The delay in the massacre's becoming an international controversy: Buruma, *Wages of Guilt*, pp. 117–18. For a useful summary of recent debates about Nanjing from the Japanese point of view, see Askew. Using a survey by conservative Japanese magazine *Shokun!*, Askew categorises the Japanese deniers as members either of the 'Illusion School' (zero to a few casualties; mainly executions of illegally disguised Chinese soldiers), the 'Middle-of-the Road School' (casualties in their tens of thousands; atrocities committed) or the 'Great Massacre School' (100 000 to 200 000 killed in indiscriminate massacres). The article also contains a useful bibliography. For a review of *Honda Katsuichi*, see Drea; for a Chinese-American scholar's point of view, see Yang; and Fogel; for an idiosyncratic US (Japanese resident) denialist point of view, see Bohn, in which he concludes, 'This was a battle in wartime. The civilian deaths are regrettable'.

Pages 77–8, *The Rape of Nanking*: Much of this section of the chapter, including the quotes, is drawn from Benson, a long (9800-word) and detailed feature article. It backgrounds much of Chang's work and life prior to her suicide in California, in November 2004, when Chang shot herself with a replica Civil War revolver. There was some conjecture that she had been adversely affected by the fanatical response that her book had aroused in Japan, but the more generally accepted reason for her suicide is a combination of post–book tour (*The Chinese in America*) exhaustion and bipolar disorder. Her suicide note, for example, showed evidence of paranoid fantasies. Chang's book had been criticised on three counts: minor errors of a typographical or technical nature (poor editing did not help); more substantial errors in producing evidence (including photographic evidence); and over-simplification of Japanese history. The minor errors were eagerly seized upon by Japanese nationalist opinion, but the overall impact of the book remained relatively undiminished.

Page 78, 'I wrote *Rape of Nanking* . . .': I Chang, media interview, n.d., cited in De Pasquale.

Page 78, 'After reading several file cabinets' worth . . .': I Chang, p. 220, also cited in *China News Digest*, 24 February 1998, and in Benson.

Pages 78–9, 'Whether it was morning or night . . .': K Pak, memoir, trans. C Berndt, unpublished honours thesis, University of North Carolina, Chapel Hill, 1996, cited in Horn. See also Stetz & Oh; and Y Tanaka. For a bland version of events, see the Japanese Cabinet Councillors' Office on External Affairs, in which the following statement appears: 'It is virtually impossible to determine the total number of comfort women, as no document has been found which either indicates their total number or gives sufficient grounds to establish an estimate'. The statement goes on to admit that there was a 'great number'. For journalistic accounts of the continuing campaign for recognition and recompense, see 'Japanese Comfort Women Ruling Overturned'; McCurry; Nozaki (a very useful scholarly summary); and Onishi.

Page 80, Senda's book: *Jugun Ianfu*, Futabasha, Tokyo, 1973. The book has not been translated into English.

Page 80, Matsui's article: 'Kankoku-Fujin No Ikita Michi' ('The Road a Korean Woman Took to Live), *Asahi Shimbun*, evening edition, 2 November 1984. The article has not been translated into English.

Page 81, 'Interviewer: What happened? . . .': M Kurumizawa, video testimony, n.d. but c. 1990s, cited in Gold, p. 45. See also Barenblatt. Most of this section is drawn from Barenblatt; Gold; and Harris.

Page 83, unrepentant and intransigently racist to the end: Barenblatt, p. 226; Gold, pp. 139–40.

NOTES

Pages 83–4, Akiyama's account: 'Saikin Sen wa Jumbi Sareteita!' ('Bacteriological Warfare Preparations Were Already Complete!'). The account has not been translated into English.

Pages 84–8, New nationalism and the Society: Buruma, *Wages of Guilt* and *Inventing Japan*; Larimer; McCormack; McNeill, 'Japan's History Wars and Popular Consciousness'. The term for 'the Society' in Japanese is 'Tsukurakai'.

Page 84, not solely a Japanese attempt at a cover-up: For useful analyses of the post-war period, see Bix; and Dower. For the best modern survey of the whole topic of western responsibility for and reaction to Japanese wartime atrocities, and for a more current analysis that suggests that recent controversies are a product of assertive Japanese nationalism and denial ranged against increasing emphasis on patriotic (that is nationalistic) education in China, see Yoshida. This ties in with Pamuk's views on the new bourgeois nationalism in Chapter 1. For MacArthur, SCAP and the post-war period, see Yoshida pp. 71–7.

Page 88, 'The masochistic slant . . .': N Fujioka, speech, Foreign Correspondents' Club of Japan, Tokyo, 25 February 1999, reproduced at www.jiyuu-shikan.org/e/education.html

Pages 89–91, Ienaga's story and quotes: Ienaga, *Japan's Past, Japan's Future*. In 2001, following a mainly Canadian and US initiative, Ienaga was nominated for a Nobel Peace Prize; the winner that year, however, was Kofi Annan. Ienaga died in December 2002.

For multilingual translations of the current government-approved middle-school textbooks, see the JE Kaleidoscope website. An example of the style and substance of the *New History Textbook*:

> The leaders of the independence movements in these countries [former western colonies] cooperated with the Japanese military in order to achieve their independence. However there was also resistance to the fact that Japan forced the people of the occupied areas to learn Japanese and pray at Shinto shrines. Anti-Japanese guerilla activities, in collaboration with the Allied forces, also occurred. (*New History Textbook*, rev. edn, p. 15.)

For part of the text and the Table of Contents of the revised edition, see www.je-kaleidoscope.jp/english/text8.html

Pages 91–3, Manga and Denial: Ashby; McNeill, 'Japan's History Wars and Popular Consciousness'. McNeill's article starts with the alarming paragraph:

> Ko Bunyu's comic book Introduction to China is not for the fainthearted. In 300 graphic pages, it claims that the Chinese are incapable of democracy, practice cannibalism, and have the world's leading sex economy. In one sequence, famous political figures say the country is the source of most of Asia's contagious diseases. In another, illustrated with naked, spread-eagled women, China is said to have exported 600 000 'AIDS-infested' prostitutes.

In the comic book, things then go from bad to worse. For manga and revisionism, see Wisniewski; Pons, 'A Cartoonist Rewrites History'; and Layland, 'A Comic Book View of History'. For a detailed study of Kobayashi's work, see Clifford; the use of 'analects' in the title is almost certainly an ironic reference to Confucius's *Analects*, Prime Minister Koizumi's favourite reading (his favourite listening is Elvis Presley). For Kobayashi placed in a wider context, see Morris-Suzuki, pp. 185–205; part of Morris-Suzuki's overall thesis is that, in Japan, while denial may be losing in academic discourse, it appears to be winning the popular debate.

Note that for reasons of space and concision, this chapter is unable to take into account the recent controversies surrounding denialist or 'revisionist' movies in Japan and the USA. See, for example, C Eastwood's ameliatory *Letters from Iwo Jima* (2006), an account of the battle from a Japanese perspective; B Spahic and A Pick's *The Rape of Nanking* (2007), a Chang-based documentary; and 'Rape of Nanking to Be War Film "Classic"':

> China plans to depict one of the most infamous events of the Second World War, with a film version of U.S. author Iris Chang's historical account *The Rape of Nanking*. Chinese moviemakers will team up with U.S. and British filmmakers to describe the brutal massacre of Chinese civilians and burning of

NOTES

the former capital city by Japanese troops in December 1937. The movie deal was announced Monday, a day before the anniversary of Japan's Second World War surrender.

Mid-August, the anniversary of VJ Day, when this article was published, tends to produce either an outbreak of forced diplomatic amiability or a China–Japan diplomatic wrestling match. This announcement coincided with Koizumi's visit to the Yasukuni shrine. See also 'Don't Support Revisionist History':

> Earlier this year, Japanese filmmaker Satoru Mizushima announced he was going to make a film about the 1937 'Rape of Nanking', in which Japanese soldiers killed roughly 200 000 Chinese in the city over eight weeks. A number of upcoming films deal with this subject, including Bill Guttentag and Dan Sturman's documentary *Nanking*, which premiered at this year's Sundance Film Festival to great acclaim and response. So what makes Mizushima's take on the unique subject? He claims the Nanking massacre is a 'myth' and his film will 'correct' the falsehoods perpetrated by the other movies. Referring to *Nanking*, he said it was 'based on fabrications and gives a false impression' of the Japanese military's actions.

Page 91, *The Japan Times* estimated in 2003: Ashby.

Page 92, 'If you really want to look …' and 'becoming comfort women …': Y Kobayashi, *Taiwan Ron*, cited in Pons, 'A Cartoonist Rewrites History'.

Page 93, 'even the Chinese Communist Party …': Y Kobayashi, interview, cited in 'Drawing up Battle Lines'.

Page 94, SCAP: The acronym stands for 'Supreme Commander of the Allied Powers', the title held by MacArthur after World War II during the Allied Japanese occupation; it also refers to the occupation administration.

Page 95, 'it being far from our thought …': Hirohito.

Pages 99–100, Koizumi and the constitution: This section is based mainly on the following sources: 'A Familiar Ring to Koizumi's

Speech'; Akaha; 'Article 9, Iraq and Revision of the Japanese Constitution'; 'China Moves to Fourth'; Curtin; 'Growth Competitive Index Ratings'; 'Japan Renews Call'; 'Koizumi Apologises'; 'Koizumi: No Shift'; Koizumi, 'General Policy Speech' and 'Statement'; Masaki; Mizuho; Nabeshima; Samuels; Takahashi.

Pages 100–1, Koizumi's work was taken up: This section is based on Junkerman. Abe, who initially adopted a softly-softly diplomatic approach, followed his party's line at home with a denial of the comfort women atrocities. (Moynihan.) Abe resigned in September 2007 after a succession of scandals and poor poll results. He was succeeded by the more cautious Yasuo Fukuda.

4 BRITISH COMMUNISM AND TWO DECADES OF DENIAL

Full chapter: In this chapter, the term 'the Party' refers to the Communist Party of Great Britain.

Page 102, gathered for their regular weekly staff: Mcleod, pp. 127–32.

Page 104, 'Who fights for Communism . . .': B Brecht, *The Measures Taken*, 1960. My thanks to Lendvai (p. 143) for pointing me to this apposite quote. Brecht's reference, in his play about following the party line, was not ironic.

Page 105, 'in a Revolutionary State . . .': H Pollitt, cited in Morgan, Cohen & Flinn, p. 222. The authors point out that while some questioned the second proposition, few questioned the first.

Page 106, The major figures on trial: Trotsky, an opponent of Stalin, was tried *in absentia* and sentenced to death. Zinoviev was a former head of the Comintern. Kamenev and Bukharin, both accused of terrorism, were senior CPSU figures.

Page 106, The final figures: Applebaum's statistics (*Gulag*, p. 520) are approximate and, considering the size of the camp system, are, pro rata, less appalling than the Nazi figures for their camp system. Unlike the Nazi concentration camps, the Gulags were largely populated by political prisoners and criminals (bearing in mind that there was a broad range of alleged criminality in the Soviet Union), and there was

NOTES

a steady flow of detainees in and of released prisoners out. For example, at the height of the Great Terror, 'counter-revolutionaries' convicted under Section 58 of the constitution made up 12 per cent of the total Gulag population, and at the time of Stalin's death, in 1953, they formed approximately 25 per cent. See Overy, pp. 615–16.

Page 107, 'the workers don't worry . . .': H Pollitt, cited in Morgan, Cohen & Flinn, p. 223.

Page 107, 'Comrade Gallagher, it is best . . .': G Dimitrov, cited in Beckett, *Enemy Within*, p. 72. Cohen was arrested after the detention of her husband, Max Petrovsky, who was then shot. Another Party member, Pearl Rimmer, asked Pollitt to intercede on behalf of her own arrested husband, George Fles, a Dutch communist. Pollitt's reply, in part, was: 'What can I do? They won't listen to me'. (Beckett, *Enemy Within*, p. 72.) Party members must have been wondering what was going on, with so many 'counter-revolutionaries', whom they knew personally to be solid communists, suffering arrest, imprisonment and execution. One of the consequences of ideologically unsound queries made by formerly compliant Party leaders was that the Soviet authorities started measuring Pollitt up for a show trial of his own, in case they should ever feel that they needed to get their hands on him. The putative charge? Mild public disagreement with the 1930s Soviet military build-up and with Stalin's 'socialism in one country' policy. The real issue? Concern about Pollitt's political reliability after his Cohen intercession. In the end, the Comintern decided not to act against him: it was better to have a usefully biddable and locally admired general secretary whom they knew than a useless, dead one—and to have to start the political grooming all over again. And anyway, the British Party was small beer in the Comintern's scheme of things. It could not compare in size or influence either with the French Communist Party or with the banned Italian organisation.

Page 108, recruiting Party members as NKVD agents: It was, according to Andrew & Mitrokhin, a Party leader's duty to assist in undercover work. For example, in 1936, NKVD undercover agent Arnold Deutsch checked with Pollitt about recruiting Norman John

('James') Klugmann as an NKVD 'illegal', or undercover agent. (Andrew & Mitrokhin, pp. 82–3.) Klugmann was an executive member and the Party's official historian. He had been parachuted in to Yugoslavia as a British special agent during the war, and after 1945 he played an active part in running the Party and maintaining ideological purity in the 1940s and 1950s. At the same time, MI5 was busy bugging the Party's meetings.

Page 108, 'the greatest anti-fascist victory . . .': J Strachey, *Daily Worker*, 1 April 1938, cited in Eaden & Renton, p. 66. At that time, there was a view among Party members that the collapse of capitalism was at hand. J Klugmann, for example, wrote that 'we simply knew, all of us, that the revolution was at hand. If anyone had suggested it wouldn't happen in Britain for say thirty years, I'd have laughed myself sick'. (Cited in Andrew & Mitrokhin, p. 82.) Klugmann's point of view explains, to some extent, the Party's long-held view of 1930s Soviet wrongdoings.

Page 108, 'the measures against . . .': Beckett, *Enemy Within*, p. 73.

Page 108, 'attack Anglo-Soviet relations . . .': *Daily Worker*, n.d., cited in Beckett, *Enemy Within*, p. 72. Beckett also comments that 'the article must rank as one of the most weaselly and discreditable pieces ever written, with its fastidious refusal even to mention the name of a woman whom every leading Communist in Britain counted as a friend'.

Page 109, 'They did not know everything . . .': Beckett, *Enemy Within*, p. 143.

Page 109, 'One has to appreciate . . .': P Cadogan, cited in Morgan, Cohen & Flinn, p. 56. The authors comment that 'even if they did not pray, for many communists the party had a churchlike character grounded in the systemic nature of communist thoughts and the acts of faith its practice required'.

Page 110, 'The fundamental facts . . .': H Pollitt, cited in *Inprecor*, 19 March 1938; and in Morgan, Cohen & Flinn, p. 223. The comment, first published in the Party's often impenetrably ideological magazine, was made after the major show trials had ended.

NOTES

Page 110, 'Next to sex . . .': Hobsbawm, *Interesting Times*, p. 73.

Page 111, 'The Soviet-Nazi [*sic*] pact . . .': B Moore, Sheffield Communist Party and Peace Council, cited in Eaden & Renton, p. 79. On page 80, the authors comment that 'although the reaction of the party's chief ideologue, Palme Dutt, to Labour's entry into a [Churchill-led] Coalition government was to claim in inimitable . . . style that this was further evidence of Labour's fascisisation, the position of the party was gradually shifting'.

Pages 112 and 13, 'I still can't understand . . .' and 'a shock to everybody . . .': J Friell, cited in Mellini, an introductory essay for the retrospective exhibition *Fallen Angel! The Political Cartoons of Jimmy Friell*, in 2007.

Page 113, 'The Soviet leaders . . .': D Hyde, *I Believed*, cited in Eaden & Renton, p. 68.

Page 114, urging a struggle on two fronts: See Fryer, 'Francis King & George Matthews'. Fryer also points out that on 14 September 1939, the *Daily Worker* received a telegram from the Soviet Union saying that it was a 'robber war' on both sides. Pollitt, still struggling with the new line, suppressed the telegram. Campbell accused Dutt of the 'most vile factional methods', which may explain some of the more duplicitous and slanderous events that occurred in 1956.

Pages 114–15, 'The victory of imperialism . . .': P Dutt, cited in Gollancz, p. 176, the Left Book Club's 1941 collection of essays of the war.

Page 115, 'Don't lose your pride . . .': Letter to H Pollitt from his mother, n.d. but c. September 1939, cited in Beckett, *Enemy Within*, p. 96.

Page 115, 'No Unity with the Chamberlain Socialists': Beckett, *Enemy Within*, p. 92.

Pages 115–16, 'We started by saying . . .': J Campbell, cited in Beckett, *Enemy Within*, pp. 94–5.

Page 116, 'Smash the fascist bastards . . .': H Pollitt, cited in Morgan, p. 109. Morgan's view is that Pollitt had 'a "class" instinct'; in other words, he knew and had an attachment to what would appeal to working-class supporters, and he also knew what would not appeal. Morgan writes that 'Dutt's casuistries appalled Pollitt as much by their wild unreality as by their cynicism'.

Page 117, 'The enemies of Communism . . .': H Pollitt, in 'The British Road to Socialism', cited in Eaden & Renton, p. 116; reproduced at www.marxists.org/history/international/comintern/sections/britain/brs/1951/51.htm#1

Page 119, 'The principle of collective leadership': A Mikoyan, speech given to the Twentieth Party Congress, Moscow, February 1956, published in the *Daily Worker*, cited in Mcleod, p. 49. According to Mcleod, Mikoyan's admission was front-page news across the world, except for in the *Daily Worker*, whose editorial staff buried it on the back page.

Page 119, 'by our excesses . . .': A Fadeyev, cited in Mcleod, p. 103. During the period of August to November 1956, the Party executive seemed more concerned about the activities of *The Reasoner* than about Soviet interventions in eastern Europe.

Page 121, 'You mustn't say . . .': M Bennet, cited in Mcleod, p. 118. This was a particularly sensitive issue, since, at that time, the Party in London had a substantial number of Jewish members, mainly split between East End–based working-class supporters and a north London middle-class element, with concentrations in the north London suburbs of Hampstead and neighbouring Swiss Cottage and Golders Green. Dutt was opposed to any examination of the issue before and after Stalin's death and, in 1953, took his pro-Stalin position to the point of asking Hyman Levy to write an article explaining why the Jewish doctors had been guilty. Levy refused, but Andrew Rothstein, apparatchik *par excellence*, obliged. The article appeared in *Labour Monthly*'s March 1953 edition (with publication date slightly delayed), after Stalin had died and after the doctors had been released and cleared. (Mcleod, p. 123.)

Page 121, Poznan rioters: Mcleod, p. 97. To the north, events in Poland included the reinstatement of the formerly discredited and imprisoned

Wladyslaw Gomulka as head of the Polish United Workers' Party, and, to the south, in Yugoslavia, Tito's defiance of Soviet hegemony led to a rapprochement with the Kremlin. Both events initially produced the feeling in Budapest that peaceful transformation might be possible. Gomulka's speech to the central committee of the Polish Communist Party was reproduced in full in the major Hungarian newspapers on the first day of the demonstrations. Events in Budapest, according to Lendvai's chronology (pp. 251–3), unfolded as follows:

Tuesday 23 October: Student-inspired demonstrations and uprising with some fatalities at the radio station. Gero 'invites' Soviet troops to intervene.

Wednesday 24 October: Infuriated by the official attempts at suppression, loose coalitions of mainly working-class insurgents loot a variety of arms repositories. Fighting begins in earnest on the Pest side of the Danube, in and around the Grand Boulevard and Ulloi Avenue. Gero is replaced by Nagy, who declares martial law.

Thursday 25 October: Fighting intensifies, with fatal casualties on each side totalling over 100.

Friday 26 October: More fighting around the (Pest side) Killian barracks and the Corvin passage. The insurgents, having learned their street-fighting technique from Soviet partisan movies, continue to savage the Soviet forces. Ulloi Avenue is jammed with the burned-out wreckage of Soviet tanks and trucks.

Saturday 27 October: The Nagy government is formed.

Sunday 28 October: Nagy announces a ceasefire.

Monday 29 October: The AVH is abolished. The Suez crisis is about to take over front pages.

Tuesday 30 October: Horrific public humiliation, mutilation and lynching of AVH operatives by a group of insurgents. The Soviets say they will conduct a negotiated withdrawal from Budapest.

Wednesday 31 October: The Soviets, anxious about any knock-on effect, decide on a second, more powerful intervention.

Thursday 1 November: Nagy says Hungary will withdraw from the Warsaw pact.

Friday 2 November: Khrushchev secretly informs Romania, Bulgaria and Czechoslovakia about proposed plans to crush the revolt. Tito secretly supports a second intervention.
Saturday 3 November: Mindszenty makes a 'reactionary' speech.
Sunday 4 – Thursday 9 November: Reinforced Soviet troops intervene. The revolt is crushed. Nagy is replaced by Kadar.

Page 122, an estimated 2652 Hungarian fighters: The figures are taken from Sebestyen, pp. 136, 164, 175, 184, 277. Until recently, casualties were thought to have numbered around 40 000, a hugely exaggerated figure. In 1948, the AVH (State Security Office) replaced the AVO (State Security Department), but in general usage the AVH were, in 1956, still called the (more easily pronounced) AVO, in much the same way that Russians referred to the NKVD, MVD and KGB as 'Chekists', a reference to the Lenin-period CHEKA.

Page 123, a bourgeois reactionary capitalist media: The Beaverbrook *Daily Express*, for example, under the inspired leadership of Arthur Christiansen (one of the great twentieth-century newspaper editors), was right on top of the issue with, among others, their experienced and respected correspondent Sefton Delmer sending regular despatches from Budapest. A comparison of the two newspapers in October and November 1956 easily demonstrates the socialist cloud-cuckoo land in which the *Daily Worker*'s editorial staff was living.

Page 125, 'This was no counter-revolution . . .': Fryer, *Hungarian Tragedy*, p. 24.

Page 125, 'gangs of reactionaries . . .': *Daily Worker*, 1 November 1956, cited in Mcleod, p. 140.

Pages 127–8, 'If the Soviet intervention . . .': Fryer, *Hungarian Tragedy*, p. 66.

Page 128, 'What about my story?': Fryer, *Hungarian Tragedy*, p. 72.

Page 128, *Daily Worker*'s staff petition: While others say there were nineteen signatories, MacEwen himself put the figure at sixteen. The petition said, in part, that

NOTES

the imprisonment of Edith Bone in solitary confinement without trial for seven years, without any public inquiry or protest from our Party even after the exposure of the Rajk trial had shown that such injustices were taking place, not only exposes the character of the regime, but involves us in its crimes. (MacEwen, p. 28.)

A hardline majority on the executive committee rejected MacEwen's criticisms and issued a statement supporting the Soviet intervention. A week later, MacEwen resigned from the *Daily Worker* over that and the Fryer business.

Page 129, The term 'maverick': An analysis of *Daily Worker* front pages between 22 October and 20 November:

22–24 October. News from Poland dominated reporting, with no mention of Hungary.

25 October. Headline: 'Hungarian Workers Answer'. Strapline: 'Armed Groups Defend Factories against Wreckers' (referring to alleged counter-revolutionary activities). Editorial began: 'Counter-revolution in Hungary staged an uprising in the hours of darkness on Tuesday night'.

26 October. Headline: 'Hungary and Poland Promise Change: More Democracy is the Keynote' (the tone at this stage suggesting that Nagy was running a Soviet-friendly reformist socialist government).

27 October. Headline: 'New Govt for Hungary' (even more optimistic). Strapline: 'Trade Union Representation in Broad Basis Body' (a claim that would appeal to Party membership).

29 October. Headline: 'Cease-Fire Is Ordered: Soviet Troops Are to Leave Budapest At Once' (a reference to the first intervention).

30 October – 4 November. Suez took over and dominated the news.

5 November. Headline: 'New Hungarian Anti-Fascist Govt in Action: Soviet Troops Called In to Stop White Terror' (a reference to the second intervention).

6 November. Suez dominated. Hungary was second lead, with: 'Budapest Says Fascists Caused New Bloodshed'.

7–8 November: Hungary was dropped from the front page.

9 November: A small item (1 column inch) appeared with: 'Gabriel, the *Daily Worker*'s distinguished cartoonist, has severed his connection with the paper because he "profoundly disagrees" with our policy over Hungary'. On the same page: 'A Call for the Defeat of Armed Rebel Bands Still Resisting Soviet Forces in Hungary'.

10–22 November: Suez continued to dominate. There were occasional references to the new Kadar regime, for example on 22 November: 'Life in Hungary Returning to Normal—Kadar'. Two further post-uprising headlines appeared, including on 16 November: 'Kadar: Hungary Stays Socialist: Russia Agrees Not to Deport Anyone Declares Premier'. Almost the final word came on 20 November, with the headline: 'Kadar Reveals the Facts: Hungarian Govt Acted to Save World Peace'.

All in all, the headlines and stories represent a depressing display of the survival of the Stalinist ethic. Next to the 'Kadar' article on 16 November was a small comment: 'Peter Fryer and the *Daily Worker*', with a version of Fryer's letter of resignation, plus the newspaper's reply, which began, 'We did not publish Peter Fryer's first report because it was an unbalanced estimate of the past eleven years and not an objective account of what he saw and heard. His interpretation of what he saw and heard was politically even more unbalanced'. In an act of revenge, the editorial even quoted anti-communist S Delmer, the *Daily Express*'s correspondent in Budapest, as a source contradicting Fryer's positive reports about the insurgents: 'In exchange for the departing terror [30 October] of the Red tanks we are now faced with the terror and anarchy of mob rule', a reference to the lynching of the AVH officers.

Page 130, 'What fools we were': D Lessing, cited in Cornwell. Lessing has written (retrospectively) about her relationship to Stalinism and Trotskyism (and Clancy Sigal) in her autobiography, *Walking in the Shade* (vol. 2, pp. 146–62). She also remembers trying to sell the *Daily Worker* to the genteel and surprised inhabitants of Cheltenham.

Page 130, Amis, Conquest, Kamm and Pryce-Jones: Amis attacked Hobsbawm in his *Koba the Dread*, referring to his 'yes' as disgraceful.

NOTES

(Hobsbawm counter-attacked in an interview with Hunt in which he said that *Koba the Dread* 'isn't an original or important book. It brings nothing that we haven't known except perhaps about his personal relations with his father'.) Conquest's attack on Hobsbawm was made in his 1999 memoir; Kamm's main thrust appeared in a *Times* article published on 23 July 2004; and Pryce-Jones pulled no punches in a *National Review* piece entitled 'Stalin's Professor—The Awful, Influential Career of E.J. Hobsbawm—Communist and Historian' and in a *New Criterion* article entitled 'Eric Hobsbawm: Lying to the Credulous'. In the *Review* article, Pryce-Jones accused Hobsbawm, a Jewish anti-Zionist, of a callous solution to the Middle East conflict: 'I have myself heard him propose that a nuclear bomb be dropped on Israel because—as another matter of arithmetic—it is better to kill a few million Jews now rather than 200 million people in the nuclear exchange that is bound eventually to occur in the Middle East'. Hitchens, a fan and friend of Conquest, was critical but much less unkind in 'Eric the Red', a *New York Times* review of Hobsbawm's 2002 memoir, *Interesting Times*.

Page 130, Hobsbawm's answer: Cited in Sexton. Sexton's 'NB' is a celebratedly bitchy insiders' column. The acidulous Sexton later became literary editor of the *Evening Standard*, radio critic of *The Sunday Telegraph* and a judge of the Man Booker Prize.

Page 131, 'it does not much matter . . .': Hobsbawm, *Age of Extremes*, p. 393. Most of Hobsbawm's commentary on this topic can be found on pp. 387–94.

Page 131, in some conservative circles: For example, *The Spectator* described him as arguably the UK's 'greatest living historian'. (Caute.)

Page 131, *Reflections on a Ravaged Century*: The reference is on p. 10.

Page 132, 'You didn't have the option . . .': E Hobsbawm, cited in Sexton. According to Sexton, Hobsbawm repeatedly made this argument.

Page 132, 'The months in Berlin . . .': Hobsbawm, *Interesting Times*, p. 55.

Page 132, 'The Soviet intervention . . .': Hobsbawm, *Interesting Times*, p. 207.

Page 133, 'Contemporary history is useless ...': Hobsbawm, 'Could It Have Been Different?'.

Page 133, 'Why I stayed ...': E Hobsbawm, cited in Hunt. Hobsbawm also maintains in *Age of Extremes* that pressure from the (apparently strong and successful) post-war communist alternative pushed the west into a more socially democratic political framework. Were they still alive, Harold Macmillan, Robert Menzies, Dwight Eisenhower and Charles de Gaulle might disagree, as might the victims of the Stasi, the AVH and the KGB.

Page 134, an after-the-event history: See Hobsbawm, *Interesting Times*, pp. 205–10. P Anderson, a leading Irish Marxist historian who was well treated in Hobsbawm's memoir, comments that *Interesting Times* is a bitter memoir and that 'scarcely an item in this sour retrospective withstands careful scrutiny'.

Page 134, suppressed Nagant revolver: For those readers who may want to take me to task for suggesting that a revolver can be suppressed, the 1895 model Nagant is an unusual, closed firing system revolver that uses a Bramit suppressor. Because of its low velocity, its reliability and its suppressibility, the Nagant made an ideal NKVD execution and assassination weapon. The NKVD also used the Walther PPK automatic, but, unlike revolvers, automatics have a tendency to jam.

5 TALES OF HEARTLESS DENIAL FROM THE BALKANS

Full chapter: The term 'Bosniak' is used to mean Bosnian Muslims. 'Serbs' generally refers, in this chapter, to all ethnic Serbs, while 'Serbians' and 'Serbia' are references to the Serbian republic. This chapter focuses primarily on the 1991–95 conflict. The later conflict in Kosovo had some similarities and some differences. For example, learning from what happened to their co-religionists in Bosnia, the (Muslim) Kosovo nationalist movement, including members of the ferocious Kosovo Liberation Army, deliberately committed brutal atrocities against Kosovo Serbs in order to excite predictable Serbian over-reaction, instigate a classic revolutionary war and drive the Serbs out of northern Kosovo. With the help of NATO intervention, the tactic has largely succeeded and, in November 2007, Kosovar secessionists, promising independence from Serbia, gained an electoral victory in what had become a United Nations (UN) protectorate, an alarming development for the few remaining Serbs, who largely boycotted the election. For Serbs generally, the Kosovo independence movement was always an opportunistic grab for the land that plays a major part in Serb heritage and history, and Kosovo's unresisted unilateral declaration of independence in 2008 has effectively reduced Serbia to a homogenised rump state, in one way much as Milosevic wanted, but in another way considerably smaller than Greater Serbia.

Page 137, 'The Srebrenica graves ...': Stover. The heavily protected forensic team, auspiced by the Hague's international war tribunal in 1996, was a multinational group led by US forensic anthropologist William Haglund.

Page 137, Radovan Karadzic and Ratko Mladic: Karadzic was president of the self-styled Bosnian *Republika Sprska*. Mladic was in command of the Bosnian Serb troops that captured Srebrenica. At the time of writing, both are still on the run, indicted war criminals by the International Criminal Tribunal for Yugoslavia (ICTY).

Page 138, an estimated 97 000: The figures are conservative and are taken from the Sarajevo-based Research and Documentation Center's 2007 *Annual Report*, Sarajevo, January 2008, www.idc.org.ba/aboutus/REPORT_2007.pdf, constructed from three years of research. The centre is funded by the Norwegian government, the Swedish Helsinki Committee, the US government and the UN. The figures for the missing are based on information supplied to E Vulliamy by the International Commission on Missing Persons. (Suljagic, p. 195.)

Page 139, Serbians seeing themselves as victims: See, for example, Pesic's comprehensive survey of Serb defensiveness and Milosevic's remarkable speech to the Serbian Fourth Party Congress of the SPS, in which he asked how the Jews would have felt if their persecution had been justified by charges that they had been perpetrating genocide against the German people. He then suggested that the Serbs were the Jews of the current generation. (Milosevic is cited in Ramet, pp. 47–8.)

Page 139, '[Serb nationalist] historical revisionism ...': Ramet, p. 47.

Page 140, 'No-one should dare to beat you': S Milosevic, speech in Kosovo Polje, April 1997, cited in Silber & Little, p. 37. There is some conjecture that Milosevic, as a Communist Party official, was actually talking to the Kosovo police, not the crowd who had turned up at the demonstration with truckloads of throw-sized rocks. Nevertheless, his comment was seen by the crowd as a call to defend their position against Kosovo's Muslim majority. (Silber & Little, p. 38.) Silber was Balkans correspondent for the *Financial Times*, and Little covered the war as BBC Radio and Television correspondent. Their detailed and highly regarded book is critical of Milosevic's role in the Balkans conflicts of the 1990s, arguing that Belgrade instigated a long-term plan to establish a Greater Serbia by force and that Milosevic was ruthlessly unscrupulous; for example, in 2004, he was implicated in the assassination of his former friend and mentor Stambolic. Milosevic was found dead on 11 March 2006 in his prison cell during the course of his ICTY trial; he had died of heart failure. Interestingly, at that time, the deputy chief prosecutor, Geoffrey Nice, was not convinced that he would have been given a guilty verdict, following the retraction of evidence by at least one key witness. (G Nice, in *Milosevic on Trial*.)

Page 141, 'transformed, set afire by Kosovo': I Stambolic, cited in Silber & Little, p. 38.

Page 141, 'Milosevic told me ...': JM Mendiluce, cited in Silber & Little, p. 222.

Page 142, Slovenia viewed as dispensable by Milosevic: One large hole in the denialist argument that Milosevic was keen to keep the federation and was forced into defensiveness by the separatist ambitions of the rest of Yugoslavia is the relative ease with which the tiny republic of Slovenia, a major contributor to the Yugoslav economy, was allowed to go. Milosevic did not care about Slovenia because there were no significant Serb communities in that part of the world, and he was therefore prepared to trade off a homogenised Greater Serbia against the loss of Slovene funding.

Pages 142–3, Glina murders: Glenny, pp. 499–500.

Page 144, Milosevic condoned a campaign: There was clear evidence available from 1995 onwards that Belgrade was behind the Bosnian Serb ethnic cleansing. More recently (2006–07), a post-mortem case against Milosevic was consolidated by Serbian Supreme Defence Council transcripts of discussions about direct Serbian involvement, which were made available to the International Court of Justice but kept back from the ICTY (although later leaked to the press). The growing body of evidence has shown that in 1993 more than 1800 JNA officers and non-commissioned officers were deployed to Bosnia by Belgrade under the supervision of the secret 30th Personnel Centre of the general staff, a figure that had grown to 4000 by 1994. There are also verbatim records of meetings in which the role that Serbian forces prepared for and played in the massacre at Srebrenica was discussed; these reports confirm Colonel Nikolic's evidence (see below). The International Court of Justice approved Belgrade's request to keep the documents secret; 'We could not believe our luck', said Vladimir Djeric, one of the Serbian team at the hearings. (Cited in Simons.)

Page 144, The JNA's support of the BSA: The JNA had 50 per cent of its forces permanently stationed in Bosnia, which also contained more than 55 per cent of the nation's military industry and munitions sites. This concentration of armaments came about because Bosnia had been selected as Yugoslavia's redoubt in case of invasion. In each region of Yugoslavia, territorial reserve defence forces provided a large pool of weapons-trained support for ethnic militias. (Nation, p. 150.)

Page 145, several hundred foreign Islamic fighters: Estimates vary, but the likelihood is that 100 or so foreign fighters, including some al Qaeda members, entered the conflict in 1992 and were initially used in anti-Serb small-unit combat operations as shock troops in central

Bosnia. By the end of 1993, as many as 1500 fighters, approximately half of whom were Arab, may have entered the country. At the end of the war, an estimated 500 foreign fighters remained behind. (Sito-Sucic.)

Page 145, 'differed considerably' in their 'fighting methods': Judge J-C Antonetti, in 'Summary of the Judgement for Enver Hadzihasanovic and Amir Kubura', ICTY, The Hague, 15 March 2006, www.un.org/icty/hadzihas/trialc/judgement/060315/hadz-sum060315.htm, cited in Warrell. This is a polite way of saying that they committed war crimes.

Page 145, 'There is nothing quite like . . .': Vulliamy, *Seasons in Hell*, cited in Silber & Little, p. 250.

Page 147, 'A walk down any side street . . .': Silber & Little, p. 310. The Catholic cathedral is situated in the narrower part of Marshal Tito Street, before it reaches the junction with Ferhadia Street, both streets then turning into more of a boulevard.

Page 147, 'condemned to death': A Izetbegovic, cited Silber & Little, p. 309.

Page 148, UNPROFOR: UNPROFOR troops in Bosnia commonly experienced mortar, grenade and sniping attacks by Muslims allegedly attempting to provoke UN fire on Serb positions and hoping to widen the conflict and increase their level of international support. There is some evidence of disdain among the UNPROFOR troops for the rag-tag nature of the Bosniak forces, who were regarded less as victims and more as dangerously volatile irregulars. (Rohde, pp. 101–2.) British general Sir Michael Rose, no friend of the Bosniaks, had no doubts about what had happened on 4 and 5 February 1994: 'The analysis of the craters indicates with certainty that the mortars were fired from Bosnian Serb positions . . . I don't accept the Serb denial. Firing into such a populated area is unacceptable. Those responsible must be confronted with their criminal actions'. (Cited in Heinrich.) Proceedings at the ICTY in the trial of Stanislav Galic, BSA corps commander, in 2003, appeared to demonstrate unequivocally that the BSA had been responsible for both shellings. Galic was sentenced to twenty years' imprisonment.

NOTES

Page 148, Major Jose Labandeira, announced: Heinrich.

Page 149, 'Near the center of the town . . .': D Erdemovic (based on his recollections), cited in Rohde, p. 169.

Page 149, 'Get on with it . . .': M Jolovic, BSA Drina Wolves brigade commander, radio instructions, Srebrenica, 14 July 1995, played at the ICTY, the Hague, cited in Marquand.

Pages 149–50, 'The bullet strikes that you see . . .': D Manning, in *Milosevic on Trial*. Manning was on secondment to the ICTY as an investigator in 2002–03. This sequence was shot in a large disused farm building near Srebrenica in which approximately 1000 Bosniaks were murdered in July 1995.

Page 150, lightly armed defenders: The Srebrenicans were armed mainly with AK-47s, light machine guns and limited-range shoulder-fired anti-tank weapons. The BSA used, or could call upon, JNA heavy assets including MiG-21 fighters, armoured personnel carriers, World War II–vintage T-34 and (more modern) T-54 and T-55 tanks, 82- and 120-millimetre mortars, at least one 155-millimetre howitzer, Russian-model VBR multiple rocket launchers (updated versions of the dreaded 'Stalin Organs' of World War II), and self-propelled triple 20-millimetre BOV-3 and dual 30-millimetre BOV-30 automatic cannons, originally designed for use against low-level anti-aircraft artillery but deadly as close- and medium-range anti-personnel artillery. (See Lucarevic; Nation; Silber & Little; Suljagic; and various television news items of the conflict.)

Page 151, Naser Oric: Oric, a former bodyguard to Milosevic, was the kind of impulsive and cruel local chieftain often thrown up during civil war chaos. Little more than a dangerous but charismatic ruffian, he also allegedly ran the black market in Srebrenica. As for his fighting skills, he boasted of killing and decapitating Serbs, becoming a focus for morbid western tabloid curiosity. His Serbian equivalent was the notorious gangster Arkan (Zeljko Raznatovic), who was eventually assassinated in Belgrade in a contract killing on 15 January 2000. Arkan was an indicted war criminal; among other crimes, he had led the Serb paramilitaries in the massacre of Croatian civilians at Vukovar.

Page 151, attacks on Serb villagers: The figures for Serb casualties at the hands of Oric's men vary wildly, according to sources, but the best estimates are about 300 or above, of which more than half would probably have been military casualties. Justifiably, Oric became a figure of hate for Bosnian Serbs and was indicted for war crimes by the ICTY, eventually receiving, from the Serb point of view, a very light sentence: 'Tribunal judges today convicted Naser Oric, a former senior commander of Bosnian Muslim forces in and around Srebrenica, of failing to take steps to prevent the murder and cruel treatment of a number of Serb prisoners in the former UN "safe area". They sentenced Oric to two years' imprisonment'. ('Naser Oric Convicted'.) Having served time, Oric was released at the time of his sentencing.

Page 151, sacked two local Serb villages: In a classic case of denialist projection, BSA general Milan Gvero stated that the attack was the Bosniaks' fault: they were 'trying to bring the attention of that little town they have already used as a joker in the pack ... They have recently burned down the village of Visnjica and massacred its inhabitants'. (Cited in Rhode, p. 130.) The Visnjica attack occurred on 26 June, with apparently one Serb soldier killed and three civilians wounded. (Rhode, p. 128.) The (generally reliable) Sarajavo-based Research and Documentation Center cites 119 civilian and 424 combatant casualties in Serb villages near Srebrenica for 1995—too many civilians, but far from the many hundreds or even thousands claimed by Serb propagandists.

Page 152, 'Here we are on 11 July 1995 ...': R Mladic, in BSA footage shown at *The Prosecutor of the Tribunal against Radovan Karadzic, Ratko Mladic* (1995) IT-95-5/18, ICTY, the Hague, 3 July 1996, p. 535, www.un.org/icty/transe5&18/960703it.htm, cited in *The Death of Yugoslavia*. Mladic was referring to the 12 July orthodox feast of Saint Peter and Saint Paul and to an 1804 Serb rebellion brutally crushed by Ottoman forces, of whom the Dahijas were the Turkish janissary leaders. Mladic's comment illustrates the significance of religious identity and the longevity of the Serbian cultural memory.

NOTES

Page 152, 'That is how we deal with our enemies': R Mladic, cited in Silber & Little, p. 349.

Page 152, 'Don't be afraid of anything . . .': R Mladic, BSA footage, cited in 'Statement of Facts and Acceptance of Responsibility: Tab A to Annex A to the Joint Motion for Consideration of Plea Agreement between Momir Nikolic and the Office of the Prosecutor', ICTY, the Hague, 6 May 2003, www.un.org/icty/mnikolic/trialc/facts030506.htm

Pages 152–3, 'At that time Lt. Colonel Popovic told me . . .': M Nikolic, in *The Prosecutor v. Momir Nikolic* (2003) IT-02-60, cited in 'Tab A to Annex A to the Joint Motion for Consideration of Plea Agreement between Momir Nikolic and the Office of the Prosecutor', ICTY, the Hague, 6 May 2003, www.un.org/icty/mnikolic/trialc/facts030506.htm. According to Nikolic, the units involved in massacres at Potocari, Bratunac and Zvornik included the Ministry of the Interior special police force, the Drina corps military police, Drina Wolves of the Zvornik brigade, sections of the 10th Sabotage detachment, sections of the 65th Protection regiment's military police, Bratunac brigade's 2nd and 3rd Infantry battalions, Bratunac brigade military police and Serb civilian police. On appeal, Nikolic's sentence was reduced from twenty-seven to twenty years' imprisonment. On July 2006, Popovic, together with six other senior Serb officers, was arraigned before the ICTY for genocide and other crimes.

Page 153, 'One thousand prisoners of war . . .': V Seselj, in *The Prosecutor of the Tribunal against Vojislav Seselj* (2003) IT-03-67, ICTY, the Hague, 8 November 2007, p. 1858, www.un.org/icty/transe67/071108IT.htm, cited in 'Serb Nationalist Rejects UN Court', BBC News, 8 November 2007, http://news.bbc.co.uk/2/hi/europe/7084506.stm

Page 154, 'I warn you . . .': R Karadzic, speech prior to the war's outbreak, cited in *The Death of Yugoslavia*.

Page 154, 'we give full guarantees . . .': R Karadzic, press conference, cited in *The Death of Yugoslavia*.

Page 154, 'in the Serbian tradition . . .': S Milosevic, in *Milosevic on Trial*.

Page 155, 'standard police operation' and 'I don't remember . . .': N Pavkovic, in *Moral Combat*.

Page 155, 'Mr Milan Babic . . .': D Ognjanovic, in *Milosevic on Trial*.

Pages 155–6, 'The Zvornik [ethnic cleansing] operation . . .': V Seselj, in *The Death of Yugoslavia*, cited in Silber & Little, p. 224. While later incarcerated in the Hague for war crimes, Seselj, a florid nationalist, held the leading ticket for the Radical Party in the 2007 Serbian general election.

Page 156, Tudjman's palace was rocketed: The Serbs also blamed the Croatians for attacking their own town of Dubrovnik, and they argued that the Croats and Muslims were besieging themselves at Sarajevo. (Ramet, p. 47.)

Pages 156–7, OESC 2006 survey: 'Public Opinion in Serbia'.

Page 157, 'Hungry for controversy . . .': Vulliamy, 'Poison in the Well of History'. Evans, author and editor of *The Sunday Times* from 1967 to 1981, pioneered modern British investigative journalism in the 1970s. Since then he has retained his celebrity status, arguably through his marriage to Tina Brown, another well-known journalist-editor. Young is a controversial British journalist and author of *How to Lose Friends & Alienate People*. The ICA is the Institute for Contemporary Art in London.

Page 158, miscellaneous make-up: The denialists have included the little-known and ultimately unsuccessful activist group International Committee to Defend Slobodan Milosevic, diligent bloggers such as Unrepentant Marxist (Louis Proyect), the neo-Nazi Stormfront website, the Serbian Orthodox Church's Patriarch Pavle, and M Yelesiyevich, editor of the implausibly titled *Ratko Mladic: Tragic Hero*, Unwritten History Inc., New York, 2006.

Page 158, mirror image of assorted far-right: The Revolutionary Communist Party, a splinter group of a splinter group, and *Living Marxism* had some pragmatic, for lack of a better word, links with right-wing libertarianism. According to Pallister, Vidal and Maguire,

Living Marxism supporters re-grouped as the Institute of Ideas, a microscopic radical group that shares its concerns about genetically modified food (a government plot), government plans to interfere with independent thought (speed limits and smoking bans are bad) and sex (paedophiles are misunderstood) with such libertarian groups as the Reason Foundation, the Heritage Foundation, the Hudson Institute, the Cato Institute, Families for Freedom and the Association of British Drivers, most of whom are also part of a loose libertarian coalition known as the Freedom Network. In 2000, Claire Fox, the director of the Institute of Ideas, denied that her organisation and *Living Marxism* were or had been fronts for well-funded, right-wing post-Reaganite groups. (Pallister, Vidal & Maguire 'Life after Living Marxism: Fighting for Freedom'.) In 2007, she was listed sixty-fourth in *Time Out*'s 'London Movers and Shakers List 2006' and was named as the capital's 'No. 3 Activist'.

Page 159, 'One night, while I was going through the pictures ...': T Deichmann, cited in Campbell, 'Atrocity, Memory, Photography', part 1, p. 13. Campbell's two detailed articles form a devastatingly critical analysis of Deichmann and *Living Marxism*'s point of view. Campbell's conclusion, which will sound familiar to any student of denialist techniques, was that

> the claims of Deichmann and *LM* are erroneous and their arguments flawed. The major reason for this is the partial, selective and partisan manner in which they presented their case. The journalists they criticised were not interviewed, and the inmates who survived the camps in the Prijedor region were ignored. Positive interpretations were given to isolated statements by prisoners, while the overwhelming number of countervailing views that emphasised the negative were overlooked. (Campbell, 'Atrocity, Memory, Photography', part 1, p. 25.)

Pages 159–60, 'In the eyes of many ...': T Deichmann, cited in Campbell, 'Atrocity, Memory, Photography', part 1, p. 12.

Page 160, supporters of the *Living Marxism* case: 'Any objective observer reading this record of biased judicial treatment would be forced to conclude that the trial's verdict was shaped by political hostility'. (Editorial, World Socialist Web Site, ICFI, 25 March 2000, www.wsws.org/articles/2000/mar2000/livm-m25.shtml) *Living Marxism*'s political case—of NATO-capitalist collusion encouraged by the Sarajevo government—had support from US-based Marxist conspiracy theories, including the twin (daft) ideas that a US-controlled oil pipeline was to be built through (unstable and mountainous) Bosnia and that US meddling in the Balkans after 1995 was to gain control of a lead mine in Kosovo. (Walls.)

Pages 160–1, 'I remember when Penny Marshall . . .': F Alic, cited in Harding.

Page 161, 'Part of a plan . . .': Johnstone, p.117.

Page 161, 'A Serb commission's final report . . .': 'Bosnian Serbs Said to Admit Role in '95 Killings', Associated Press, reproduced in *The New York Times*, 9 November 2004, www.nytimes.com/2004/11/09/international/europe/09serb.html

Page 161, 'Last month the government . . .': Agence France, press release, 8 November 2004.

Page 161, 'The International Court of Justice . . .': United Nations News Centre, 26 February 2007.

Page 162, 1998 piece in *Covert Action Quarterly*: 'Misinformation: TV Coverage of a Bosnian Camp', *Covert Action Quarterly*, no. 65, fall 1998.

Page 162, Serb crimes: Johnstone, pp. 92–108.

Page 163, 'veterans of the war . . .': Johnstone, p. 67. The list of suppositional statements is on p. 67.

Page 164, the nine-page analysis of events at Srebrenica: Johnstone, pp. 108–18.

Page 164, 'The difficulty in knowing the truth . . .': Johnstone, p. 109.

Page 164, the convoys were used to smuggle weapons: Much of the weapons smuggling was carried out by small groups of Bosniaks who used familiar mountain trails to bypass Serb lines. The arms, generally infantry weapons and ammunition, came from Turkey and Iran through a (generally) complicit Croatia and with tacit and unofficial US support. There is at least one recorded instance of a Sarajevo-Srebrenica UN convoy being stopped and searched for weapons by the Serbs. Approximately 8000 rounds of AK-47 and light machine gun (LMG) ammunition were discovered. That amounts to about two rounds apiece for each AK-47 of the defenders of Srebrenica, bearing in mind that the average cyclic rate of fire for one LMG is between 700 and 800 rounds per minute. On the other hand, Lucarevic, head of the Sarajevo Military Police (in reality, Bosniak shock troops) from 1992 to 1993, discusses, in his account of the siege of Sarajevo, the ingenuity required in the smuggling of arms and explosives into the city via UNPROFOR convoys, using oxygen cylinders with false compartments (pp. 201–5) and false-bottomed containers (pp. 246–9). However, by mid-1993, the BSA and UNPROFOR had both realised that they were being deceived in this fashion, effectively ending any chance of sustained and large-scale Bosniak arms smuggling via UNPROFOR convoys.

Page 165, 'has aroused the strong suspicion of a calculated sacrifice': Johnstone, p. 112.

Page 165, 'the number of Muslims killed . . .': Johnstone, p. 114.

Page 166, 'Part of a plan of genocide? . . .': Johnstone, p. 117. Johnstone takes a narrow view of genocide, demanding demonstrable long-term planning with 'intent to destroy, in whole or in part, a national racial or religious group' (the 1948 Geneva Convention definition) and claiming, on that basis, that the Bosniaks and the Croats could also be charged with genocide because they attacked Serbs. The part she missed out was the ICTY's refinement of that original definition during the trial of Radislav Krstic, a former BSA general who assisted with the killings at Srebrenica, on 2 August 2001. (*The Prosecutor v. Radislav Krstic* (2001) IT-98-33-T, 'Judgement', ICTY, The Hague, 2 August 2001, www.un.org/icty/krstic/TrialC1/judgement/index.htm) The amendment says that the part must be 'a substantial part of the group' and is further clarified in the ICTY's 2004 judgment against Krstic's appeal (at which his sentence was reduced from forty-six to thirty-five years' imprisonment): 'the intent requirement of genocide under Article 4 of the [ICTY] Statute is . . .

satisfied where evidence shows that the alleged perpetrator intended to destroy at least a substantial part of the protected group'. (*The Prosecutor vs Radislav Krstic* (2004) IT-98-33-A, 'Judgement', ICTY, The Hague, 19 April 2004, p. 4, www.un.org/icty/krstic/Appeal/judgement/krs-aj040419e.htm) The ICTY and the Appeals chamber also found, in 2001 and 2004 respectively, that 'genocide was committed in Srebrenica in 1995', a verdict upheld by the International Court of Justice on 26 February 2007 in a judgment which cleared Serbia of direct involvement in genocide but which found that Belgrade had breached international law by failing to prevent genocide at Srebrenica. (www.icj-cij.org/presscom/index.php?pr=18978&pt=1891=6&p2=1)

Page 167, 'History doesn't offer …': N Chomsky, in *Manufacturing Consent.*

Page 168, Brockes–Chomsky interview: The only easily accessible version is on Chomsky's website, at www.chomsky.info/onchomsky/20051031.htm

Page 171, 'in trying to understand …': Johnstone, 'The Bosnian War Was Brutal But It Wasn't a Holocaust'.

Page 171, 4500 words: This is about the length of a scholarly article. As a point of comparison, this chapter contains 2500 words on Srebrenica. Interestingly, in the first part of her book, Johnstone cites Silber and Little's *Yugoslavia* eight times as an authoritative and corroborating source without any reference to one of the authors' major theses, which is essentially that Milosevic was a devious, brutal and rampant nationalist.

Page 171, 'by encouraging the secession of republics …': Herman & Peterson, part 4, p. 47, reproduced at www.monthlyreview.org/1007herman-peterson4.php

Page 173, 'The [Srebrenica] massacre is a lie': M Milovanovic, in Suljagic, p. 192.

Page 173, 'the murder, often in …' and 'Serb nationalists…': Weitz, p. 220.

NOTES

6 FAILING THE SCHOLARLY TEST

Full chapter: This chapter focuses on Windschuttle's views as expressed in *The Fabrication of Aboriginal History* and on the collection of responses in Manne's *Whitewash*. (Citations from *Fabrication* use the 2003 reprinted edition.) There are other books on the debate, including Attwood's excellent *Telling the Truth about Aboriginal History* and the far less good 2004 *Washout* by 'writer and businessman' J Dawson, which is basically a Windschuttle defence through repetition. While the former sells reasonably well, the latter has effectively sunk without trace. Dawson's contribution, however, did display two memorable moments. First, on *Washout*'s rear cover, Dawson is described as having discovered that historians had 'abandoned their patriotic oath to defend the truth'. Second, and to his credit, Dawson has asked for references to his work to be removed from the notorious Adelaide Institute's website.

Page 174, Pseudohistory: There are several definitions of the term, but a common understanding, adopted in this chapter, is that pseudohistory is a form of writing that purportedly adopts the appearance and style of historical scholarship to propagate an undeclared or cryptic ideological, metaphysical or personal point of view. This is distinctly different from a historian who has a declared position and writes from that perspective. For an example of a recent pseudohistorical work, see B Anzulovic, *Heavenly Serbia: From Myth to Genocide*, NYU Press, New York, 1999, a study of the nationalist myth of a Greater Serbia. The book has been sharply criticised for its (anti-Serb) ideological position and for its unconvincing use of sources. For another example cited by authorities, see G Menzies, *1421: The Year China Discovered the World*, Bantam Press, London, 2002, which outlines Menzies's controversial assertion known as the 1421 hypothesis. See Finlay.

Page 174, Tasmanian archives: To avoid confusion, Van Diemen's Land and Tasmania will be cited throughout the chapter as 'Tasmania', even though the term was not adopted until 1855.

Page 175, Sydney as a centre of intellectual debate: In the 1960s the Sydney Push, a loose and anarchical collection of post-beat intellectuals and artists, was the prominent intellectual elite of the day. In the 1970s, youthful radical intellectualism coalesced around the University of Sydney and the Vietnam war debate. Several of the 1970s radicals later turned into conservative commentators. See Windschuttle's website, The Sydneyline, on which some interesting claims are made:

> Since the nineteenth century, Sydney has generated a way of thinking that amounts to a distinctive intellectual tradition. It is not exclusive to Sydney, nor has it ever been the mainstream position in this city, but this is where it has established itself and thrived. It can be identified by what it is for and against ... It has a low opinion of: anything beginning with 'post', especially postmodernism, poststructuralism and postcolonialism; anything ending with 'studies', especially cultural studies, gender studies, peace studies and environmental studies. (www.sydneyline.com/About.htm)

Having said that, Melbourne has its own rightist community, in which the dominant force is the Institute of Public Affairs. Melbourne's neo-conservatives, it may be argued, tend to be less exaggerated in their behaviour than their Sydney counterparts.

Page 175, appointment to the board of the ABC: This was one in a number of contentious political appointments to the ABC board by conservative prime minister John Howard. Other appointees included Liberal Party numbers man and banker Michael Kroger (1998), Howard supporter Ron Brunton (2003) and Murdoch columnist Janet Albrechtsen (2005). Each time an appointment was made, Howard was accused of stacking the board, and he later admitted that the Kroger appointment was indeed political. As it happened, there was an alleged intervention by Kroger to get Shier appointed, and there was an allegation that Windschuttle and the others were involved in blocking the ABC's publication of a controversial book about Howard supporter Sydney shock jock Alan Jones.

Page 176, something of an icon: The Holocaust denial website of the self-styled Adelaide Institute regularly reports Windschuttle's doings.

Of course, Windschuttle does not have much control over this apparent interest in his point of view by the Adelaide Institute's 'master', convicted Holocaust denier Fredrick Töben. Interestingly, though, a hagiographical review of Windschuttle's 2004 book *White Australia* by author and *Quadrant* contributor RJ Stove was published in the far-right, racially obsessed US magazine *The Occidental Quarterly*. Here is a taste:

> It is not obvious why anyone would actively seek the title of 'Australia's best living historian'. What is perfectly obvious is that nowadays, Keith Windschuttle alone among Australians consistently threatens the historiographical preeminence of Geoffrey Blainey. One suspects that Blainey himself hails this development. Any major thinker cherishes competitors talented enough to be worth fretting about. He may, as Newton said of himself, stand on giants' shoulders; but he can never be content with his exalted location if his only confreres are earthbound midgets. (RJ Stove, 'Goodbye to All That: Reflections on White Australia', *The Occidental Quarterly*, vol. 5, no. 1, spring 2005, http://theoccidentalquarterly.com/archives/vol5no1/rjs-windschuttle.html)

Page 176, Windschuttle's interpretation of Australian settlement by European colonists: See Flood, pp. 96–132; Davison, Hirst & Macintyre, including R Broome's entry; and Hirst, pp. 80–103. For a useful summary of the pre-Windschuttle debates, see Attwood & Foster, pp. 1–30).

Page 177, 'liberal fantasy': Hirst, p. 82.

Page 177, 'passionate advocates' Flood, p. 108.

Page 177, 'Since 1985, the dissidents . . .': Windschuttle, *The Killing of History*, p. 9.

Page 178, even by his supporters: See, for example, Henderson, 'The Battle Is Not to Be Left Behind'.

Page 178, shallow but highly dogmatic leftism: The impression given by friends, former friends and colleagues at the time was that

Windschuttle had a lower middle class chip on his shoulder and was not that deeply immersed in socialist doctrine, but did enjoy obsessional verbal sparring, to the extent that he exasperated many of those who knew him well. For a moderately balanced, journalistic view of several of his personality traits, see Cadzow. Windschuttle seems to have given very few print interviews after the unflattering write-up by Cadzow in May 2003. On 24 November 2003, *The Australian* did publish a Windschuttle-sympathetic interview by the conservative writer F Devine ('Lured Back into the Fray by Cromwell of the South Seas'—a reference to Paul Keating), and there was Marsh's 2005 luncheon interview for the *Financial Times*'s feature column 'Lunch with the FT', in which Windschuttle, described as 'small [and] slightly stout', relaxed for his overseas audience over oysters and a raw kingfish salad. Since then, however, Windschuttle seems to prefer calling the shots by writing his own pieces for the press. For more perspectives on Windschuttle's character, see Gould (a former Windschuttle comrade but friend no longer).

Page 179, spotted by Bob Gould himself: Gould.

Pages 179–80, 'Academia didn't live . . .': Marsh.

Page 180, 'Keith Windschuttle argues . . .': Sykes.

Page 181, 'incomprehensible and odious gauntlet': Windschuttle, 'The Poverty of Media Theory'.

Page 181, synthesising technique: There is nothing unreasonable in criticising the more bogus and contradictory aspects of postmodernism; Terry Eagleton does it all the time. The problem is that Windschuttle is unreasonable in his muddled précis, which amounts to an over-ripe critique pandering to superficial prejudices. A better analysis may be found in the more rigorous work of philosopher C Norris, especially in his book *What's Wrong with Postmodernism? Critical Theory and the Ends of Philosophy*, Johns Hopkins University Press, Baltimore, MD, 1990. Windschuttle makes two very brief references to Norris's work, in *The Killing of History*, pp. 25, 38n.

Page 182, friendly glow of the limelight: Cadzow.

NOTES

Page 182, 'No one who disagrees with them ...': Windschuttle, *The Fabrication of Aboriginal History*, p. 6.

Page 182, The three rules of Windschuttleism: For a wonderful example of Windschuttleism at work, see Bendle, a venomously inaccurate and highly exaggerated review of B Kiernan's *Blood and Soil: A World History of Genocide and Extermination from Sparta to Darfur*, Yale University Press, New Haven, CT, 2007; and see Kiernan, an angry but forensic reply and dissection. Bendle's article attacked Kiernan, among other things, for unfairly blaming Europeans for genocide and was based on a longer piece in *Quadrant*, published at a time when Windschuttle was newly appointed editor of the conservative magazine.

Pages 182–3, 'It is not the friends he has lost ...': For further discussion of Windschuttle's tempestuous relations with former friends and colleagues, see Cadzow.

Page 183, inspired by a book review: The book under review was R Moran, *Massacre Myth*, Access Press, Perth, 1999.

Page 183, 'The trouble is ...': K Windschuttle, cited in Marsh.

Page 184, Henry Reynolds's historical practice: Windschuttle, *The Fabrication of Aboriginal History*, p. 6.

Page 184, 'This series has been written ...': By mid-2008 only one book had been published in the 'series'. A second has been promised for late 2008, about the Stolen Generation.

Page 184, bourgeois bigotry: While constructed by Windschuttle in tabloid terms, the *Fabrication* debate has generally featured in the middle-class broadsheet press and in the ABC, with its predominantly middle-class constituency. See, for example, M Ricketson's brief summary and assessment in 'Footnotes to a War', *The Sydney Morning Herald*, 13 December 2003, www.smh.com.au/articles/2003/12/15/1071336875054.html

Page 184, Robert Manne: Manne is arguably Windschuttle's most formidable critic. He became a thorn in the flesh of neo-conservatives

277

when his 1990s editorship of *Quadrant* turned the magazine towards a more centrist line, inviting, for example, left liberals such as philosopher Raimond Gaita to contribute. Furthermore, Manne took up the Stolen Generation as a cause, and his espousal of Indigenous Australian issues was the last straw as far as the journal's board was concerned. Manne was replaced in 1997 by the colourful and bibulous rightist PP ('Paddy') McGuinness, who died in 2008 to encomia from the Sydney Right and an obituary in the *Australian Financial Review* of such vitriol from Paul Keating that it shocked even those who were used to Keating's abrasive style.

Page 185, Testing the Windschuttle Technique: All quotes from *The Fabrication of Aboriginal History* in this section are taken from pp. 1–10 unless stated otherwise.

Page 185, 'But historians should report . . .': Windschuttle, 'Why I'm a Bad Historian'.

Page 185, prepared as a PhD: Although the PhD is now the basic training program for scholarship in history, there are many successful historians and historical writers who never completed doctoral studies, including Henry Reynolds, Les Carlyon, Richard White, Manning Clark, EH Carr and, indeed, Geoffrey Blainey. (AJP Taylor, having successfully completed his doctoral dissertation, turned down the title.) These have instead relied on the quality of their scholarship and their writing, and on the respect of their peers, to make their reputations. Windschuttle abandoned his own PhD studies and threatened *The Bulletin* with legal action when an article made reference to his non-completion. *The Bulletin* apologised. At the same time, it is important to remember that there are good PhDs and bad PhDs, just as there are good universities and bad universities, good examiners and bad examiners.

Page 187, Geoffrey Blainey's odd, populist views: In the 1980s, Blainey developed a public anxiety that the multicultural nature of Australian society and the demand for Indigenous Australian rights would lead to a break-up of the Commonwealth, at a time, he believed, when Australia was threatened by Indonesian expansionism. This position gained him some prominent friends on the Right of

NOTES

politics and lost him almost every friend on the Left. Blainey was not alone in his anxiety, as Clark has commented:

> There is quite a well-known image of John Howard after the Wik decision in 1996 holding up a map of Australia on the [ABC's] 7.30 Report. Looking grave, the Prime Minister warned of the unending disputes the High Court had just invited. Showing in bright red great swathes of the continent that were under 'threat' from potential Aboriginal land claims, the map was a graphic image of division.

Page 187, Stuart Macintyre: Macintyre's professional and former personal involvement in communism has been a constant refrain in the Murdoch press's attacks on his allegedly subversive influence in the history community. At the same time, Macintyre's professional support for Blainey as a historian, through, for example, convening a Melbourne celebration of Blainey's work in November 2000, earned him the opprobrium of several of his leftist colleagues. See Gare et al.

Page 188, The Reynolds–Blainey controversy: For a good and balanced discussion of the controversy, see Macintyre & Clark, Chapter 5. See also 'Blainey Quits', *The Sydney Morning Herald*, 24 November 1988: 'The controversy over his views on Asian immigration, he said, "might have been a small component, but very small"'; and L Schwarz, 'Blainey's Views Appear to Have Cost Him His Post', *The Sydney Morning Herald*, 25 August 1988: 'A protest vote against the historian by eleven student representatives, whose votes may have been crucial in a closely contested election, are cited as a likely reason for his failure'. Blainey's successor was Dr Marion Adams, a scholar in Germanic studies, generally regarded as slightly to the right of centre politically. A discussion that I had in 2008 with an academic staff member who was closely involved at the time of the Blainey business suggested two things: that there was a level of incredulity and consequent annoyance among electors that Blainey would stand for a third time; and, more importantly, that a strong female constituency in the electors wanted a female dean. My source rejected the idea that anti-Blainey student representatives were influential in the outcome.

Pages 188–90, NMA and Jewish Museum links: The genocide argument dominates Windschuttle's worldview, but, in characteristic fashion, he sees it as an absolute comparison with the Holocaust. For a more detailed discussion of what the term 'genocide' has come to mean, see Chapter 5.

Page 189, Michael McKernan: 'Homegrown Advantage', *Eureka Street*, vol. 11, no. 3, April 2001.

Page 190, Vivienne Rae-Ellis's *Black Robinson*: For a detailed account of this case, see Tasmanian author C Pybus, in Manne (ed.). Pybus says that the book was rejected because of its 'offensive and inaccurate assertions about Tasmanian Aborigines, most notably that they routinely engaged in cannibalism'. Rae-Ellis also alleged that George Robinson used hypnotism on his guides, a claim greeted with scorn. According to Pybus, scholarly reviews of the Rae-Ellis book were 'uniformly critical' (p. 259).

Page 191, 'footnotes are one of the principal reasons …': Windschuttle, *The Fabrication of Aboriginal History*, p. 133.

Page 191, 'Scholarly history distinguishes itself …': Windschuttle, *The Fabrication of Aboriginal History*, p. 132.

Page 192, chardonnay-drinking: See, for example, J Albrechtsen, article on industrial relations sub-headed 'Despite Labor's Chardonnay-Fuelled Bleatings …' *The Australian*, 13 February 2008.

Page 192, 'small businessman': Statement made at a meeting attended by the author, 18 September 2007.

Page 193, in at least one of his allegations: Windschuttle, *The Fabrication of Aboriginal History*, pp. 131–4, 358–9.

Page 193, 'historians are always making up figures': L Ryan, *Sunday*, television program, Channel 9, Sydney, 25 May 2003. Ryan's 'what was she thinking of?' response was to questions from Helen Dalley, a seasoned and intelligent interviewer, about Ryan's 'guesstimate' of Indigenous Australian deaths.

NOTES

Page 194, Methods for recording numbers of deaths: Ironically, thanks to the Nazis' grisly bookkeeping tendencies, the picture for the Holocaust is much clearer than it is for other genocidal atrocities.

Page 194, 'As demonstrated below ...': Windschuttle, *The Fabrication of Aboriginal History*, p. 137.

Page 195, 'To support her death toll ...': Windschuttle, *The Fabrication of Aboriginal History*, p. 49.

Page 196, 'For almost twenty years ...': Windschuttle, 'The Struggle for Australian Values in an Age of Deceit'.

Page 197, 'at least seventeen cases ...': This is a repeated topic in Windschuttle's road shows. See, for example, Windschuttle, 'White Settlement in Australia' and 'Social History, Aboriginal History and the Pursuit of Truth'.

Page 198, doubling up: An example of this is the extermination controversy, where one side argues that settlers were out to extirpate, or exterminate, Indigenous Tasmanians and the other side says there is no evidence for such a conclusion. See Windschuttle, *The Fabrication of Aboriginal History*, pp. 340–2.

Page 199, So far, Windschuttle's reply has been based on denial, additional straw-man reasoning and counter-attack: This was the case at the time of writing, at least. Windschuttle did promise a point-by-point refutation back in 2003, as follows: 'I will examine all of [Ryan's] claims with fully referenced documentation, plus those of the other authors in *Whitewash*, in a book I am currently preparing that replies to all my critics and discusses several broader issues about the methodological practices and professional ethics of Australian historians'. (Windschuttle, '*Whitewash* Confirms the Fabrication of Aboriginal History', cited in F Töben, 'Keith Windschuttle Replies to His Critics', Adelaide Institute, Adelaide, October 2003, www.adelaideinstitute.org/Dissenters/windschuttle1.htm)

For a characteristic piece of Windschuttle conflation, red herring-ism, question avoidance and question begging, see his article

'The Return of Postmodernism in Aboriginal History'. Furthermore, in attempting to refute J Boyce's point about the use of French sources for a 1793 French landing (see Appendix), Windschuttle, in characteristic fashion, switches the argument to an 1807 French landing, ignoring the 1793 claim altogether. See Windschuttle, 'No Slander in Exposing Cultural Brutality', *The Australian*, 29 December 2003, reproduced at www.sydneyline.com/Fabrication%20one%20year%20on.htm. Windschuttle had already publicly dismissed criticism of the blunder as an inconsequential error in an ABC Television discussion with Stuart Macintyre, when he said: 'That's the most minor issue that anyone could possibly raise' ('Authors in History Debate'), and yet still persisted with the mistake three months later. On the other hand, Windschuttle has unearthed some sloppy commentary by Australian historians regarding the use of the words 'genocide' and 'Holocaust', but these are really obtuse lapses rather than signs of a concerted plot. See The Sydneyline website.

Pages 199–200, 'I bin born la bush . . .': P Patrick (mistakenly dismissed by Windschuttle as a reliable source), statement, 2003, cited in Manne (ed.), p. 215.

Page 200, *Fabrication* is a disaster area: In what is essentially a dark and mean-spirited volume, there are some lighter moments. Here are two. The first is Windschuttle's minor but revealing clanger in his mini-biography of William Broughton, appointed by Governor Arthur to be the chair of the 1830 Aboriginal Committee. Attempting to bolster Broughton's credibility as a gentleman and a scholar, Windschuttle states that Broughton had two degrees, a 'BA and MA from Cambridge University' (pp. 116–17), little realising that they are the same degree. At Cambridge, and at Oxford, it is possible to convert a BA to an MA, for a small fee, nine terms after graduation, but, once converted, the BA becomes redundant. This is sloppy work by Windschuttle.

The second reference is equally embarrassing. In an attempt to discredit mainstream views that Flinders Island was an inhospitable place to dump Indigenous Tasmanians, Windschuttle points out that a contemporary account of the island's weather in November 1831, written by J Bonwick, purportedly exaggerated its miserably cold and windy character. Windschuttle goes on: 'Anyone who cares to check with the [modern-day] Australian Bureau of Meteorology will find that the temperature that day would probably have reached a pleasant 18.5 degrees Celsius' (p. 230). This is an assertion clearly written by a Sydneysider used to a Mediterranean-style climate. Anyone who lives in or around the Bass Strait knows that it is one of the most treacherous seas in the world, where the high-summer weather can be violently changeable, with sudden, massive drops in temperature, freezing gales and horizontal rain.

Page 200, 'If a source doesn't fit . . .': Evans, p. 255.

Page 201, 'I don't have any kind of political agenda . . .': D Irving, interview, *The Homes Show*, television program, New Zealand, 4 June 1993, cited in Evans, p. 27.

Pages 201–3, Windschuttle and Irving comparisons: While conservative commentators complain when Windschuttle is compared, in whatever circumstances, with Irving, *The Australian*'s editor Chris Mitchell was not averse to making his own claim that Manning Clark, Blainey's predecessor as Australia's best known historian, was 'the David Irving of the Left'. (*The Australian*, 11 June 1997, cited in Macintyre & Clark, p. 71.)

Page 202, Windschuttle and racism: Bearing in mind Windschuttle's reputation for resorting to threats of legal action, J Quiggin, a leftist academic at the University of Queensland, has been intrepid enough to state: 'The word "racist" has become taboo in Australian intellectual debates, but I find it difficult to think of an alternative characterisation of Windschuttle's version of cultural relativism'. (J Quiggin, 'Repudiating the Past: John Quiggin Scrutinises Keith Windschuttle', Evatt Foundation, Sydney, 26 January 2003, http://evatt.org.au/news/169.html) For a Howardite response to J Boyce's comment on Windschuttle, see A Shanahan, 'Windschuttle's Word Twisted as the Left Insists He Is a Racist', *The Canberra Times*, 24 June 2006.

Windschuttle certainly seems to have a special interest in the politics of race. In 2004 he published *White Australia*, an attack on conventional views of the history of Australian race relations (arguing that the Australian policy of exclusion on racial grounds was not racial). In February 2008, five days before the Labor government's national apology to Indigenous Australians, *The Australian* published a Windschuttle article which said: '"Sure let's apologise to the Stolen Generations, and pay them billions", declares Keith Windschuttle'. (K Windschuttle, 'Don't Let the Facts Spoil the Day', *The Australian*, 9 February 2008.)

Page 203, 'It is not difficult to see . . .': Windschuttle, *The Fabrication of Aboriginal History*, p. 403.

Page 204, There are variations on this theme: For an example of this technique at work, see *The Australian*'s orchestrated attack on Monash University English educator Ilana Snyder, whose views were described as 'barking mad'. See T Livingstone, 'Skills Tests Put Students at Odds', news feature, 2 February 2008, www.theaustralian.news.com.au/story/0,,23146976-12332,00.html%3Ffrom%3Dpublic_rss; 'A Resistant Reading of Postmodernism', editorial, 2 February 2008, www.theaustralian.news.com.au/story/0,25197,23145541-16741,00.html; K Donnelly, 'In Plain English, A War Worth Fighting', feature, 2 February 2008, www.theaustralian.news.com.au/story/0,25197,23145537-7583,00.html; L Slattery, 'A Fraternity Built on Oversensitivity', feature, 5 February 2008, www.theaustralian.news.com.au/story/0,25197,23158670-7583,00.html; and *The Australian* letters column, 5–8 February 2008. *The Australian*'s opinion editor between 2001 and 2008, T Switzer, a sometime Quadranteer, seems to have been an important behind-the-scenes influence on the newspaper's relentless attack on the Left during the Howard years of 1996 to 2007. See, for example, J Albrechtsen's revealing encomium 'Room for All at the Table of National Debate', *The Australian*, 5 March 2008, in which she disingenuously, and very oddly, describes Switzer, a confirmed Howardite, as a 'pluralist' who, with 'editor-in-chief Chris Mitchell . . . has been constantly embroiled in those swirling controversies [Culture Wars]'. She adds, 'To be sure Switzer was no saint . . . [some] would claim that he succumbed to putting crude ideological labels on groups and individuals who defied simplistic categorisation'. See also Switzer, 'Conservatives Are No Longer Losing the Culture Wars', *Quadrant*, vol. L1, no. 10, October 2007, http://quadrant.org.au/php/article_view.php?article_id=3643. Switzer retired from *The Australian* in February 2008, just three months after John Howard lost his parliamentary seat and Howard's conservative coalition lost the general election.

Page 205, Cronulla riots: These were ethnic clashes at the beachside suburb of Cronulla largely between western suburbs youths and locals ('Lebs' and 'Skips'). The 'riots' provoked John Howard into making an assimilationist Australia Day speech in January 2006, promising a 'root and branch' renewal in Australian history in schools.

Page 205, Manne's plagiarism accusation: Manne accused Windschuttle of 'soft' plagiarism. See G Elliott, 'Trouble in the Press Gang', *The Australian*, 1 November 2003. *The Australian* seems to have acted as Windschuttle's research assistant in this case. See B Lane, 'Historian No Plagiarist', *The Australian*, 1 December 2002. In 2008, Manne was the object of a trivial and allegedly vexatious plagiarism accusation by Windschuttle in *Quadrant*'s May edition (see, for example, Jewel Topsfield, 'Copycat Barbs Ignite New Front in Culture War', *The Age*, 6 June 2008). Manne subsequently published in the June 2008 edition of *The Monthly* 'Keith Windschuttle and Robert Edgerton: A Comparison of Texts', a careful, weighty and very interesting analysis of Windschuttle's own alleged plagiarism of US author Robert Edgerton's work—the point at issue in the original 2003 'soft plagiarism' accusation. The battle continues.

Page 206, 'raped by a voracious media': L Ryan, Australian Historical Association conference, *The Australian*, 6 July 2004.

Page 206, 'Historians Cry "Media Rape"': E Higgins, *The Australian*, 6 July 2004. However, a few historians present at the conference at which Ryan made her accusation did their profession no favours by agreeing that a moratorium on speaking out against each other was a good idea, much to *The Australian*'s delight and proving the point that, while some historians may write capably about past politics, they may not necessarily be any good at the practice of current politics. The generality of historians at the conference sensibly seemed to consider the moratorium a very bad idea. See E Higgins & B Lane, 'Critics Slam Plan for Ethics Gag on Historians', *The Australian*, 5 July 2004.

Page 206, unofficial public relations department: *The Australian* contacted both Ryan's publishers and the University of Newcastle vice-chancellor's office in an attempt to take the campaign more deeply into Ryan's home territory. See B Lane, 'Publisher Discusses Defects Claims with Historian', *The Australian*, 11 January 2003.

Pages 206–7, 'Howard, who is reading . . .': 'Prime Mover', *The Sydney Morning Herald*, 18 December 2004.

Page 207, They had been waiting: Paul Keating had a firmly anti-colonialist view of history. In 1996, Howard saw Keating's demise and his own accession as an opportunity for redressing the Keating view. See J Howard, Sir Thomas Playford Memorial Lecture, Adelaide, 5 July 1996, cited in Macintyre & Clark, pp. 136–7. During the course of the 'History Wars' and the broader 'Culture Wars', critics of the Howard approach were universally characterised by neo-conservative commentators as 'Howard haters'.

Page 207, oblivious to the manifest faults in Windschuttle's book: Ron Brunton (anthropologist) and Gerard Henderson (conservative think-tanker) did express some doubts about Windschuttle's tone and technique. For example:

> Dr Brunton, a consultant anthropologist, said the Windschuttle book was 'very effective in showing that the conventional view, which I certainly had, has got some very, very serious weaknesses'. But Dr Brunton was troubled by Mr Windschuttle's tone. 'There is a lack of a sense of tragedy about [Indigenous Tasmania] in the book'. He was not convinced by Mr Windschuttle's conclusion, in the context of the guerilla warfare argument, that Tasmanian Aborigines had no concept of land ownership. While his book pointed out that vocabularies of Aboriginal language lacked words for 'land', 'possess' or 'property', it concedes an indigenous concept of ownership of

game, such as kangaroos. 'There is an inconsistency, a contradiction in his own argument', Dr Brunton said. (B Lane, *The Australian*, 28 December 2002.)

Henderson, when he was still writing for *The Age*, commented in similar vein in a review of *White Australia* which also touched on *Fabrication*. (G Henderson, 'The Trouble with Keith Windschuttle', *The Age*, 7 December 2004, www.theage.com.au/news/Gerard-Henderson/The-trouble-with-Keith-Windschuttle/2004/12/06/1102182220823.html)

Page 208, 'of the causes that Quadrant . . .': J Howard, 'A Tribute to Quadrant', speech at *Quadrant's* fiftieth anniversary dinner, 3 October 2006, cited in *Quadrant*, vol. L, no. 11, November 2006, http://quadrant.org.au/php/article_view.php?article_id=2290; and Errington & van Onselen, p. 377. See D Shanahan, 'Howard Rallies Right in Culture Wars Assault', *The Australian*, 4 October 2006, www.theaustralian.news.com.au/story/0,20867,20521768-601,00.html: '[Howard] pointed to *Quadrant's* defence of Keith Windschuttle's questioning of Aboriginal history'.

Page 208, 'The responsibility of the historian . . .': K Windschuttle, in 'Authors in History Debate'.

Page 209, Past debates about Indigenous Australian history: There is a strong argument that conservative opposition leader Brendan Nelson's response to Labor prime minister Kevin Rudd's landmark Sorry Day speech on 13 February 2008 reflected elements of Windschuttleism, with its references to good intentions, Christianity and colonisation. (Anna Clark, in discussion with the author.)

Page 209, 'By abandoning truth and objectivity . . .': Windschuttle, *The Fabrication of Aboriginal History*, p. 403.

Addendum: Using Nielsen's Bookscan statistics, the relative lifetime sales figures (as at February 2008) for the major books associated with this chapter are as follows:

The Fabrication of Aboriginal History (Windschuttle): 5604

The History Wars (Macintyre & Clark): 4856

Whitewash (Manne (ed.)): 3896

Telling the Truth about Aboriginal History (Attwood): 1940

The Killing of History (Windschuttle): 665

CODA

Page 210, Mugabe's regime denied: Godwin, 'Mugabe's Academic Mugs'.

Page 210, Zimbabwe was racked by post-election violence: Godwin, 'The Desperate Throes of a Master Election-rigger'.

Page 210, 'no crisis in Zimbabwe': Cave.

Page 210, badly caught out by the devastating cyclone: 'Burma's Twin Disasters: A Cyclone and the Generals'.

Page 214, Nielsen Bookscan figures for *Fabrication*: These are based on figures supplied by Nielsen in February 2008 to the author, who queried the lowish figures for *Fabrication* with Macleay Press on 3 March 2008. He received no reply.

Page 214, 'The number of elementary errors in *Fabrication* …': J Boyce, in Manne (ed.), pp. 17–18.

BIBLIOGRAPHY

All webpages and websites listed were viewed in May 2008 unless otherwise stated.

Books

Adorno, TW et al., *The Authoritarian Personality*, Harper, New York, 1950.
Akcam, T, *From Empire to Republic*, Zed Books, London, 2004.
——*A Shameful Act: The Armenian Genocide and the Question of Turkish Responsibility*, Metropolitan Books, New York, 2006.
Allport, G, *The Nature of Prejudice*, Addison-Wesley, Reading, MA, 1979.
Amis, M, *Koba the Dread*, Talk Miramax Books, New York, 2003.
Andressen, C, *A Short History of Japan: From Samurai to Sony*, Allen & Unwin, Crows Nest, NSW, 2002.
Andrew, C & V Mitrokhin, *The Mitrokhin Archive: The KGB in Europe and the West*, Allen Lane, London, 1999.
Applebaum, A, *Gulag*, Allen Lane, London, 2003.
Attfield, J & S Williams (eds), *1939: The Communist Party of Great Britain and the War*, Lawrence & Wishart, London, 1984.
Attwood, B, *Telling the Truth about Aboriginal History*, Allen & Unwin, Crows Nest, NSW, 2005.
Attwood, B & SG Foster (eds), *Frontier Conflict: The Australian Experience*, National Museum of Australia, Canberra, 2003.
Balakian, P, *The Burning Tigris: The Armenian Genocide and America's Response*, HarperCollins, New York, 2003.
Banac, I, *The Diary of George Dimitrov 1933–1949*, Yale University Press, New Haven, CT, 2003.
Barenblatt, D, *A Plague upon Humanity: The Secret Genocide of Axis Japan's Germ Warfare Operation*, HarperCollins, New York, 2004.
Barkan, E, *The Guilt of Nations: Restitution and Negotiating Historical Injustice*, Johns Hopkins University Press, Baltimore, MD, 2000.
Bartov, O, *Hitler's Army: Soldiers, Nazis, and War in the Third Reich*, Oxford University Press, New York, 1991.
Bartov, O (ed.), *The Holocaust: Origins, Implementations, Aftermath*, Routledge, London, 2000.

Beckett, F, *Enemy Within: The Rise and Fall of the British Communist Party*, Merlin Press, Woodbridge, Suffolk, 1998.
—— *Stalin's British Victims*, Sutton Publishing, Stroud, 2004.
Bix, H, *Hirohito and the Making of Modern Japan*, HarperCollins, New York, 2000.
Bloxham, D, *The Great Game of Genocide*, Oxford University Press, Oxford, 2005.
Bone, E, *Seven Years Solitary*, Bruno Cassierer, Oxford, 1966.
Brooks, RL (ed.), *When Sorry Isn't Enough: The Controversy over Apologies and Reparations for Human Injustice*, NYU Press, New York, 1999.
Broome, R, 'Massacres', in G Davison, J Hirst & S Macintyre (eds), *The Oxford Campanion to Australian History*, rev. edn, Oxford University Press, Melbourne, 2001, pp. 418–19.
Buruma, I, *Wages of Guilt*, Jonathan Cape, London, 1994.
—— *Inventing Japan: From Empire to Economic Miracle*, Phoenix, London, 2005.
Buruma, I & A Margalit, *Occidentalism: The West in the Eyes of Its Enemies*, Penguin, New York, 2004.
Callaghan, J, *Cold War, Crisis and Conflict: the CPGB 1951–1968*, Lawrence & Wishart, London, 2003.
Campbell, G, *The Road to Kosovo: A Balkan Diary*, Westview, Boulder, CO, 2000.
Chang, I, *The Rape of Nanking*, Basic Books, New York, 1997.
Cohen, S, *States of Denial: Knowing about Atrocities and Suffering*, Polity Press, Cambridge, 2001.
Churchill, W, *A Little Matter of Genocide: Holocaust and Denial in the Americas 1492 to the Present*, City Lights Books, San Francisco, 1997.
Clendinnen, I, *The Aztecs: An Interpretation*, Cambridge University Press, Cambridge, 1991.
—— *Reading the Holocaust*, Text, Melbourne, 1998.
Conquest, R, *The Great Terror: A Reassessment*, Oxford University Press, Oxford, 1990.
—— *Reflections on a Ravaged Century*, Norton, New York, 1999.
Cooper, J, *Cognitive Dissonance: 50 Years of Classic Theory*, Sage, Los Angeles, 2007.

BIBLIOGRAPHY

Dadrian, VN, 'The Role of the Special Organisation in Armenian Genocide during the First World War', in P Panayi (ed.), *Minorities in Wartime: National and Racial Groupings in Europe, North America, and Australia during the Two World Wars*, Berg, Providence, RI, 1993.

—— *The History of the Armenian Genocide: Ethnic Conflict from the Balkans to Anatolia to the Caucasus*, Berghahn Books, New Providence, RI, 2003.

Dawson, J, *Washout*, Macleay Press, Paddington, NSW, 2004.

Dovidio, JF, P Glick & LA Rudman (eds), *On the Nature of Prejudice: Fifty Years after Allport*, Blackwell, Malden, MA, 2005.

Dower, JW, *Embracing Defeat: Japan in the Wake of World War II*, WW Norton, New York, 1999.

Eaden, J & D Renton, *The Communist Party of Great Britain since 1920*, Palgrave, Basingstoke, 2002.

Einstein, L, *Inside Constantinople: A Diplomatist's Diary during the Dardanelles Expedition April–September 1915*, John Murray, London, 1917.

Errington, W & P van Onselen, *John Winston Howard: The Biography*, Melbourne University Publishing, Melbourne, 2007.

Evans, RE, *Telling Lies about Hitler: The Holocaust, History and the David Irving Trial*, Verso, London, 2002.

Festinger, L, *When Prophecy Fails: A Social and Psychological Study of a Modern Group That Predicted the Destruction of the World*, University of Minnesota Press, Minnesota 1956.

—— *A Theory of Cognitive Dissonance*, Row Peterson and Company, Evanston, IL, 1957.

—— *Conflict, Decision & Dissonance*, Tavistock, London, 1964.

Finkelstein, N & R Birn, *A Nation on Trial: The Goldhagen Thesis and Historical Truth*, Henry Holt, New York, 1998.

Firer, R & S Adwan, *The Narrative of the Israeli-Palestinian Conflict in History and Civics Textbooks of Both Nations*, Herlag Hahnsche Buchhandlung/Georg-Eckert-Institut, Hannover, 2004.

Fogel, J (ed.), *The Nanjing Massacre in History and Historiography*, University of California Press, Berkeley, CA, 2000.

Flood, J, *The Original Australians: The Story of the Aboriginal People*, Allen & Unwin, Crows Nest, NSW, 2006.

Fryer, P, *Hungarian Tragedy*, New Park Publications, London, 1986.

Fulbrook, M, *German National Identity after the Holocaust*, Polity Press, Cambridge, Cam., 1999.

Gagnon, VP, Jr, *The Myth of Ethnic War: Serbia and Croatia in the 1990s*, Cornell University Press, Ithaca, NY, 2004.

Gare et al., *The Fuss That Never Ended: The Life and Work of Geoffrey Blainey*, Melbourne University Publishing, Melbourne, 2003.

Gellatley, R & B Kiernan (eds), *The Specter of Genocide: Mass Murder in Historical Perspective*, Cambridge University Press, New York, 2003.

Gibney, F, *Honda Katsuichi. The Nanjing Massacre: A Japanese Journalist Confronts Japan's National Shame*, ME Sharpe, Armonk, NY, 1999.

Gilbert, M, *The Holocaust: A History of the Jews of Europe during the Second World War*, Holt, New York, 2003.

Glenny, M, *The Balkans 1804–1999: Nationalism, War and the Great Powers*, Granta, London, 2000.

Gold, H, *Unit 731: Testimony*, Yenbooks, Tokyo, 1996.

Goldhagen, D, *Hitler's Willing Executioners: Ordinary Germans and the Holocaust*, Abacus, London, 1998.

Gollancz, V (ed.), *The Betrayal of the Left*, Victor Gollancz, London, 1941.

Harmon-Jones, E & J Mills (eds), *Cognitive Dissonance: Progress on a Pivotal Theory in Social Psychology*, American Psychological Association, Washington, 1999.

Harris, SH, 'Japanese Biomedical Experimentation during the World-War-II Era', in *Military Medical Ethics*, vol. 2, The Textbooks of Military Medicine, Borden Institute, Washington, 2003.

Heer, H & Naumann, K (eds), *The War of Extermination: Crimes of the Wehrmacht 1941–44*, Berghahn Books, New York, 2000.

Heer, H et al., *The Discursive Construction of History: Remembering the Wehrmacht's War of Annihilation*, Palgrave Macmillan, Basingstoke, Hampshire, 2007.

Hewsen, RH, *Armenia: A Historical Atlas*, University of Chicago Press, Chicago, IL, 2001.

Hicks, G, *The Comfort Women: Japan's Brutal Regime of Enforced Prostitution in the Second World War*, WW Norton, New York, 1995.

Hirst, J, *Sense and Nonsense in Australian History*, Black Inc. Agenda, Melbourne, 2005.

Hobsbawm, E, *Age of Extremes: The Short History of the Twentieth Century 1914–1991*, Michael Joseph, London, 1994.
——*Interesting Times: A Twentieth-Century Life*, Pantheon, New York, 2002.
Hovannisian, R (ed.), *The Armenian Genocide: History, Politics, Ethics*, St Martin's Press, London, 1992. 'Turkish Historiography and the Unbearable Weight of 1915' by FM Gocek.
——*Remembrance and Denial: The Case of the Armenian Genocide*, Wayne State University Press, Detroit, MI, 1999.
Hyde, D, *I Believed: The Autobiography of a Former British Communist*, Heinemann, London, 1951.
Ienaga, S, *The Pacific War 1931–1945*, Pantheon Books, New York, 1979.
——*Japan's Past, Japan's Future: One Historian's Odyssey*, Rowman & Littlefield, Lanham, MD, 2001.
Johnstone, D, *Fools' Crusade: Yugoslavia, NATO and Western Delusions*, Pluto Press, London, 2000.
Kaye, HJ, *The British Marxist Historians*, Polity Press, Cambridge, Cam., 1984.
Kershaw, I, *Hitler: 1936–1945: Nemesis*, Allen Lane, London, 2000.
——*The Nazi Dictatorship: Problems and Perspectives of Interpretation*, Arnold, London, 2000.
Kevorkian, RH, 'Facing Responsibility for the Armenian Genocide? At the Roots of a Discourse That Legitimises Mass Violence', in H Lukes-Kiese (ed.), *Turkey Beyond Nationalism: Towards Post-Nationalist Identities*, Palgrave, New York, 2006.
Klein, L & B Simon, 'Identity in German Right Wing Extremism', in B Klandermans & N Mayer (eds), *Extreme Right Activists in Europe: Through the Magnifying Glass*, Routledge, Abingdon, Oxon., 2006.
Lendvai, P, *1956: One Day that Shook the Communist World*, Princeton University Press, Princeton, NJ, 2008.
Lessing, D, *Walking in the Shade: Volume Two of My Autobiography*, Flamingo, London, 1998.
Lewy, G, *The Armenian Massacres in Ottoman Turkey: A Disputed Genocide*, University of Utah Press, Salt Lake City, UT, 2005.
Lipstadt, D, *Denying the Holocaust: The Growing Assault on Truth and Memory*, The Free Press, New York, 1993.

——— *History on Trial: My Day in Court with David Irving*, Ecco-HarperCollins, New York, 2005.

Longerich, P, *The Unwritten Order: Hitler's Role in the Final Solution*, Tempus, Stroud, Glos., 2003.

Lucarevic, K, *The Battle for Sarajevo*, TZU, Sarajevo, 2000.

McCarthy, J (ed.), *The Armenian Rebellion at Van*, University of Utah Press, Salt Lake City, UT, 2006.

Macintyre, S & A Clark, *The History Wars*, Melbourne University Publishing, Melbourne, 2003.

Mcleod, A, *The Death of Uncle Joe*, Merlin, Woodbridge, Suff., 1997.

Mann, M, *The Dark Side of Democracy: Explaining Ethnic Cleansing*, Cambridge University Press, Cambridge, 2005.

Manne, R, *The Culture of Forgetting: Helen Demidenko and the Holocaust*, Text, Melbourne, 1996.

Manne, R (ed.), *Whitewash: On Keith Windschuttle's Fabrication of Aboriginal History*, Black Inc. Agenda, Melbourne, 2003.

Melson, R, *Revolution and Genocide: On the Origins of the Armenian Genocide and the Holocaust*, The University of Chicago Press, Chicago, IL, 1992.

Miller, DE & LT Miller, *Survivors: An Oral History of the Armenian Genocide*, University of California Press, Berkeley, CA, 1999.

Minow, M, *Between Vengeance and Forgiveness*, Beacon Press, Boston, MA, 1998.

Morgan, K, *Harry Pollitt*, Manchester University Press, Manchester, Lancs., 1993.

Morgan, K, G Cohen & A Flinn, *Communists and British Society 1920–1991*, Rivers Oram, London, 2007.

Morris-Suzuki, T, *The Past within Us: Media, Memory, History*, Verso, London, 2005.

Nation, RC, *War in the Balkans, 1991–2002*, Strategic Studies Institute, Carlisle, PA, 2003.

Overy, R, *The Dictators: Hitler's Germany and Stalin's Russia*, Allen Lane, London, 2004.

Overy, R & A Wheatcroft, *The Road to War*, Macmillan-BBC, London, 1989.

Pamuk, O, *Snow*, Faber & Faber, London, 2004.

Pyle, KB, *Japan Rising: The Resurgence of Japanese Power and Purpose*, Public Affairs, New York, 2007.

Raphael, S, *The Lost World of British Communism*, Verso, London, 2006.
Rees, L, *Horror in the East: Japan and the Atrocities of World War II*, Da Capo Press, Cambridge, MA, 2001.
——*Auschwitz: The Nazis & the Final Solution*, BBC Books, London, 2005.
Robson, L, *A History of Tasmania*, vols 1 & 2, Oxford University Press, Melbourne, 1983–91.
Rohde, D, *Endgame: The Betrayal and Fall of Srebrenica, Europe's Worst Massacre since World War II*, Farrar, Strauss & Giroux, New York, 1997.
Ryan, L, *The Aboriginal Tasmanians*, 1st & 2nd edn, Allen & Unwin, Crows Nest, NSW, 1981 & 1996.
Sandler, J, with A Freud, *The Analysis of Defense: The Ego and the Mechanisms of Defense Revisited*, International Universities Press, New York, 1985.
Sebestyen, V, *Twelve Days: Revolution 1956*, Phoenix, London, 2006.
Seraphim, S, *War Memory and Social Politics in Japan, 1945–2005*, Harvard East Asian Monographs, Harvard University Asia Center, Cambridge, MA, 2006.
Service, R, *Comrades: A History of World Communism*, Harvard University Press, Cambridge, MA, 2007.
Shepherd, B, *War in the Wild East: The German Army and Soviet Partisans*, Harvard University Press, Cambridge, MA, 2004.
Sherif, M & C Hovland, *Social Judgment*, Yale University Press, New Haven, CT, 1961.
Shermer, M & A Grobman, *Denying History: Who Says the Holocaust Never Happened and Why Do They Say It?*, University of California Press, Berkeley, CA, 2002.
Silber, L & A Little, *Yugoslavia: Death of a Nation*, Penguin, London, 1997.
Stannard, DE, *American Holocaust: Columbus and the Conquest of the New World*, Oxford University Press, New York, 1992.
Stetz, M & B Oh (eds), *Legacies of the Comfort Women of World War II*, ME Sharpe, Armonk, NY, 2001.
Stover, E & G Peress, *The Graves: Srebrenica and Vukovar*, Scalo Publishers, Zurich, 1998.
Suettinger, R, *Beyond Tiananmen: The Politics of U.S.–China Relations*, Brookings Institute Press, Washington, DC, 2003.

Suljagic, E, *Postcards from the Grave*, The Bosnian Institute, London, 2005. Afterword by E Vulliamy.

Suvorov, V, *Icebreaker: Who Started the Second World War?*, Hamish Hamilton, London, 1990.

Tanaka, T, *Hidden Horrors: Japanese War Crimes in World War II*, Westview Press, Boulder, CO, 1996.

Tanaka, Y, *Japan's Comfort Women: Sexual Slavery and Prostitution during World War II and the US Occupation*, Routledge, London, 2002.

Taylor, F, *Dresden: Tuesday 13 February 1945*, Bloomsbury, London, 2005.

Tipton, EK, *Modern Japan: A Social and Political History*, Routledge, London, 2002.

Torpey, J, *Making Whole What Has Been Smashed: On Reparations Politics*, Harvard University Press, Cambridge, MA, 2006.

Vörster, J, *The Wehrmacht in the National Socialist State: A Structural-historical Analysis*, Military History Series Volume 2, R Oldenburg Verlag, Munich, 2007.

Vulliamy, E, *Seasons in Hell: Understanding Bosnia's War*, St Martin's Press, New York, 1994.

Walker, CJ, *Armenia: The Survival of a Nation*, Routledge, London, 1990.

Weitz, ED, *A Century of Genocide: Utopias of Race and Nation*, Princeton University Press, Princeton, NJ, 2003.

Windschuttle, K, *Unemployment: A Social and Political Analysis of the Economic Crisis in Australia*, Penguin, Ringwood, Vic., 1979.

—— *The Media*, 1st, 2nd & 3rd edn, Penguin, Ringwood, Vic., 1984, 1988 & 1989.

—— *The Killing of History*, Macleay Press, Paddington, NSW, 1994.

—— *The Fabrication of Aboriginal History*, 1st & 2nd edn, Macleay Press, Paddington, NSW, 2002 & 2003.

Yoshida, T, *The Making of the 'Rape of Nanking': History and Memory in Japan, China, and the United States*, Oxford University Press, New York, 2006.

Journal and Internet Articles

Anderson, P, 'The Age of EJH', review of E Hobsbawm's *Interesting Times*, *London Review of Books*, 3 October 2002, www.lrb.co.uk/v24/n19/ande01_.html

Askew, D, 'The Nanjing Incident: Recent Research and Trends', *Electronic Journal of Contemporary Japanese Studies*, 4 April 2002, www.japanesestudies.org.uk/articles/Askew.html

Bohn, M, 'The Nanking Incident: One American's Personal Perspective', *Japan Echo*, vol. 28, no. 2, 2001.

Cadzow, J, 'Who's Right Now?', *Good Weekend,* 17 May 2003.

Campbell, D, 'Atrocity, Memory, Photography: Imaging the Concentration Camps of Bosnia—the Case of ITN versus *Living Marxism*', *Journal of Human Rights* (University of Connecticut), part 1: vol. 1, no. 1, March 2002, pp. 1–33; part 2: vol. 1, no. 2, June 2002, pp. 143–72.

Caute, D, '*Interesting Times: A Twentieth-Century Life*: Great Helmsman or Mad Wrecker', *The Spectator*, 19 October 2002, www.spectator.co.uk/the-magazine/books/20259/great-helmsman-or-mad-wrecker.thtml

Dadrian, VN, 'Children as Victims of Genocide: The Armenian Case', *Journal of Genocide Research*, vol. 5, no. 3, September 2003.

Darville, H, 'Irving's Berlin: Helen Darville Speaks with David Irving', *Australian Style*, March 2000, reproduced by Fairfax Are Yellow, at www.geocities.com/fairfax_are_yellow/manne.html

De Pasquale, S, 'Nightmare in Nanking', *Johns Hopkins Magazine*, vol. 49, no. 5, November 1997, www.jhu.edu/~jhumag/1197web/nanking.html

Deichmann, T, 'The Picture that Fooled the World', *Living Marxism*, February 1997.

Drea, E, '*Honda Katsuichi. The Nanjing Massacre*: A Japanese Journalist Confronts Japan's National Shame', *H-Japan*, November 1999, www.h-net.org/reviews/showpdf.cgi?path=2293944868556

Dutt, RP, 'Notes of the Month', *Labour Monthly*, May 1956.

Einstein, L, 'The Armenian Massacres', *Contemporary Review*, vol. 616, April 1917.

Eley, G, 'Hull, Isabel V., *Absolute Destruction: Military Culture and the Practices of War in Imperial Germany*', *The English Historical Review*, vol. 121, no. 492, 2006, pp. 869–72.

Finlay, R, 'How Not to (Re)write World History: Gavin Menzies and the Chinese Discovery of America', *Journal of World History*, vol. 15, no. 2, June 2004.

Fryer, P, 'Francis King & George Matthews (eds.), *About Turn: The British Communist Party and the Second World War*', *Revolutionary History*, vol. 3 no. 4, Autumn 1991, www.revolutionary-history.co.uk/backiss/Vol3/No4/RevKing.html

Glikson, M, 'A Censored Discourse: Contradictions in the Structure of the Gallery of the First Australian', Marxist Interventions, Australian National University, Canberra, n.d., www.anu.edu.au/polsci/marx/interventions/gallery.htm

Gott, R, 'Living through an Age of Extremes', *New Statesman*, 23 September 2002, www.newstatesman.com/200209230039

Gould, B, 'Deconstructing the 1960s and 1970s: An Open Letter to Keith and Liz Windschuttle', Ozleft, Sydney, 30 June 2000, www.gouldsbooks.com.au/ozleft/windschuttle.html

'Growth Competitive Index Ratings 2005 and 2004 Comparisons', World Economic Forum, 27 September 2005, www2.weforum.org/site/homepublic.nsf/Content/Growth+Competitiveness+Index+rankings+2005+and+2004+comparisons.html

Herman, ES & D Peterson, 'The Dismantling of Yugoslavia: A Study in Inhumanitarian Intervention (and a Western Liberal-Left Moral Collapse)', *Monthly Review*, vol. 59, no. 5, October 2007, pp. 1–64, www.monthlyreview.org/1007herman-peterson1.htm

Hobsbawm, E, 'Could It Have Been Different?', *London Review of Books*, vol. 28, no. 22, 16 November 2006, www.lrb.co.uk/v28/n22/hobs01_.html

Holdwater, 'The Other Side of the Falsified Genocide', Tall Armenian Tale, 12 June 2007, www.tallarmeniantale.com

Horn, D, 'Comfort Women', *Endeavors Magazine*, vol. 13, no. 2, January 1997, http://research.unc.edu/endeavors/win97/comfort.html

Horowitz, IL, '*Revolution and Genocide: On the Origins of the Armenian Genocide and the Holocaust*', *American Political Science Review*, vol. 87, no. 2, June 1993.

Junkerman, J, 'Japan's Neonationalist Offensive and the Military', *Japan Focus*, 27 December 2007, www.japanfocus.org/products/topdf/2302

Kemenetzky, DA, 'The Debate on National Identity and the Martin Walser Speech: How Does Germany Reckon with Its Past?', *SAIS Review*, vol. 19, no. 2, summer–fall 1999, pp. 257–66.

Kolbert, E, 'Dead Reckoning: The Armenian Genocide and the Politics of Silence', *The New Yorker*, 24 February 2008, www.newyorker.com/archive/2006/11/06/061106crbo_books2

Labi, A, 'Conference in Turkey on Armenian Question Is Canceled Under Government Pressure', *The Chronicle of Higher Education*, 27 May 2005.

Larimer, T, 'National Colours', *Time Asia*, vol. 154, no. 6, 16 August 1999, www.time.com/time/asia/asia/magazine/1999/990816/cover1.html

Layland, P, 'A Comic Book View of History', *Quarterly Bulletin* (Australian National University), vol. 2, no. 2, June 2001, http://rspas.anu.edu.au/qb/articleFile.php?searchterm=2-2-2. Poetry by T Morris-Suzuki.

Leader, 'Haunted by the Past', *The Guardian*, 23 January 2007, www.guardian.co.uk/commentisfree/2007/jan/23/comment.turkey

Lehman, S, 'A Matter of Engineering', *Atlantic Monthly*, February 1990, www.theatlantic.com/doc/199002/electric-chair

Levene, M, 'Illumination and Opacity in Recent Holocaust Scholarship', *Journal of Contemporary History*, vol. 37, no. 2, 2002, pp. 275–92.

MacEwen, M, 'The Day the Party Had to Stop', *Socialist Register*, vol. 13, 1976, pp. 24–42, http://socialistregister.com/socialistregister.com/files/SR_1976_MacEwan.pdf

McNeill, D, 'Media Intimidation in Japan: A Close Encounter with Hard Japanese Nationalism', *Electronic Journal of Contemporary Japanese Studies*, 27 March 2001, www.japanesestudies.org.uk/discussionpapers/McNeill.html

——'Japan's History Wars and Popular Consciousness', *Japan Focus*, 1 May 2007, www.japanfocus.org/products/details/2413

Marquand, R, 'Why "Never Again" Recurred', *Christian Science Monitor*, 14 July 2005, www.csmonitor.com/2005/0714/p01s04-woeu.html

Mellini, P, 'Fallen Angel! The Political Cartoons of Jimmy Friell', The Political Cartoon Society, n.d., www.politicalcartoon.co.uk/html/history/fallen-angel.html

Messerschmidt, M, 'The Wehrmacht and the Volksgemeinschaft', *Journal of Contemporary History*, vol. 18, no. 4, 1993, p. 719–44.

Mizuho, F, 'The Constitution is Japan's Pledge of Peace to the World', *Japan Focus*, 16 January 2006, www.japanfocus.org/products/details/1717

Moses, AD, 'Structure and Agency in the Holocaust: Daniel Goldhagen and His Critics', *History and Theory*, vol. 37, no. 2, May 1998.

Nozaki, Y, 'The "Comfort Women" Controversy: History and Testimony', *Znet*, 31 July 2005, viewed 20 February 2006, www.zmag.org/znet/view/Article/5719

Oren, M, 'The Mass Murder They Still Deny', *The New York Review of Books*, vol. 54, no. 8, 10 May 2007.

Pamuk, O, 'On Trial', *The New Yorker,* 19 December 2005, www.newyorker.com/archive/2005/12/19/051219ta_talk_pamuk

Pesic, V 'Serbian Nationalism and the Origins of the Yugoslav Crisis', *Peaceworks* no. 8, United States Institute of Peace, April 1996, pp. 1–42, www.usip.org/pubs/specialreports/early/pesic/pesic.html

Pons, P, 'A Cartoonist Rewrites History', *Le Monde Diplomatique*, October 2001, http://mondediplo.com/2001/10/09manifesto

Pryce-Jones, D, 'Stalin's Professor—The Awful, Influential Career of E.J. Hobsbawm—Communist and Historian', *National Review*, 15 October 2001.

—— 'Eric Hobsbawm: Lying to the Credulous', *The New Criterion* 21 January 2003, http://newcriterion.com:81/articles.cfm/hobsbawm-pryceyones-1824

Quiggin, J, 'The "Fabrication" of Aboriginal History', Evatt Foundation, University of New South Wales, 26 January 2003, http://evatt.org.au/news/169.html

Ramet, SP, 'The Denial Syndrome and Its Consequences: Serbian Political Culture since 2000', *Communist and Post-Communist Studies*, vol. 40, no. 1, March 2007, pp. 41–58.

Reemtsma, JP, 'Two Exhibitions—A Review', Hamburg Institute for Social Research, Hamburg, 12 July 2005, www.his-online.de/CMS.asp?ID=8718444&Mode=Master

Riggs, DW, 'Understanding History as a Rhetorical Strategy: Constructions of Truth and Objectivity on Debates over Windschuttle's Fabrication', *Journal of Australian Studies*, no. 82, 2004.

Rosefielde, S, 'Incriminating Evidence: Excess Deaths and Forced Labour under Stalin: A Final Reply to Critics', *Soviet Studies*, vol. 39, no. 2, April 1987.

Sexton, D, 'NB', *The Times Literary Supplement*, 28 October 1994, p. 16 (review of E Hobsbawm interview on *The Late Show*, BBC Television, 24 October 1994).

BIBLIOGRAPHY

Shermer, M, 'Giving the Devil His Due', *eSkeptic*, 2 March 2006, www.skeptic.com/eskeptic/06-03-02.html

'Shiro Azuma', *Time Asia,* 16 January 2006.

Shlomowitz, R, 'Keith Windschuttle's Contribution to Australian History: An Evaluation', *Australian Economic History Review,* vol. 45, no. 3, November 2005.

Stover, E, 'Investigating Mass Murder', *Frontline World*, Public Broadcasting Corporation, 26 March 2006, www.pbs.org/frontlineworld/stories/bosnia502/graves.html

Suny, R, '*The History of the Armenian genocide: Ethnic Conflict from the Balkans to Anatolia*', *Slavic Review*, vol. 55, no 3, Autumn 1996.

Switzer, T. 'Conservatives Are No Longer Losing the Culture Wars', *Quadrant*, vol. LI, no. 10, October 2007.

'The Battle for Turkey's Soul', *The Economist*, 5 May 2007.

Waine, A, 'Martin Walser', *The Literary Encyclopaedia*, 17 March 2007.

Wakisaka, M, 'Uyoku: The Japanese Right Wing', *Electronic Working Paper*, School of East Asian Studies, University of Sheffield, vol. 2, no. 2, 20 March 2004, viewed 15 February 2006.

Walls, D, 'Dubious Sources: How Project Censored Joined the Whitewash of Serb Atrocities', *New Politics*, vol. 9, no. 1, summer 2002, www.wpunj.edu/icip/newpol/issue33/walls33.htm

Welch, SR, '"Harsh but Just"? German Military Justice in the Second World War: A Comparative Study of the Court-Martialling of German and US Deserters', *German History*, vol. 17, no. 3, 1999.

Windschuttle, K, 'The Myth of Frontier Massacres in Australian History, Part I: The Invention of Massacre Stories', *Quadrant*, October 2000, reproduced at www.sydneyline.com/Massacres%20Part%20One.htm

——'The Myth of Frontier Massacres in Australian History, Part II: The Fabrication of the Aboriginal Death Toll', *Quadrant*, November 2000, reproduced at www.sydneyline.com/Massacres%20Part%20Two.htm

——'The Myth of Frontier Massacres in Australian History, Part III: Massacre Stories and the Policy of Separatism', *Quadrant*, December 2000, reproduced at www.sydneyline.com/Massacres%20Part%20Three.htm

——'Whitewash Confirms the Fabrication of Aboriginal History', *Quadrant*, October 2003, reproduced at www.sydneyline.com/Manne%20debate%20Quadrant.htm

———'The Return of Postmodernism in Aboriginal History', *Quadrant*, vol. L, no. 4, April 2006, http://quadrant.org.au/php/archive_details_list.php?article_id=1959

———'Why I Left the Left', *Quadrant,* vol. L, no. 6, June 2006, http://quadrant.org.au/php/article_view.php?article_id=2063

———'The Struggle for Australian Values in an Age of Deceit', *Quadrant,* vol. LI, nos. 1–2, January 2007, http://quadrant.org.au/php/archive_details_list.php?article_id=2390

Wisniewski, M, 'War and Memory', *Kansai Time Out*, February 2004.

Yang, D, 'Convergence or Divergence? Recent Historical Writings on the Rape of Nanjing', *The American Historical Review*, vol. 104, no. 3, June 1999, www.historycooperative.org/journals/ahr/104.3/ah000842.html

Newspaper Articles and Media Releases

'A Familiar Ring to Koizumi's Speech', *Asahi Shimbun*, 21 January 2006.

Applebaum, A, 'Tehran's Holocaust Lesson', *The Washington Post*, 12 December 2006, p. A27, www.washingtonpost.com/wp-dyn/content/article/2006/12/11/AR2006121101163.html

Arsu, S, 'Editor of Turkey's Armenian Paper Is Killed', *The New York Times*, 19 January 2007, www.nytimes.com/2007/01/19/world/europe/19cnd-turkey.html?hp&ex=1169269200&en=e33786f3af02d03c&ei=5094&partner=homepage

'Article 9, Iraq and Revision of the Japanese Constitution', *Asahi Shimbun*, 3 November 2003.

Ashby, J, 'Manga Culture Ignites Craze in Media Market Overseas', *The Japan Times*, 14 August 2003, search.japantimes.co.jp/cgi-bin/ek20030814br.html

Barnard, A, 'Conference in Iran on Holocaust Begins', *The Boston Globe*, 12 December 2006, www.boston.com/news/world/middleeast/articles/2006/12/12/conference_in_iran_on_holocaust_begins/

Bendle, M, 'Were We Really Worse Than Hitler?', *The Australian*, 27 March 2008, www.theaustralian.news.com.au/story/0,25197,23436688-7583,00.html

Benson, H, 'Historian Iris Chang Won Many Battles: The War She Lost Raged Within', *San Francisco Chronicle*, 17 April 2005,

www.sfgate.com/cgi-bin/article.cgi?f=/c/a/2005/04/17/
CMGCNBQRRP1.DTL
'Bill Censoring Online Content That Insults Ataturk Is Signed into Law',
   Reporters without Borders, Paris, 24 May 2007, www.rsf.org/article
   .php3?id_article=22273
Birch, N, 'Outspoken Armenian Editor Shot Dead in Istanbul Street
   Attack', *The Guardian*, 20 January 2007, www.guardian.co.uk/media/
   2007/jan/20/pressandpublishing.turkey
—— 'Seven Held over Killing of Turkish Journalist', *The Guardian*,
   22 January 2007, www.guardian.co.uk/media/2007/jan/22/
   pressandpublishing.turkey
'Blainey Quits', *The Sydney Morning Herald*, 24 November 1988.
'Bosnian Serbs Apologize for Srebrenica Massacre', *The New York Times*,
   11 November 2004, www.nytimes.com/2004/11/11/international/
   Europe/11serb.hmtl
Broomby, R, 'Protest Fears over War Crimes Exhibition', BBC News Online,
   28 November 2001, news.bbc.co.uk/1/hi/world/europe/1680579.stm
Burke, J, 'Mystery of a Killer Elite Fuels Unrest in Turkey', *The Observer*,
   4 May 2008, www.guardian.co.uk/world/2008/may/04/turkey
   .thefarright
'Burma's Twin Disasters: A Cyclone and the Generals', *International Herald
   Tribune*, editorial, 6 May 2008, www.iht.com/articles/2008/05/
   06/opinion/edburma.php
Cave, P, 'Zimbabwe Election Deadlock No Crisis: Mbeki', ABC News
   Online, 12 April 2008, www.abc.net.au/news/stories/2008/04/12/
   2215246.htm
Childs, D, 'Alfred Dregger: Robust and Controversial German Politician',
   The Independent, 12 August 2002, www.independent.co.uk/news/
   obituaries/alfred-dregger-639589.html
'China Moves to Fourth in Global GDP Rankings', Reuters-*China Daily*,
   14 December 2005, www.chinadaily.com.cn/english/doc/2005-12/
   14/content_503281.htm
Chrisafis, A, 'Turkey Warns France over Armenian Genocide Bill', *Guardian
   Unlimited*, 11 October 2006, www.guardian.co.uk/world/2006/oct/
   11/turkey.eu

'Clinton Calls Emergency Meeting', *The Age*, 7 February 1994.

Cornwell, J, 'Beguiling Narrator', interview with Doris Lessing, *The Australian*, 30 December 2006, www.theaustralian.news.com.au/story/0,20867,20975196-5001986,00.html

Craig, O, 'David, What on Earth Would Mother Think?', *The Daily Telegraph*, 25 February 2006, reproduced at www.fpp.co.uk/Austria/arrest_2005/DTel_Nicky.html

Curtin, JS, 'At the Shrine, Koizumi's Dangerous Game', *Asia Times*, 6 January 2004, www.atimes.com/atimes/Japan/FA06Dh02.html

Daily Express, 20 October – 30 November 1956 (articles, comments and letters referring to events in Hungary).

Devine, F, 'Lured Back into the Fray by Cromwell of the South Seas', *The Australian*, 12 September 2003.

Dodson, L et al., 'Prime Mover', *The Sydney Morning Herald*, 18 December 2004, www.smh.com.au/news/federal-election-2007-news/prime-mover/2007/11/19/1195321650843.html

'Don't Support Revisionist History', *AsianWeek*, 27 July 2007.

'Drawing up Battle Lines', *The Standard*, Chinese Business Daily, 11 August 2005.

Erlich, R, 'Right Wing Rising: Japanese Nationalists Use Comics, Film, Punk Rock to Recruit Youth', *San Francisco Chronicle*, 10 July 2001, www.sfgate.com/cgi-bin/article.cgi?file=/chronicle/archive/2001/07/10/MN211532.DTL

Fisk, R, 'Remember the First Holocaust', *The Independent*, 28 January 2000.

'Funeral Held for Japan Veteran Who Admitted Taking Part in Rape of Nanking', *Time Asia*, 16 January 2006.

Godwin, P, 'Mugabe's Academic Mugs', *The Times*, 17 June 2007.

——'The Desperate Throes of a Master Election-rigger', 2 April 2008, *The Independent*, www.independent.co.uk/opinion/commentators/peter-godwin-the-desperate-throes-of-a-master-electionrigger-803497.html

Hale, E, 'Who Is Abu Mazen?', *USA Today*, 25 March 2003.

Harding, L, 'Second Front: A Shot That's Still Ringing', *The Guardian*, 12 March 1997.

Harvey, B, 'Mass Protests at Editor's Funeral', Associated Press, reproduced in *The Guardian*, 24 January 2007, www.guardian.co.uk/media/2007/jan/24/pressandpublishing.turkey

Heinrich, M, 'Carnage as Serb Gunners Shell Market', *The Sunday Age*, 6 February 1994.

Henderson, G, 'The Battle is Not to Be Left Behind', *The Age*, 24 December 2002, www.theage.com.au/articles/2002/12/23/1040511005690.html

——'The Trouble with Keith Windschuttle', *The Age*, 7 December 2004, www.theage.com.au/news/Gerard-Henderson/The-trouble-with-Keith-Windschuttle/2004/12/06/1102182220823.html

Herald Sun, 1988–2008 (articles, comments and letters referring to K Windschuttle).

Herwig, M, 'Holocaust Denier on Trial: The Swastika Wielding Provocateur', *Spiegel Online*, 16 January 2006, www.spiegel.de/international/spiegel/0,1518,395810,00.html

Higgins, E, 'Who's still afraid of Keith Windschuttle?', *The Australian*, 22 July 2004, reproduced at www.sydneyline.com/Who's%20afraid%20of%20KW.htm

Hitchens, C, '"Interesting Times": Eric the Red', *The New York Times* 24 August 2003, www.nytimes.com/2003/08/24/books/review/24HITCHET.html?pagewanted=1&ei=5007&en=d5d57a9b145f5f4e&ex=1377057600&partner=USERLAND

——'Anti-Sovietchik No. 1', *The Wall Street Journal*, 3 February 2007, www.opinionjournal.com/editorial/feature.html?id=110009618

Hunt, T, 'Man of the Extreme Century', *The Observer*, 22 September 2002, http://books.guardian.co.uk/departments/history/story/0,,796548,00.html

'Japan Renews Call for UN Security Council Seat', AFP, 16 September 2005, reproduced in *China Daily*, www.chinadaily.com.cn/english/doc/2005-09/16/content_478448.htm

'Japanese Comfort Women Ruling Overturned', CNN, 29 March 2001, http://edition.cnn.com/2001/WORLD/asiapcf/east/03/29/japan.comfort.women.02

Johnstone, D, 'The Bosnian War Was Brutal, but It Wasn't a Holocaust', *The Guardian*, 23 November 2005.

Kamm, O, 'It takes an intellectual to find excuses for Stalinism', *The Times*, 23 July 2004, www.timesonline.co.uk/tol/comment/thunderer/article460555.ece

Keegan, J, 'The Trial of David Irving—and My Part in His Downfall', *The Daily Telegraph*, 12 April 2000, www.telegraph.co.uk/htmlContent.jhtml?html=/archive/2000/04/12/nirv512.html

Kiernan, B, 'Try Reading My Book with Both Eyes', *The Australian*, 3 April 2008, www.theaustralian.news.com.au/story/0,25197,23473719-7583,00.html

Kifner, J, 'West Blamed for Market Carnage', *The Sydney Morning Herald*, 7 February 1994.

'Koizumi: No Shift in Article 9 for UN Security Bid', *Asahi Shimbun*, 25 August 2004, www.globalpolicy.org/security/reform/cluster1/2004/0825bid.htm

'Koizumi Apologizes for Japan's World War II Legacy', *Voice of America*, 15 August 2005, www.voanews.com/english/archive/2005-08/2005-08-15-voa6.cfm

Kuderna, M, 'Bomb Attack Hits Hitler Exhibit', Associated Press Online, 9 March 1999, viewed 15 October 2006.

Laity, P, 'The Great Persuader', *The Guardian* 1 September 2007, http://books.guardian.co.uk/departments/politicsphilosophyandsociety/story/0,,2160101,00.html

Lawson, C, *Daily Express* from 2 November 1956 onwards (articles on E Bone).

McCurry, J, 'Discomfit Women', *The Guardian* 14 June 2005, www.guardian.co.uk/world/2005/jun/14/worlddispatch.secondworldwar

Marsh, V, 'Lunch with the FT: The History Wars', *Financial Times*, 26 August 2005, http://us.ft.com/ftgateway/superpage.ft?news_id=fto082620051042247498

Masaki, H, 'Japan Rethinks Strategy for Gaining Permanent U.N. Security Council Seat', *The Japan Times*, 19 May 2002, http://search.japantimes.co.jp/cgi-bin/nn20020519a3.html

Meldrum, A, 'South African Government Ends Aids Denial', *The Guardian*, 28 October 2006.

Moynihan, S, 'Abe Ignores Evidence, Say Australia's "Comfort women"', *The Age*, 3 March 2007, www.theage.com.au/news/world/abe-ignores-evidence-say-australias-comfort-women/2007/03/02/1172338881441.html

BIBLIOGRAPHY

Nabeshima, K, 'The Year of Koizumi's Exit', *The Japan Times*, 1 January 2006, http://search.japantimes.co.jp/cgi-bin/eo20060101kn.html

'Naser Oric Convicted', press release OK/MOW/1094e, ICTY, The Hague, 30 June 2006, www.un.org/icty/pressreal/2006/p1094-e.htm

'Neo-Nazis in Germany: Right-Wing Violence on the Rise', *Spiegel Online*, 17 October 2006, www.spiegel.de/international/0,1518,443063,00.html

'New PA "Prime Minister" Denies Holocaust', IsraelNationalNews.com, 3 September 2003, viewed 8 August 2007.

Onishi, N, 'Denial Reopens Wounds of Japan's Ex-Sex Slaves', *The New York Times,* 8 March 2007, www.nytimes.com/2007/03/08/world/asia/08japan.html

Pallister, D, J Vidal & K Maguire, 'Life after Living Marxism: Banning the Bans', *The Guardian*, 8 July 2000.

——'Life after Living Marxism: Fighting for Freedom—to Offend, Outrage and Question Everything', *The Guardian*, 8 July 2000, www.guardian.co.uk/uk/2000/jul/08/davidpallister.johnvidal1

'Radical Longs for Death Penalty', *The Australian*, 10 November 2007.

'Rape of Nanking to Be War Film "Classic"', Canadian Broadcasting Corporation, 14 August 2006, www.cbc.ca/arts/story/2006/08/14/nanking-film.html

'Scarred by History: The Rape of Nanjing', BBC News Online, 11 April 2005, http://news.bbc.co.uk/1/hi/world/223038.stm

Schwarz, L, 'Blainey's Views Appear to Have Cost Him His Post', *The Sydney Morning Herald*, 25 August 1988.

'Serb Nationalist Rejects UN Court', BBC News, 8 November 2007, http://news.bbc.co.uk/2/hi/europe/7084506.stm

Simons, M, 'Genocide Court Ruled for Serbia without Seeing Full War Archive', *The New York Times*, 9 April 2007, www.nytimes.com/2007/04/09/world/europe/09archives.html?_r=1&pagewanted=1&n=Top/News/World/Countries and Territories/Serbia&oref=slogin

Sito-Sucic, D, 'Muslim Fighter Begins Testimony in Bosnia Trial', Reuters, 7 September 2007, www.reuters.com/article/latestCrisis/idUSL07470729

Sokatch, D & DN Myers, '"Never Again" for Armenians Too', *Los Angeles Times*, 1 May 2007, www.latimes.com/news/opinion/la-oe-myers1may01,0,3937946.story?coll=la-opinion-rightrail

Soylemez, Y, 'Ottoman Armenians Discussed', *Turkish Daily News*, 23 October 2005.

Steele, J, 'The Real Struggle Is Inside Turkey, Not on Its Borders', *The Guardian*, 15 June 2007, www.guardian.co.uk/commentisfree/2007/jun/15/turkey.comment

Sykes, R, 'History Without Morality', *The Sydney Morning Herald*, 10 December 1994.

Takahashi, K, 'China vs Japan—It's Not Just a Soccer Game', *Asia Times*, 7 August 2004, www.atimes.com/atimes/japan/fh07dh01.html

'Testing Two Leaders: George Bush, in Denial', *The New York Times*, 29 January 2004

The Age, 1988–2008 (articles, comments and letters referring to K Windschuttle).

The Daily Worker, 20 October – 30 November 1956 (articles, comments and letters referring to events in Hungary).

The Sydney Morning Herald, 1988–2008 (articles, comments and letters referring to K Windschuttle).

Traynor, I, 'Serbs Vote for the "Future or the Past"', *The Age*, 20 January 2007.

——'Serbia Jails Srebrenica Death Squad after Video Exposes Massacre', *The Age*, 12 April 2007.

'Turkey Pulls Plug on YouTube over Ataturk "Insults"', Associated Press–*The Guardian*, 7 March 2007, www.guardian.co.uk/world/2007/mar/07/turkey

'Turkish Court's Ban of Armenian Conference is Circumvented', *International Herald Tribune*, 24 September 2005.

Underwood, K, 'German Exhibit of Nazi-Era Art Raising Debate', CNN, 25 February 1997, www.cnn.com/WORLD/9702/25/germany.exhibition

Vulliamy, E, 'Poison in the Well of History', *The Guardian*, 15 March 2000, www.guardian.co.uk/itn/article/0,2763,184815,00.html

Watt, DC, 'History Needs Its David Irvings', *Evening Standard*, 11 April 2000.

Windschuttle, K, 'Why I'm a Bad Historian', *The Australian*, 12 February 2003.

Wise, MZ, 'Bitterness Stalks Show on Role of the Wehrmacht', *The New York Times*, 6 November 1999, http://query.nytimes.com/gst/fullpage.html?res=9E0DE1DC163AF935A35752C1A96F958260

Speeches, Papers, Reports and Guides

Akaha, T, 'US-Japan Security Alliance Adrift?', paper presented at the annual meeting of Asian Studies on the Pacific Coast, Asilomar, CA, June 1997.

Cabinet Councillors' Office on External Affairs, 'On the Issue of Wartime "Comfort Women"', The Ministry of Foreign Affairs of Japan, Tokyo, 1993, www.mofa.go.jp/policy/postwar/issue9308.html

Clark, A, 'Moving Forward in a Time of Fear', paper delivered at the Manning Clark House Day of Ideas conference, Perth, 2 August 2003, www.manningclark.org.au/papers/ANNACLARK.html

Clifford, R, 'Cleansing History, Cleansing Japan: Kobayashi Yoshinori's Analects of War and Japan's Revisionist Revival', *Nissan Occasional Paper Series*, no. 35, Nissan Institute of Japanese Studies, St Anthony's College, Oxford, 2004, www.nissan.ox.ac.uk/nops/nops35.pdf

Fullerton, M, '"Germany for the Germans": Xenophobia and Racist Violence in Germany', Human Rights Watch, Helsinki, April 1995, www.hrw.org/reports/1995/Germany.htm

Hirohito, 'Text of Hirohito's Radio Rescript', *The New York Times*, 14 August 1945.

Irving v. Penguin & anr. (2000), transcript, reproduced at www.holocaustdenialontrial.com/trial/transcripts

Jahnke, E & Kallinich, J, 'Shattering a Myth—the Wehrmacht Exhibition in the Kunst-Werke Berlin', *Bulletin of the European Museum Forum*, Bristol, January 2002.

Koizumi, J, 'Statement by Prime Minister Junichiro Koizumi', The Ministry of Foreign Affairs of Japan, Tokyo, 15 August 2005, www.mofa.go.jp/announce/announce/2005/8/0815.html

——'General Policy Speech by Prime Minister Junichiro Koizumi to 164th Session of the Diet', Prime Minister of Japan and His Cabinet, Tokyo, 20 January 2006, www.kantei.go.jp/foreign/koizumispeech/2006/01/20speech_e.html

McCormack, G, 'Holocaust Denial à la Japonaise', JPRI Working Paper no. 38, Japan Policy Research Institute, University of San Francisco, CA, October 1997, www.jpri.org/publications/workingpapers/wp38.html.

Macintyre, S, 'On "Fabricating" History', Blackheath Philosophy Forum, Upper Blue Mountains, NSW, 16 March 2003, reproduced at http://evatt.org.au/publications/papers/92.html

'Public Opinion in Serbia: Views on Domestic War Crimes Judicial Authorities and the Hague Tribunal', Belgrade Center for Human Rights, Belgrade, December 2006, www.osce.org/documents/srb/2007/03/23518_en.pdf

Samuels, RJ, 'Constitutional Revision in Japan: The Future of Article 9', paper presented at the Brookings Institute Center for Northeast Asian Policy Studies Roundtable, Washington, DC, 15 December 2004, www.brookings.edu/events/2004/1215japan.aspx

'Stories of an Exhibition: Two Millenia of German Jewish History', exhibition guide, Jewish Museum of Berlin, Berlin, 1978.

'The British Road to Socialism: Programme Adopted by the Executive Committee of the Communist Party', Communist Party of Great Britain, 1951, reproduced by Marxists Internet Archive at www.marxists.org/history/international/comintern/sections/britain/brs/1951/51.htm

Warrell, H, 'Command Responsibility Convictions', Global Policy Forum, Institute for War and Peace Reporting, New York, 17 March 2006, www.globalpolicy.org/intljustice/tribunals/yugo/2006/0317comresponsibility.htm

Wildt, M, U Jureit & B Otte (eds), 'Crimes of the German Wehrmacht: Dimension of a War of Annihilation 1941–1944', exhibition brochure, trans. P Bradish, Hamburg Institute for Social Research, Hamburg, 2004.

Windschuttle, K, 'The Poverty of Media Theory', paper to Journalism Education Association annual conference, University of Canterbury, Christchurch, December 1995, published in revised form in *Quadrant*, March 1998, reproduced at www.sydneyline.com/Poverty%20of%20Media%20Theory.htm

—'Social History, Aboriginal History and the Pursuit of Truth', debate with S Macintyre, Blackheath Philosophy Forum, Upper Blue Mountains, NSW, 1 March 2003, www.sydneyline.com/Blackheath%20philosophy%20forum.htm

—'White Settlement in Australia: Violent Conquest or Benign Colonisation?', speech at Melbourne Trades Hall, Melbourne, 5 March 2003, www.sydneyline.com/RMIT%20debate%20with%20Grimshaw.htm

Radio and Televisions Programs

'Authors in History Debate', *Lateline*, television program, ABC Television, Australia, 3 September 2003.

'Fabricating Aboriginal History', *Sunday*, television program, Channel 9, Willoughby, NSW, 25 May 2003.

Manufacturing Consent: Noam Chomsky and the Media, television documentary, Necessary Illusions, Finland, 1992.

Milosevic on Trial, television documentary, TV2 Danmark, Denmark, 2007.

Moral Combat: NATO at War, television documentary, British Broadcasting Corporation, London, 2000.

Mr Death: The Rise and Fall of Fred A. Leuchter, Jr., documentary, Channel Four Films, UK, 1999.

The Death of Yugoslavia, television documentary series, British Broadcasting Corporation, London, 1995.

The Serbs' Last Stand, television documentary, British Broadcasting Corporation, London, 1998.

'Whitewash versus the Fabrication of Aboriginal History', *Book Talk*, radio program, ABC Radio, Australia, 13 September 2003.

Websites

Adelaide Institute, www.adelaideinstitute.org
Armenian Genocide Information & Recognition, www.genocide1915.info
Armeniapedia, armeniapedia.org

Focal Point Publications, www.fpp.co.uk
Holocaust Denial on Trial, www.holocaustdenialontrial.com
International Criminal Tribunal for the Former Yugoslavia,
    www.un.org/icty
Japan Focus, www.japanfocus.org
JE Kaleidoscope, www.je-kaleidoscope.jp
Louis Proyect, The Unrepentant Marxist, http://louisproyect.wordpress.com
Serbianna, www.serbianna.com
Stormfront, www.stormfront.org
Tall Armenian Tale, www.tallarmeniantale.com
The Emperor's New Clothes, www.emperors-clothes.com
The Sydneyline, www.sydneyline.com
World Socialist Web Site, www.wsws.org

INDEX

Abdul'ahad Nuri, Bey, 12
Abe, Shinzo, 100–1, 250
Adams, Marion, 279
Adams, Phillip, 204
Adelaide Institute, 42, 273, 274–5
Ahmadinejad, Mahmoud, 42
AIDS, vii, 210
Ainley, David, 129
Akcam, Taner, 8, 12, 18, 229; *From Empire to Republic*, 229; *A Shameful Act*, 227
Akiyama, Hiroshi, 83
Albrechtsen, Janet, 204, 274, 284–5
Ali, Tariq, 168
Alic, Fikret, 146, 159, 160–1, 162
Allport, Gordon, 226; *The Nature of Prejudice*, xi
Amis, Martin, 130; *Koba the Dread*, 258–9
Anderson, P, 260
anti-Semitism, 39–40, 44, 45, 48, 55, 58, 59, 60, 61, 66, 94, 142, 226, 237, 239; neo-Nazi, x, 41, 214; Stalinist, 120–1, 123, 125, 254
Anzulovic, B: *Heavenly Serbia*, 273
Applebaum, Anne, 41, 70, 106, 250
Ararat (Egoyan), 234
Arkan (Zeljko Raznatovic), 265
Armenia, 29, 34, 35
Armenian massacres of 1915–16, 3–4, 10–15, 16–17, 18, 19–20, 34, 212, 227, 230–2, 233; and Armenian propaganda and exaggeration, 29, 30–1, 33, 233; as genocide, 2, 7, 13–14, 15, 16, 18, 23, 24, 25, 29, 30, 34, 35, 36; as Holocaust, 7, 16, 30–3, 34; Kemakh gorge incident, 20, 21–4, 230, 233; as reprisals, 9, 24, 26; and Turkish denial of, viii, xiii, xv, 2, 4–5, 24–9, 32, 35, 210–11, 213, 229, 230, 234

Armenians (Turkish), 1, 4, 8, 21; atrocities by, 4, 12, 24, 26; as Christian minority, 5, 6; deportations, 10–11, 12, 14, 15, 19, 20; diaspora, 4, 36, 229; resentment and suspicion of, 6–7, 8, 9, 10, 12, 13, 14, 16, 23, 30; and Russia, 6–7, 9, 10, 12, 24, 26, 212
Asahi Shimbun, 76, 85
Ataturk, Kemal, xv, 5, 25, 27, 28
Atlantic Monthly, 60
Attlee, Clement, 117
Attwood, Bain, 192; *Telling the Truth about Aboriginal History*, 273
Auschwitz. *See* Holocaust; Nazism
Auschwitz (Rees), 235
Australia: bigotry in, 176, 184; conservatives in, 176, 187, 189, 191–2, 203–8, 274, 278–9, 284–5, 286, 287; and historical denial, x, xv, 174, 176, 177, 183, 186, 200, 201, 202, 214; 'History Wars' 175, 177, 182, 183–4, 185, 186–99, 204–8, 281, 282–3, 286; Indigenous Australians and European settlement, 175, 176, 182, 184, 188–9, 192, 193, 202, 214, 277, 282; land rights, 184; racism in, 176
Australian, 203, 204, 205–6, 214, 276, 284, 285
Australian Broadcasting Corporation, 175, 274
Australian Institute of Aboriginal and Torres Strait Islander Studies, 190
Australian Style, 47
Azuma, Shiro 73, 77, 244; *My Nanking Platoon*, 245

Babic, Milan, 155
Balkans, the: conflict and atrocities in, xviii, 17–18, 33, 64, 137–8, 142,

143–56, 160–7, 168, 171–2, 261, 262, 265, 266, 267, 271; memory in, 143; NATO role in, 165, 270; and Serb denial of atrocities in Bosnia, xv, 138–9, 145, 148, 153–7, 158, 166, 172–3, 263, 264, 266; western (Marxist) denial of Serb atrocities, xiii, 156–60, 161–7, 168, 169–70, 171–2, 203, 268, 269; *see also* Bosnia; Croatia; Kosovo; Serbia
Barenblatt, Daniel, 82
Bartov, Omer: *Hitler's Army*, 242; *The Holocaust*, 235
Beaverbrook, Lord, 116
Beckett, Francis: *Enemy Within*, 108–9, 252
Benedict, Ruth: *The Chrysanthemum and the Sword*, 97
Bennet, Mick, 102, 121, 125
Berlin, xix; Holocaust memorial, 213; Jewish Museum, 38–9, 188, 189, 213
Bevin, Ernest, 116
biological warfare, 82, 83, 84
Blainey, Geoffrey, 186, 187–8, 190, 198, 275, 278–9, 283
Blair, Tony, 131
Bloxham, Donald, 12, 13, 18, 229; *The Great Game of Genocide*, 227
Bolsheviks: as Jewish-inspired, 40, 43
Bone, Edith, 127, 128, 257
Bonwick, J, 282
Bormann, Martin, 238
Bosnia, 144–51, 164–7, 169, 173; Bosnian Serbs, 137–8, 141, 143, 145–53, 154–6, 164, 166–7, 168, 171, 263, 264; foreign Islamic fighters in, 145, 263–4; Serbian forces in, 144, 263, 265, 267; Srebrenica massacre, xviii, 137–8, 149, 152–3, 154, 161, 164, 170–1, 173, 263, 265, 271; UNPROFOR in, 144, 150, 151, 164, 264, 271; *see also* Balkans, the

Boston Globe, 237
Boyce, James, 214, 282
Brecht, Bertolt, 104, 250
Britain: class divisions in, 112, 118; fascism in, 106, 112; Labour Party, 116, 131; Revolutionary Communist Party, 158, 268; *see also* Communist Party of Great Britain
Brockes, Emma, 168–70
Broome, Richard, 177
Broughton, William, 282
Brunton, Ron, 274, 286–7
Bubitz, Ignatz, 67
Bukharin, Nikolai, 106, 250
Bulletin, 278
Bunyu, Ko, 248
Burma, 210
Buruma, Ian, 77, 245; *Wages of Guilt*, 96–7
Bush, George W, vii, viii
Butz, Arthur R: *The Hoax of the Twentieth Century*, 59

Cadogan, Peter, 109
Cambodia: genocide in, xviii, 34, 179
Campbell, Johnny, 109, 112, 115, 125, 129, 215, 253
Carto, Willis, 43, 55, 56, 57
Casey, Dawn, 188
Chamberlain, Neville, 116
Chang, Iris, 245; *The Rape of Nanking*, 77–8, 244, 245–6, 248
China, 75, 84, 98–9; Japanese occupation in, 73–8, 79, 81; massacre at Tiananmen Square, vii, viii; and Sino-Japanese relations, 75–6, 85, 96, 99; *see also* Nanjing
Chomsky, Noam, 162, 163, 167, 168–70
Christiansen, Arthur, 256
Churchill, Winston, 44, 46, 47, 117
Cicek, Cemil, 27
Clark, Manning, 283

INDEX

Clifford, Rebecca, 93
Clinton administration, 166
Cohen, Rose, 107, 251
Cold War, 75, 80, 83, 118, 212
Cole, David, 58, 241
colonialism: and military brothels, 80
comics, 91; *see also* manga
Comintern, 107, 113, 114–15, 251
communism. *See* Comintern; Communist Party of Great Britain; Soviet Russia/USSR
Communist Party of Great Britain: *The British Road to Socialism*, 118; and dirty tricks, 129; knowledge of the Great Terror, 107, 108, 109; maxims of, 105; members purged in Soviet Russia, 106, 107, 251; post-war fortunes, 118; providing shelter, 109, 110–11; and 'realistic Marxism', 131; twists and turns in response to Soviet actions and policies, viii, x, xii, xv, 102–4, 106–10, 111–17, 119–21, 123–30, 132, 133, 135, 214–15, 252, 253, 254, 256–8; and unquestioning loyalty, 110, 113, 119, 132
Conquest, Robert, 130; *The Great Terror*, 131*; Reflections on a Ravaged Century*, 131, 259
Cosic, Dobrica, 139
Covert Action Quarterly, 162
Croatia, 142, 156, 157, 265; designs on Bosnia, 144, 166; Ustase atrocities, 142–3
culture, 97; Japanese, 73, 95–6; Serb, 139

Dadrian, Vahakn, 18
Daily Express, 128, 256
Daily Herald, 108
Daily Worker (London), 102–3, 108, 114, 116, 119, 120, 121, 123–5, 126–9, 132, 215, 253, 254, 256, 257–8
Daily Worker (US), 119, 120, 128

Dalley, Helen, 280
Darville ('Demidenko'), Helen, 47, 238–9; *The Hand That Signed the Paper*, 47, 238
Dawson, J: *Washout*, 273
de Gaulle, Charles, 260
Deichmann, Thomas, 158, 159–60, 162, 269
Delmer, Sefton, 256
Deng Xiao-Ping, vii, viii, 85
denial, 241; historical, viii–ix, x–xvi, 158, 171, 202, 210, 226; political, vii–viii; *see also* Armenian massacres of 1915–16; Australia; Balkans, the; Communist Party of Great Britain; Holocaust denial (western); Japan
Deutsch, Arnold, 251
developing nations, 36, 37
Devine, Frank, 204, 276
Diamond, Dorothy, 108
Dimitrov, Georgi, 107, 114
Dink, Hrant, 1–3, 34, 228, 229
Dink, Rakel, 2–3
Discussion, 108
Djemal, Pasha, 6, 8
Djeric, Vladimir, 263
Donnelly, Kevin, 204
Dreger, Alfred, 65
Dresden, xix, 45–6, 69
Duke, David, 42
Dutt, Palme, 115, 116, 119, 124, 129, 158, 253, 254

Eagleton, Terry, 276
Eichmann, Adolf, 52
Einstein, Lewis, 14, 30
Eisenhower, Dwight, 260
Ekran, Bey, 11
Enver, Pasha, 6, 8, 9, 10, 11, 17, 27, 230
Erdemovic, Drazen, 149
Erdogan, Recep Tayyip, 1, 3, 34, 35, 37, 228

315

'ethnic cleansing', xviii, 33, 138, 144, 147, 150, 154, 155–6, 166, 168, 172, 213
Evans, Harold, 157, 268
Evans, Richard, 46, 49, 50–1; *Exhibition for War and Peace* (Tokyo), 77; *Telling Lies about Hitler*, 45, 53, 200, 238, 239–40

Fadeyev, Alexander, 119
fascism, 106, 112, 114, 116, 126, 142
Faurisson, Robert, 59, 168
Festinger, Leon: *A Theory of Cognitive Dissonance*, xii
Financial Times, 276
Fisk, Robert, 31
Fles, George, 251
Flood, Josephine: *The Original Australians*, 176–7
Focal Point Publications, 59, 238
Folks-sztyme, 120
Foot, Michael, 116
Fox, Claire, 269
France: stance on Turkey, 36, 229
Franco, Francisco, 106
Freud, Anna, xii, xiii
Freud, Sigmund, xii
Friell, Jimmy, 112, 113, 128
Fryer, Peter, 123, 124–5, 126–8, 129, 215, 253, 258; *Hungarian Tragedy*, 124
Fujioka, Nobakazu, 86, 88, 98; *History Not Taught in Schools*, 91
Fukuda, Yasuo, 250
Fukushima, Mizuho, 101

Gaita, Raimond, 277
Galic, Stanislav, 264
Gallagher, Willie, 107, 115
Gardner, Llew, 128–9
Gauweiler, Peter, 65
genocide, xvi–xix, 34, 63, 88, 242, 277, 280; in Australia, 193, 198, 199; in the Balkans, 138, 147, 153, 154, 161, 166, 172, 271–2; and 'ordinary' Germans, 66; *see also* Armenian massacres of 1915–16; Holocaust, the
German political parties and groups, 236; Christian Social Union, 65, 68; Die Republikaner, 68; German National Party, 65, 68; National Democratic Party, 65, 67, 236
Germany: invasion of Russia, 116–17; Jewish population, 39; military tradition and character, 62–3, 64, 242; Nazi Germany, 16, 17, 18, 34, 46, 52, 64, 69, 114, 211; post-war, 36–7, 87, 97, 213; Turkish minority in, 37; Wehrmacht and atrocities, 43, 62, 63–5, 67–8, 242
Gero, Erno, 122, 255
Gilbert, Martin: *The Holocaust*, 235
globalisation, 36, 37, 164, 167, 179, 196
Goering, Hermann, 32
Goldhagen, Daniel, 65; *Hitler's Willing Executioners*, 66, 68, 69, 209, 243
Gollan, John, 126
Gomulka, Wladislaw, 255
Gould, Bob, 175, 179
Gray, Justice Charles, 48
Greenland, Hall, 175
Griffiths, Leon, 128
Guardian, 170, 228
Gul, Abdullah, 35, 211
Guttman, Roy, 146
Gvero, Milan, 266

Haglund, William, 261
Hamburg, xix, 46
Hamburg Institute for Social Research, 63, 64, 67
Harding, Luke, 158
Hasluck, Paul, 186
Hayal, Yasin, 2, 3
Healy, Gerry, 128
Heer, Hannes, 65, 67
Henderson, Gerard, 286–7
Herman, Edward S, 158, 171

INDEX

Heydrich, Reinhard, 32, 52, 53
Himmler, Heinrich, 18, 50, 53
Hiranuma, Takeo, 87
Hirohito (emperor), 94–5, 211
Hiroshima, xix, 88, 92, 95
Hirst, John, 177
historians and reputation, 53–4, 240
history (discipline), xvi, 181, 182, 184, 185, 186–7; historians' quarrel in Germany, 69, 242, 243; revisionism in, xiv, 60–1
Hitler, Adolf, xv, 26, 30, 45, 46, 69, 113, 114; accession to power, 106; admiration for, 57; and the Armenians, 31, 32, 33, 234; and extermination of the Jews, xiv, 49, 50–1, 52, 53, 234
Hobsbawm, Eric, 110–11, 130–5, 258–9; *Age of Extremes*, 130, 131, 135, 260; *Interesting Times*, 260
Holocaust, the, xvi, xvii, xviii, 26, 31–3, 39, 41, 56, 67, 281; memorialisation of, 30, 66, 189, 190; plans and program for extermination of the Jews, 16, 17, 32, 50–3, 64, 97, 235
Holocaust denial (western), viii, xiv, xv, 39–53, 54–62, 65, 68, 69, 70, 168, 173, 201–2, 214, 236–7, 241; arguments of, 42–3; combating, 40–1, 47, 55, 70; and Islamist propagandists, 41–2; laws against, 49, 57, 61, 168, 213; and neo-Nazism, 41
Honda, Katsuichi, 85; *A Journey to China*, 76
Hovannisian, Richard: *The Armenian Genocide*, 227
Howard, John, xv, 187, 204, 206–7, 274, 279, 285, 286
human rights, vii, x, 36, 37, 226
Human Rights Watch, 236
Hungary: fascism in, 126; uprising of 1956, xii, 102–3, 120, 121–3, 124, 125–8, 129, 132, 255–8
Hyde, Douglas, 113

Ienaga, Saburo, 89–90, 213, 247; *The Pacific War*, 90
Ignatieff, Michael, 130, 135
Ihsan, Bey, 11
immigration, 37, 41; and xenophobia, 69
imperialism, 116, 158, 162, 172
India, 98
Inonu, Ismet, 24, 233
Inprecor, 108
Institute for Historical Review (IHR), 43, 55–6, 57–60, 62, 70, 240
Iraq War, vii
Irving, David, 39, 43–5, 53, 61, 69, 70, 200–2, 203, 214, 238, 283; *The Destruction of Dresden*, 45–6; *Goebbels*, 47, 50, 51; *Hitler's War*, 51, 54; libel case against Penguin and Deborah Lipstadt, 44, 46–9, 54–5, 61, 62, 160, 237, 240; misrepresentations by, 49, 50–2, 203, 239–40
Irving, Nicholas, 44
Ishihara, Shintaro, 87
Ishii, Shiro, 82, 83
Israel, Jared, 158, 160
Istanbul, 2, 3, 6, 11
Itakura, Yoshiaki, 76
Izetbegovic, Alija, 147, 165

Japan: Allied occupation of, 80, 85, 94, 211; and behaviour of military in Asia, 71–2, 73–4, 88; Class A war criminals, 87, 95, 212; and 'comfort women' scandal, 73, 78–81, 84, 88, 90, 92, 101, 212, 246; (official) historical denial in, xiii, xv, 71–3, 75, 76–7, 78, 81, 84, 85, 86–91, 92, 93, 94, 95, 96–7, 99, 101, 210–11, 212, 213, 245, 248, 250; and international authority, 98, 99, 100–1; new nationalist politicians, 87, 92; relations with China, 96; relations with the US, 98; school history texts in, 86–7, 88, 89, 90–1, 93, 99, 247

surrender, 94–5; Unit 731 chemical and biological warfare group: atrocities, 73, 81–4, 88, 90, 95; *yakuza* criminal gangs, 72, 85, 244; Yasukuni shrine, 92, 100, 101, 249; *see also* manga; Nanjing; nationalism and ultra-nationalism
Japan Times, 91
Jacques, Martin, 131
Jennings, Peter, 147
Jewish Clarion, 120
Johnson, Thomas T, 56
Johnston, Monty, 109
Johnstone, Diana, 170, 203; *Fools' Crusade*, 158, 161–7, 168, 169, 170, 271, 272
Jolovic, Milan, 149
Jones, Alan, 274
Journal of Historical Review, 60
Judgment (Israel), 160
Junkerman, John, 101

Kadar, Janos, 123, 256
Kadishman, Menashe: *Fallen Leaves*, 38–9
Kamenev, Lev, 106, 250
Kamm, Oliver, 130, 259
Karadzic, Radovan, 137, 146, 148, 150, 154, 156, 162, 172, 261
Keating, Paul, 207, 276, 278, 286
Keegan, John, 53, 54
Kempner, Robert, 44–5
Kennedy, Robert, 45
Khrushchev, Nikita, 103, 118, 119, 256
Kiernan, B: *Blood and Soil*, 277
Kirakossian, Arman, 34
Kirov, Sergei, 105, 106
Kitano, Masaji, 82, 83
Klugmann, NJ 'James', 251–2
Knobloch, Charlotte, 236
Knopwood, Robert, 195, 197
Kobayashi, Yoshinori, 92–3, 98, 248; *Manifesto for a New Pride*, 92; *On Taiwan*, 92; *On War*, 91, 92, 93, 101; *On the Yasukuni Question*, 92, 93

Kohl, Helmut, 64
Koizumi, Junichiro, 92–3, 99–100, 248, 249
Kojiro, Tomohiro, 85
Korea (South), 73; and Japan, 81
Korean War, 75, 84, 118
Kosovo, 140–1, 154, 155, 213, 260–1, 261
Kroger, Michael, 274
Krstic, Radislav, 271
Kucan, Milan, 141, 142
Kurumizawa, Masakuni, 81

Labandeira, Jose, 148
Labour Monthly, 108, 119
Lane, Bernard, 286
Left Book News, 108
Lemkin, Raphael, xvi, xviii
Lenin, Vladimir, 135
Lepsius, Johannes: *Der Todesgang des Armenischen Volkes*, 23
Lessing, Doris, 130, 157, 258
Leuchter, Fred, 60, 241; *Auschwitz (The Leuchter Report)*, 59
Levy, Hyman, 254
Lewy, Guenter, 15, 16, 18; *The Armenian Massacres in Ottoman Turkey*, 227
Libeskind, Daniel, 38
Little, Allan, 147, 262
Lipstadt, Deborah, 46, 53, 55, 60, 61, 168; *Denying the Holocaust*, 47
Living Marxism, 158–60, 162, 169, 268–70
Los Angeles Times, 30

MacArthur, Douglas, 85, 94
McCalden, David (Lewis Brandon), 43, 55, 57
McDougall, George, 103
MacEwen, Malcolm, 102, 128, 256
McGuinness, PP, 278
Macintyre, Stuart, 187, 192, 279, 282
MacKenzie, Lewis, 148
McKernan, Michael, 189

INDEX

Macleay Press, 180, 181, 183
Mcleod, Alison, 102, 215; *The Death of Uncle Joe*, 124, 254
Macmillan, Harold, 260
McNeill, David, 71–2, 85, 244
McNeill, Keiko, 71–2
McQueen, Humphrey, 186
Maehara, Seiji, 100
Mahameed, Khaled, 237
manga, 91–2, 93; and historical denial in Japan, 92, 248
Manne, Robert, 184, 192, 205, 208, 277–8, 285; *The Culture of Forgetting*, 239
Manning, Peter, 149–50
Mao Tse-tung, 75
Marsh, Virginia, 179, 180, 182–3
Marshall, Penny, 146, 160
Matsui, Iwane, 76
Matsui, Yayori, 80, 85
Matthews, George, 119, 129
Mazen, Abu, 42, 236–7
Mbeki, Thabo, vii, viii, 210
Meanjin, 189
media, 28, 123, 167, 168, 172, 173, 178, 179, 181, 204–5, 214, 262, 277, 279; ITN, 146, 160, 169, 170; *see also* individual newspapers and magazines
Melson, Robert, 33, 34, 234
Mende, Erich, 65
Mendiluce, Jose Maria, 141
Menzies, G: *1421*, 273
Menzies, Robert, 260
Merdzanic, Idriz, 160
Mermelstein, Mel, 55, 56, 62
Mikoyan, Anastas, 119, 254
Milanovic, Milos, 172–3
Milosevic, Slobodan, xv, 139, 140–1, 142, 143, 144, 154, 155, 156, 162, 172, 261–3, 272
Mindszenty, Cardinal Jozsef, 126, 256
Mitchell, Chris, 204, 283, 284
Mizushima, Satoru, 249

Mladic, Ratko, 137, 150, 151, 152, 153, 162, 172, 261, 266
Mohammed cartoons: responses to, 2, 237
Mommsen, Hans, 54
Moore, Bill, 111
Moran, R: *Massacre Myth*, 277
Morgenthau, Henry, 7, 13, 30, 229
Morioka, Masahiro, 87
Morris, Jan, 186
Morrison, Herbert, 116, 117
Morris-Susuki, Tessa, 248
Mosley, Oswald, 106, 112
Mugabe, Robert, 210
Murdoch, Rupert, 179
Mussolini, Benito, 106

Nagasaki, xix, 88, 92, 95
Nagy, Imre, 122, 123, 255, 256, 257
Nanjing: Japanese military atrocities in, 71, 73–8, 84, 88, 90, 92, 97, 244–5, 248–9
Narcissism and grandiosity, xiv–xv, 201
nationalism and ultra-nationalism: in China, 247; Croatian, 142, 143; in developing nations, 35–6; in Germany, 45, 68, 236, 242; in Japan, x, 71–2, 73, 77, 78, 84, 85–9, 91, 92–3, 94, 95, 96, 98–9, 244; Serbian, x, 138–9, 140–1, 142, 143, 145, 155, 156, 157, 167, 172, 213, 268, 272; in Turkey, xiii, 1, 2, 3, 6, 9, 7–8, 17, 25, 27–8, 35, 228
National Museum of Australia (Canberra), 188–90
National Vanguard, 58
Nazism, 48, 57, 66, 88, 112, 281; concentration camps of, 49, 50, 55, 56, 64, 97, 146, 250; gas chambers, 59; and racism, 41; *Schutzstaffeln* (SS), 18, 51; *see also* Holocaust, the; neo-Nazism
Nazi–Soviet pact, 111–14

319

Nelson, Brendan, 287
neo-Nazism, x, 41, 45, 57, 58, 67, 69, 70, 213–14, 236, 268
New Criterion, 183
New History Textbook (Japan), 86–7, 90–1, 247
New York Times, 161
Nice, Geoffrey, 262
Nigeria: Biafran atrocities, 33, 34
Nikolic, Momir, 152–3, 166, 263, 267
Nomura, Shusuke, 85
Norris, Christopher: *What's Wrong with Postmodernism?*, 276

Occidental Quarterly, 275
Ognjanovic, Dragoslav, 155
Okamura, Yasuji, 79
Oran, Baskin, 35
Oren, Michael, 30
Oric, Naser, 151, 164, 165, 265, 266
O'Shaughnessy, Kathleen, 108
Ottoman (Turkish) Empire, 5–6, 17–18, 24–5; Committee for Union and Progress (CUP), 7–8, 9, 10, 11, 12, 13, 14, 18, 230; foreign interventions in, 5–6, 12, 25; Ittihadist (Young Turks) government, 6–7, 13, 15, 17, 23, 27; Kurds in, 14, 19, 20, 22; (non-Islamic) minorities in, 4, 5–6, 8; Special Organisation, 13, 14, 16–17, 18–19; and Turkish (Islamic) nationalism, 6, 9, 7–8, 17, 25; in World War I, 6, 8–11, 15, 24, 26; Young Turk movement, 8, 25; *see also* Armenian massacres of 1915–16; Turkey
Owen, Frank, 116
Oxley, John, 195, 197

Pak, Kumjoo, 79
Palestinians: and Holocaust denial, 42
Pamuk, Orhan, 2, 3, 35–6, 37, 247
Patrick, Peggy, 199–200
Patterson, Frank, 102

Pavkovic, Nebojsa, 155
Paxman, Jeremy, 48, 49
Pearson, Christopher, 204
Pelemis, Milorad, 149
Penguin (publisher), 53, 160
Peterson, David, 171
Petrovsky, Max, 251
Pilger, John, 168
Poland, 121, 254–5
Pollitt, Harry, 107–8, 109, 110, 112, 113, 115, 116–17, 119, 124, 251, 253–4; *How to Win the War*, 114
Popovic, Vujadin, 152, 267
postmodernism, 179, 181, 182, 204, 276
Pot, Pol, 34, 179
prejudice, xi, xv, 226; *see also* anti-Semitism; racism
Pryce-Jones, David, 130, 132, 259
pseudohistory, 202, 273
Pybus, Cassandra, 280

Quadrant, 183, 192, 203–4, 208, 214, 277, 278
Quiggin, John, 283

racism, 83, 196, 203, 226, 236; and atrocities, 75; in Australia, 176, 201, 202; in the Balkans, 143; and 'comfort women', 79–80; and culture, 93–4, 283; and immigration, 41; in Japan, 86, 96
Rae-Ellis, Vivienne, 280; *Black Robinson*, 190
Raggatt, Howard, 189
Rajk, Laslo, 121, 123–4
Rakosi, Matyas, 122
Ramet, Sabrina, 139
Reasoner, The, 119, 254
Reemtsma, Jan Philipp, 62
Refik, Ahmet, 5
Rehn, Olli, 37
Reynolds, Henry, 174, 175, 177, 184, 186, 187, 188, 190, 193–4, 198–9, 208

Reynolds News, 126
Riefenstahl, Leni, 94
Rimmer, Pearl, 251
Robertson (Gilbert), 193, 223, 224
Robinson, George, 198, 280
Robson, Lloyd, 174, 197
Roosevelt, Franklin D, 47
Rose, Sir Michael, 264
Rothstein, Andrew, 254
Rudd, Kevin, 214, 287
Rwanda, 30, 34
Ryan, Lyndall, 174, 190, 193–5, 197, 198, 199, 206, 208, 280, 281, 285
Ryan, Peter, 190

Sabit, Erzincanh, 11
Sakir, Bey, 10, 11, 230, 231
Samast, Orgun, 2
Samistat Publishers, 241
Saville, John, 119, 129
Schröder, Gerhard, 68
Seidler, F: *Fahnenflucht*, 242
Senda, Kako, 80
Serbia, 137, 156–7, 163–4, 171, 213, 261, 272; Chetniks, 143; Croatian Serbs, 142–3; cultural memory in, 266; Kosovan Serbs, 155, 260–1; Serb expansionism, 143, 144, 151, 163, 171, 172, 261–2, 263; Serbian mythology of victimhood, 138, 139–40, 141, 172; *see also* Balkans, the; Bosnia; nationalism and ultra-nationalism
Seselj, Vojislav, 153, 154, 155–6, 268
sexual slavery, 78–81, 88
Shermer, Michael, 61
Shokun!, 245
Silajdzic, Haris, 147
Silber, Laura, 147, 262
Simon Wiesenthal Center, 55, 58
Singapore, 82
Slansky, Rudolf, 121
Slovenia, 142

Smith, Bradley, 58
Snyder, Ilana, 284
socialism, 108, 178, 204; in Germany, 106
Society for the Making of New School Textbooks in History (Japan), 86, 87–8, 91, 92
Soviet Russia/USSR: Communist Party of the Soviet Union (CPSU), 8, 105, 110, 111, 113, 120, 133; Great Terror, 106, 109, 130, 251; Gulags, xvii, 106, 134, 250–1; Moscow show trials and purges, 103, 105–6, 107–8, 111, 121, 133–4, 179, 260; Romanov royal family, 17; and Stalinist repression in eastern Europe, xii, xvii, 102–3, 121–3, 127–8, 215, 254, 255–6, 260
Spiegel Online, 236
Springhall, Dave, 115
Staley, Tony, 189
Stalin, Joseph, xii, xv, 102, 104, 109, 110, 113, 120–1, 135; death and denunciation of, 118–19, 254; and repression, 105, 132, 134; western belief in, x, 111, 114
Stambolic, Ivan, 140, 141, 262
Stove, RJ, 275
Stover, Eric, 137
Strachey, John, 108
Sudan: Darfur massacres, 30
Suez crisis, 122, 255, 257
Suny, Ronald, 34
Switzer, Tom, 284–5
Sydney, 175, 273–4; Book Arcade, 175
Sydney Morning Herald, 206
Sykes, Roberta, 180

Tadic, Dusko, 159
Talat, Pasha, 6, 7, 8, 13, 27, 230
Tanaka, Masaaki: *The Fabrication of the 'Nanjing Massacre'*, 76

Tanaka, Toshiyuki: *Japan's Comfort Women*, 80
Taylor, AJP, 61; *The Origins of the Second World War*, 60
Taylor, Frederick, 46; *Dresden*, 45, 238
Tehlirian, Soghomon, 230
terrorism, 27, 69
Teutonophilia, 42, 64
Theil, Georges: *Heresy in 21st Century France*, 42
Thompson, Edward, 119, 129, 131
Tito (Josef Broz), 140, 255, 256
Töben, Fredrick, 42, 275
Treatment of Armenians in the Ottoman Empire 1915–16, The (Bryce and Toynbee), 227
Trevor-Roper, Hugh, 209
Trotsky, Leon, 105, 106, 250
Trotskyism, 105, 108
Tsumura, Hideo, 94
Tudjman, Franjo, 142, 144, 156
Turkey, 16; Anatolia, 17, 18, 19–20, 33, 230; censorship in, 28, 34–5 and the European Union, 25, 36–7, 212, 228; external image of, 25; Islamic extremism in, x, 2, 3; isolationism in, 37; Justice and Development Party (AKP), 3, 228; media in, 28; and western intervention, 37; *see also* Armenian massacre of 1915–16; Armenians (Turkish); nationalism and ultra-nationalism; Ottoman (Turkish) Empire
Turkish Daily News, 28
Turkish legal code, 213; Article 301, xiii–xiv, 25, 28, 34
Turkish War of Independence, 16

Under Western Eyes (Conrad), 228
United States, 167; conservatism in, 180, 181; history wars in, 181; Holocaust Memorial Day, 30; *see also* biological warfare; war crimes

Vehip, Pasha, 230
Vietnam War, 76
Vulliamy, Ed, 145, 146, 157, 158, 169, 173

Walker, Christopher, 19, 23
Walser, Martin, 66, 67, 68
war crimes, 45–6, 88, 95, 171, 172, 233; and Allied silence, 75, 80, 83, 84–5; in the Balkans, 154, 264, 266, 267; German, 65, 67, 97; Japanese, 72–5, 78, 80, 82, 83, 84, 97; tribunals and trials, xviii, 44, 75, 83, 86, 87, 92, 95, 155, 159, 211, 261, 271
War of Extermination (Germany; book and exhibitions), 63–5, 67–8, 69, 242
Washizumu, 92
Waterman, Alec, 120
Watt, Donald Cameron, 53, 54
Weber, Mark, 58, 60
Weitz, Eric, xvii; *A Century of Genocide*, 173
Welcome to Sarajevo (Winterbottom), 148
Wiesenthal, Simon, 58
Whitewash (ed. Manne), 184, 196, 199, 214, 216–25, 281
Williams, Ian, 146
Windschuttle, Keith, 174, 175–6, 177–82, 205–6, 274, 276, 277, 278, 282–3; and denial, 200, 201, 202; *The Fabrication of Aboriginal History*, 183–99, 202, 207–9, 214, 282, 286–7, 288; and history method, 190, 191, 194, 195–7, 199, 200, 203, 208, 209, 281–2; *The Killing of History*, 178, 181, 192, 199, 276; *The Media*, 178, 179; *Unemployment*, 178; *White Australia*, 275, 283, 287
Wise, Stephen, 58
World War I, 6, 9, 24, 63, 112, 211
World War II, 34, 60, 67, 101, 103–4, 142, 143, 253; Britain in, 116–17;

Germany in, 63–6, 111–14; Japan in, 75, 78, 90, 92, 94, 211; and Soviet Russia, 67, 83, 111–14; and United States, 87, 88, 95; *see also* Holocaust, the; Holocaust denial (western); war crimes

Yagoda, Genrikh, 105
Yehip, Mehmet, 11
Yelesiyevitch, M, 268
Yezhov, Nikolai, 105
Young, Toby, 157, 268

Yugoslavia, 137, 139, 140, 143, 158, 255; disintegration of, 138, 141, 142, 167, 171, 262
Yugoslavia (Silber and Little), 262, 272
Yun, Chung-Ok, 80–1

Zimbabwe, 210
Zinoviev, Grigory, 106, 250
Zündel, Ernst, 43, 55, 57, 58, 59, 60, 61, 69, 70, 214, 241; *Hitler's Antarctic Bases*, 56

BF
175.5
.D44
T39
2008